The Promised End

Challenges in Contemporary Theology

Series Editors: Gareth Jones and Lewis Ayres
University of Birmingham and Trinity College, Dublin

Challenges in Contemporary Theology is a series aimed at producing clear orientations in, and research on, areas of 'challenge' in contemporary theology. These carefully co-ordinated books engage traditional theological concerns with mainstreams in modern thought and culture that challenge those concerns. The 'challenges' implied are to be understood in two senses: those presented by society to contemporary theology, and those posed by theology to society.

Already published

These Three are One
David S. Cunningham

After Writing
Catherine Pickstock

Mystical Theology
Mark A. McIntosh

Engaging Scripture
Stephen E. Fowl

Torture and Eucharist
William T. Cavanaugh

Sexuality and the Christian Body
Eugene F. Rogers, Jr

On Christian Theology
Rowan Williams

The Promised End
Paul S. Fiddes

Forthcoming

Alien Sex: The Body and Desire in Cinema and Theology
Gerard Loughlin

THE PROMISED END

Eschatology in Theology
and Literature

Paul S. Fiddes

First published 2000

2 4 6 8 10 9 7 5 3 1

Blackwell Publishers Ltd
108 Cowley Road
Oxford OX4 1JF
UK

Blackwell Publishers Inc.
350 Main Street
Malden, Massachusetts 02148
USA

British Library Cataloguing in Publication Data
A CIP catalogue record for this book is available from the British Library.

Library of Congress Cataloging-in-Publication Data
Fiddes, Paul S.
    The promised end : eschatology in theology and literature / Paul S. Fiddes.
        p. cm. — (Challenges in contemporary theology)
    Includes bibliographical references and index.
    ISBN 0-631-22084-4 (alk. paper) — ISBN 0-631-22085-2 (pbk. : alk. paper)
    1. Eschatology. 2. Eschatology in literature. 3. Christianity and literature. I. Title. II.
Series.
BT821.2.F53 2000
291.2'3—dc21
                                                                                00-028940

Typeset in 10½ on 12½pt Bembo
by SetSystems Ltd, Saffron Walden, Essex
Printed in Great Britain by TJ International, Padstow, Cornwall

This book is printed on acid-free paper.

Dedicated to my son Benjamin

1978–1998

Is this the promised end?
(Shakespeare, *King Lear*)

What we call the beginning is often the end
And to make an end is to make a beginning.
The end is where we start from.
                    (T. S. Eliot, *Little Gidding*)

CONTENTS

PREFACE

Sending out this book to a wider audience, I want to express my appreciation to a number of universities and colleges who have provided me with my initial hearers. During the past five years, I have given lectures in which some of the ideas in this book have been tried out, and the best kind of testing has been through the response of students and fellow-teachers. Chapters 1–6 formed the substance of a lecture series, given in successive years, in the Faculty of Theology of the University of Oxford. Earlier versions of these chapters were also given as guest lectures at the University of Wales, Bangor; in the Edwin Stephen Griffiths Lectures in the Department of Religious and Theological Studies of the University of Wales, Cardiff; in special lectures at the Universities of Timisoara and Oradea in Romania; and as the Gheens Lectures for 1994 in The Southern Baptist Theological Seminary, Louisville, Kentucky. In addition, I wish gladly to acknowledge the stimulation and good company of a succession of my doctoral students during this period, and among them especially Fanie du Toit, Lindsay Robertson, Jeremy Law, and Andrew Moore. In what follows they may recognize fragments of conversation together over the years, and for their contributions I offer my thanks.

Regent's Park College
Oxford
Easter 2000

ACKNOWLEDGEMENTS

Excerpts from 'Ash Wednesday' and *Four Quartets* in *Collected Poems 1909–1962* by T. S. Eliot © 1969 by Valerie Eliot, are reprinted by permission of Faber and Faber Ltd.

Excerpts from 'Ash Wednesday' in *Collected Poems 1909–1962*, copyright 1930 and renewed 1958 by T. S. Eliot, are reprinted by permission of Harcourt, Inc.

Excerpts from 'Burnt Norton' in *Four Quartets*, copyright 1936 by Harcourt, Inc. and renewed 1964 by T. S. Eliot, are reprinted by permission of the publisher.

Excerpts from 'East Coker' in *Four Quartets*, copyright 1940 by T. S. Eliot and renewed 1968 by Esme Valerie Eliot, are reprinted by permission of Harcourt, Inc.

Excerpts from 'The Dry Salvages' in *Four Quartets*, copyright 1941 by T. S. Eliot and renewed 1969 by Esme Valerie Eliot, are reprinted by permission of Harcourt, Inc.

Excerpts from 'Little Gidding' in *Four Quartets*, copyright 1942 by T. S. Eliot and renewed 1970 by Esme Valerie Eliot, are reprinted by permission of Harcourt, Inc.

Excerpts from the poem 'Byzantium' in *The Collected Poems of W. B. Yeats* (Macmillan, 1950) © Michael B. Yeats, are reprinted by permission of A. P. Watt Ltd. on behalf of Michael B. Yeats. Also reprinted with the permission of Scribner, a Division of Simon & Schuster from *The Collected Poems of W. B. Yeats*, revised second edition edited by Richard J. Finneran. Copyright 1933 by Macmillan Publishing Company; copyright renewed © 1961 by Bertha Georgie Yeats.

Excerpts from *Waiting for Godot* and *Endgame* by Samuel Beckett are copyright (1956, 1958), and are reprinted by kind permission of the publishers, Faber and Faber Ltd. and the Grove Press.

Excerpts from the poem 'Dance' in *A Fragile City* by *Michael O'Siadhail* © 1995 Michael O'Siadhail, are reprinted by kind permission of the author and Bloodaxe Books Ltd.

Quotations from *The Holy Bible, Revised Standard Version* and *New Revised Standard Version* © 1946, 1952 1989 Division of Christian Education of the National Council of the Churches of Christ in the United States of America, are used by permission.

Chapter One

FACING THE END

Many modern novelists seem to find it difficult to bring their books to an end. I am not only referring here to the increase in the *size* of novels, although this is an alarming phenomenon which some commentators blame on the use of the word processor; it is, after all, so much easier to go on adding material when a page does not have to be retyped as a consequence. Nor is this a trivial observation. The advance of technology may be giving scope for making clear what has been the case all along, that there is an inherent openness of meaning about a text that can never be brought to a final close. This is a truth to which I intend to return often in this book, although the unpleasant fact that the computer may encourage writers to indulge a lack of discipline should also warn us that we need to consider *limits* to openness. At this opening moment, however, I am concerned with the difficulties of 'closure' in a narrower sense than mere size. I am thinking about the problem of an appropriate end to a plot, about the nature of 'the last things' – the *eschata* – of a narrative.

The Problem of Closure

In his novel *The French Lieutenant's Woman*, John Fowles relates the obsession of Charles Smithson with a mysterious young governess, Sarah Woodruff. Charles, a Victorian gentleman and amateur paleontologist, is investigating the fossils around Lyme Regis when he becomes intrigued by the tragic and silent figure of Sarah, who apparently carries with her the sorrow of being deserted by her French lover. He has a one-night affair with her, discovers she has invented the story of her ruin, and painfully breaks his engagement with his fiancée with the intention of marrying the enigmatic Sarah. However, Sarah has now disappeared without trace. After several years of fruitless searching, he finally discovers her living in the bohemian household of Gabriel and Christina Rossetti. After a stormy interview, he comes to understand her need to find her own identity rather than being a mere extension of others' lives; he meets the child of their brief and passionate union, the scene ends with 'the pressure of lips upon auburn hair',[1] and we are left with the clear impression that they will marry. It is a happy, if uneasy, ending.

But there are still half a dozen pages of the novel left, and the novelist chooses at this point to appear in the narrative *in persona*, as 'the sort of man who cannot bear to be left out of the limelight . . . for whom the first is the only pronoun' and who has now 'got himself in *as he really is*'.[2] This impressario-like figure stares at the Rossettis' house 'with an almost proprietary air', takes out his watch, and turns back the hands by a quarter of an hour. We find ourselves back in the middle of the meeting between Charles and Sarah, but this time there is no mutual understanding; he bitterly accuses her of cruelty, refuses her implicit offer of a liaison without marriage as making him into 'the secret butt of this corrupt house . . . the pet donkey', misses seeing the child, and storms off to a lonely exile in America. The narrator bids us not to think that 'this is a less plausible ending to their story'. After all, Charles has found 'an atom of faith in himself, a true uniqueness, on which to build'. He has learnt that life cannot be reduced to one riddle and one solution, however well Sarah fits the role of the Sphinx; though with agony in his heart, he can venture onto the 'unplumb'd, salt, estranging sea'.[3]

These are the alternative endings provided, though we immediately become aware that the options are not exhausted. There could have been others as well; as Fowles himself points out, life is not to be shrunk to one riddle. The film of *The French Lieutenant's Woman*, written by Harold Pinter and directed by Karel Reisz, presents the two alternatives in an ingenious way, though in doing so it does perhaps reduce the options to two only. The movie is a film within a film, relating the story of the actors who play Charles and Sarah and the affair on which they embark, as well as the Fowles' story itself; at the end, Charles and Sarah are reunited, but the actor who plays Sarah breaks the relationship with her fellow actor and

---

[1] John Fowles, *The French Lieutenant's Woman* (London: Pan Books, 1987 [1969]), p. 393.
[2] Ibid., p. 394.
[3] Ibid., pp. 398–99.

leaves him deserted. The 'film within the film' opts for the first ending, and the 'film outside the film' for the second.

Another modern novelist, Julian Barnes, has the narrator of his novel *Flaubert's Parrot* protest against this kind of multiple ending. He mocks at the idea that a hesitant and ambiguous ending somehow reflects reality:

> When the writer provides two different endings to his novel (why two? why not a hundred?), does the reader seriously imagine that he is being 'offered a choice' and the work is reflecting life's variable outcomes? Such a 'choice' is never real, because the reader is obliged to consume both endings. In life, we make a decision – or a decision makes us – and we go one way; had we made a different decision (as I once told my wife, though I don't think she was in a condition to appreciate my wisdom), we would have been elsewhere. The novel with two endings doesn't reproduce this reality; it merely takes us down two diverging paths.[4]

The narrator therefore suggests that if novelists really wanted to simulate the spectrum of possibilities in life, they would supply a set of sealed envelopes at the back of the book, in various colours. Each would carry clear labels such as 'Traditional Happy Ending', 'Traditional Unhappy Ending', 'Modernist Arbitrary Ending', 'End of the World Ending', 'Dream Ending' and so on. Readers would be allowed only one, and would be obliged to destroy the envelopes they did not select.

Of course, Barnes is giving us here a satire on the belief that novels *should* be realistic, that they *should* mirror life. The narrator, Geoffrey Braithwaite, is an amateur Flaubert enthusiast, who is trying to find the stuffed parrot that served as a model for the parrot Loulou in Flaubert's short story, *Un Coeur Simple*. He is a realist critic, who thinks that he will find the author's true voice and intention if he can only establish various hard facts about Flaubert's life, including the train timetable by which he travelled to meet his mistress, and above all if he can find the parrot. Finding the creator's voice will, he believes, in some way also throw light on his own life story, and in particular enable him to come to terms with his wife's suicide.

But the parrot of Flaubert's story is a mystical beast, an inspiration for the poor maid Felicité's religious feelings, sheltering her with its wings like the Holy Ghost. We realize that no factual information will ever bring us to this parrot. Geoffrey sets out in a scholarly way to resolve the dispute

---

[4] Julian Barnes, *Flaubert's Parrot* (London: Picador, 1985 [1984]), p. 89.

between two rival Flaubert museums, each claiming to preserve the original parrot, which Flaubert borrowed from the Museum of National History and returned there. The book ends with his discovery that the museum had owned fifty similar parrots, and the curators of the two museums, confronted with this largesse, had 'read to themselves Flaubert's description of Loulou . . . And then they chose the parrot which looked most like his description.'[5] It seems that the text had created the referent, rather than the other way round. As Alison Lee wittily suggests, it is the readers and critics of the novels who are all Flaubert's parrots.[6] Arguing that neither museum might have chosen rightly, Geoffrey persists in viewing the remains of the collection in a dusty attic. Three remain, their once-bright colours dimmed by a covering of pesticide, and the novel ends with Geoffrey staring at them and thinking, 'Perhaps it was one of them.'

The end of the book, like its fantastic text which is a ragbag of historical research, literary criticism and story, subverts the realism it pretends to support. The narrator constantly undermines his own obsessions with finding the reality behind the text, as in the little piece about realistic endings quoted above, where his logical case is blown apart by the passing ironic comment, 'as I once told my wife, though I don't think she was in a position to appreciate my wisdom'. Though the book purports to have one, semi-realistic ending, it implies several ways of closure; we are left in uncertainty about whether the narrator is pleased or disappointed by the failed quest for the parrot ('. . . it was an ending and not an ending . . . Well, perhaps that's as it should be', he reflects at one point),[7] and we do not know whether or not the quest has helped him to rationalize his wife's suicide, or in what way.

The reluctance to close a novel has been magnified in recent writing, and shortly we shall be investigating some movements of thought in our contemporary culture to which critics refer when they dub Fowles and Barnes as 'postmodern' novelists.[8] Yet it cannot be denied that the reader demands some kind of closure to a narrative. Frank Kermode judges that we are predisposed to seek what he calls '*pleroma*, fullness, the fullness that

[5]   Ibid., p. 187.
[6]   Alison Lee, *Realism and Power. Postmodern British Fiction* (London: Routledge, 1990), p. 39.
[7]   Barnes, *Flaubert's Parrot*, p. 189.
[8]   See e.g. Linda Hutcheon, *A Poetics of Postmodernism. History, Theory, Fiction* (London and New York: Routledge, 1990), pp. 44–8, 77–8, who classifies such novels as 'metafiction.'

results from completion'.[9] Paul Ricoeur notes that in our age the traditional paradigms of narrative are under threat, and particularly the dictum of Aristotle that a myth is 'an imitation of an action that is whole and complete in itself';[10] but however ambiguous, unexpected or inconclusive the ending might be, Ricoeur rightly maintains that anti-closure must have a limit; beyond a certain boundary we no longer have a work of art or any confidence in language to arrange what happens in life into a meaningful form.[11] Our samples from Fowles and Barnes thus leave us with two questions. Why do we demand some kind of ending to a story, and why does an end seem more difficult to achieve today than before? But by now you may be asking a different question altogether; is this a book about theology at all?

Theology and Literature – a Dialogue

In fact, there is a remarkable convergence going on between theologians and literary critics in their focus upon eschatology. Among the theologians, Jürgen Moltmann has been influential in claiming that eschatology is not just an appendix to Christian doctrine, to be abandoned to the enthusiasms of fanatical sects and revolutionary groups; since eschatology is the doctrine of Christian hope and witnesses to the God of hope, it is 'the medium of Christian faith as such, the key in which everything is set, the glow that suffuses everything here in the dawn of an expected new day.'[12] In the same tones, literary critics declare that the basic nature of texts is eschatological, and that this dimension is too important to be left to the minority interests of science fiction and disaster novels.[13] Indeed, Jacques Derrida

[9]   Frank Kermode, 'Waiting for the End' in Malcolm Bull (ed.), *Apocalypse Theory and the Ends of the World* (Oxford: Blackwell, 1995), p. 251.
[10]   Aristotle, *Poetics* 50b.23–25; see Paul Ricoeur, *Time and Narrative*, vol. 2, transl. K. McLaughlin and D. Pellauer (Chicago and London: University of Chicago Press, 1985), p. 20.
[11]   Ibid., p. 22.
[12]   Jürgen Moltmann, *Theology of Hope. On the Ground and Implications of a Christian Eschatology*, transl. J. Leitch (London: SCM Press, 1967), pp. 15–16.
[13]   See, e.g. Frank Kermode, *The Sense of an Ending. Studies in the Theory of Fiction* (Oxford: Oxford University Press, 1968), pp. 5–17, and 'Lawrence and the Apocalyptic Types' in C. B. Cox and A. E. Dyson (eds), *Word in the Desert* (London: Oxford University Press, 1968), pp. 14–38; Brian McHale, *Postmodernist Fiction* (London and New York: Routledge, 1989), pp. 65–8; Patricia Waugh, *Practising Postmodernism.*

claims that the apocalyptic mood of the nuclear age 'has been dealt with more "seriously" in texts by Mallarmé, or Kafka, or Joyce, for example, than in present-day novels that would offer direct and realistic descriptions of a "real" nuclear catastrophe.'[14] All texts are eschatological, both in being open to the new meaning which is to come to them in the future, and also in being 'seriously' open to the horizon which death gives to life, though the relation between this openness and the interior 'eschaton' of the closure of narrative is debated as vigorously as theologians debate realized and future eschatology.

Nor is the appeal to eschatology as the basic mood of theology and literary creation just an accidental convergence. On the one hand the Christian understanding of the last things – the final advent of the Lord of the cosmos, the last judgement, heaven and hell – is located in a story, the death and resurrection of Jesus Christ, and is dependent on certain basic texts. On the other hand, literary critics are generally concerned not only about the text but about human existence, human society, human hope and especially (as we shall see) the threat of death. We may regard our agenda as being set by Prospero in Shakespeare's *Tempest*, contemplating in one apocalyptic sweep the end of the magical play he has produced on his island, the end of life and the end of the cosmos:

> . . . be cheerful, sir.
> Our revels now are ended. These our actors,
> As I foretold you, were all spirits, and
> Are melted into air, into thin air:
> And, like the baseless fabric of this vision,
> The cloud-capp'd towers, the gorgeous palaces,
> The solemn temples, the great globe itself,
> Yea, all which it inherit, shall dissolve,
> And, like this insubstantial pageant faded,
> Leave not a rack behind. We are such stuff
> As dreams are made on; and our little life
> Is rounded with a sleep.[15]

Reading Modernism (London: Edward Arnold, 1992), pp. 7–16; Fredric Jameson, 'Progress Versus Utopia' in Brian Wallis (ed.), *Art After Modernism: Rethinking Representation* (Boston: David Godine, 1984), pp. 239–52. On science fiction and eschatology, see David Ketterer, *New Worlds for Old: The Apocalyptic Imagination, Science Fiction and American Literature* (New York: Anchor, 1974).

[14] Jacques Derrida, 'No Apocalypse, Not Now (full speed ahead, seven missiles, seven missives)', *Diacritics* 14/2 (1984), pp. 27–8.

[15] Shakespeare, *The Tempest*, IV.1.147–58.

In a previous study, *Freedom and Limit*, I have set out in some detail what I believe to be a fruitful method of 'dialogue' between creative literature and the work of the doctrinal theologian.[16] There I propose a relationship of mutual influence without confusion, where the images and narratives of literature can help the theologian to make doctrinal statements, while at the same time doctrinal thinking can provide a perspective for the critical reading of literary texts. There is, admittedly, a fundamental difference between the nature of literature and doctrine. Poetic metaphor and narrative rejoices in ambiguity and the opening up of multiple meaning; doctrine will always seek to reduce to concepts the images and stories upon which it draws – including those within its own scripture. Literature emphasizes the playful freedom of imagination, while doctrine aims to create a consistent and coherent system of thought, putting into concepts the wholeness of reality that imagination is feeling after. Of course, doctrinal statements are bound to go on using symbol and metaphor since it is not possible to do without analogies in speaking of God as infinite and transcendent Reality. I certainly do not mean to suggest that doctrine is 'literal' speech about God in contrast to the images of poetry. But doctrine uses metaphor in an attempt to *fix* meaning, to define and limit a spectrum of possible interpretations. In short, literature tends to openness and doctrine to closure.

However, because no doctrine can be absolute or final, it needs to be constantly broken open by the impact of image and story in changing times and situations. Creative literature can also help the theologian in deciding between various options of interpretation; there are alternative ways in which the multiple meanings of the metaphors and stories of faith might be fenced around by concepts, and imaginative writing can enable the theologian to make judgements. For instance, with regard to eschatology we might ask whether there is any reason to prefer a doctrine of resurrection to the immortality of the soul. The questions of identity and personal life involved have been well argued from the viewpoint of philosophy of religion, but the study of a novelist such as Doris Lessing will show that there are aspects that can be overlooked within such a narrow discussion (see chapter 4). On the other hand, Christian belief and doctrine can provide a reader with a perspective for the interpretation of literary texts. As E. H. Gombrich aptly puts it, 'the innocent eye sees

[16] Paul S. Fiddes, *Freedom and Limit. A Dialogue between Literature and Christian Doctrine* (Basingstoke: Macmillan Press, 1991), pp. 15, 33–5.

nothing.'[17] Without imputing religious intentions to the author where they do not exist, the attempt of theologians to achieve a coherent grasp of patterns of human experience can make readers sensitive to aspects of experience within and beyond the text that they might otherwise miss. In particular we shall find that theological reflection on the nature of an 'end' to personal and cosmic existence will make us more aware of the way that texts are orientated towards an end, and the effect this has upon the consciousness of the reader.

Such a dialogue is not to be entered upon in a purely pragmatic manner, just to see if it might happen to work. There is a theological justification for embarking upon it in the first place, which again I have worked out in detail in my earlier study. I suggest that images and stories on the one hand, and concepts on the other, are all to be understood as *responses* to revelation. None are *identical* with revelation, for in revelation we are concerned with the self-disclosure of God's own being, not with the transmission of a message or even a picture. Nor is this revelation to be limited to the Bible, though the Hebrew and Christian scriptures are witness to revelation in an exceptional way. Wherever God opens God's own self to draw human persons into relationship with the divine life, there will be response of varying kinds, including that of the imagination. Only this universal self-opening of God can justify the making of connec-tions between theology and other 'writings' in our culture, of whatever kind. On this basis, I want further to prepare for a dialogue between theology and literature on the theme of eschatology by considering, with the help of four literary critics, the way in which all texts are eschatological. Throughout this book I shall be returning to these four basic approaches, represented by Frank Kermode, Northrop Frye, Jacques Derrida and Paul Ricoeur.

The End Organizes the Human Story:
Frank Kermode

In his influential study, *The Sense of an Ending* (1966), Frank Kermode argues that the end of a narrative brings a concord between its beginning, middle and conclusion. The denouement of a novel creates a pattern for the action within it, organizing past, present and future in a way that

[17]   E. H. Gombrich, *Art and Illusion. Studies in the Psychology of Pictorial Representation* (Oxford: Oxford University Press, 5th edn, 1983), p. 271.

overcomes the mere successiveness of time as measured by the clock.[18] The sense that the story is working towards an ending turns mere *chronos* (the 'tick-tock' of the clock) into moments of *kairos*, points of time filled with the significance of being part of a larger fulfilment. Thus all fiction provides 'paradigms of concord' overcoming discord, meeting a basic human need for consolation. Because of the expectation of the end, disorganized time can be 'humanized'. We may summarize Kermode's proposal by observing that the end both organizes and unifies the whole.

Now, Kermode goes on to suggest that the organizing of time within fiction is a model for the way we find a pattern for time in the world itself.[19] Like Prospero in his valedictory speech, we make an analogy between the book and the world. We project concord-fictions onto the scene of our personal history and world history. To make sense of the mere successiveness of history ('just one damn thing after another') we give it a plot, a story, which is unified by its ending. In the Christian West we have read history according to the narrative of the Christian drama of creation and redemption, organized by its ending in the apocalypse of the new creation. Apocalypse depends, Kermode observes, on a 'concord of imaginatively recorded past and imaginatively predicted future'.[20] Here the shaping of time within a book has been especially influential in our understanding of time on the world scene, because the Christian view of the world has been shaped by a *particular* book (the Bible) which ends with the apocalyptic Revelation of John of Patmos. Of course we must add, as does Mark Taylor,[21] that this 'emplotment' of history has not been understood by Christians as a mere *projection* of a concord fiction, but as the *discovery* of relations between events which have been plotted by the divine Logos into a scheme of promise and fulfilment, and which are sustained in their coherence by the presence of the Logos. History is regarded as God's story, and when the story has been revealed to us through the Bible, we can make sense of history.

But the influence does not just run one way, from story to history. Kermode observes that changes in our understanding of the end of history have had their effect on the writing of literature. Since the Reformation there has been a 'wearing out' of the paradigm of concordance on the

---

[18] Kermode, *The Sense of an Ending*, pp. 37, 45–7.
[19] Ibid., pp. 6–10, 54–60.
[20] Ibid., p. 8.
[21] Mark C. Taylor, *Erring. A Postmodern A/theology* (Chicago and London: University of Chicago Press, 1984), p. 59.

world scene. A lack of confidence in history as God's story has appeared among us. In particular, the expectation that an end will come to the world and history has been weakened. The 'end' as an objective event has been generally demythologized in two directions. First, people have become more preoccupied with the individual ending of their own death; and second, the sense of an ending to history has been modified into a crisis of perpetual 'transition' from one age to another.[22] It is as if we are always living at the end of one era and moving into another, though we feel this acutely at the end of a century, such as the one we are facing now.[23] Whether in the crisis of death or transition, the end is now immanent, rather than imminent.

In fact, Kermode points out that the scenario of apocalypse as contained in the Book of Revelation puts some emphasis upon episodes of transition, with the terrors of the three and a half year reign of 'the Beast' forming a bridge into the 'millennial' reign of Christ (Revelation, chapter 13), and a final period of decadence coming before the final judgement (20:7–10).[24] As thinkers have used the code of apocalypse to trace a pattern in history, they have often identified their place in history with the help of the symbols of terrors or decadence, and have felt themselves living in an age of transition. In the work of Joachim of Fiore, for example, the present is interpreted as a transitional stage between the ages of the Son and the Spirit. Kermode's argument is that while apocalyptic images keep their vividness, they have come to be understood as pointing to a situation of crisis rather than a cosmic end itself, that is, the individual crisis of death and the social crisis of being 'at the end of an age'. This change of paradigm on the world scale has had its impact upon the book, as Kermode suggests that creative writers have become preoccupied with the crises of death and transition.

If we return now to our earlier question as to why modern authors find it so difficult to end their novels – the problem of closure – then I suggest that Kermode's analysis offers us some clues. He observes that the end of a book organizes the time-flow within it; but if this is designed in order to produce a sense of transition, the result must be deeply ambiguous. It will impose a kind of pattern on time and event ('the end of an

---

[22] Kermode, *The Sense of an Ending*, pp. 6, 88–9 (on death), 100–03 (on transition).
[23] Ibid., pp. 115–18. In his later essay, 'Waiting for the End', Kermode maintains his view that people always feel themselves to be in an age of transition, and Postmodernism is identified as another form of transition.
[24] Kermode, *The Sense of an Ending*, pp. 12–13.

era'), but it will also easily slip back into mere successiveness. Some writers, such as Samuel Beckett, portray human life in a perpetual state of transition, crying out for an apocalypse that never comes; his characters wait for the end, but all they get is a vain passing of time. Later we shall be looking at Beckett's plays more closely, but it may suffice for the moment to quote from *Endgame*, where Clov cries out, 'Then how can it end?'; Hamm asks, 'You want it to end?' and Clov replies, 'I want to sing'.[25] For song to be possible, time has to be organized with a beginning and an end. But if a story reflects the experience of constant crisis, it is difficult to construct any end.

The difficult of closure is deepened by another factor. Novels have always had to balance their organization with a sense of contingency. There must be an ending to the book which gives it form and shape, yet if a narrative is *too* concordant and consolatory, it will neglect the haphazardness we know in 'real life'.[26] Thus, maintains Kermode, novels have always preserved a tension between a reflecting of accidental reality on the one hand, and the form of the story, which demands a harmony between past, present and future, on the other. A check on consolation can be provided, for example, through irony, paradoxes, or the disconfirming of expectations. But today this check and balance is harder to manage since there is a loss of the sense of history as a divine fiction; viewing history through the lens of Christian story gave a confidence that contingencies would either arrange themselves into patterns, or be resolved in final harmony.[27]

Thus, for several reasons, if we have lost confidence in an ending to the world and history, there will be a deep suspicion about providing an end to any story. But, we might say, even if closure has been undermined by perpetual transition, it is surely still demanded because we all face the ending of our own deaths. Kermode in fact suggests that because the end of a narrative 'humanizes' the time within it, we are consoled in the face of our death. At the close of a novel or play we are left as the surviving remnant, projecting ourselves 'past the End, so as to see the structure

---

[25] Samuel Beckett, *Endgame. A Play in One Act* (London: Faber and Faber, 1964), p. 46.

[26] Kermode, *The Sense of an Ending*, pp. 160–4. Iris Murdoch develops a similar tension between the proper consolations and the potential deceptions ('magic') of the unity of a work of art; see *The Fire and the Sun. Why Plato Banished the Artists* (Oxford: Clarendon Press, 1977), pp. 77–80, and *Metaphysics as a Guide to Morals* (London: Chatto and Windus, 1992), pp. 80–89.

[27] There is a classical statement of this by Paul in Romans 8:18–23.

whole, a thing we cannot do from our spot of time in the middle'.[28] So we are enabled to place our own death within the context of the whole.

Kermode's stress here upon the way that facing an end brings unity to passing moments of time has some affinities with Martin Heidegger's early thought about 'being towards death'. In his work, *Being and Time*, Heidegger finds that the unity of self is based not in any kind of underlying substance but in an enduring through time; the self finds its identity in sameness through past, present and future. However, in actuality our self is broken through a failure to bring our experience of past, present and future into a harmony.[29] Heidegger further suggests that a movement of the will, fixed upon some master concern, will achieve a unifying of the self in time, and he identifies this concern as a concentration upon the fact of death. From the perspective of the non-being that confronts us in death we can be awoken to an authentic way of being in life.

Throughout this study I am going to argue that any Christian view of eschatology must take the fact of death seriously, as the 'last enemy' that the Apostle Paul identifies.[30] Biblical writers view the human person as a psychosomatic unity; the soul is not a survival capsule which can simply float through death unscathed. The New Testament hope for eternal life is in the resurrection of the body and personality together, when God acts to conquer death. Death itself then cannot be our 'final concern' in the way that Heidegger proposes; but we may agree with John Macquarrie and Paul Tillich that facing the shock of the nothingness of death will alert us to God who is our final concern,[31] and it is openness to the God of promise that will bring an integration to a broken existence.

Even, then, if a vision of the end of the world has been lost, it seems that the end of a book or play might still help us to accept and confront our own end, and so bring our lives into a whole. But the increased difficulty that writers find in making a closure is, I suggest, a sign that in our modern Western society we also find it hard to face the fact of death. Ours is a society that evades death, by shutting it away in elaborate funeral arrangements, by not allowing space to grieve, by pretending aging does

[28] Kermode, *The Sense of an Ending*, pp. 7–8.
[29] Martin Heidegger, *Being and Time*, transl. J. Macquarrie and E. Robinson (Oxford: Basil Blackwell, 1973), pp. 236–7, 279–80.
[30] 1 Corinthians 15:26.
[31] John Macquarrie, *Principles of Christian Theology*, revised edn (London: SCM Press, 1977), pp. 86–8, and *Studies in Christian Existentialism* (Philadelphia: Westminster Press, 1965), pp. 45–57; Paul Tillich, *Systematic Theology. Combined Volume* (Welwyn: James Nisbet & Co., 1968), vol. I, pp. 210–20.

not happen through the use of cosmetics and surgery; even the constant display of death on our television screens, whether in news programmes or violent films, evades the fact of death. Death has been packaged as virtual reality, as a media event.

In this study I shall be suggesting that, although the reluctance in our modern culture to acknowledge endings makes closure more difficult than ever before, literature has the power to recreate the sense of an ending, to awaken us through its endings to the greater endings of death and apocalypse. In any case, we should challenge Kermode's general assumption that in our age an end to the cosmos is inconceivable, and so apocalypse must be totally demythologized into death and transition. Modern cosmology is uncovering a finite universe, not in steady state but having a beginning in a 'Big Bang', and an ending in the alternative scenarios of either collapse into itself ('Big Crunch') or expansion to a point where temperature can no longer support life ('Heat Death').[32] On the much smaller scale of the history of the earth, a total end is conceivable rather earlier through such horsemen of the apocalypse as nuclear warfare, toxic poisoning, asteroid collision or destruction of the ozone layer. I do not mean that the acts of God in creation and consummation can be simply *coordinated* with any of these points, as this would limit the freedom of God;[33] but the sense that our universe *has* a story makes more reasonable the belief that God *gives* it a story, which may lead us in turn to put some limits to the demythologizing of the eschaton.

But if the end of all things is totally demythologized, and if at the same time a direct analogy is drawn between the world and the book, the result will be that all concord fictions, *including literary ones*, must somehow be consoling deceptions. The two assumptions taken together mean that the end of a book is a lie – comforting, but no less a lie. As Paul Ricoeur points out, 'a divorce is thus established between truthfulness and consolation.' Ricoeur aptly accuses Kermode's study of ceaselessly oscillating

. . . between the inescapable suspicion that fictions lie and deceive, to the extent that they console us, and the equally invincible conviction that fictions

---

[32] Which alternative is the most likely appears to depend on the density of the universe; see Stephen Hawking, 'The future of the universe' in L. Howe and A. Wain (eds), *Predicting the Future* (Cambridge: Cambridge University Press, 1993), pp. 8–23; Paul Davies, *The Last Three Minutes. Conjectures about the Ultimate Fate of the Universe* (London: Weidenfeld and Nicholson, 1994), pp. 67–81.

[33] This point plays a significant part in the plot of John Updike's novel, *Roger's Version* (New York: Fawcett Cress, 1986).

are not simply arbitrary, inasmuch as they respond to a need . . . to impress
the stamp of order upon the chaos of existence, of sense upon nonsense, of
concordance upon discordance.[34]

This amounts, concludes Ricoeur, to regarding the relation between
literature and human action and suffering as 'consolation reduced to a vital
lie'. I have already suggested that the problem here may come from the
first assumption, that a cosmic ending must be completely demythologized.
Ricoeur himself diagnoses the problem as lying in the second assumption
– in a too easy correspondence established between literature and life,
fiction and reality, the book and the world. Ricoeur acclaims Kermode's
insight that narrative aims at bringing new concords to the discord of time,
or (in Ricoeur's phrase) 'refigures time',[35] but he doubts whether the
impulse for this can be found in either a 'horror of the unformed' in
everyday experience, or in coping with the fear of death.[36] His own tracing
of the roots of this impulse find, as we shall see, that there is an orientation
of human being towards possibility and hope.

Kermode of course recognizes that the work of the poet and the novelist
reaches beyond *mimesis* (imitation of the world) to *poesis* (invention), but
perhaps his view of books as world-models and the world as booklike relies
on a correspondence that does not sufficiently recognize the new world of
possibility that a literary text can create, and so neglects its power to
redeem as well as to console. The parallel that Kermode draws between
the world and the book is illuminating; we do need a sense of an ending
to bring organization and wholeness to our time. However, he leaves little
room (in this study at least)[37] to say anything positive about *lack* of closure.
Difficulty with endings is not entirely to be regretted; as I aim to show,
the openness of endings has a great deal to do with the creative and

---

[34]   Ricoeur, *Time and Narrative*, vol. 2, p. 27.

[35]   Ibid., pp. 100–105.

[36]   Ibid., p. 28. Here Ricoeur opposes Heidegger's view that 'being towards death' is
the primary form of authentic existence: see *Time and Narrative*, vol. 1, transl. K.
McLaughlin and D. Pellauer (Chicago and London: University of Chicago Press,
1984), pp. 60–4, 84–7, and *Time and Narrative*, vol. 3, transl. K. Blamey and D.
Pellauer (Chicago and London: University of Chicago Press, 1988), pp. 92–6.

[37]   In his *The Genesis of Secrecy. On the Interpretation of Narrative* (Cambridge, Massachusetts: Harvard University Press, 1979), Kermode suggests that lack of definite
closure prompts us to make our own closure, even if to do so we have to construct a
secret narrative hidden beneath the surface of the manifest one; see pp. 63–4, 70–3.

redemptive power of texts. But closure also has a place, as Kermode reminds us.

The End Discloses a Desired World: Northrop Frye

Northrop Frye is one critic who is deeply suspicious of the kind of correspondence that Kermode proposes between the patterns of meaning in a piece of literature and patterns of event in the external world. According to Frye, a novel or poem does not reflect the reality of the world around us, but points to a world that is *desired*. We shall see that in working the implications of this out, Frye at least hints at a positive view of resistance to closing a text.

In his book *The Great Code: The Bible and Literature*, Frye finds that the images and plot of the Bible, as in all literature, are 'centripetal' rather than 'centrifugal'; their meaning comes from relating internally to each other, not in relating to an external referent: 'The centripetal aspect of a verbal structure is its primary aspect, because the only thing that words can do with any real precision or accuracy is hang together.'[38] Any particular verbal sign in a literary text, if taken as an isolated unit, has an external referent of some kind; but there is no external correspondence to the coming of signs together into a network or pattern. When, for example, Jesus says 'I am the door' (John 10:9) we know what doors are. But the meaning of the statement, what is *signified* by the signifiers, has no external referent; we cannot find a door in the world that is the kind of door to which this statement points. To think we could would be to find Flaubert's parrot, or in this case an idolatry.

In stressing the sealed world of the text Frye sounds like a member of the 'structuralist' school of criticism, though it is probably better to regard him as 'structural' in approach rather than conforming to structuralism in every respect.[39] Ferdinand de Saussure, the founding father of structuralism, maintained that verbal signs in a text should be studied as an inter-related system in their own right, and not as reflections of any external reality.[40]

[38] Northrop Frye, *The Great Code. The Bible and Literature* (London: Ark Paperbacks, 1983), p. 60.
[39] This distinction is suggested by Anthony C. Thiselton, *New Horizons in Hermeneutics. The Theory and Practice of Transforming Biblical Reading* (London: HarperCollins, 1992), p. 91.
[40] Ferdinand de Saussure, *Course in General Linguistics*, transl. W. Baskin (London: Peter Owen, 1960), pp. 68–70.

Since a sign has only an arbitrary relation with the object to which it refers (its referent), its meaning (what is signified) is to be found in its relation to other signs, and in particular its *difference* from them. A literary text thus has an autonomy; it is not owned by the author, and its meaning is not to be found by investigating the author's intention. Rather, we must employ tools of structural analysis to find the inherent meaning of a text, or the meaning of the text in its own right. In a development from earlier structuralism, the anthropologist Lévi-Strauss maintained that while sign systems are culturally variable, there are deep laws governing the grammar of the systems, which are universal and embedded in the collective mind.[41] The individual subject is to be de-centred, and the author detached from the text, as 'myths think themselves through people'.

Echoes of this later kind of structuralism resound in Frye,[42] and in particular in the way that Frye handles the issue of the *ending* of a work. According to Frye, any narrative or plot may be called a myth, and he identifies four universal forms of myth – comedy, romance, tragedy and irony – of which the two great organizing patterns are the tragic and the comic.[43] Tragedy is about human isolation, and comedy about human integration.[44] A 'comic' ending expresses the fundamental human desire for harmony, and a tragic ending is a broken comedy where the desire remains unfulfilled. To make its effect, tragedy only has to tell the story of natural human life, in its state of alienation, without moving on to redemption; tragedy is a prelude to the desired end of comedy which it glimpses from time to time.[45] The end of a story thus articulates not the individual intention of the author, but the desire of the collective subject of the human race. The verbal structure of the text is a kind of utopian dreaming, an alternative to the world in which we live.[46] Frye comments, apparently with approval, that in much contemporary criticism there is the feeling that 'it is really language that uses man, and not man that uses language'.[47]

Frye thus describes the Bible, in Blake's phrase, as the 'Great Code of Art'; it not only exemplifies but clearly makes manifest the universal

---

[41]   Claude Lévi-Strauss, *Structural Anthropology*, transl. C. Jacobson and B. G. Schoepf (London and New York: Basic Books, 1963), pp. 62–3, 210ff.

[42]   See Frye, *The Great Code*, p. 22.

[43]   Northrop Frye, *Anatomy of Criticism* (Princeton: Princeton University Press, 1971), pp. 161–2, *The Great Code*, p. 73.

[44]   Frye, *Anatomy of Criticism*, pp. 35–7, 43.

[45]   Ibid., p. 215.

[46]   Ibid., p. 170: 'Happy endings do not impress us as true but as desirable.'

[47]   Frye, *The Great Code*, p. 22.

grammar of mythology. Its narrative structure he proposes to be a U-shaped divine comedy, tracing a movement from perfection down to alienation and back to perfection again, and this curve is both the total shape and the pattern for many shorter cycles on the way. As with all narrative endings, its ending expresses human desire for the Kingdom of God and its metaphors express the unity and integration of this spiritual kingdom:

> The entire Bible, viewed as a 'divine comedy' is contained within a U-shaped story . . . one in which man, as explained, loses the tree and the water of life at the beginning of Genesis and gets them back at the end of Revelation. In between, the story of Israel is told as a series of declines into the power of heathen kingdoms . . . each followed by a rise into a brief moment of relative independence.[48]

Now, if the desire expressed by a creative text comes to a focus in its ending, there is bound to be something unresolved about the closure, since ideals 'are seldom defined or formulated'. Thus, while for Kermode the end is open because actuality forbids too much consolation, for Frye the end is open just because it is *not* actuality. Frye suggests that something 'comes to birth' at the end of a comedy, a society that has broken free of old and restrictive legal forms.[49] At the beginning of a comedy an absurd, irrational or life-denying law is usually present, whose advocates try to block the happiness of the heroes. There is the law in *A Midsummer Night's Dream* that compels obedience to parents in the choice of a husband, the decree in *As You Like It* that banishes first the rightful Duke and then Rosalind to the forest, the pedantic oath in *Love's Labour's Lost* that forbids the company of women in the court, the vicious laws against adultery made by Angelo in *Measure for Measure*, and above all the typifying of legalism itself in the bond of Shylock in *The Merchant of Venice*. But at the end life wins out over legalism, and the new society which emerges will be the contrary of habit, ritual bondage and oppressive law. Frye points out that this kind of refusal of closure is somewhat negative; it is simply a reaction *against* what is fixed or defined by the advocates of law, 'who want predictable activity'. Little can be said about this open society except what it is *not*. 'Whatever reality is, it's not that.' We may simply be given

---

[48]   Ibid., p. 169.
[49]   Frye, *Anatomy of Criticism*, pp. 163–70.

to understand that the newly-married couple, for example, will 'get along in a relatively . . . clear-sighted manner'.[50]

Frye finds that the apocalyptic vision of John of Patmos, standing at the close of the biblical comedy, has the same kind of anti-legal openness in its ending.[51] The apocalypse apparently ends with the restoring of the water and the tree of life, the two elements of the original creation that had been lost, but this vision is followed by an 'upward metamorphosis' to something else, a 'second apocalypse' opened by the invitation to *drink* the water of life. A new vision begins in readers' minds as soon as they have finished reading. The 'last judgement' is the climax to the whole series of fantastic ordeals and trials in the narrative, determined by the system of law that arbitrates between good and evil, and which (according to Frye) objectify 'repressed mental forms'; it is when the reader has passed through the judgement that 'the law loses its last hold on us'. We enter the desired world in which the ego and its guilt has disappeared, and the promise is given: 'behold I make all things new' (Rev. 21:15).

Thus the cataclysmic end to the order of nature symbolizes a destruction of the way of seeing that order which keeps us confined to the world of time and history as we know them. This destruction of our conventional structures of understanding is what all art is intended to achieve, and what all scripture aims to do. Apocalypse means 'unveiling', and as the final phase in a sequence of phases of revelation within the total biblical story, this narrative unveils the true meaning of all previous scriptures, providing a glittering array of anti-types to Old Testament texts. 'His dragons and horsemen and dissolving cosmos were what he saw in Ezekiel and Zechariah, whatever or however he saw on Patmos'.[52] The 'wonders' of the vision are not what will happen, but the inner meaning of all that has happened and is happening now; they express the mysteries of the kingdom of God and the mystery of iniquity.

Frye offers the important insight that endings which achieve harmony are based in desire, which Blake truly understood to be a form of the imagination. In exploring later the idea of Christian hope that transcends human desire, we must not leave desire behind. As Blake also sees, desire cannot be contained within law.[53] But Frye's account is based too much in

50   Ibid., p. 169.
51   Frye, *The Great Code*, pp. 136–8.
52   Ibid., p. 135.
53   See e.g. William Blake, *The Marriage of Heaven and Hell*, Plates 5–8, 'The Garden of Love' in *Songs of Experience, Milton, A Poem*, Book 2, plates 40–1.

the uncovering of archetypal patterns already laid down in human imagin-ation.[54] In his analysis of the Apocalypse of John, for example, he misses the way that the unfolding of the vision itself, in its main features, *undermines* the structures of law. The Judgement of The Great White Throne does not operate by the usual rules of a law court; as G. B. Caird points out, what the books recording people's deeds contain is determined by what God in his mercy decides to remember or forget (see Rev. 18:5), and before the ledgers are scrutinized by the auditors, another book is opened, the lamb's book of life, whose contents must be thrown into the balance. 'Into the scale in men's favour are set the gracious, predestining purpose of God and the redemptive love of him who died to ransom men for God'.[55] We are reminded of Paul's use of the image of justification, employing legal language to defeat (or debunk?) a legal vision of life.[56] The colourful ordeals of the preceding visions also express, despite their military imagery, the triumph of suffering witness to the Word of God over oppressive decrees of worldly powers and authorities. The martyrs who go to their deaths under sentence from a Roman judge have no weapon except their words of testimony, but these are like a fire in their mouths (11:5, the scene of the two witnesses). The lamb triumphs through the power of his wounds and the bloody martyrdom of his followers, in a reversal of human expectations about power.[57]

The basic archetypal pattern that Frye finds is the shaping of biblical narrative into a U-shaped curve. But, as I have explained elsewhere,[58] this is actually a reading imposed upon scripture under the influence of Augustine, understanding human alienation to be the result of fallenness from a perfect original creation; in fact, as Irenaeus perceived early in Christian theology, the Old Testament does not portray a perfect, but an immature, original state of human life.[59] The curve, returning to an upper

[54] While Frye's structuralism is moderate, he does accept the notion of archetypes, if cautiously: see *Anatomy of Criticism*, p. 99–102.

[55] G. B. Caird, *A Commentary on the Revelation of St. John the Divine* (London: Adam & Charles Black, 1966), p. 259.

[56] See e.g. Romans 3:23–5. On this, see Paul S. Fiddes, *Past Event and Present Salvation* (London: Darton, Longman and Todd, 1989), pp. 86–8.

[57] Revelation 5:12, 12:11, 19:15. These observations are in accord with the proposal by René Girard, that apocalyptic pictures can be used to unmask the 'law' of redemptive violence: see Girard, *Things Hidden from the Foundation of the World*, transl. S. Bann and M. Matteer (London: Athlone Press, 1987), p. 251f.

[58] See my *Freedom and Limit*, pp. 47–52.

[59] Irenaeus, *Adversus Haereses*, 4.38.

level from which it begins, betrays Frye's structural preoccupations with
internal relations of the text such as inversion, equivalence, and opposition.
This shape of the story undermines an openness to the future, and so tends
to restrict eschatology to the unveiling of timeless truth. The weight of a
structural approach will inevitably be towards the closure of a narrative,
however much Frye tries to inject some openness into the end.

Frye takes a similarly archetypal approach to the nature of poetic images.
Within the movement of a myth is a pattern of metaphors that have a
unified structure and support the myth's shape. Here Frye identifies three
basic kinds of images: the apocalyptic express *the desired world*, the demonic
express the world that desire totally rejects, and the 'analogical' express
human experiences which are intermediate to the apocalyptic and demonic
extremes.[60] The colourful images of the Book of Revelation recapitulate
metaphors we have met many times in the pages of scripture, apocalytic
images that unveil the object of our desire or the spiritual kingdom: 'The
apocalyptic world, the heaven of religion, presents . . . the categories of
reality in the forms of human desire, as indicated by the forms they assume
under the work of human civilization'.

'The Biblical Apocalypse', suggests Frye, 'is our grammar of apocalyptic
imagery'.[61] He finds such imagery to be drawn first from the upper half
of the natural cycle – the sphere of youth, spring and the energy of life;
here the main images are the tree and the water of life, which appear in
the garden of Eden and re-appear in the heavenly Jerusalem. Then there
are images drawn from pastoral, agricultural, and urban life which represent an idealized transformation through human work and desire of the
animal, vegetable and mineral worlds. The main images here, corresponding to these three worlds, are flocks (animal/ pastoral), harvests and gardens (vegetable/ agricultural), cities and roads (mineral/ urban). As we
follow the U-shaped curve of the biblical narrative from alienation to
resurrection, we encounter these images on the upper slope of the curve,
suggesting 'a nature transformed into an environment with human meaning'. Finally there are the apocalyptic images for human life itself – the
metaphors of a human being as king (representative form), bridegroom
(individual form) and bride (social form). The demonic forms of the last
two images are also prominent in the Book of Revelation, namely the

---

[60]   Frye, *Anatomy of Criticism*, pp. 141, 147, 151; in *The Great Code*, pp. 139–43, Frye
applies this threefold classification to biblical imagery.
[61]   Frye, *Anatomy of Criticism*, p. 141.

Beast – probably symbolizing Nero – (individual) and the Great Whore (social).[62]

This structural approach to image has, I suggest, some real gains for a Christian eschatology. As with the shape of a narrative, we need to allow the patterns of images within the text of scripture to make their own imaginative impact, to let them create concepts in their own right rather than to subject them immediately to external systems of thought, or to demythologize from an alien perspective. This point has been made forcibly by Frye's near-namesake, Hans Frei, in relation to biblical narrative.[63] With regard to our study of eschatology we shall find this to be essential as we explore the metaphor of resurrection and the narrative pattern of promise and fulfilment.

Thus, Frye finds an opening up of the end of narrative in the *effect* that it has upon us as readers. In Frye's view, because a literary text does not *represent* the outside world, it does not follow that there is no *relation* at all between them. The 'Prague School' of structuralism had already added that a work of art, autonomous as it is, can renew our perceptions of the world by drawing attention to its own structure, and by undermining the conventional sign systems with which we normally work. Language itself can shape consciousness.[64] Frye builds on this perception, characterizing myths and metaphors as 'rhetorical', that is, having the power to persuade. They are not 'rhetorical' in the sense of being figures of speech that we construct to illustrate or decorate our arguments or our account of history; rather, metaphor has a structure of universal meaning that can produce and sustain any number of arguments or interpretations, just as myth can sustain a number of historical applications. Metaphor and myth create concepts and histories. Myths in this way have a social function and a social concern: 'they are the stories that tell a society what is important for it to know, whether about its gods, its history, its laws, or its class structure.'[65]

With this emphasis on rhetoric and the social concern of myth, Frye is already drifting away from orthodox structuralism, and moves away more dramatically when he proposes that one particular text, the Bible, may be

---

[62] Frye, *The Great Code*, pp. 142–4, 165–6.
[63] Hans W. Frei, *The Eclipse of Biblical Narrative. A Study in Eighteenth and Nineteenth Century Hermeneutics* (New Haven: Yale University Press, 1974).
[64] See e.g. Roman Jakobson and Morris Halle, *Fundamentals of Language* (The Hague: Mouton, 1956).
[65] Frye, *The Great Code*, p. 33.

regarded as 'God's rhetoric'. God is the final speaker behind the biblical text; its kerygma expresses the rhetoric of God accommodated to human intelligence, and this Word has been incarnated in history in Christ. The author is certainly absent from the book, as is the case with all books, but the book invokes a 'presence' which lies behind the text; while the text does not *represent* the historical appearance of the Word, it enables this background presence to be recreated forwards in the reader's mind.[66] Moreover, the universal human desire expressed in the comic shape of myth and in the apocalyptic images it contains is a desire for the Kingdom of God, and this has a reality beyond the objective world.

But for all this, Frye's account of a desired world keeps the world of the text self-enclosed in its own reality. Structuralism as a whole deserves the stricture that it escapes from history in a search for certainty. It loses the human subject facing the realities of politics, labour and social change in exalting the new subject of the system of language itself. As Terry Eagleton rightly affirms, language is practised by persons in a social context, and this demands a valuation of the importance and truth of a text that structuralism refuses to give.[67] There are the seeds of an advance beyond idealism in Frye's concern with the rhetorical power of a text, but logically this should lead us to break out of the structural prison of language. If a piece of literature has persuasive power, then there are speakers who are seeking to persuade and hearers being persuaded in particular social contexts. A text is a performance with actors and audience. As Eagleton puts it, even when it is not considered as the speech act of a particular historical author, it constructs 'subject positions'; it embodies an intention to achieve certain effects, and this means a reference to historical life.[68] It is difficult, for instance, to see why Frye's analysis of the ending of a text or the apocalyptic nature of images should result in a rhetoric that encourages freedom in society, as Frye as a good liberal democrat believes they do. If these patterns of meaning are autonomous within the text, then the way in which they apply themselves to social life seems quite arbitrary. An analysis of the structure of a text is a useful tool in discovering how it makes its effects, but a study of text as 'rhetorical discourse' means taking its place in history more seriously.

[66] Ibid., pp. xx, 138.
[67] Terry Eagleton, *Literary Theory. An Introduction* (Oxford: Blackwell, 1983), pp. 111–12.
[68] Ibid., p. 120.

Biblical Eschatology and Openness

We have now surveyed two answers to our original question about the effect the ending of a text has upon both the text and the reader. First, the end organizes and unifies the whole; second, the end expresses a desired world. The closure will be incomplete, however, for various reasons. Lack of conviction in our modern culture about a cosmic end and a reluctance to face the fact of death will make literary endings more difficult, while the anti-legalistic nature of desire will always resist what is fixed and predictable. It seems that a satisfactory ending of a text would integrate closure and openness, and in the next chapter I propose to explore the way that an attitude of hope might achieve this in both literature and theology.

This balance between openness and closure is, I want to argue, fundamental to a truly religious view of the end of all things. There has to be a certainty about the overcoming of evil and the triumph of God's purposes, but the freedom of God and the freedom of human beings to contribute to God's project in creation also demands an openness in the future. Here, however, we need to make some distinctions in our terminology, since not all types of eschatological literature allow for this balance in the same way. When I use the term 'eschatology' in this book I mean a concern for 'last things' in general. The end in view may be of various kinds; it might be the end *of* history and the cosmos, or it may be an end *in* history such as the Old Testament prophets envisaged.

When the prophets spoke of 'the day of the Lord', or 'that day' or 'the latter end of times'[69] they had in view a decisive turn of events in history, a day when Yahweh would act to vindicate his faithful people and judge both their oppressors and the unfaithful in the nation itself (though this last expectation was surprising and unwelcome to many who took a more nationalistic view of the 'Day'). The imagery of cosmic disturbance and dissolution which accompanies this expectation is not to be taken literally; it may be the traditional language of theophany, or imagery enlisted from creation myths (protology), or even 'end of the world' imagery applied metaphorically to a historic event.[70] Jeremiah describes such a day as one

---

[69] See e.g. Amos 5:18–20, 8:8–9; Isaiah 2:12–21, 13:9–11; Jeremiah 4:23–6; Zephaniah 1:14–16, 2:2–4; Joel 1:15, 2:28–32.
[70] See Stanley Frost, *Old Testament Apocalyptic. Its Origins and Growth* (London:

in which the sky rolls up like a scroll and the stars fall, but we realize as we read on that this picture of cosmic collapse is metaphor for a foreign army coming over the hill and razing Jerusalem to the ground.[71] It was appropriate to use such dramatic imagery, as the Day would be a moment after which nothing would ever be the same again. We might then call this category of expectation *prophetic eschatology*. In later prophecy the hope for a 'golden age' of peace and stability developed out of 'the Day of the Lord', but it was not until about the mid-third century BC that 'apocalyptic' appeared in which the end was now considered to be the passing away of the present order of reality altogether into a future age – that is, the end *of* history.

A second category is therefore the *apocalypse* as a literary type, the apocalypses of the later Jewish and early Christian tradition, written between about 250 BC and 100 AD.[72] These are a kind of writing marked by a dualism between this world and another world, where the 'other world' may be either spatially or temporally located, or both. That is, the apocalypse may offer revelation *both* about a parallel reality going on in heaven, and about the final destiny of the world and individuals in 'the age to come'.[73] The *apocalypse* claims that this revelation has been received through a vision (including otherworldly dream journeys) or through the mediation of angels. When both kinds of dualism are *strongly* present, there is a sense of predetermination and thus 'closure'; the battle against principalities and powers in the heavenly places will be inevitably duplicated on earth, and the already existing heavenly kingdom will be 'inserted into human history'[74] bringing it to an end. This end is also usually regarded as imminent; the readers of the apocalypse are living in the crisis of the last times. However, some apocalypses (especially the

---

Epworth Press, 1952), pp. 32–5, 234–8; G. B. Caird, *The Language and Imagery of the Bible* (London: Duckworth, 1980), pp. 113–15.

[71] Jeremiah 4:23–26, cf. 1:14–15, 10:22.

[72] Examples are: The Book of Daniel, I Enoch (Ethiopic Book of Enoch), II Enoch (Slavonic Book of Enoch), Apocalypse of Abraham, Apocalypse of Zephaniah, II Esdras (or 4 Ezra), II Baruch, the Apocalypse of John (i.e. Book of Revelation). D. S. Russell provides a useful classification in *The Method and Message of Jewish Apocalyptic 200BC-AD100* (London: SCM Press, 1964), pp. 36–40.

[73] J. J. Collins includes both the spatial and temporal element in his definition of apocalyptic: see Collins (ed.) *Apocalyptic; the Morphology of a Genre, Semeia* 14 (1979), p. 9.

[74] André Lacocque's phrase: in *Daniel in his Time* (Columbia, S.C.: University of South Carolina Press, 1988), p. 89.

'Ascent' apocalypses) are only concerned with a spatial dualism and not at all with a temporal ending; this has led one scholar, Christopher Rowland, to claim that the basic nature of apocalypse is not eschatology at all, but the disclosure of divine secrets through revelation, and so a discovery of the will of God.[75] After all, *apocalupsis* means an 'unveiling'. Apocalypses certainly vary in the emphasis given to the two kinds of dualism, and less stress laid upon details of a parallel world in heaven will generally result in a more open view of the future.

A third category is therefore *apocalyptic eschatology*, a kind of eschatology that envisages the end of history and cosmos, and which may (or may not) be a feature of *apocalypses*. It is this, as a mode of expectation, that mainly concerns us in this study rather, than the literary genre of *apocalypses*. Some scholars also use a fourth category, the term '*apocalyptic*' or 'apocalypticism' to refer to a broad historical 'movement of mind', an eclectic mood that surrounded and gave birth to the apocalypses, and we shall find this useful occasionally.[76] To speak of 'apocalyptic eschatology' does not then, I suggest, in itself presume a predetermined view of the future, nor the imminence of the end, such as is found in some apocalypses. This kind of eschatology is, however, marked by the confidence that God will bring the divine purposes to completion, and so by a concern for the sovereignty of God. D.S. Russell comments that: 'Such prophecies declare not a predetermined programme which is to work itself out . . . with exact precision . . . but rather a divine principle which sees God in control of events rather than events in control of God.'[77] However, even the word 'control' here implies a degree of determinism that may not be reflected in all apocalyptic eschatology (in parts of the Book of Revelation, for instance), and which I myself do not wish to affirm in developing a view of the future.

Apocalypses as a genre have a strong momentum towards the organization and unification of history from the perspective of the end. This intention of God, in the words of André Lacocque, 'constitutes the secret of the universe'.[78] In the expression of such hope, heaven and earth merge

---

[75] Christopher Rowland, *The Open Heaven. A Study of Apocalyptic in Judaism and Early Christianity* (London: SPCK, 1982), p. 14.

[76] See Klaus Koch, *The Rediscovery of Jewish Apocalyptic* (London: SCM Press, 1972), pp. 18–33; D. S. Russell, *Divine Disclosure. An Introduction to Jewish Apocalyptic* (London: SCM Press, 1992), pp. 13, 24–6.

[77] D. S. Russell, *Daniel. An Active Volcano. Reflections on the Book of Daniel* (Edinburgh: Saint Andrew, 1989), p. 15.

[78] Lacocque, *Daniel in His Time*, p. 89.

together, the transcendent and the mundane combine, and this age coalesces with the age to come. Thus, events of past history leading up to the present moment are arranged into a significant pattern, and narrating them in this way gives the reader confidence that the leap into the future consummation will also take place. In the Book of Daniel, events are traced leading up to the decree of Antiochus, the suspension of the daily offering in the Temple and the very edge of the Maccabean revolt (167 BC); at this point[79] the writer launches into the future, predicting the destruction of the Desolator and the resurrection of the dead. In the Book of Revelation we have coded descriptions of the persecution of the Christian church under successive Roman Emperors leading up to the present moment of writing (probably in the latter part of the reign of Domitian), when the seer finally moves into the future with the fall of the Roman Empire or Babylon (chapters 17–19) followed again by the resurrection. As with Kermode's view of the organizing power of the end of any narrative, this stresses closure, and in the case of a cosmic end may seem quite determined. The dualistic scenario is often marked by a pessimism about this world and this age, as if it cannot be redeemed, but only replaced.

But we also notice in the wild images of desire in apocalyptic some of the resistance to legalism that we find in Frye's account of a comedy; in fact, one of the roots for apocalyptic may have been a reaction against the growth of a theocracy in Israel after the Babylonian exile, when it was assumed that the living voice of prophecy had come to an end, that the prophets could now be regarded as transmitters of the law, and that the hopes of previous generations had been buried in the walls of the restored Jerusalem, the rebuilt Temple and the new priestly establishment. Although apocalyptic writers were also believers in theocracy, they wanted to assert – suggests Otto Plöger[80] – that God's purposes could not be so neatly defined, that there was a 'surplus' of meaning from past prophecies not yet fulfilled. While the weight in *apocalypses* is certainly towards closure, there is thus still a note of openness; this is especially evident in the apocalypse included in the New Testament – the Book of Revelation – and I believe it is even stronger in the apocalytic eschatology to be found elsewhere in the New Testament, and notably in Paul's vision of the renewed cosmos.

[79]   That is, the very last phrase of Daniel 9:27 about the 'decreed end', which is expanded in 11:40–45.
[80]   Otto Plöger, *Theocracy and Eschatology* (Oxford: Blackwell, 1968), pp. 110–15.

Closure and Openness in Ending

I began with a modern novel that ends with an ambiguity about whether lovers were reconciled or divided for ever. This kind of ambiguity about closure is not unique to the modern age, though perhaps it is harder to close novels now than ever before. We need only compare them with a nineteenth century realistic novel such as Dickens' *Great Expectations* to see the point. This novel appears to have some problems about closure, as Dickens actually supplied two endings, though he only printed one. He first wrote an ending in which Pip meets the mysterious and cruel Estella in passing in a London street, many years after they parted; he learns that she too has been marked by suffering in the years that have passed, and she assumes he is happily married. Under pressure from friends, Dickens then substituted a happier ending in which Pip and Estella meet in the garden of the ruined house where they had grown up together and where she was schooled by Miss Haversham to break men's hearts; they acknowledge that each has suffered, and it appears that they determine never to part again.

Apart from the inconceivability of Dickens providing both endings at once, as does Fowles, there is another crucial difference. As Martin Meisel points out in his essay on the ending of *Great Expectations*,[81] the physical ending to the book is not the thematic end; this has already come when Pip returns to the blacksmith's cottage after years in the East, and finds little Pip there (chapter 59). The happiness of Joe Gargery and Biddy with their little son 'in his likeness' underlines Pip's own moral failure in life, his loss of true values in chasing the illusory 'great expectations', and it affirms 'the possibility of individual and social redemption in the children'.[82] There is a complex relation then, between the 'thematic ending' (the return to the forge) and the 'fictive ending' (the last chapter);[83] but unlike the twentieth century 'postmodern' novel, the author's authoritative voice, his moral intention and his social realism are not subverted whichever fictive ending is appended.

[81] Martin Meisel, 'The Ending of *Great Expectations*' in Norman Page (ed.), *Hard Times, Great Expectations and Our Mutual Friend. A Casebook* (Basingstoke: MacMillan, 1979).

[82] Meisel, 'The Ending of *Great Expectations*', p. 128.

[83] We may compare the distinction between 'narrative' and 'fictive' ending made by Paul Ricoeur, *Time and Narrative*, vol. 2, pp. 21–22, though he makes no reference to *Great Expectations*.

I cannot agree with Meisel, however, that the final chapter can only be a postscript. We *are* interested in the relationship between Pip and Estella; we want to know what happens to them. Actually, Dickens's finally chosen ending is not unambiguously happy; a cloud of uncertainty hangs over the syntax in the final sentence. We can make it a happy ending if we wish, but we could read it in a more uncertain way.

> 'We are friends,' said I, rising and bending over her, as she rose from the bench.
> 'And will continue friends apart,' said Estella.
> I took her hand in mine, and we went out of the ruined place; and, as the morning mists had risen long ago when I first left the forge, so the evening mists were rising now, and in all the broad expanse of tranquil light they showed to me, *I saw no shadow of another parting from her.*[84]

He saw none. But was there none? A closure has been achieved at the forge, but the desire for a new world expressed in Pip's 'great expectations' cannot be so neatly achieved.

---

[84]   Emphasis mine.

Chapter Two

DEFERMENT
AND HOPE

Novels which offer nightmare visions of the future, or *dystopias*, usually include the banning of books that are seen to be a threat to the oppressive authorities. In Ray Bradbury's science fiction classic, *Fahrenheit 451*, for example, the main character, Guy Montag, is a fireman. But these firemen do not put fires out; their job is to make them, using kerosene sprays to burn books – hence the title, since 451 degrees F. is the temperature at which book paper catches fire and burns, and the firemen wear the symbolic number emblazoned on their helmets. In fact, when they discover collections of books they punish the owner by burning down the entire house in which they are found, and sometimes incinerate the owner along with them. The book begins with Montag's joy in his job:

> It was a pleasure to burn. It was a special pleasure to see things eaten, to see things blackened and changed. With the brass nozzle in his fists, with this great python spitting its venomous kerosene upon the world, the blood pounded in his head, and his hands were the hands of some amazing conductor playing all the symphonies of blazing and burning to bring down the tatters and charcoal ruins of history.

But Guy gradually becomes uneasy about his job, collects some forbidden books himself, becomes word-drunk on the Book of Job and the poetry of Matthew Arnold, has his own house burnt down and becomes a dissident on the run, chased by the mechanical hound whose jaws contain a lethal hypodermic. In this often prophetic novel, Bradbury offers (through the mouth of an old man) a significant reason why the authorities have forbidden all books. The point is not just that books contain subversive ideas, unwelcome to authorities. The book itself *as a medium* has been banned as dangerous. The walls of people's living rooms have been entirely replaced by huge television screens, so that they are surrounded by the characters of their favourite soap operas, and live in a world of virtual reality. The old man points out that:

> '. . . you can't argue with the four wall televisor. Why? The televisor is "real". It is immediate. It has dimension. It tells you what to think and blasts it in. It *must* be right. It *seems* so right. It rushes you on so quickly to its own conclusions your mind hasn't time to protest, "What nonsense!".' . . .
> 'My wife says books aren't "real".'
> 'Thank God for that. You can shut them, say, "Hold on a moment" . . . Books can be beaten down with reason . . .'[1]

Books are dangerous just because they are open in meaning. They invite a plurality of interpretations. Immediate speech, whether it is a person speaking in the flesh, or in the virtual reality of television, seems more 'real', and so more convincing. Imaginatively, long before the coming of the movement called postmodernism, Bradbury has seized on a theme that has occupied Derrida, Roland Barthes and others. Jacques Derrida points out that a written text calls attention to the *absence* of the author, while oral speech seems to affirm the *presence* of the speaker and so offers a communication which claims to mirror 'reality' objectively.[2] But in fact we are sign-users, whether the signs are written or not. All our discourse is a kind of "writing", a system of signs, not just the written text, and so it is all open to contradiction and expansion of meaning. Books just make this clear. In their openness books deflate the pretensions of those who want to oppress others with their vision of reality, and who seem to carry conviction when they speak forcibly in person.

In *Fahrenheit 451* there is in fact a coming together of the speaker and the book when Guy finds refuge among a company of people who are living books; they have all memorized one text and preserve it in hope for the future, passing it on to their children. One of them explains:

---

[1] Ray Bradbury, *Fahrenheit 451* (London: Flamingo/Harper Collins, 1993 [1954]), p. 92.
[2] Jacques Derrida, *Speech and Phenomena, and Other Essays on Husserl's Theory of Signs*, transl. D. B. Allison (Evanston: North Western University Press, 1973 [1967]), pp. 129–40, cf. Derrida's *Writing and Difference*, transl. A. Bass (London: Routledge, 1978), pp. 175–8 and *Of Grammatology*, transl. G. C. Spivak (Baltimore and London: Johns Hopkins University Press, 1976 [1967]), p. 30.

'I am Plato's *Republic*. Like to read Marcus Aurelius? Mr. Simmons is Marcus
. . . And this other fellow is Charles Darwin, and this one is Schopenhauer,
and this one is Einstein . . . we are also Matthew, Mark, Luke and John . . .
Why, there's one town in Maryland, only twenty-seven people, no bomb'll
ever touch that town, is the complete essays of a man named Bertrand
Russell. Pick up that town, almost, and flip the pages, so many pages to a
person . . .'[3]

Guy resolves to become the Book of Ecclesiastes, and perhaps – daringly
– the Book of Revelation.

The End Defers Meaning: Jacques Derrida

We turn from this chilling picture of a future where books are subversive
because they can be 'argued with', and we consider a group of critics who
seek to subvert all the attempts which are made to control others through
imposing a *total vision* of the world and history. I mean the disturbing
prophets of 'deconstruction', who are part of the movement calling itself
'postmodernism', and chief among whom was (and is) Jacques Derrida.
They come with both a political and a literary critique of all 'structuralism'.
Politically they are opposed to any appeal to universal structures of
meaning, Grand Stories, total theories or metanarratives, as they suspect
that these are simply ideologies under another name, designed by powerful
groups in society to manipulate and dominate.[4] They are thus eager to
demystify (or debunk) all the myths of modernity by which we try to
make sense of the world as a whole, whether these are religious, economic
or political. A prime target of deconstructive modernism has been the
'American Dream'; a myth closer home to us in the UK has probably been
the 'freedom of the markets'. But even the earlier 'masters of suspicion'
like Marx and Freud have to be unmasked.

With regard to the language of texts, these critics of modernism both
build upon and contradict the earlier literary movement called 'structuralism'. Here they fasten upon the concept of '*difference*' in the analysis by the
founding father of 'structuralism', Ferdinand de Saussure. Saussure had seen
the meaning of a verbal sign as being established through its relational
difference from another sign. As he puts it, 'two signs a and b are never

---

[3]   Bradbury, *Fahrenheit 451*, pp. 158–61.
[4]   See Jean-François Lyotard, *The Postmodern Condition. A Report on Knowledge*, transl.
G. Bennington (Manchester: Manchester University Press, 1984), pp. 27–40.

grasped as such by our linguistic consciousness, but only the difference between a and b.'[5] Let me invent an example. The meaning of the signifier 'book' is not established by any similarity of the sound 'book' or the shape of the word 'book' on the page to the actual physical appearance of a book. It is established through its difference from such signifiers as 'newspaper' or 'magazine' or even 'CD ROM'; it is also established through difference from other sounds such as 'back' or 'buck' or 'boot' or 'bark'.

So for Saussure, and the structuralists who follow him, a written text is a sealed world of its own. The network of verbal signs within it does not reflect the everyday world, but must be studied as an inter-related system in its own right. A literary text has an autonomy; it is not owned by the author and its meaning is not to be found by investigating the author's intention. In the previous chapter we saw some echoes of this structural approach in Northrop Frye, for whom the world of the text does not refer to the world around us, but expresses deep-laid human desire. For structuralists, the meaning of words and phrases comes from their relation to each other, and particularly their difference from each other.

Derrida, however, pounces upon this proposal; he points out that a relation of difference can be infinitely expanded as all signs differ from all others. So *différence* in the spatial sense of distance between things becomes *différence* in the temporal sense of 'deferment' or postponement of meaning. Derrida coins the word *différance* (with an *a*) to evoke both these senses of difference at once – *differing* and *deferring* – without simply combining them; *différance* hovers between the two and cannot be trapped in any category, but it certainly results in a dispersal of meaning.[6] So if we accept the insights of structuralism itself about the network of language, we can never reach any final point in interpretation of a text. It is endlessly open in meaning, and there can be no archetypal structures such as the comedy of desire that Frye discerns.

According to the deconstructionists, meaning is not immediately present in a sign. Because signifiers become the signified to which new signifiers point, meaning is dispersed down an infinite chain of signs.[7] When we read a sentence, final meaning is suspended or postponed; it is still to come.

---

[5]   Ferdinand de Saussure, *Course in General Linguistics*, transl. W. Baskin (London: Peter Owen, 1960), p. 116.

[6]   Jacques Derrida, 'La Différance', in Derrida, *Margins of Philosophy*, transl. A. Bass (Chicago: University of Chicago Press, 1982), pp. 6–15.

[7]   Derrida, *Of Grammatology*, p. 7.

'The text practises the infinite deferral of the signified' (Roland Barthes).[8] There can certainly be no 'transcendental signifier', that is, one signifier that acts as a foundation or unity for all others, whether this be Reason, class warfare or the Oedipus complex. Nor can there be a 'transcendental signified' – that is, a concept which is present even without signifiers and which exceeds the chain of signs, so acting as the cause of all meaning in the text – such as God.[9] *Différance* itself is not a concept that can be *thought*; there is a continual 'flickering, spilling and defusing of meaning' which 'can *show* us something about nature of meaning and signification which it is not able to formulate as a proposition.'[10]

A verbal sign is what it is only because it is *not* something else. It can be called a 'trace', first because it does not correspond to a 'thing in itself' in the world, but only offers a clue or a hint to it (as structuralists had stressed), and second because it contains the mark of what it differs from or of what is still to come. It traces out a future track for the reader, throwing itself forward in reference to other traces which are yet to be.[11] In this way a text, as Barthes stresses, involves the reader in generating a plurality of meanings; it draws the reader in to share in the pleasurable play which it produces in the absence of either the author or the referent.[12] For Derrida, the trace is thus 'foundational absence'. But we ourselves are not exempted from this world of traces that stand 'under erasure'; our selfhood also is in question.[13] Because we always use verbal signs, even when we search our own minds, we are creatures of traces, never fully present to others or to ourselves.

In a later chapter we are going to tackle this critique of full or immediate presence, which in some versions of deconstruction (but not in Derrida himself) has become an onslaught on the very idea of 'presence' altogether. Our concern here, however, is specifically with the sense of an ending in texts, and there are two essays of Jacques Derrida that have a particular interest – 'Of an Apocalyptic Tone Newly Adopted in Philosophy' (1980) and 'No Apocalypse, Not Now' (1984). In the first, Derrida proposes that

---

[8]   Roland Barthes, 'From Work to Text', in Josué V. Harari (ed.), *Textual Strategies. Perspectives in Post-Structuralist Criticism* (Ithica: Cornell University Press, 1979), p. 76.

[9]   Jacques Derrida, *Positions*, transl. A. Bass (Chicago: University of Chicago Press, 1981), pp. 19–20; cf. *Of Grammatology*, pp. 49–50.

[10]   Terry Eagleton, *Literary Theory. An Introduction* (Oxford: Blackwell, 1983), p. 134.

[11]   Derrida, *Speech and Phenomena*, pp. 135–41.

[12]   Roland Barthes, *The Pleasure of the Text*, transl. R. Miller (London: Jonathan Cape, 1976), pp. 78–80.

[13]   Derrida, *Writing and Difference*, pp. 221–31.

all texts are apocalyptic in the sense that they defer the final unveiling of meaning to the future; *apocalypses* as a genre are simply self-conscious about doing this.[14] Here Derrida confesses that he has become intrigued by the resonance of the appeal 'Come!' throughout the text of the Book of Revelation. The invitation accompanies the opening of the first four of the seven seals (Revelation 6:1–8), the showing of the judgement of the Great Harlot (17:1), and the showing of the bride of the Lamb in the heavenly Jerusalem (21:9). Above all, the book ends with the invitation 'Come' issued by the Spirit and the Bride, to which the visionary responds 'Come, Lord Jesus'. There is, says Derrida, an elusiveness about this appeal that sums up the apocalyptic nature of texts.[15] It is unclear in the first place who the speaker or author of the invitation is. Jesus is on the face of it the one who says 'stay awake, I am coming soon' (22:7, 12, 20); he is the narrative voice which is heard from behind John's back (1:9–11). But throughout the text there is a differential multiplication of messages, a complex interaction of narrative voices and narrating voice so that one is often not clear who speaks or writes, or who addresses what to whom. There is an interlacing of 'narrative sending', which Derrida evidently identifies as an open series of signifiers and signified.

At the very beginning of the book, for instance, God is said to give a revelation to Christ, who gives it to his angel, who gives it to John who gives it to the reader (Rev. 1:1–2). Yet all this is summed up as somehow being 'the testimony *of* Jesus Christ.' Indeed, the interaction of messengers may be even more complex than Derrida supposes, if we follow the example of several New Testament scholars (including Richard Bauckham), who identify those who 'read aloud the words of the prophecy' as prophets who take the messages to the churches.[16] The confusion as to who is speaking also comes out into the open in the final chapter, with the mingled voices of the angel, Jesus, John, the Spirit, the Bride and 'the one who testifies', but every speech in the book is mediated through a narrator who is apparently not simply John. The recurrent invitation 'Come' thus resists any assimilation to ideology, since one cannot deduce its origin and so the issuing authority. 'Come' cannot be made into an object to be

[14] Jacques Derrida, 'Of an Apocalyptic Tone Newly Adopted in Philosophy', transl. J. Leavey, in Harold Coward and Toby Foshay (eds), *Derrida and Negative Theology* (Albany: State University of New York Press, 1992), pp. 57–8.

[15] Ibid., pp. 52–6.

[16] Richard Bauckham, *The Climax of Prophecy. Studies on the Book of Revelation* (Edinburgh: T. & T. Clark, 1993), pp. 85–6.

examined or categorized, it points to an absent place that is not described, and it is addressed to recipients who are not identified in advance. Derrida concludes that 'I do not know what come *is*',[17] though he knows what it does. 'Come' is the apocalyptic tone itself, the apocalypse of the apocalypse, without message, without messengers, without senders or destinations.[18] In this single word Derrida is able to sum up deconstructionist convictions about the *absences* of the writer and the referent from a text, that enable the reader to find inexhaustible meaning within it.

What 'Come' *does* is to break open the ending of the narrative. When we think that everything is neatly wrapped up through the Last Judgement into either the heavenly Jerusalem or the lake of fire, there is heard once more the word 'Come'! The invitation is issued to drink of the water of life. The apocalypse breaks into the apocalypse, so that even though the readers are forbidden to add to the actual length of the text or subtract from it, the book cannot be sealed up (22:10, 18–19). The Book of Revelation depicts the end of the cosmos, and provides what seems to be the definitive ending to a story; but even this ending deconstructs itself, and so disperses meaning rather than completing it. The apocalyptic tone of every text is the invitation 'come' issued to the reader: come and find ever more in the superabundant store of meaning in the text. Adapting a phrase of Barthes, we may say: come and play!

We recall from the previous chapter that for Frank Kermode, facing the end of a text, like facing death, brings everything into a whole. For Derrida, by contrast, the end of the text opens everything up, postponing meaning into the future.

Death and the Other

The failure to reach closure is also shown by another feature of the ending of a text. The end, whether of a novel or a poem, is only felt to be an ending if it excludes certain possibilities. Even in the multiple endings of a novel by John Fowles, it cannot include all alternatives. The structuralist critics found the pattern of myths and images precisely in making these alternatives and polarities – good or evil, higher or lower, inside or outside, male or female, presence or absence. The deconstructionists point out that the alternative, the disruptive Other which is excluded, will always re-

---

[17]   Derrida, 'Of an Apocalyptic Tone', p. 65.
[18]   Ibid., p. 66.

emerge. It just cannot be suppressed. Some kind of untidiness, some impasse will occur in the narrative which upsets the closure so that the end is ruptured. Like the pod of a plant bursting open and scattering its seeds, the end of a text bursts and spreads its words.[19] There is always 'surplus' of meaning.

Though Derrida does not appeal to the comedies of Shakespeare at this point, they seem to me to be the classic instance of ruptured endings. Someone always stands outside the dance that ends the action; there is always someone absent from the feast of harmony that celebrates the happy ending. For example, *The Merchant of Venice* excludes Shylock, *Twelfth Night* excludes Malvolio, *Much Ado about Nothing* excludes Don John, and in *As You Like It* the melancholy Jacques excludes himself: 'to see no past-time, I'.[20] Without the exclusions there could be no ending to the plot, and yet the absence of the Others troubles the ending and casts a dark shadow over it; their viewpoint and their experience cannot be simply obliterated. The circle of concord cannot be complete, the measures of the dance are broken.

Now, Derrida suggests that a major Otherness which we try to exclude is death; joining letters together to form lines, the book closes the gaps and attempts 'to fill the hole . . . the dangerous hole' of death.[21] As does Kermode, he suggests that the concords of fiction console us in the face of death; yet he stresses that the Other remains. In completing itself, the book actually reveals that it includes the other it struggles to exclude. Thus, taking death seriously, the end undermines itself and is always open; it serves to disperse the meaning of the text. Again, I suggest a Shakespearean paradigm; in *Love's Labour's Lost* the pleasant courtship games and the 'dance of the Nine Worthies' is finally disrupted by the news of the death of the King of France: 'The King your father – Dead'. In the face of this blow it is clear that the amusing antics of the lovers, drunk with words, can be no basis for marrriage. This 'latest minute of the hour' is, in the words of the French Princess,

> A time, methinks, too short
> To make a world-without-end bargain in.

The end is fractured, open for meaning to be found in the future:

[19] Jacques Derrida, 'Limited Inc abc', *Glyph* 2 (1977), p. 197, cf. *Writing and Difference*, pp. 298–9.
[20] William Shakespeare, *As You Like It*, V.4.194.
[21] Derrida, *Writing and Difference* pp. 297–8, cf. p. 71: 'Death strolls between letters'.

> Our wooing doth not end like an old play;
> Jack hath not Jill . . .[22]

Death, for Derrida, is thus a 'gift' in the sense that all gifts stand outside the processes of exchange and subvert the closed structures of commerce.[23] However, in his later essay, 'No Apocalypse, Not Now', Derrida modifies his view of the powerful 'otherness' of death. There must be a horizon of the strange and the wholly other in which 'literature can come to life and . . . experience its own precariousness, its death menace and its essential finitude'.[24] But the death of an *individual* can be tamed by culture, and softened into symbolism so that it loses its impact of otherness. Rather, we can now envisage obliteration through nuclear warfare, which would mean total destruction/death of the human archive of literary and juridical texts. This, suggests Derrida, is 'the only possible referent of any discourse'. The only referent that is 'absolutely real' is one with the scope of an absolute nuclear catastrophe, that 'would irreversibly destroy the entire archive and all symbolic capacity, would destroy the "movement of survival" . . . at the very heart of life'. As the absolute effacement of any possible 'trace', it is 'the only ineffaceable trace', and so 'literature and literary criticism cannot speak of anything else, they can have no other ultimate referent, they can only multiply their strategic maneuvers in order to assimilate that unassimilable wholly other.'[25]

So, quite in contrast to Kermode's demythologizing of a cosmic end into a sense of transition, Derrida finds a cosmic end to be the catastrophe that really puts an 'end' to the closure of fictional endings, and so opens them for expansion of meaning. Occasionally, Derrida also allows an even more powerful Otherness to enter his writing, a presence that can only be indicated by its absence. There is an unreachable and nameless primordial 'space', which Plato designated the *khora*, whose traces disturb all our closures.[26] Though Derrida denies that the *khora* is God and that he is constructing a negative theology, it seems that something like an apophatic

---

[22] William Shakespeare, *Love's Labour's Lost*, V.2.781–2, 866–7.
[23] Jacques Derrida, *The Gift of Death*, transl. D. Wills (Chicago and London: Chicago University Press, 1995 [1992]) pp. 49–52, 83–7; more generally on the subversive power of gifts, see Derrida, *Given Time: I. Counterfeit Money*, transl. P. Kamuf (Chicago and London: Chicago University Press, 1992), pp. 14–17, 29–35.
[24] Derrida, 'No Apocalypse, Not Now', *Diacritics* 14/2 (1984), pp. 26–7.
[25] Ibid, p. 28.
[26] Jacques Derrida, 'How to Avoid Speaking: Denials', transl. K. Frieden, in Coward and Foshay (eds), *Derrida and Negative Theology*, pp. 104–10; see also chapter 8 below.

idea of God, together with the ideas of death and the nuclear eschaton, act as milieu for writing; they enable us to recognize absence and 'primal lack' in the being of the self-as-trace. There is at least a 'family resemblance' between approaching God through negative attributes, and approaching a text by affirming that a 'trace' is 'neither this nor that, neither inside nor outside, neither present nor absent . . . it is written completely otherwise.'[27]

Openness and Relativism

How shall we assess the Derridean apocalypse? How shall we learn from this riddling Jacques, spiritual successor to the ironic philosopher of *As You Like It*? We can, I believe, learn a good deal about the openness of meaning of texts, the dangers of over-polarization of truths, and the impact of the horizon of death and eschaton in opening up meaning by dispersing it.[28] I began my first chapter by observing that modern writers who have been influenced by the mood of postmodernism find it difficult to bring their books to a close, and we have seen this illustrated in John Fowles and Julian Barnes; now we can see why it is difficult. The end always seems to undermine itself. There is a truth here, that meaning will always expand, that we will always find something new in a story or metaphor; but the inability to make an end also means a loss of confidence in any value and meaning at all.

In this connection, Derrida's exegesis of the Book of Revelation is quite fascinating. He misses all the buoyant confidence in the book, all the certainty that God will in the end triumph over the forces of evil. The many colourful images in the book all affirm that the victory belongs to the Lamb, and that the Lamb conquers through his suffering; not by military might but through the wounds of the cross all empires will bow to him. Derrida then misses the note of hope. But he does catch an important flavour of the book; the repeated command 'come' and the mixture of voices are not a confusion – they are a deliberate opening up of the future. As I proposed in my first chapter, our eschatology may take the form of saying that while the end is certain, God can always do new things;

---

[27]   Derrida, 'How to Avoid Speaking', p. 74.

[28]   After all, as Valentine Cunningham points out in critique of Derrida, there is a long tradition in Christian thought of God's veiling God's self in the very act of self-revelation: Cunningham, *In the Reading Gaol. Postmodernity, Texts and History* (Oxford: Blackwell, 1994), pp. 400–2.

God fulfils promises in unexpected ways, and we can hear the divine voice of promise in many ways. While the end is certain, it is also open because of the freedom of God, and because of the freedom God gives to human beings to contribute to the project of creation.

Apocalyptic does have an open quality about it, and Derrida rightly finds this openness in the Book of Revelation as a type of every book. But the openness becomes mere relativism. No less than with 'structuralism', there is a flight in deconstruction from both history and values. While Terry Eagleton seeks to defend Derrida on the *latter* score, he admits that deconstruction was born from a disillusionment with political action: he notes the failure of the student-workers' uprising in France in 1968, and suggests wryly that 'unable to break the structures of state power, post-structuralism found it possible instead to subvert the structures of language.'[29] An alternative to social action was found in the 'erotic frissons of reading (the pleasure of the text)'.

Eagleton maintains, however, that it was the American disciples of Derrida who drew the conclusion that 'values', 'truth', 'certainty' and 'the real' were to be dismissed as mere metaphysics, and Valentine Cunningham has a good deal of fun with the fact that Derrida's word *jeu* (the 'play' of the text) was translated as 'game' and even 'free play' by American scholars.[30] While Derrida proposed that there was no absolute ground for truth and certainty (in some 'transcendental signified'), this does not mean they lack all meaning. The American excesses towards total relativism, in Derrida's own view, left untouched the ideologies of American society that needed criticism. A case can be made that Derrida's main concern is not to deny the existence of any truth or meaning, but to unmask the logic (the 'logocentrism') by which political and social structures exercise domination. With this attack upon repressive ideology we return to the concerns of apocalyptic, for Derrida rightly notes the revolutionary nature of the apocalypses of the early Christian world, their seemingly bizarre texts encoding messages of resistance against the powers that be. In a useful piece of self-criticism, Derrida admits that even apocalyptic can become a tool of mastery and a lust for power; those who announce the end to an epoch, an end to history, to the subject and to God, who vie with each other to go one better in 'eschatological eloquence', must have their motives examined.[31] That is, even the apocalyptic announcement of postmodernism

---

[29] Eagleton, 'Literary Theory', p. 142.
[30] Ibid., pp. 145–7; Cunningham, 'In the Reading Gaol', p. 57.
[31] Derrida, 'Of an Apocalyptic Tone', pp. 48–51.

must be demystified. This check too he finds in the pattern of the Book of Revelation, which follows the main bulk of its apocalypse with a further apocalypse, the appeal to 'come' breaking in upon the new Jerusalem. So he ends his essay on 'Apocalyptic tone' with a challenge addressed to himself and his own motives:

> But what are you doing, all of you will still insist, to what ends do you want to come when you come to tell us, here and now, let's go, come, the apocalypse, it's finished, I tell you this, that's what's happening.[32]

Yet for all this Derrida gives many hostages to fortune, and there is an inevitable relativism in his denial of polarities and alternatives. When he says that the apocalypse of the appeal 'Come' is 'an apocalypse without apocalypse, without vision, without truth, without revelation . . . an apocalypse beyond good and evil'[33] we can understand the basic iconoclastic intention, but it abandons us to wandering in a world of traces with little sense of self-identity and without any possibility of arrival.

It is here that we need to balance openness with closure. We need to combine the sense that the end always brings something new (Derrida, and just a hint in Northrop Frye) with the confidence that the end organizes the whole (as expressed by Frank Kermode) – and it is here that a theology of hope can help us.

The End Opens Hope: Paul Ricoeur

The philosopher Paul Ricoeur takes up many of the insights from the critics we have surveyed so far, and gives them a new perspective within the horizon of hope. I am treating him as the last of the four theorists, not because he comes last chronologically (although he does comment on all three of them) but because he seems to have a genius for the reconciling of conflicting thought, and because his philosophy of hope points us in the direction we are journeying in these studies.

With Northrop Frye, Ricoeur agrees that narratives and metaphors express human desire. Out of an overflowing surplus of being, human existence is orientated forwards in a passion to be, and this is the true basis

---

[32] Ibid., p. 67.
[33] Ibid., p. 66.

of hope.[34] Here he picks up the idea of a 'surplus' or 'excess' of meaning from Derrida, but gives it another direction from the endless straying and playing which Derrida commends; the result of the surplus in human life is not to *defer*, but to give us *hope*. Ricoeur agrees with both Frye and Derrida that stories and poems do not refer directly to the world around us; they are not mere imitations (like a photograph). But they do refer to the *real world*, says Ricoeur, that is to the world as it can be. The world of the text is referring to a world less 'behind' than 'in front of' the text.[35]

Like Frye, Ricoeur finds that texts are eschatological because they express possibilities rather than actualities; they describe not how things are, but how they *might be*. They point to a way of being beyond the greediness of the ego and the split of the consciousness between subject and object. But here Ricoeur takes a step beyond Frye, for whom all possibilities are already contained within the universal structures of meaning within human existence. For Frye, the desired world is already buried in the consciousness from whence it can be resurrected. For Ricoeur, human being is *possibility itself*, and out of this fecund capacity the imagination can create genuinely new possibilities which are not simply repetitions of the past and present; symbol and myth refer to a reality which is yet to come and which they help to create. 'Fiction changes reality', maintains Ricoeur, 'in the sense that it both "invents" and "discovers" it.'[36] Imagination offers possibilities to the will, which adopts them and forms *projects* which are not dependent upon conditions in the present. Such projects are not unreal just because all the conditions for them do not exist here and now, as the world includes 'what *is to be done* by me'. Human existence means that 'the possible precedes the actual and clears the way for it.'[37] There are obvious affinities here with *The Principle of Hope* of Ernst Bloch, as Bloch speaks of 'the ontology of the not yet' and 'real-possibilities' as the objects of hope.[38]

---

[34] Paul Ricoeur, 'Freedom in the Light of Hope', transl. R. Sweeney, in Paul Ricoeur, *The Conflict of Interpretations*, ed. Don Ihde (Evanston: Northwestern University Press, 1974), pp. 405–7, 410–11, and *History and Truth*, transl. C. Kelbley (Evanston: Northwestern University Press, 1965), pp. 126–7.

[35] Paul Ricoeur, *Interpretation Theory. Discourse and the Surplus of Meaning* (Fort Worth: Texas Christian University Press, 1976), p. 87.

[36] Paul Ricoeur, 'The Function of Fiction in Shaping Reality', *Man and World* 12 (1979), p. 127.

[37] Paul Ricoeur, *Freedom and Nature: The Voluntary and the Involuntary*, transl. E. V. Kohak (Evanston: Northwestern University Press, 1966 [1950]), pp. 48, 54.

[38] Ernst Bloch, *The Principle of Hope*, vol. I, transl. N. Plaice, S. Plaice and P. Knight (Oxford: Blackwell, 1986), pp. 235–49.

All this provides a new slant on the question of 'the world of the text'. Ricoeur agrees with Frye and Derrida, with structuralists and post-structuralists, that the verbal signs of a text do not refer to the actual world around us. But poetic and fictional language is still mimetic of the 'real world', when this is understood as a reality which is to be and which it helps to make. *Mimesis* is the '*creative* imitation' of reality.[39] There is an extralinguistic reference, but 'the world of the text' is referring to a world which 'the text unfolds before itself'.[40] In this context, Ricoeur can take up the old dispute between those who find the meaning of the text to be in its autonomy, and those who find it to be open in meaning and made ever new through the participation of the reader. There is room in interpretation for both objective analysis of the text in its own right ('explanation') *and* for existential involvement ('understanding'). We must have regard for both the sense of a text (what it says) *and* its meaning (what it is talking about).[41] In a hermeneutics of suspicion the critic unmasks the ideologies that lie hidden in the text, and in a hermeneutics of retrieval the critic is willing to listen to the symbols that lead to truth. As Ricoeur puts it, 'the idols must die, so that the symbols may live.'[42] On the basis of analysis of the text (explanation), the reader joins in the play of the text in developing new possibilities for human existence (understanding), which can then effect the reader's self-understanding here and now through evoking feeling (appropriation); affects are effects. The world of the text *refers* to future reality and not to the present, but it *transforms* human reality here and now.[43] Here Ricoeur agrees with Frye that narrative and metaphor have revelatory and rhetorical power.

With Kermode, Ricoeur finds that the new world of the text consists in the reshaping of time. From the perspective of its ending, a narrative integrates beginning, middle and end into a temporal whole; it 'configures'

---

[39] Ricoeur pairs together *mimesis* (imitation) and *muthos* (composition): *Time and Narrative*, vol. 1, transl. K. McLaughlin and D. Pellauer (Chicago: University of Chicago Press, 1984), pp. 32–7. On this pairing, see James Fodor, *Christian Hermeneutics. Paul Ricoeur and the Refiguring of Theology* (Oxford: Clarendon Press, 1995), pp. 185–91.

[40] On the 'world of the text', see Paul Ricoeur, 'Towards a Hermeneutic of the Idea of Revelation' in *Essays on Biblical Interpretation*, ed. Lewis S. Mudge (Philadelphia: Fortress Press, 1980), pp. 98–100.

[41] Ricoeur, *Interpretation Theory*, pp. 87–8.

[42] Paul Ricoeur, *Freud and Philosophy. An Essay on Interpretation*, transl. D. Savage (New Haven: Yale University Press, 1970), p. 531.

[43] Ricoeur, 'The Function of Fiction', pp. 134–9.

time as a painting configures space and light.[44] But as we have seen, Ricoeur does not draw an immediate *analogy* between this and our emplotment of eschatology in individual experience and on a cosmic scale. The temporal configuration of a literary plot (what Ricoeur calls *mimesis₂*), has reference to a world of future possibilities and this has an indirect effect, through feeling, upon the refiguring of human consciousness of time in the present (*mimesis₃*).[45] He *does* agree with Kermode, at least implicitly, that the organizing effect of the end of a plot cannot be simply transferred to our experience of death, and here he explicitly takes issue with Heidegger.

He welcomes Heidegger's perception that human being is essentially temporal, and that it 'projects itself ahead of itself' by being aware of possibilities.[46] Human being is *Dasein* – being there – that is, thrown into the facticity of the world but with the capacity to form possibilities and choose between them. Possibility means we stand before an open future. However, Ricoeur disagrees with Heidegger that the 'master possibility' that orientates life and shapes the temporal flow into a whole is death. The total orientation of life upon death, maintains Ricoeur, is only one way of being human, as the basic structure of human existence is full of possibilities.[47] Facing death resolutely is a Stoic ethic, but another conception of possibility is the Christian being-towards-eternity. In *Time and Narrative* Ricoeur considers Augustine's meditations on the nature of time, which is measured or 'narrated' within the extension (*distentio*) of the human soul.[48] As does Heidegger later, Augustine registers the sense of being torn asunder by time ('I am divided between time gone by and time to come');[49] but he suggests that only engagement or direction (*intentio*) of the soul towards its stability in eternity will bring a sense of wholeness. Eternity is a 'limiting

---

[44] Ricoeur, *Time and Narrative*, vol. 2, transl. K. McLaughlin and D. Pellauer (Chicago: University of Chicago Press, 1985), pp. 21–8.

[45] Ibid, p. 20; *Time and Narrative*, vol. 1, pp. 64–76.

[46] Martin Heidegger, *Being and Time*, transl. J. Macquarrie and E. Robinson (Oxford: Blackwell, 1962), pp. 183–90; Ricoeur, *Time and Narrative*, vol. 3, pp. 253–8. On the use of Heidegger by Ricoeur, see Kevin J. Vanhoozer, *Biblical narrative in the Philosophy of Paul Ricoeur. A Study in Hermeneutics and Theology* (Cambridge: Cambridge University Press, 1990), pp. 19–32.

[47] Ricoeur, *Time and Narrative*, vol. 3, transl. K. Blamey and D. Pellauer (Chicago: University of Chicago Press, 1985), pp. 233–5; cf. pp. 75–96. For Heidegger on 'being-towards-death', see *Being and Time*, pp. 301–11.

[48] Ricoeur, *Time and Narrative*, vol. 1, pp. 26–30.

[49] Augustine, *Confessions*, XI.29. This is Ricoeur's paraphrase; Augustine writes 'I fall into dissolution amid the times (*in tempora dissilui*)'.

concept' for understanding and healing time. Ricoeur concludes that, according to Augustine, an orientation towards 'the eternal present', which 'strikes time with nothingness', deepens temporality rather than abolishing it. He then draws a comparison here with the way that fiction replaces mere chronology with human time and thus also deepens time. It is necessary 'to confess what is other than time' (*chronos*) in order to probe deeper into it.

However, if literature should help us to 'refigure' our consciousness of time into an orientation towards eternity, we are bound to ask whether this takes death seriously enough. Even if we do not follow Heidegger in regarding death as our ultimate concern and our master possibility, we cannot deny that human existence has a being-towards-death. Ricoeur himself asks the question as to whether there is an irreducible 'disjunction' between the two alternative orientations in Augustine and Heidegger. He offers the hope that his own reflections on narrativity 'may aid us in thinking about eternity and death at the same time'.[50] In this present study I am suggesting that we shall need a different concept of eternity from Augustine's eternal present (and so simultaneity of time) if we are ever to bring hope and realism together.

At the root of Ricoeur's quarrel with Heidegger is his conviction that we cannot arrive at self-understanding (which is his goal) by immediate existential awareness, such as reflection on the experience of death. We come to self-understanding only through the mediation of symbol and narrative because they express the human desire to be. In a new version of Pascal's 'wager' on the existence of God, Ricoeur breaks through the circle of hermeneutics by saying 'I wager that I shall have a better understanding of man . . . if I follow the indication of symbolic thought.'[51] At the same time, this is a wager that the world of the text does refer to the reality of future possibilities. Metaphor plays a critical part in this process within the discourse of narrative, for just as narrative 'configures' the different moments of past, present and future into a whole, so metaphor configures dissimilar objects in the world into a new whole in order to '*redescribe* reality'. There is a parallel between the closure of a text, which unifies the whole action, and the 'closure' made by putting two dissimilar things together that are being compared. However, the closure does not result, as Frye supposes, in the closed circle of an inner (centripetal) self-reference

---

50   Ricoeur, *Time and Narrative*, vol. 1, p. 86.
51   Paul Ricoeur, *The Symbolism of Evil*, transl. E. Buchanan (Boston: Beacon Press, 1969), p. 355.

and a hypothetical or merely virtual reality. The tension between the terms of comparison in a metaphor generates a fictive experience which we can only call 'seeing as'.[52] When we say 'this is and is not' we see the world 'as not yet', and we open up the play of possibilities. Ricoeur agrees with Frye that the wholeness of a poem articulates a mood, but this does more than exist within the poem itself; 'seeing as' is 'a way of being rooted in reality; it is an ontological index.'[53]

Ricoeur thus understands texts as eschatological, but not only in the sense that they defer meaning forwards, as in Derrida's thought; in their very meaning, in their sense (structure) and reference (creating a new world) they present a hope by which human beings can live.

Hope and a Passion for the Possible

Now, in his portrayal of hope and possibility Ricoeur has two theological conversation partners, Jürgen Moltmann and Eberhard Jüngel. Ricoeur greeted Moltmann's book on *The Theology of Hope* with great enthusiasm. In his essay 'Freedom in the Light of Hope' (1968) Ricoeur commends Moltmann's stress upon a religion of promise rather than a religion of presence; he strongly approves Moltmann's finding of revelation to consist in the giving of a promise that opens up the future rather than in an epiphany of eternal being.[54] Ricoeur thus takes Moltmann's emphasis upon promise and fulfilment into his own focus upon the 'surplus' in language and being. Moltmann points out that in the Jewish-Christian experience, history is generated by the expectation of fulfilment, and when the fulfilment of promise comes it is perceived as being not an end of the promise but a renewal of it; Ricoeur comments that 'this designates an increase, *a surplus*, a 'not yet' which maintains the tension of history'.[55]

Above all, the resurrection of Jesus does not close off the promise of God when it fulfils it, but opens our expectations by directing our hope to

---

[52] Paul Ricoeur, *The Rule of Metaphor. Multi-disciplinary Studies of the Creation of Meaning in Language*, transl. R. Czerny (London: Routledge & Kegan Paul, 1986), pp. 209–11.

[53] Ibid., pp. 148, 245.

[54] Jürgen Moltmann, *Theology of Hope*, transl. J. Leitch (London: SCM Press, 1967), pp. 42–5; Ricoeur, 'Freedom in the Light of Hope', pp. 404–8.

[55] Ricoeur, 'Freedom in the Light of Hope', p. 405, cf. pp. 409–10; Moltmann, *Theology of Hope*, pp. 194–7, 124–33.

the future resurrection from the dead.[56] Ricoeur finds 'freedom in the light of hope' to be 'the meaning of my existence in the light of the Resurrection, that is, as reinstated in the movement which we have called the future of the Resurrection of the Christ.' This hope is a 'living contradiction' of reality as it is; the superabundance of the 'how much more' (Rom. 5:12–20) is 'in spite of' death. So Ricoeur finds the cross of Jesus symbolizes a denial of everything in present reality that hope transcends; it is, as it were, God's judgement upon present actuality.[57]

Thus far it may seem that Ricoeur and Moltmann are speaking in harmony, and indeed both are indebted to the 'ontology of the not yet' in Ernst Bloch. Moltmann follows Bloch in saying that 'promise announces the coming of a *not yet* existing reality from the future of the truth'.[58] He agrees with Bloch and Ricoeur that the object of hope is not a 'calculable' future extrapolated from present actuality, but a 'desirable' future which contradicts the power structures of the present. So the future is a 'new pattern of transcendence', creating a revolutionary consciousness.[59] But there is a significant difference in the way that Moltmann and Ricoeur speak of what the resurrection of Jesus promises. Ricoeur agrees with Moltmann's analysis of its 'tendential' character, its pointing towards a new *creatio ex nihilo* in the resurrection of all; but for Ricoeur, the tendency lies in the symbol of resurrection itself – 'in *its* future, the death of death'; for Moltmann, its tendency lies in 'the future of *Jesus Christ*'. That is, the resurrection for Moltmann promises the coming of Jesus to his glory, and our resurrection is only in this context. Moltmann's concept of 'the God who comes' thus has a more radical discontinuity with present reality than does Ricoeur; the new possibilities of the new creation come entirely (it would seem) from the future coming of Jesus. To use another formulation of Moltmann's, they come from *adventus* and not from *futurum*.[60] Hope must be in the God of resurrection who does altogether new and unexpected things, not in the resurrection itself as a phenomenon in human life.

---

[56] Ricoeur, 'Freedom in the Light of Hope', p. 406; cf. Moltmann, *Theology of Hope*, p. 85.

[57] Ricoeur, 'Freedom in the Light of Hope', pp. 409–10.

[58] Moltmann, *Theology of Hope*, p. 85.

[59] Jürgen Moltmann, *The Future of Creation*, transl. M. Kohl (London: SCM Press, 1979), pp. 9–12.

[60] Ibid., pp. 29–31; cf. Moltmann's *The Way of Jesus Christ. Christology in Messianic Dimensions*, transl. M. Kohl (London: SCM Press, 1990), pp. 317–18, and *The Coming of God. Christian Eschatology*, transl. M. Kohl (London: SCM Press, 1996), pp. 25–6.

We are not surprised when, in the second part of his essay, Ricoeur goes on to maintain that 'the passion for the possible must graft itself onto real tendencies, the mission onto a sensed history, the superabundance onto signs of the Resurrection, wherever they can be deciphered.'[61] He suggests that, by opposing the promise to the Greek *Logos*, Moltmann intends to indicate the 'innovation of meaning' in promise, its irruption into a closed order, its looking to the novelty of the new creation which 'catches us unawares'. 'Resurrection surprises by being in excess in comparison to the reality forsaken by God.'[62] But this novelty, urges Ricoeur, must make us think or it would pass us by like 'a flash without a sequel' (a 'flash in the pan', we might say), and so it must be grounded in *a way of thinking* in the present. While possibilities are novel in not being present in particular form in the consciousness, they *are* rooted in the human *capacity* for excess, and so this 'passion for the possible' can be analysed through a revision of Kant's theory of the postulates of the reason.

There seems to be a sharp contrast here between Ricoeur and Moltmann. For Moltmann, the promised future depends entirely upon 'the God who comes' in the coming of Jesus Christ, and not at all in the structure of human existence, not even in its 'passion for the possible'.[63] The future Kingdom can certainly be anticipated in the present, through actions of resistance and even revolution against the *status quo*; but the restless dreams that motivate the struggle for freedom will only produce what is truly 'new' if they are prompted solely by the hope engendered by the resurrected Jesus. In his later work Moltmann has laid greater stress on the dialectic between discontinuity and *continuity*, between the new creation and present experience; he has detected ever-wider signs in history and the cosmos of the 'tendency' towards the future contained in the resurrection of Jesus. But he has still resisted finding any conditions for these possibilities in human existence itself. I shall, however, be arguing for a link between a human 'passion for the possible' in the present, and the unexpectedness of new creation in the future; a study of *King Lear* in the following chapter will begin the case.

Eberhard Jüngel is a second theologian who has been in dialogue with Ricoeur about the nature of the possible. More interested than Moltmann

---

61   Ricoeur, 'Freedom in the Light of Hope', p. 412.
62   Ibid., p. 411.
63   See Moltmann, *Theology of Hope*, pp. 225–9, and 'Ernst Bloch and Hope without Faith', in Jürgen Moltmann, *The Experiment Hope*, transl. D. Meeks (London: SCM Press, 1975), pp. 32–40.

in the working of religious language, Jüngel takes a similar approach to Ricoeur in a study on metaphor he has co-authored with him;[64] religious language, he argues, calls into question the ultimacy of actuality as its referent. Metaphor brings to speech states of affairs that are 'more than actual'; metaphor refers not to the world as it is, but as it is coming to be.[65] Jüngel affirms, moreover, that metaphor can refer to God as he is coming to the world, and so in metaphor God also comes to worldly speech.[66] In finding that being embraces possibility as well as actuality, Jüngel, like Ricoeur, seeks to reverse the long Western intellectual tradition of making actuality prior to possibility.

However, in so doing Jüngel launches a direct attack on the idea of the possible as the 'not yet', as found in Bloch and Ricoeur. In another essay, 'The World as Possibility and Actuality', he urges that the radical eschatology of the New Testament cannot be contained within the well-worn formula of 'the already and the not yet'.[67] He argues that if we define the 'possible' as the 'not yet', we are simply subordinating it once more to actuality, and reducing it to mere 'potential for actuality'. 'Not yet' defines the possible merely in negatives, and 'not yet being' is a kind of ghostly being. In Bloch's apocalyptic-messianic approach to history, actuality is only being surpassed by actuality. We will only make possibility prior to actuality if we understand it exclusively as that which God creates, and cease to define it by any tendencies in the present. 'That which God makes possible in his free love has ontological priority over that which he makes actual through our acts.'[68] Possibility thus belongs with our justification as a free gift from God. God makes possible what is possible through the resurrection of Jesus, creating it anew from nothing.

According to Jüngel, the language of metaphor thus testifies to a possible world for which we can hope, but this is established by the external agency

---

[64] Paul Ricoeur and Eberhard Jüngel, *Metapher. Zur Hermeneutik religiöser Sprache* (*Evangelische Theologie*, Sonderheft 1974). Jüngel's contribution, 'Metaphorische Wahr-heit. Erwägungen zur theologische Relevanz der Metapher als Beitrag zur Hermeneutik einer narrativen Theologie' (pp. 71–122) is quoted here in the English translation, 'Metaphorical Truth', in J. B. Webster (ed.), *Eberhard Jüngel. Theological Essays* (Edin-burgh: T. & T. Clark, 1989), pp. 16–71.

[65] Jüngel, 'Metaphorical Truth', p. 32.

[66] Ibid., pp. 59–60.

[67] Eberhard Jüngel, 'The World as Possibility and Actuality. The Ontology of the Doctrine of Justification' [1969], in Webster (ed.), *Eberhard Jüngel. Theological Essays*, p. 103.

[68] Ibid., p. 116.

of God, on whom the world is contingent. As I have already indicated, I myself believe that we must find more continuity between present actuality and the future world for which we hope than Jüngel wishes to do. But as we do so, we must not lose Jüngel's perception that possibility can only begin from a human reduction to nothingness; God not only makes possible the possible in the resurrection, but also 'makes impossible the impossible' (human sin) in the cross of Jesus.[69] Here we find the hostile 'nothingness' of a loss of relationship with God and others revealed for what it is, and we find it negated by God. The cross of Jesus does more than offer a *comparison* with the reality of hope, more than simply stand in contrast – as an actuality 'forsaken by God' – to the surprising excess of the resurrection, as Ricoeur expresses it.[70] By sharing in the cross of Jesus our actuality is *reduced* to nothingness, a 'No' which is for the sake of the creative divine 'Yes'. While Ricoeur speaks of hope as the 'freedom for the denial of death',[71] it is when we are brought into the valley of the shadow of death, by identification with the cross of Jesus, that we find hope in God's creative word, rather than in any particular future worldly actuality.[72] The Christian faith thus brings us to the hope of resurrection only by taking death seriously.

Hoping in the Face of Death

We have now surveyed four suggested effects of the end of a piece of creative writing: (1) the end organizes and unifies the whole; (2) the end expresses human desire; (3) the end defers meaning; and (4) the end opens future possibility. As we have seen, there is some truth in all of them, and we shall be returning to all four insights in constructing a dialogue between literature and Christian doctrine on the theme of eschatology. However, they clearly cannot all simply be adopted without qualification. Here and now I should declare that I find Ricoeur's account of the 'world of the text' most convincing, and most responsible in terms of our living in a world which requires personal, social and political decisions to be made. It challenges the totally non-referential account of texts in both structuralism and post-structuralism, while recognizing the overflowing 'surplus' of

---

[69]   Ibid., pp. 112, 120.
[70]   Ricoeur, 'Freedom in the Light of Hope', p. 411.
[71]   Ibid., p. 410.
[72]   Jüngel, 'The World as Possibility and Actuality', p. 114

meaning in language, rooted in the surplus of being in human existence. However, Frye alerts us, despite his rather rigid archetypes, to the way that images and narratives express the desire that must be a part of hope. Jacques Derrida, and such Christian exegetes as Robert Detweiler and Mark Taylor who have followed in his 'traces', have important insights to offer us about the impossibility of closing meaning, and about the need to suspect the ideological motives that lie hidden behind 'metanarratives' or universal theories of life. They also bear witness to the finality of death in a way that Ricoeur seems to undermine.

We began the previous chapter with examples (from John Fowles and Julian Barnes) of the difficulty that is felt in ending a novel today. From the theories we have surveyed we can begin to see some of the reasons for this. When someone has lost confidence in a cosmic end, it is hard to bring time into a whole within fiction (Kermode). Or, the energy of desire will always burst open legal structures (Frye). Or, excluded alternatives will re-assert themselves in reading a text, undermining final closure (Derrida); we must add to this last answer that, when confidence has been lost through endless meaning, it is also hard to come to any conclusions.

As Ricoeur points out, readers will only be interested in a work of fiction if their expectation that some kind of consonance will prevail seems likely to be fulfilled, but an author can choose to dissolve her plot in such a way that the readers are prompted and enabled to shape the plot themselves; despite an ambiguous or open ending, frustration will not be the last word if the reader can make order where the author denies it.[73] This kind of enabling, however, requires no less careful composition than a traditional, 'realistic' novel. This is the kind of end that opens possibility; like the ends in Christian apocalyptic it will have an openness about it, but it is the opening of hope.

I offer an example of this kind of composition, as well as a witness to the need for both narrative and reader to take death seriously, in a chapter from Julian Barnes' novel, *A History of the World in 10½ Chapters*. The novel plays a series of variations on the apocalyptic theme of Noah's Ark and the Great Flood, finding echoes of this story (and, according to Barnes, the subversive sub-plot of a tribe of woodworms who survived the flood as stowaways) in all kinds of unlikely corners of history. In the chapter 'The Survivor', Barnes tells the story of an ordinary Australian woman, Kath, who becomes deeply worried first about the ecological damage done by recent nuclear accidents, and then about the threat of an impending

---

[73] Ricoeur, *Time and Narrative*, vol. 2, p. 25.

nuclear war. Her husband Greg is an unsympathetic character, coping with the political crisis they are passing through by sitting around in bars, picking up girls and 'slapping her around a bit' on paynight. She takes matters into her own hands when the crisis deepens, stealing Greg's boat and sailing out into the deep ocean with two cats for company – male and female, the latter soon becoming pregnant. Through sunstroke, near starvation and *perhaps* radiation sickness she falls into a delirious fever, but apparently still succeeds in making landfall on a small rocky island. In her feverish dreams white-coated doctors appear, informing her that she is in a psychiatric hospital, having been picked up in a bad state in the Darwin Straits by a passing ship. War had been averted, and she is fantasizing about landing on the island as a way of escaping the reality of the breakdown of her relationship with Greg. They have labelled her as showing the guilt and rejection of 'the persistent victim syndrome', and suggest that 'There's a lot of denial in your life, isn't there? You . . . deny a lot of things'.[74] So the reader is forced to ask whether she is 'fabulating' (the doctors' word) the island or the hospital. What is the reality – is she denying her own inadequacies by imagining the island, or is she being tempted to go along with the rest of the world in denying the catastrophe they are facing? 'We've got to look at things how they are' she muses, 'It's the only way we'll survive.'[75] If she is a persistent victim, she is not the only one; 'the whole bloody world's a persistent victim' she retorts.

This short story encapsulates the hesitation over closure in much modern fiction, but readers are enabled to make a whole out of the action, whatever decision they come to. Whether Kath is on her Pacific island or in a hospital ward, the story moves towards the point that the apocalyptic crisis facing the world cannot be evaded. If Kath is in denial over her relationships, this does not excuse humanity from its own refusal to face the threat of its self-inflicted end. As another of Barnes' characters, Jean in *Staring at the Sun* realizes, life cannot be built on denial of death. When Jean is told that 'it is impossible to look at either the sun or death without blinking', she remembers the fighter pilots of her youth who trained themselves to do both.[76] With Kath, just when the text has nudged us towards thinking that she is indeed in a psychiatric ward, the ending of the story subverts this, but not in such a way as to exclude the alternative

[74] Julian Barnes, *A History of the World in 10½ Chapters* (London: Picador, 1990), p. 108.
[75] Ibid., p. 111.
[76] Julian Barnes, *Staring at the Sun* (London: Picador, 1986), p. 155.

conclusion. The openness does not leave us frustrated, but opens us to the future:

> The next day, on a small, scrubby island in the Torres Strait, Kath Ferris woke up to find that Linda [the cat] had given birth. Five tortoiseshell kittens, all huddling together, helpless and blind, yet quite without defect. She felt such love . . . She felt such happiness! Such hope![77]

---

[77]   Barnes, *A History of the World*, p. 111.

Chapter Three

TAKING DEATH
SERIOUSLY

Did Shakespeare go too far in his ending to *King Lear*? Many have protested that even tragedy does not demand the kind of catastrophe with which Shakespeare closes the play; Lear, driven insane, dies of a broken heart with the dead body of Cordelia in his arms, holding in the embrace of death his sole faithful daughter with whom he had just before been tenderly reconciled.

> And my poor fool is hang'd! No, no, no life!
> Why should a dog, a horse, a rat, have life,
> And thou no breath at all? Thou'lt come no more,
> Never, never, never, never, never!   (V.3.305–8)

The threefold 'no' and the fivefold 'never' underline an end which a chorus of characters compares to the terrors of the end of the world and the Last Judgement:

> KENT: Is this the promis'd end?
> EDGAR: Or image of that horror?
> ALBANY: Fall and cease.   (V.3.263–4)

Among other offended critics, Samuel Johnson declared that the end was unendurably painful, since Cordelia's virtue should have had its reward even if Lear deserved no better.[1] The disaster is even more shocking as the wicked Edmund need only have repented a few minutes earlier than he does to have forestalled Cordelia's execution; indeed, we feel that he might have confessed in time if some of the virtuous characters who find him

---

[1] Samuel Johnson, 'Concluding Notes' to *King Lear* in *The Plays of William Shakespeare* (1765).

dying had not made such long speeches of rebuke. Thus the ending seems not only extreme but accidental. Although wrongs have been set right and the kingdom restored to Lear, he and the guiltless Cordelia must still die. It seems a profoundly pessimistic vision of the world.

A Journey to Nothingness: *King Lear*

Players and audience felt so strongly that Shakespeare had gone too far that the writer Nahum Tate produced – in addition to metrical versions of the Psalms – a revised version of the play in 1681: Cordelia escapes death and marries Edgar who has also suffered at the hands of Edmund, his villainous half-brother; even Lear survives into a serene old age. This happy ending was the *only* form in which the play was produced for the next century and a half, until the tragic end was restored to the stage in 1834. It is highly significant that this censored version of the play also omitted all the appearances of the Fool, Lear's court jester and companion in his misery.[2] It seems that people could not tolerate *either* the extreme of tragedy *or* the presence of comedy in an essentially tragic play. We shall see that both elements are in fact subversive of a certain ideology.

For I do not think that Shakespeare has gone too far, though he has perhaps gone to the point where one can go no further. The play is a journey to absolute zero; it is the story of a man reduced to nothing, the passion story of a man stripped bare. The action proceeds remorselessly until he has nothing left that people usually build upon in their lives. He has come to the final 'no' and 'never'. He has entered apocalypse now. Frank Kermode is surely right to find this play exemplifying the Renaissance shift of interest from the literal end of the world to the personal crisis of death, the move from apocalypse to tragedy; 'tragedy assumes the figurations of apocalypse, of death and judgement, heaven and hell; but the world goes forward in the hands of exhausted survivors.'[3] Yet we should not forget that though the focus has shifted, the final apocalypse is still in the picture, as Edgar refers to Lear's agony as 'image' of the final terrors. The play, then, can stand as a paradigm for testing out the four effects of an end to a text that we surveyed in the first two chapters, and so for

---

[2]   The scenes with the Fool were not restored to the stage until 1838. For the stage history, see *King Lear*, ed. Kenneth Muir, *The Arden Shakespeare* (London: Methuen, 1964), pp. xliii-xlv. The version of the text used in this chapter comes from this edition.
[3]   Frank Kermode, *The Sense of an Ending* (Oxford: Oxford University Press, 1968), p. 82.

exploring the dialogue between creative literature and Christian doctrine about the nature of eschatology: we shall need to consider the end as organizing the whole, the end as expressing a desired world, the end as dispersing meaning and the end as opening hope.

We note in the first place the view of both Kermode and Ricoeur that the end of a work organizes and unifies the action within it, bringing it into a temporal whole. We find indeed that the non-being at the end of *King Lear*, the 'no' and the 'never', integrates the whole process of the plot. Lear's path to tragedy begins with the mistake he makes in the first scene of the play when he deprives himself of royal power in a foolish way, and so propels himself towards the nothingness of the end. The plot simply works out the action that begins when Lear divests himself of his crown, and the shape of the play is dissolution to nothing. The opening scene in which Lear strips himself of the garment of power, shaking 'all cares and business from our age . . . while we/ Unburthen'd crawl towards death' is to issue in the scene on the heath when Lear in madness tears off all his clothes, 'Off, off, you lendings; come unbutton here!' and reaches its climax at the end with Lear desperately trying to get some breath into Cordelia dead on his lap: 'Pray you, undo this button'. As the fool says, Lear has put down his own breeches. But Lear's mistake is not so much the political error of divesting himself of authority; it is the manner in which he has done it which unlooses the apocalypse.

He has chosen the recipients of his kingdom by making love a commercial matter of bargaining, and thereby stripped himself of what matters most – the fellowship of those who love him truly. He has divested himself of his daughter Cordelia and his faithful servant Kent. Lear decides to distribute his lands and rule among his three daughters and his sons-in-law according to the degree in which they can swear they love him. The two selfish daughters find no difficulty in flattering the old man and drawing their payment, but Cordelia (whom Lear loved most) is unable to play this language game and compute her love by arithmetic:

CORDELIA: *[aside]* What shall Cordelia speak? Love and be silent. . . .
LEAR: . . . what can you say to draw
     A third more opulent than your sisters? Speak.
CORDELIA: Nothing, my lord.
LEAR: Nothing?
CORDELIA: Nothing.
LEAR: Nothing will come of nothing: speak again.
CORDELIA: Unhappy that I am, I cannot heave

My heart into my mouth; I love your majesty
According to my bond; no more, nor less.   (I.1.62, 85–93)

This bond Cordelia respects is not the legal bond of Shylock in *The Merchant of Venice*, who like Lear also reduces human relationships to a commercial transaction. It is the bond of love, the harmony that ties together the elements of the universe in Elizabethan thought. This bonding that unites her to her father is the opposite of the divesting and dissolution which is the action of the play; Lear's world comes apart because he has neglected this great creative bond. His text, 'Nothing will come of nothing' is critical here, as it begins the process that ends with the 'no' and the 'never' of the end. The text, though having admirable classical authority, is a denial of the Christian doctrine of creation *ex nihilo*, achieved by the bond of 'love that moves the sun and the other stars'.[4] Ironically, by asserting that 'nothing will come of nothing' Lear will himself be propelled into nothingness; as we shall see, however, he is wrong since something *will* come from it.

Lear has despised Cordelia's bond, and so he unlooses the Great Chain of Being. In savage anger he orders her exile from the kingdom, and when the Earl of Kent contradicts his judgement he exiles him also on pain of death. In Lear's reaction we observe the beginning of the disintegration of his personality; in his passion he is breaking up: 'Come not between the dragon and his wrath!'. In this extraordinary cry, Lear's emotion becomes a kind of extension of his personality, splitting apart from himself; his wrath is taking on an existence of its own and Lear fears he is losing control of it. Throughout the play the passions of anger and lust are to take on this independent existence and become positively demonic, as we shall see in a moment.

Lear has made love a matter of commercial exchange, and his two elder daughters repay him in kind. They progressively strip him of whatever power and ceremonial dignity he has left. Since he has made love a matter of arithmetic, he ought not to be surprised when they start doing the sums. They reduce his retinue of raffish knights in rapid calculation, and to begin with Lear accepts the logical equation of love and quantity. When Goneril cuts them to fifty, he denounces her ingratitude as a 'marble hearted fiend', and curses her into sterility, but when Regan cuts the fifty knights to twenty-five, he vows to return to Goneril after all:

---

4   Dante, *The Divine Comedy. Paradiso*, 33.145.

> Thy fifty yet doth double five-and-twenty
> And thou art twice her love.   (II.4.261–2)

Lear is still calculating love by numbers, and ought not to be as astounded as he is when Goneril replies, 'what need you five?' and Regan concludes the theorem, 'What need one?' Lear begins to see the point when he replies,

> O! reason not the need; our basest beggars
> Are in the poorest things superfluous:
> Allow not nature more than nature needs,
> Man's life is cheap as beast's.   (ll. 266–9)

It is because Lear has applied the logic of numerical need that he is shortly to be reduced to the level of the beasts of the field. The fool has an apt comment on those who place their trust in the mathematics of love:

> FOOL: The reason why the seven stars are no more than seven is a pretty reason.
> LEAR: Because they are not eight?
> FOOL: Yes indeed; thou would'st make a good Fool.   (I.5.35–9)

Shakespeare is thus portraying a journey into nothingness, a path into the void, launched from Lear's angry assertion of the doctrine of equivalence: 'Nothing will come of nothing'.

Human Surplus and Excess

Here a Derridean perspective upon deferment and dispersal of meaning is instructive, and Terry Eagleton provides it in his study of the play. He suggests that Lear's appeal 'reason not the need' indicates that there is always a 'surplus' of meaning over sign. It is a mark of being human that we transcend ourselves; in every area of culture there is a 'capacity for a certain lavish infringement of exact limit,'[5] and so our language will always be superfluous to the exact need of sense. As Jacques Derrida describes it, writing works by 'difference' and so there will be a diffusing and dispersing of meaning, an endless web of signifiers and signified that can never be

---

[5]   Terry Eagleton, *William Shakespeare. Rereading Literature* (Oxford: Blackwell, 1986), pp. 81–2.

contained within a structure or system. So a text can 'show' us something that cannot be reduced to concept, as Cordelia cannot 'heave her heart into her mouth', and the blinded Earl of Gloucester confesses that he 'sees feelingly' (IV.6.150). Pre-eminently, in Cordelia's forgiveness of Lear, Eagleton discerns that there is a 'gratuitous excess of the strict requirements of justice'.

Signs will come astray from objects, and this superfluity makes us human. It challenges an ideology of exact exchange which can also take economic and political forms, for signs are not only literary but the stuff of commerce in every area.[6] There is a danger, however, in this surplus of meaning that values will be lost. As we noted in our critique of deconstruction in the previous chapter, an excess of significance can lead to relativism and norms can get over-ridden. There is capacity for destructiveness in superfluity, as Lear observes that one class in society can amass the 'superflux' entirely for itself at the expense of the poor (III.4.35). The sisters demonstrate the destructive excess of language as they vie with each other to prove their love in an inflation of words, cancelling out any kind of value for love by the piling up of negative comparisons, 'beyond what can be valued, rich or rare'. It takes the sober 'nothing' of Cordelia, or the riddling reversals of sense by the Fool, to debunk this claim for absolute meaning. It is no wonder that in his last speech Lear identifies the Fool with Cordelia; as the two truth tellers they merge into each other in his last passion: 'And my poor fool is hang'd! No, no, no life!'.

In his 'post-structural' analysis, Eagleton suggests that the end of the play thus leaves us with an unresolved contradiction; it is endemic to human nature to surpass itself, and the medium of this is language, but in this very superfluity 'values can get out of hand'.[7] We may add to Eagleton's insights the observation that the ending of the play opens itself in the moment of closure. The horizon of death (and beyond that, apocalypse) prompts our awareness of the elements that undermine closure. It seems that wrong has been judged, mistakes have reaped their bitter harvest and right has been vindicated, but the judgement of Lear leaves matters open; Cordelia the guiltless, with no fatal flaws, has been killed. The moment of justice is still awaited. Edgar has reflected earlier that 'The worst is not, so long as we can say, this is the worst . . .', and he confirms this view with the last words

---

[6]   Cf. Paul Ricoeur on the 'economy of superabundance': 'Freedom in the Light of Hope', transl. R. Sweeney, in Paul Ricoeur, *The Conflict of Interpretations*, ed. Don Ihde (Evanston: Northwestern University Press, 1974), p. 410.

[7]   Eagleton, *William Shakespeare*, p. 83.

of the play, predicting that 'we that are young, shall never see so much, nor live so long.' Kermode suggests that the mood of transition, of perpetual crisis, has replaced that of apocalypse; the end is always post-poned. While other tragedies, we notice, offer us the possibility of a society cleansed for a new beginning by the death of a notable individual, careful examination shows these also undermine themselves. Perhaps the death of Cordelia is so unendurable because it makes clear, without equivocation, that nothing has been resolved.

Edgar's words 'or image of that horror?' in response to Kent's query 'is this the promis'd end?' may not in fact indicate an *indefinite* postponement of the end as Kermode suggests ('a mere image . . . not the thing itself'),[8] but there is certainly an incompleteness about the end at which the plot has arrived, opening to new crises to come in the future. We shall shortly need to ask why the 'promise' in this play is only the negative promise of the terrors of the Last Judgement, especially as I have chosen this phrase as the title for this book.

Images of a Desired and Undesirable World

The ending, then, both organizes the action and yet subverts its own closure in deferring any final meaning. In the movement of plot towards its end, Northrop Frye also discerns (we recall) the expression of human desire: even though in tragedy this desire is felt as unfulfilled, since the redemption and integration of life expressed in comedy is not reached, yet characters are allowed to catch a glimpse of the desired world. Lear has such a vision in his scene of reconciliation with Cordelia; this is what wholeness looks like, as Cordelia's forgiveness releases him momentarily from the 'wheel of fire' on which he is bound, and patriarchal hierarchy is overcome as the father kneels to the daughter. But it is only a glimpse. As the soldiers of his foul daughters come to take them away, Lear turns the vision into a fantasy:

> Come, let's away to prison;
> We too alone will sing like birds i' th' cage:
> When thou dost ask me blessing, I'll kneel down,
> And ask of thee forgiveness: so we'll live,

---

[8] Kermode, *The Sense of an Ending*, p. 82.

> And pray, and sing, and tell old tales, and laugh
> At gilded butterflies . . .   (V.3.8–13)

This idyll is a castle in the air, as little grounded in truth as his earlier attempt to get his daughters to calculate their love. Their enemies are not going to allow them to live on into old age in a golden cage; they are going to be killed like rats in a trap. The pattern of the play is tragedy, and within this there is a unifying pattern of the kind of imagery that Frye calls 'demonic'; in contrast to apocalyptic images of integration, these are images of disintegration; they depict the world that is not desired. They mark the journey towards nothingness, portraying a world coming apart.

First there is the image of unclothing, or stripping bare; humanity is to be reduced to a state of nakedness. We have already noted Lear's divesting himself of his crown, and this image finds its most vivid example in the figure of Edgar who assumes the role of the naked madman Tom, and accompanies Lear in his mad ravings on the heath when the doors have been shut against him by his two daughters. Edgar is in fact the loyal son of the Earl of Gloucester, and has been forced to go into hiding through a plot against him by his illegitimate half-brother, Edmund. Ironically, it is meeting the supposed madman Tom that drives Lear deeper into his own real madness; Lear sees in Tom the image of humankind reduced to absolute nothing, and in his frenzy seeks to imitate Tom by tearing off his own clothes:

> Is man no more than this? Consider him well. Thou ow'st the worm no silk, the beast no hide, the sheep no wool, the cat no perfume. Ha! Here's three on's are sophisticated; thou art the thing itself; unaccommodated man is no more but such a poor, bare, forked animal as thou art. Off, off you lendings! Come; unbutton here.   (III.4.105–12).

A second major image of dissolution is that of water, not the life-giving refreshment of the river of life, but the death-dealing waters of chaos and Hades. Lear compares the storm on the heath in which he is caught, unprotected, with the primeval flood come again. Recalling the biblical texts about Noah's flood, the cataracts of heaven are opened from above, and the depths of the earth are broken open from below, so that the water pours into the world from every side:

> Blow, winds, and crack your cheeks! rage! blow!
> You cataracts and hurricanoes, spout
> Till you have drench'd our steeples, drown'd the cocks!

> . . . and thou, all-shaking thunder
> Strike flat the thick rotundity o' the world!
> Crack Nature's moulds, all germens spill at once
> That makes ungrateful man!   (III.2.1–9)

But even more potent than this storm outside is the storm within Lear's mind, and here the flood of water is a matter of tears. The whole play conspires to make Lear weep, for Lear has vowed never to do so (I.4.310–12; II.4.284–9); when he cries, he will have finally come apart, and so he fights continually against tears (V.3.23–5). He regards tears as a sign of humanity reduced to its most basic state, as he instructs the blinded Gloucester:

> If thou wilt weep my fortunes, take my eyes;
> I know thee well enough; thy name is Gloucester;
> Thou must be patient; we came crying hither:
> Thou know'st the first time that we smell the air
> We wawl and cry. I will preach to thee: mark . . .
>
> When we are born we cry that we are come
> To this great stage of fools.   (IV.6.178–85)

But Lear does weep after all; at the end, with Cordelia dead in his arms:

> Howl, howl, howl! O! you are men of stones:
> Had I your tongues and eyes I'd use them so
> That heaven's vault should crack.   (V.3.256–9)

His crying is the sign of the final disintegration of his personality; when he cries, he dies. He is reduced to absolute zero, to humanity as a piece of earth, to mere dust. So Kent aptly enquires as he weeps: 'Is this the promis'd end?'

A third chain of 'demonic' imagery concerns animals: human passions are seen as fragmenting into animal forms, into a whole pack of wild beasts. Human emotional unity is scattered into animal diversity, or as Edgar preaches in his feigned madness, 'hog in sloth, fox in stealth, wolf in greediness, dog in madness, lion in prey' (III.4.93–5). At the end point, these negative passions are depicted as demonic, and Shakespeare has drawn upon several contemporary tracts about witchcraft and demon possession for some of the most vivid vocabulary which he puts into Tom's mouth. According to Albany, Goneril's passions have taken on a deadly life of their own, so that 'humanity must perforce prey on itself/ Like monsters of the

deep' (IV.2.48). The Great Chain of Being is becoming unlinked, and so
Lear complains over the dead Cordelia:

> Why should a dog, a horse, a rat have life
> And thou no breath at all?

It is in line with this sequence of imagery that the conspirator Edmund
dedicates himself to brute Nature. He throws off all the garments of law
and custom and vows to return to basic nature:

> Thou, Nature, art my goodess; to thy law
> My services are bound . . .　　　(I.2.1–2)

We sympathize with him in the unfairness of his being socially ostracized
as the illegitimate son of Gloucester, but the solution is not to overthrow
the benefits of nature altogether:

> 　　　　　　　　　　　　　I grow, I prosper;
> Now, gods, stand up for bastards!　　(21–2)

Shakespeare is not seduced by a 'return to nature' romanticism. As in all
his plays, he shows a belief in the proper blend of nature and nurture. We
may say that he recognizes the 'excess' and 'superabundance' in human
existence (to use terms from Derrida and Ricoeur) that cannot be trapped
in either alternative alone. By excluding one polarity, Edmund has volun-
tarily returned to zero as Lear is to be propelled into it against his will. For
the moment Edmund may have succeeded in tricking Gloucester into
turning against Edgar, getting himself installed in Gloucester's earldom, and
winning the affections of both Goneril and Regan, but nothingness awaits.

The Configuring of Time

Shakespeare thus traces the descent of Lear into Nothing with this sequence
of images – unclothing, flooding, dissolving into animal passions. But we
can also find confirmed the critical view (Kermode, Ricoeur) that the
ending enables a *temporal* configuration of the action, a humanizing of the
mere successiveness of time. Here I shall ignore the configuring of time in
the sub-plot of Gloucester and his son Edgar, though this certainly deserves
attention, and consider the way that Lear's story is shaped by passing

through a sequence of 'trial scenes'. In-between the last judgement of the conclusion and the opening scene of the play, in which Lear has tried and unjustly sentenced his faithful daughter Cordelia, the passing of time is unified for Lear by three mock trials in which he plays at judging his two ungrateful daughters.

In the first of these scenes, which takes place in the raging storm of the open heath, Lear realizes for the first time the state of the naked poor. He calls upon the gods to show justice to the poor and to have vengeance upon their so-called judges who have exploited them; significantly, at this point he includes himself as chief among the oppressed: 'I am a man/ More sinn'd against than sinning' (III.2.58–9). Lear has had a glimpse of humanity in its basic state, and he expects the thunder of heaven to intervene on the side of the poor and himself. He is still confident about justice, and wants it applied. In the second of these mock trial scenes however, sheltering in a farmhouse near the castle, the journey to nothing has gone a further stage. Now as Tom, the Fool and Lear play out a court scene where Regan and Goneril are accused, the poor and the justices have their roles reversed; the beggar and the fool change places with the judges (III.6.37–8). We have gone further than demanding that the law should be applied justly for the poor; the whole order of judges has been supplanted by the poor and the mad.

In the third trial scene, out in the open country again, there is now no judgement at all. Lear realizes that in their basic state all people are equally guilty, all sinners. He calls for the beadle who lashes the back of the whore to halt his hand, for 'Thou hotly lusts to use her in that kind/ For which thou whipp'st her'. While small vices easily become apparent through the tattered clothes of the poor, 'robes and furr'd gowns hide all' (IV.6.167). This vision of universal sin does not, however, lead Lear directly to quote Paul's text in Romans 3:23, 'All have sinned and fallen short of the glory of God'. In his madness he creates an apparently anti-Pauline text: 'None does offend, none I say, none.'

> I pardon that man's life. What was thy cause?
> Adultery?
> Thou shalt not die: die for adultery! No:
> The wren goes to 't, and the small gilded fly
> Does lecher in my sight.   (IV.6.112–16)

Since all are guilty, none are guilty; no discrimination can be made between them. All are equally guilty; all are equally innocent. We have arrived at nothing:

GLOUCESTER: O! let me kiss that hand.
LEAR: Let me wipe it first; it smells of mortality.
GLOUCESTER: O ruin'd piece of Nature! This great world
    Shall so wear out to naught.   (ll. 134–7)

Looking upon Death

We have traced the way that Shakespeare propels one man, Lear, into the abyss of nothingness. He is reduced to humanity at zero, basic man with no clothing to hide his nakedness. Such an ending organizes and unifies time, defers meaning and grants a glimpse of the desired world in the midst of the undesired. But why choose to locate the ending at the zero point? Some have suggested that Lear is redeemed through his experience; through his passion story, as with Christ, life has come out of death. He has gone the furthest into death's other kingdom, and come forth in resurrection. Such commentators point to Lear garlanded in flowers like Christ wearing a crown of thorns, and they find evidence of Lear's sanctification in his reconciliation with Cordelia. But we have already noticed the element of fantasy in this; Lear is not redeemed; he is still a 'very foolish, fond old man' (IV.7.60). This tragedy cannot be forced into the Christian sequence of life through death, although Shakespeare's comedies and romances do take the form of rebirth through suffering.

Lear is not redeemed, but he does *learn*. He gains only a glimpse of the desired world, but he looks steadily upon what humanity is like here and now. He looks upon humanity at bare minimum, reduced to its basic elements, and he invites us to look too. Through his passion story his eyes are at least cleared. We are presented with the final tableau of Lear with Cordelia dead upon his lap, and the critic Helen Gardner makes the perceptive comment that this is a secular version of a *pieta*; where artists have depicted the sacred subject of Mary with the dead body of Christ in her arms, Shakespeare gives us Lear with Cordelia.[9] And all Lear can say is:

> Do you see this? Look on her, look, her lips,
> Look there, look there!   (V.3.310–11)

Some critics have suggested that Lear dies believing that Cordelia is alive after all; he is asking the bystanders to look on her lips which he believes

[9]   Helen Gardner, *King Lear. The John Coffin Memorial Lecture 1966* (London: Athlone Press, 1967).

are moving with breath, and so dies in a final delusion to crown all his others. I believe this is the wrong interpretation. Lear is simply asking us to look, to contemplate a piece of humanity, a piece of earth. This is a human being in the face of death. In a secular *pieta* Lear presents Cordelia to us as the prime example of what a man or woman is; in himself, in herself, this is all. The very finest, the most faithful, the most loving – dead. This is 'the thing itself' as Lear said earlier of the naked Tom. This is the something that comes of nothing.

The play as a whole invites us to consider this, humanity at zero. Lear's error from the beginning has been a failure of sight. He has looked upon the outward appearance of words and flattery, rather than being able to see to the heart of Cordelia. He has said, 'Nothing will come of nothing'. Continually in Shakespeare's plays, lovers suffer failure of inner sight; they do not trust the inner, intuitive vision of love and are deceived by the outward appearance of the senses. They reduce the meaning to the sign. Othello loses trust in Desdemona because of the 'evidence' of a misplaced handkerchief, while Claudio (in *Much Ado About Nothing*) shamefully rejects Hero because of the 'evidence' of an overheard conversation at a window. 'You see how this world goes' says Lear to the blind Gloucester in the last mock-trial scene, but Gloucester has only come to see how things are through his physical blinding at the command of Edmund. The scene of the gouging out of Gloucester's eyes is a horrific piece of theatre, and once again Shakespeare has been accused of 'going too far'; but only through this drastic piece of surgery to his moral sight does Gloucester come to see the truth ('I stumbled when I saw'). We are reminded of the words of Christ to the Pharisees in the Fourth Gospel (a Gospel also full of trial scenes, as New Testament scholars have shown us);[10] 'Because you claim to see, your guilt remains' (John 9:41). The trick that Edgar plays on his now blind father, pretending that the suicidal Gloucester is on the edge of the cliffs of Dover, is very painful; but only by supposedly throwing himself off the edge and finding himself alive does Gloucester discover the value of life, and the need for patience; he comes to agree with Edgar that

> . . . Men must endure
> Their going hence, even as their coming hither:
> Ripeness is all.   (V.2.9)

[10] See e.g. Anthony E. Harvey. *Jesus on Trial. A Study in the Fourth Gospel* (London: SPCK, 1976).

As in Shakespeare's comedies, the truth emerges through a confusion which has healing power. The tricks that are played can blow open the surface of things and uncover the truth which lies deep beneath. The Fool is always doing this; he turns things upside down so that the audience can see that the world was the wrong way up all the time. His jokes reverse the normal order of things, and then we suddenly see that things were disordered anyway:

> LEAR: Who is it that can tell me who I am?
> FOOL: Lear's shadow.
> LEAR: I would learn that.   (I.4.238–40)

The Fool disappears from the play with one more delighted reversal of reality: 'And I'll go to bed at noon'. So he speaks truly of his untimely death.

The need for Lear to see clearly is linked with his need to weep, for tears are the natural emotional response to seeing clearly, the feeling part of the sight pattern. Cordelia both sees and weeps, saying at the end of the first Act that she leaves her father with 'wash'd eyes', washed with tears and washed clear of motes. In the scene of reconciliation with her father, while Lear maintains a Stoic attitude, her eyes are full of 'holy water'. In his meeting with the blind Gloucester a little earlier, when Lear had asked with irony 'you see how this world goes', Gloucester had replied, 'I see it feelingly'. And at the last Lear both weeps and sees; he sees with feeling as he cries 'look here, look here'. He sees the sheer fact of death which cannot be avoided if we are to give attention to other human beings; a little later I want to suggest that he sees something else as well, but for the moment, let us concentrate upon taking death seriously.

Death the Last Enemy

In our consideration of eschatology, death is traditionally the first of the 'four last things', and it must be granted a certain priority. In urging us to look with Lear on the sheer fact of death, the play moves the theologian to take a view of the status of death.

A whole range of factors prompts us to face the finality of death for human life, that is, to regard it as the end of the whole person, and not just the cracking of an outer shell of flesh so that the butterfly of an eternal soul can emerge. In the first place, there is the modern biological view of psychosomatic unity, which fits in with the Hebrew understanding of the human being as a body *animated* by 'life' or 'breath' rather than the Greek view of a *soul imprisoned* within a body. The Hebrew view of a human person knows nothing of the dualism between soul and body that Christian tradition has absorbed from Platonism. According to the Old Testament, the *nephesh*[11] or 'life' (often translated 'soul') may certainly be distinguished from the 'flesh' (*bāśār*), but not as an independent entity, or 'ghost in the machine' that inhabits the body and could exist outside it as a personal consciousness. At death the *nephesh* is described as being breathed out, or poured out like water that has been spilt on the ground and cannot be gathered up again (Job 11:20, Isaiah 53:12, 2 Sam. 14:14). Having lost all the vitality, purpose and emotions represented by the *nephesh*, the body is in the very weakest state and is thought to inhabit Sheol as a kind of shadow ('shade') of its former self.[12] It is as if the air has been let out of a tyre and it has gone flat. The description of human vitality as *rūach* or 'breath' within the body pictures the wholeness of the human being in a similar way, although *rūach* tends to carry stronger psychical functions of intellect and will.

Death cannot be finally escaped. To be 'rescued from Sheol', a phrase that occurs many times in the Psalms, means to return to health and so only to put off dying; the *nephesh* or *rūach* begins to drain out of the body in illness, so that people who are ill stand on the very borders of Sheol from which they can be said to 'return' only if the *nephesh* returns to their body and they recover their strength (Psalm 30:1–3). For almost the whole Old Testament period Israelite faith thus had no concept of a meaningful life beyond death, asking 'can the Shades praise Yahweh?' (Psalm 88:10–12). When hope for a future life began to develop late on in Jewish belief, it had to be in terms of resurrection; that is, Yahweh must restore the vital breath to the shadowy and exhausted bodies that could otherwise only squeak and gibber in Sheol, the land of the grave. Then the whole person would be raised to life (Daniel 12:1–2).

It says much for the positive outlook on daily life that the Israelite people possessed that hopes of life beyond death took much longer to

[11]   For the wide range of meaning of this term, see Aubrey R. Johnson, *The Vitality of the Individual in the Thought of Ancient Israel* (Cardiff: University of Wales Press, 1964), pp. 3–22.

[12]   Cf. Psalm 6:5, Ecclesiastes 9:5–6. See Robert Martin-Achard, *From Death to Life. A Study of the Development of the Doctrine of the Resurrection in the Old Testament*, transl. J. Penney-Smith (Edinburgh and London: Oliver and Boyd, 1960), pp. 17–18, 36–46.

develop than in surrounding cultures. The blessing of Yahweh was perceived in physical forms such as good health, prosperity, freedom from
enemies and a large family, as well as the spiritual gift of fellowship with
God in the Temple (Psalm 42:1–5). This history of Jewish thought also
shows that death could not be *escaped* by some kind of survival capsule; it
could only be *conquered* – by resurrection. The deaths of Jesus and Socrates
have often been compared in this regard, Socrates urbanely discussing
philosophy with his friends while the poison was taking effect, Jesus in a
bloody sweat in the garden and crying out on the cross. The last words of
Socrates were a swan-song, those of Jesus a scream. As Oscar Cullman
points out,[13] the difference was that Socrates thought of himself as stepping
into immortality, his soul released from the prison-house of his body, while
Jesus as a Jew could only feel the onset of death as an attack upon life.

The finality of death can thus be felt, in the Apostle Paul's words as 'the
last enemy' (1 Cor. 15:26). But there is something ambiguous about this
finality. In exploring the sense of an ending in narratives, we have already
come to see that these ends are like death in giving a sense of unity and
organization to the whole of the story. The mortals in Homer's *Iliad* are
tragic figures, oppressed by suffering and death; but as Simon Tugwell
points out in his study of *Human Immortality*, the immortal gods who do
not have to face death are by contrast presented as leading lives of 'sublime
frivolity'.[14] Since they cannot grow old or die, nothing in the end can
make any difference to them, and they have no story worth telling, no
song worth singing. We are reminded of Lazarus in Oscar Wilde's fable
'The Doer of Good', who is found weeping by Christ; when he asks why
he is weeping, Lazarus replies, 'But I was dead once and you raised me
from the dead. What else should I do but weep'?[15]

To the positive effects of death as an ending belong the insights of
Heidegger about 'being-towards-death' and of Tillich about the 'ontological shock' of non-being;[16] only by facing up to death as a real negation can
we gain knowledge of ourselves, gain insight into being itself, and find the

[13] Oscar Cullmann, *Immortality of the Soul or Resurrection of the Dead?* (London: Epworth Press, 1958), pp. 23–7.
[14] Simon Tugwell, *Human Immortality and the Redemption of Death* (London: Darton, Longman and Todd, 1990), p. 48.
[15] Oscar Wilde, *Poems in Prose*, in *Collins Complete Works of Oscar Wilde* (Glasgow: HarperCollins, 1999), p. 901.
[16] Heidegger, *Being and Time*, transl. J. Macquarrie and E. Robinson (Oxford: Basil Blackwell, 1973), pp. 280–90; Paul Tillich, *Systematic Theology*. Combined Volume (London: James Nisbet, 1968), vol. 1, pp. 207ff.

fragments of life coming together into a whole. To this we should add Hegel's talk about the 'Golgotha of the Spirit' without which mind is not mind: 'the life of the Spirit' he says, 'is not one that shuns death and keeps clear of destruction . . . it only wins to its truth when it finds itself utterly torn asunder.'[17]

So is death a good or a bad thing? While the witnesses to whom we have appealed have made clear the finality of death, they have also made clear its ambiguity. It appears both as the last enemy, and as a proper end that gives life shape and meaning. 'Ripeness is all' says Edgar to his suicidal father in *King Lear*, but as a matter of fact much (perhaps most) death in our world is not in the ripeness of old age, or as the pinnacle of achievement. King Lear with Cordelia in his arms insists that we take death seriously, rather than as a door through which an immortal soul floats unscathed. 'Look here!' he says; look well. The end of the play thus makes the theologian enquire about the status of death in God's creation.

The biblical writers offer a picture of death that accepts its ambiguity, and offers some explanation for it. Death *as we know it* has been marked by sinfulness, that is a slipping of human life away from the purpose of God towards non-being; 'the sting of death is sin' concludes the Apostle Paul (1 Cor. 15:56). But this does not mean that the bare fact of death itself stands outside God's creative intention, and that it must have occurred as a punishment for sin. Neither Genesis chapter 3 nor Paul's theology states that human beings would not have died if sin had not entered the world. 'For you are dust, and to dust you shall return' is a simple statement about human existence (Genesis 3:19). The myth of Adam and Eve in the garden, in its own terms, does not deny that they would have died even if they had remained obedient to God, but depicts the death they experience as becoming something different, an enemy to life, making work into a miserable struggle.[18] While death in the abstract may be regarded as a natural end to life, the *actual* death we experience is a mixture in varying proportions of natural limit and hostile force. Karl Rahner describes death as having a natural element within it, but concludes that: 'The death which is actually experienced by all men individ-

---

[17]   G. W. F. Hegel, *The Phenomenology of Mind*, transl. J. Baillie (London: George Allen & Unwin, 2nd edn revised, 1949), p. 93.
[18]   So G. Von Rad, *Genesis. A Commentary*, transl. J. Marks (London: SCM, 1963), pp. 91–4.

ually cannot be identified in some naïve and unreflective manner with that natural essence of death.'[19]

Death then appears in the biblical witness as a good thing spoilt. But I suggest that this does not entirely account for its ambiguity. In what sense can it be regarded, even in *essence*, as part of the divine creative intention? The biblical symbols of the resurrection of the dead and the final day when 'death will be swallowed up for ever'[20] witness to a basic religious feeling that death has a *provisional* place at best within God's creative purpose. Death, even if unmarked by sin, does not appear as God's last word on human personal existence. Even, for instance, where death comes in a timely way at the end of a full life, it still breaks relationships and takes away the opportunity for us to express love. The Old Testament psalms portray death as a destructive force, breaking into a life which is to be valued; the destruction is lessened when death comes in old age, but there is still a tinge of regret there:

> You shall come to your grave in ripe old age
> As a shock of grain comes up to the threshing floor in its season
> (Job 5:26).

We might, with Irenaeus, regard natural death, therefore, as a provisional stage in God's purpose for the maturing of humankind, a boundary which gives a wholeness to life but which is finally to be abolished.[21] So there is a double kind of ambiguity: first, natural death considered in the *abstract* is only provisional; second, death as we *actually* know it is interfused with frustrations, untimeliness and regrets of which human beings are victims (whatever their own sins contribute to it), and this is a tragedy against which God protests. Jürgen Moltmann remarks that the feeling of sorrow for suffering is in fact a protest against it, and so to believe that God participates in the sorrow of the world is to say that God is also in protest against the conditions of natural evil, including the destructiveness of death.[22]

This perspective on the ambiguity of death does, I suggest, enable us to

[19]   Karl Rahner, *On the Theology of Death*, transl. C. Henkey (London: Burns & Oates/ Herder: Freiburg, 1961), p. 45.

[20]   Isaiah 25:8 (from an apocalyptic section inserted into the earlier collection of prophecies gathered under the name of Isaiah); 1 Corinthians 15: 54.

[21]   Irenaeus, *Adversus Haereses*, 4.38.

[22]   Jürgen Moltmann, *The Crucified God*, transl. R. A. Wilson and J. Bowden (London: SCM Press, 1974), pp. 226–7, 252.

take death with the seriousness upon which *King Lear* insists when it bids us: 'Look here'. It requires that in developing any doctrine of life beyond death we do not lose this finality. Even in the light of the story of the cross, which affirms that Christ has overcome death, we cannot diminish the reality of the death we still have to face; our concept of eternal life must throw us upon God to overcome the last enemy, rather than disparaging it as an illusion. In the next chapter I shall be suggesting that only a concept of resurrection meets these requirements.

Creation from Nothing

Shakespeare's play thus prompts us to shape our doctrine in a certain way, measuring up to the demand to look unflinchingly on the face of death. But the dialogue between literature and Christian doctrine also works the other way round, as Christian faith can offer a perspective upon our reading of literary texts. Here there is something to be said about the portrayal of the divine in *King Lear*. Some commentators have found this to be an essentially pagan play, showing a disillusioned atheism towards the likelihood of the beneficial intervention of the gods.[23] Certainly, the progress of the mock trial scenes is marked by an increasing doubt about the thunder of heaven; in the last of these scenes Lear remembers 'when the rain came to wet me once and the wind to make me chatter, when the thunder would not peace at my bidding' (IV.6.102–4). Lear is no longer confident that the thunderbolts of the gods will strike at the guilty and vindicate the innocent. Gloucester offers one interpretation of this, taking a view of the arbitrary nature of divine behaviour common in the classical world: 'as flies to wanton boys, are we to the Gods;/ They kill us for their sport' (IV.1.35–6). Lear's own conclusion appears to be far more agnostic, and in fact we can see from a theological perspective that his doubts about the transparency of divine providence are not pagan at all, but a thoroughly Reformation position.

Luther opposed a 'theology of glory', a God who could be demonstrated from the appearance of the world.[24] This play's agnosticism towards natural

---

[23] See, e.g. William R. Elton, *King Lear and the Gods* (San Marion, CA: Huntingdon Library, 1966).

[24] Luther, *Heidelberg Disputation* (1518), Thesis 21; also Theses 19 and 20; *Luther: Early Theological Works*, Library of Christian Classics, vol. 16, ed. and transl. J. Atkinson (London: SCM Press, 1962), pp. 290–2.

theology, that is, the attempt to prove the existence and justice of God from the state of the world, is a typically Reformation 'agnosticism'. Luther finds God not openly displaying himself in thunder, but hidden in the suffering of the cross of Jesus Christ. The *deus revelatus* is the *deus absconditus*, veiling divine power and glory in weakness. This play does not, of course, offer the positive statement of a *theologia crucis* to complement its denial that God can be justified from the course of history, and in this way we may regard it as a pre-Christian, or proto-evangelical play.

The play is also of the Reformation in seeing humankind as reduced to nothing *in itself*. Lear's conclusion, 'None does offend' is a riddling way of affirming that 'all have sinned', but it has a greater shock value than the expected text, and so underlines its impact. It indicates that no true justice, values, or moral order can be built on human nature *by itself*. Few Reformation thinkers would have denied that there is any spark of goodness at all within the natural person, and most thought of the image of God in humankind as being marred rather than totally destroyed; so the 'nothingness' which Lear is driven to recognize is to be seen in Reforma-tion perspective not as a matter of total evil, but as a fundamental loss of relationships. It is a more pernicious 'nothing' than the absolute *nihil* from which the universe was created, since it is the 'negating nothing' which is a turning away from communion with God.[25] In Reformation terms, this 'nothing' must be recognized in all its destructiveness before salvation can come. Lear is, from a Christian perspective, altogether wrong that 'nothing will come of nothing'. Humanity is reduced to nothingness in judgement as a prelude to justification by grace through faith alone, and not by human actions. As Luther puts it, 'God destroys all things and makes us out of nothing and then justifies us.'[26] The play does not take the next step of moving from the nothing to the 'something' of creation 'from nothing' through justification, but it cries out for the step to be taken. At the end we feel that something more must be said, and the play leaves the audience to say it.

Eberhard Jüngel helpfully relates justification as a kind of creation *ex nihilo* to the Christian understanding of hope.[27] The whole Aristotelian

---

[25] For a discussion of this distinction, see Paul S. Fiddes, *The Creative Suffering of God* (Oxford: Clarendon Press, 1988), pp. 210–14.

[26] Martin Luther, *Die zweite Disputation gegen die Antinomer* (Weimar Gesamtausgabe, 39/I, 470); cited in Jüngel, 'The World as Possibility and Actuality', [1969] in J. B. Webster (ed.) *Eberhard Jüngel. Theological Essays* (Edinburgh: T. & T. Clark, 1989), p. 107.

[27] Jüngel, 'The World as Possibility and Actuality', pp. 107–116.

tradition (from which, we may add, the text 'nothing will come of nothing' comes)[28] assumes the priority of actuality over possibility. But the doctrine of justification makes possibility prior to actuality, as we *become* righteous in God's sight before we *act* righteously. The hope we have in the future is not in the development of present actualities, but hope in God who distinguishes the possible from the impossible. In the death of Christ, affirms Jüngel, God 'makes impossible the impossible', that is, God negates the nothingness of sin; and in the resurrection of Jesus God makes possible the possible. Those who are justified have faced up to the nothingness revealed in the death of Christ, and they trust in the promise of the resurrection that God will bring new possibilities to the world from beyond it. The possible world to which Christian language testifies is generated from without, by God in the freedom of divine love.[29] This possibility has ontological priority over whatever we make through our own activity.

The ending of *King Lear* seems then to support Jüngel's view of hope and the possible, over against Ricoeur's understanding of these factors. We recall (see chapter 2) that Ricoeur, like Jüngel, affirms the priority of possibility over actuality, but that he sees this to be rooted in the nature of human existence as itself being full of possibilities. Tragedy, however, and especially a tragedy as complete as *King Lear*, does not appear to portray a possible world arising from the surplus of meaning in human existence, but brings us to a blank nothingness which demands nothing less than a new creation through the Word of God. There is something to be said, nevertheless, for Ricoeur's understanding of 'deliverance *within* tragedy' rather than *from* it.[30] With regard to tragedy, Ricoeur does not argue that it directly *portrays* a possible world that delivers us from the present world. This would be to reduce symbol to concept and make speculation out of spectacle. The course of classical tragedy, for example, is a conflict between the wrath of God and the wrath of the human hero, between divine predestination to disaster and the freedom of the hero in struggling against it. (This is not, by the way, the shape of Shakespearean tragedy, though Gloucester does take this view of the 'sport' of the gods). Ricoeur's point in taking this example of divine–human struggle is to show that, as

---

[28] The proverbial tag, *ex nihilo nihil fit*, is not found in Aristotle himself, but cf. 'everything that is produced is something produced from something and by something': Aristotle, *Metaphysics*, 1049b.24–9.

[29] Jüngel, 'The World as Possibility and Actuality', pp. 115–17.

[30] Paul Ricoeur, *The Symbolism of Evil*, transl. E. Buchanan (Boston: Beacon Press, 1969), pp. 227–31.

theology, it would be highly unsatisfactory; but it is to be understood as a myth, which refers to a possible world by providing the opportunity for our *participation* within it.

The tension of the myth, which cannot be directly theologized, draws the observer into the tragic chorus that weeps and sings with the hero, and so into a 'sphere of feelings'. Ricoeur singles out the two feelings identified by Aristotle, Fear and Pity, and especially the 'merciful gaze' of pity 'which no longer accuses or condemns.'[31] This is the possible world, a world in which there is a 'tragic wisdom' created by suffering, a world which can remake our actual world through the modalities of feeling.

We can find support for this kind of possibility as we recall the meeting between the mad King and the blind Earl, when Gloucester affirms that he sees the world 'feelingly'. It flits into Lear's mind that Cupid is depicted wearing a blindfold, and he retorts:

> I remember thine eyes well enough. Dost thou squiny at me?
> No, do thy worst, blind Cupid; I'll not love.   (IV.6.138–9)

Cupid is portrayed blindfold in Renaissance iconography to indicate that people in love see each other not with the outer senses but with an inner, intuitive sight, as we read in *A Midsummer Night's Dream*,

> Love sees not with the eyes, but with the mind,
> And therefore is wing'd Cupid painted blind.   (I.1.234–5)

Lear will not cry; he fails to see; he will not love. But through his reduction to nothing he is brought to tears, to sight and, I suggest also, to love. The something that comes of nothing in this play is not only a clear view of death, but some glimpse of love. In all Shakespeare's tragedies, something is affirmed at the end; even in the midst of the wreck of lives, something of value is rescued, held up for us to see and then fixed for ever in story by the event of death. Here, at the end, Lear is reduced to gazing upon human being reduced to nothing; but I suggest that we are drawn into feeling something else that has the seeds of possibility within it. Transfusing this nothingness is Lear's love for Cordelia in the face of death, love with no future, no reconciliation to come, no eternal felicity promised. This is love in the face of bare mortality. Humankind reduced to zero can still learn to love: 'my poor fool' says Lear, 'look on her lips'. The play

---

[31]   Ibid., p. 231.

succeeds if we are willing to look, and it goes as far as it possibly can to make us look.

I believe, then, that we can combine the two dimensions to which Jüngel and Ricoeur draw our attention. First, hope is more than the actualizing of what is potentially present in human life; it is hope in God to whom we turn for the creation of new possibilities in the face of nothingness. But second, the ending of *King Lear* shows us that there is also a 'surplus' in human existence which, though it can be abused, opens up the possibility of redescribing the world. This is more than reaching towards a 'desired' world, which can become fantasy. It is an actuality which has the power of the 'not yet'. Are these two dimensions of hope reconcilable? Must we say that the second is simply inferior to the first, as Jüngel suggests in his essay 'The World as Possibility and Actuality'? We shall be looking further at this question in a later chapter,[32] but for the moment I suggest that all depends upon where we see grace and revelation at work. Perhaps we may see the surplus of being and meaning in human existence as evidence of the pressure of divine grace already there at the foundation of personal life, not just as a natural phenomenon.

After all, if the nothingness to which Lear is propelled can turn us towards the need for justification, it is not only in the cross of Jesus that the divine verdict on human life is revealed. It is revealed in the 'wheel of fire' upon which Lear is bound.

---

[32] See chapter 6, pp. 168–73.

Chapter Four

A QUESTION OF
IDENTITY

A favourite device in science fiction is the 'body transporter', perhaps most well known in the version that appeared in the television series *Star Trek*, accompanied by the immortal line 'beam me up, Scottie'. More convenient and faster than conventional transport over huge distances, it is portrayed as dissolving the body into its component atoms, and somehow re-assembling the body in another location. In fictional accounts where a scientific explanation of the device is offered, the process is one of *replication*: a scanner destroys the present brain and body of the travellers while making an exact record of the state of all their cells, the vital information is transmitted by radio wave to the desired destination and there a replicator creates out of new matter brains and bodies exactly like the old ones.[1] The travellers lose consciousness while being scanned, and wake up in the new body which appears to them just like their former one. This common feature of science fiction has been attractive to both philosophers of mind and to theologians, as it raises the interesting question: is the replica *the same person*?

Resurrection and the Idea of Replication

For philosophers such as Derek Parfit, who uses the illustration in his book *Reasons and Persons*, the 'Teletransporter' (as he names it) provides a thought

---

[1]   This is the technique described in the Hollywood movie, *The Fly* (1986). Lawrence Krauss, *The Physics of Star Trek* (London: HarperCollins/Flamingo, 1997), pp. 67–71, points out that the *Star Trek* episodes are ambiguous about whether only digital bits of information are transported, or atoms of the body along with them. My present argument addresses the former scenario.

experiment which enables us to test out questions of personal identity. By considering the case of Parfit with his blueprint beamed to Mars, he is able to explore what it means to be a person – Parfit – existing over time.[2] For theologians such as John Hick, the scenario of replication provides an analogy with the doctrine of the resurrection of the body, and enables him to test out the coherence of the belief that God, after death, somehow remakes us with a new body.[3] The two issues of personal identity and resurrection are of course deeply connected; if we are recreated by God and given a new body are we the same persons as we were when we were alive? These are questions I want to explore in this chapter. If the resurrection of the body in the face of death is indeed central to Christian eschatology, as I have argued that it is, then the question of identity becomes an urgent one. It justifies us playing, at least for a while, with the idea of replication and with a *Star Trek* theology. Would an exact replica be the same person?

John Hick's answer is yes, though with certain qualifications. The replica must have exact bodily similarity, have the same memories as the original, and be the only instance of the person. Identical body *plus* memory *plus* uniqueness would enable us to claim that the replica is 'the same person as the original.'[4] We should add that an identical body includes an identical brain state, and the 'memory' will include the consciousness of being the same person as before, with identical 'beliefs, habits and mental propensities.' I must admit that Hick does not refer to teletransportation as directly as Parfit does; rather he gives us the scenario of someone disappearing suddenly from one location – say a lecture in London – and a replica of the kind described 'appearing' in another place – say New York. In this case 'the only reasonable and generally acceptable decision would be to acknowledge identity'.[5] However, for support of this case he appeals to the work of the cyberneticist Norbert Wiener, who proposed the theoretical possibility of transmitting by radio the coded form of a human body and brain and re-embodying the human being at the other end. The pattern of a human being, claimed Wiener, could be 'telegraphed' from one country to another and then reconstituted. Hick approves of Wiener's conclusion that psycho-physical individuality does not depend upon the numerical

---

[2] Derek Parfit, *Reasons and Persons* (Oxford: Clarendon Press, 1984, repr. 1989), pp. 199–226.

[3] John Hick, *Death and Eternal Life* (London: Collins, 1976), pp. 279–88.

[4] Ibid., pp. 280, 283.

[5] Ibid., p. 280.

identity of the different parcels of matter used, but upon the pattern or code they exemplify. Writing as long ago as 1950, Wiener appears to be the grandfather of the teletransporter.

Of course, Hick's interest is not in the travel industry, but in applying the same idea to resurrection. It is equally reasonable, he proposes, to believe that God re-embodies the same person in another space from our finite world. Appealing to the insights of modern physics about the possibility of 'plural spaces within a single superspace', he believes that we could be reborn in another physical world in another space, perhaps another 'sub-space within this unimaginably vast and complex universe', or in a parallel universe.[6]

At first sight, this seems a strong defence of the New Testament idea of the resurrection of the body, in contrast to the Greek view of survival beyond death through the immortality of the soul. It stresses God's recreating of the whole individual being, body and personality, after death. The image of resurrection accepts the psychosomatic unity of the human being, it affirms the goodness of the body and of material existence here and now, and it fits in with our everyday perceptions that a body is necessary for communication with others and orientation to an external environment. By contrast, the idea of immortality of the soul is dualistic, regarding the soul as the essence of the human being that is separable from the body and that can exist without it. This makes the body merely accidental, contingent upon the 'really important' component of the soul. As we have already seen in the previous chapter, neither the Old or New Testament supports this idea of a soul, whether in the Platonic version of an immortal *psyche*, or in the Cartesian version of the Ego. Where the word 'soul' is used in scripture it refers to the personal life that upholds and energizes the body, and it is not considered to have any survival prospects outside the body. For these reasons I prefer to use the word 'personality' instead of soul, though the term is still helpful in indicating that there is a dimension of the whole personality which is open towards God, and which is never satisfied until it finds its rest in God.

---

[6]   John Hick, 'A Possible Conception of Life After Death' in Stephen T. Davis (ed.), *Death and Afterlife* (London: Macmillan, 1989), pp. 191–2, 195; cf. Hick, *Death and Eternal Life*, pp. 279–80, 289–90.

Problems about Identity

The analogy between resurrection and a replica, with or without inter-planetary travel, is not, however, completely convincing. The image of resurrection evokes continuity with our present bodily existence, but can a person beyond death really be the same purely on grounds of an identi-kit reconstruction? The break between death and resurrection, however brief, seems to be a gulf in which identity will be swallowed up for ever unless there is some kind of continuing link between the old person and the new.

The philosopher Kai Nielsen, for example, asserts that a mere replica body plus memory would not be sufficient for identity. Nielsen is the fascinating case of a philosopher who believes neither in God nor in life after death, but who has for many years argued vigorously that resurrection of the body is a coherent concept *if* one is a religious believer, while immortality of the soul is never so. According to Nielsen, if one believes in God then it is reasonable to grant God power to resurrect persons in a beyond death existence; but survival through an immortal soul is incoher-ent as mind and character are dependent for their activities on a body in causal interaction with the world around.[7] Moreover, he argues, the only criterion for identity in a disembodied existence would be memory, and memory can be a fallible instrument for recognizing others and even oneself.[8] However, by a coherent concept of resurrection Nielsen means the gathering together of the actual physical particles that made up the original person. Continuity of identity can only be secured if the atoms that have constituted the former body are brought together and re-energized. The link between the old and new person would be the particles of his body.

In taking this view of resurrection Nielsen is in line with the Church Fathers and the medieval scholastics. Augustine, for example, declares:

> For the earthy matter of which mortals' flesh is created is never lost to God: but into whatsoever dust or ashes it be dissolved, into whatsoever vapours or mists it flee away, into whatsoever substance of other bodies it be converted, or even into the very elements, into whatsoever animals' or

---

[7] Kai Nielsen, 'The Faces of Immortality' in Davis (ed.), *Death and Afterlife*, pp. 1–28.

[8] Ibid., p. 14. Thus far he is in agreement with Terence Penelhum, *Survival and Disembodied Existence* (London: Routledge and Kegan Paul, 1970), pp. 55–62.

men's food it be reduced, so as to be changed into their flesh, it returns in a moment of time to that human soul which in the first place made it animate . . .'[9]

According to Aquinas, 'if the body of the man who rises is not to be composed of the flesh and bones which now compose it, the man who rises will not be numerically the same man.'[10] For both Augustine and Aquinas, the power of divine omnipotence to reconstitute the same matter cannot be defeated even by a person's being eaten by fishes or cannibals and, as a modern philosopher, Nielsen agrees that it is not logically impossible. On the other hand, according to Nielsen, a *replica* of (say) Hans cannot *be* Hans; the argument is that since persons are unique, there can only be one instance of each one.[11] The criterion of uniqueness is not satisfied by there only being one replica. Nielsen, of course, does not think there actually will be a resurrection of the literal sort he describes, as he believes that belief in God, and therefore in life beyond death, is 'groundless'.

Together with virtually all modern theologians, I do not want to take this over-materialistic view of resurrection. Scientifically, our knowledge about transfer of energy and the constant replacement of cells in our bodies through time makes the problems of re-assembly even more tortuous than the Fathers imagined. But more important than this, if the promise of new creation is to have the power of challenging and changing the present, as I have already suggested it does (in line with Moltmann, Ricoeur and Bloch to different degrees), then the re-assembly of our actual bodies would be as much a 'calculable future' and as much a projection of the present as the continuing of a ready-made survival capsule of an immortal soul. Nor does the New Testament substantiate such a view. Jesus is portrayed as having risen in a transformed body, a 'body of glory', which has discontinuity as well as continuity with his earthly existence. A pericope that has good claim to be based in the discourse of Jesus himself[12] warns us against supposing that certain bodily activities like marrying will persist in the coming resurrection (Mark 12:18–27). The Apostle Paul's term, a 'spiritual body' (1 Cor. 15:44), has a kind of internal tension and contradiction that

---

[9]   Augustine, *Enchiridion*, 88; transl. Ernest Evans (London: SPCK, 1953), p. 76.

[10]   Thomas Aquinas, *Summa Contra Gentiles*, 4.84.

[11]   Kai Nielsen, 'God, the Soul and Coherence', in Davis (ed.), *Death and Afterlife*, p. 151.

[12]   Ben Witherington, *Women in the Ministry of Jesus* (Cambridge: Cambridge University Press, 1984), pp. 32–35.

opens up multiple meaning rather than constricting us to one understanding: while the most obvious meaning is that the resurrection body will be completely energized by the Holy Spirit of God, in contrast to our present bodies that are energized by a 'natural' life force, this by no means exhausts the meaning of this tantalizing phrase.

Paul's analogy of the seed in 1 Corinthians 15 ('what is sown is perishable, what is raised is imperishable', v.42) does not support the extreme continuity ascribed to the resurrection body by Augustine and Aquinas. Paul is not thinking in modern biological terms of a smooth, continuous development between the seed and the plant. He assumes, as was common in his time, that the seed *dies* in the earth; it is sown as a 'naked kernel', and God then 'gives it a body'. There will be no wheat growing from the seed unless a body is created for it. Thus his analogy for resurrection resists both a crude materialism and the over-spiritualization of the Corinthian church to whom he was writing, who seem to have assumed that the resurrection had already happened in the form of enjoying life in the divine Spirit here and now. If we are to follow the track of thought opened up by the image of a 'spiritual body' we shall think of something analogous to the material body we know now, with its powers of expression, interaction and communication, but nevertheless its 'own kind of body' (1 Corinthians 15:35–41). We shall hope for continuity *and* discontinuity; the question is whether a 'replica' would provide this.

Nielsen does not actually quote the 'teletransporter' scenario in attacking the identity of a proposed replica, though it is evident that, if he did, he would deny the traveller to Mars to be the same person who left earth. However, the advantage of our considering this fictional device is that it forces us to consider some of the implications of resurrection as the creation of a replica; in facing imaginatively how *we* would feel about travelling to Mars by teletransporter rather than by the slower mode of the spaceship, we are being forced to face up to our beliefs both about personal identity and the possibility of life beyond death. It leaves us, I suggest, with a certain discomfort about the idea of survival in the form of a replica, whether or not the replica has exact bodily similarity.

Derek Parfit admits the disturbing nature of the scenario (destruction and replication), though he is only concerned about questions of personal identity, not resurrection, for reasons that will shortly become clear. However, he suggests that our reluctance to enter the teletransporter and press the green button, though understandable, would not be rational. His view is that the replica would probably not be the same person – 'we should probably decide not to call my Replica me'[13] – but that this loss of personal identity 'does not matter'. Being destroyed and replicated is 'about as good as ordinary survival',[14] that is, being teletransported is no better and no worse than the way we normally survive from day to day. This rather extraordinary response to the scenario is based in Parfit's view of the nature of the person, which is a modified reductionism (or what he calls at one point a dualist reductionism). He holds that a person consists in a set of mental and physical experiences or events, and the relations between them; this is a kind of 'bundle' theory in which a person is characterized by 'connectedness':

> . . . persons exist. And a person is distinct from his brain and body, and his experiences. But persons are not separately existing entities. The existence of a person, during any period, just consists in the existence of his brain and body, and the thinking of his thoughts, and the doing of his deeds, and the occurrence of many other physical and mental events.[15]

We notice that Parfit's view is not a simple reductionism where person ('I') is simply equivalent to brain (such as is held, for example, by Thomas Nagel).[16] Mental events, argues Parfit, should be recognized as being different from physical events.[17] Moreover, the 'person' cannot be reduced to any one component part of the bundle (the brain, for example), but is a kind of corporate whole, like a nation. The person *can* also be regarded as a subject, doing certain things, in the same way that a nation can be said to act as a whole. But the person is 'nothing but' the sum total of events. Personal *identity* consists in this connectedness together with physical and mental continuity between sets of experiences over time. Thus the replication of 'me' through a scanning device does not strictly issue in the same person. My replica has a psychological continuity with me – what Parfit calls relation R – since he has exactly the same attitudes, memories and beliefs. But this continuity is caused in an abnormal way (by the scanner/replicator) compared with the way it usually happens in my daily existence through the action of my brain, and so there is also no physical continuity; this means that I am probably not the same person as my replica. But Parfit

---

[13] Parfit, *Reasons and Persons*, p. 285.

[14] Ibid., p. 201.

[15] Ibid., p. 275.

[16] See, e.g. Thomas Nagel, *The View from Nowhere* (New York: Oxford University Press, 1986), pp. 37–45.

[17] Parfit, *Reasons and Persons*, p. 241.

stresses that personal identity is not what matters as I think about 'my' future. Personal identity often coincides with 'what matters' to me, but it need not.[18]

Parfit's response to the scenario of teletransportation is, in fact, a religious one. He is asking what his ultimate concerns are as he looks to his future, and especially as he looks to his death; he decides that what really matters to him is that there will be future valuable experiences both before and after his death that are connected *in some way* to his present experience; but the manner of connection may be quite indirect and different from that which he experiences in his own identity now. What matters is 'relation R', not the cause of it. This liberates him from a fear of death, and frees him from concern for self into being concerned for others. As he acknowledges, this is close to the Buddhist 'loss of self', or loss of a centred subject; from this perspective, we are less anxious about the future, as 'we would have for ourselves in the future only the concern that we would have for a mere replica' of ourselves.[19] There is still a difference, Parfit testifies, between 'my life' and the life of other people, but the difference is less; other people are 'closer'.[20]

An extension of this thought experiment should make this clear. Suppose, suggests Parfit, that instead of being destroyed immediately by the scanner I lived on for a short period in my present body, while my replica lived on Mars (Parfit calls this the 'branch-line case'). I ought to be happy for him, after my death, to live with my wife, care for my children and carry on my career. My reluctance to enter the scanner and travel by teletransportation would thus show that I have an unhealthy preoccupation with my own ego from which I need to be released. It also shows that I think there is some kind of 'deep fact' about 'me' that the device will fail to reproduce. When I fear that 'I' will never get to Mars, says Parfit, it is because I think there will be something missing that cannot be produced by this unusual means of causing my psychological continuity. However, asserts Parfit, there is no such 'deep fact'. He sums up: 'Teletransportation is about as good as ordinary survival . . . ordinary survival is about as bad as being destroyed and replicated'.[21]

Parfit's reflections are highly valuable for our concern about future hope.

[18]   Ibid., pp. 282–3.
[19]   Derek Parfit, 'A Response [to Grant Gillett]', in Arthur Peacocke and Grant Gillett (eds.), *Persons and Personality* (Oxford: Blackwell, 1987), p. 91.
[20]   Parfit, *Reasons and Persons*, p. 281.
[21]   Ibid., pp. 279–80.

Although Hick hails Parfit's discussion as supporting his view of a 'replica',[22] his enthusiasm is surely misconceived. Parfit puts his finger on the key point; if another causation replaces the normal cause of our day-to-day personal continuity, the resulting replica cannot be the same person.[23] This is an observation to which I want to come back, because I believe that it does not necessarily rule out resurrection as God's re-creation of us *ex nihilo* after death. It does, however, highlight the inadequacy of a mere 'replica' idea, and urges us towards a view of re-creation that is more than reproduction. God cannot be conceived as an omnipotent scanner-replicator; there must be something else involved in a new act of creation.

Parfit also challenges us to consider why we would *want* to have a centred, unitary subject at the heart of personal identity. Is it merely egoism, causing us anxiety about future, death and suffering that we would be better rid of in a Buddhist loss of self? Though Parfit, in his modified reductionism, allows that the person can sometimes act as a corporate subject (as a nation would), his 'bundle' theory of a person means that 'we could describe any person's life in impersonal terms'. In explaining the unity of a life, we could simply talk about various experiences or actions and their interconnections, without claiming that it is the life of a particular person.[24] In terms of resurrection (which Parfit of course does not deal with), this leads us to ask why we should *want* the resurrected person corresponding to 'me' to be exactly the same as I am. Some answers immediately spring to mind: we may say that unless there is continuity of identity doubt is cast upon the value of our present existence with its trials and decisions; justice for the victims of life does not seem to be satisfied; and the faithfulness of God to the servants of God is not clear if divine promises are to be fulfilled to a different person from the one to whom they were made. But are all these answers simply ways of asserting our own ego? After all, the Old Testament shows us that the Hebrew people managed for a very long time with a view of after-life in terms of survival through one's children or the continuing existence of the tribe, based on an intense awareness of 'corporate personality'. In developing an understanding of resurrection we must take care both to preserve what is worth preserving about the individual while avoiding egocentricity, to keep centredness of subject without self-centredness.

[22] John Hick, 'Response to Nielsen' in Davis (ed.), *Death and Afterlife*, p. 32.
[23] Parfit, *Reasons and Persons*, pp. 242, 285–9.
[24] Ibid., p. 251.

Closing the Gap: A Modified Dualism?

We have probably wrung all the lessons we can from the science-fiction scenario of teletransportation, but we are left with a problem regarding resurrection. It seems that the break between death and re-creation cannot be easily closed with the idea of an exact replica. The gulf remains.[25] It gapes wide if resurrection is believed to happen, not immediately after death, but at some future moment of the renewal of the whole cosmos associated with the ideas of the Last Judgement, the *parousia* (appearing) of Christ and the coming of the Kingdom. As I have been arguing, I judge that only such a hope in a new creation will provide the influence to change present conditions, but the gap is still there even if the *parousia* is demythologized and resurrection is believed to happen immediately after death; however short the gap, there is still a going of the person out of existence and a consequent creation *ex nihilo*.

This leads some theologians to make the move of filling the gap with a modified kind of dualism, that is with a *temporary* disembodiment of the soul. While insisting that the ultimate and proper destiny of the human being is the resurrection of the body, it is suggested that the continuing of a disembodied soul through death into an interim period would solve the problem of continued identity, as this soul would finally be reunited with a recreated body and link the new person to the older version. Indeed, the new body could be quite unlike the old one as replication would no longer be the criterion. This combination of a disembodied soul with resurrection is a popular solution, and while it has very widespread precedent in classical Christian thought (for example, in Aquinas and Augustine) it has been recently argued most strongly by Stephen T. Davis.[26] Indeed, while John Hick does not advance it explicitly as a solution to the problem of discontinuity, he has now added it to his replica theory so that implicitly at least the replica is bolstered up by it: 'Let us entertain the hypothesis, then, that after bodily death consciousness continues, in a now disembodied

---

[25] In face of the gap, Penelhum concludes agnostically that 'there is no compelling reason' for either affirming or denying bodily continuity: faced with a replica-person we would simply have to decide. See Terence Penelhum, *Survival and Disembodied Existence*, pp. 93–102.

[26] Stephen T. Davis, 'The Resurrection of the Dead' in Davis (ed.), *Death and Afterlife*, pp. 119–144, and 'Is Personal Identity Retained in the Resurrection?', *Modern Theology*, 2 (1986), pp. 229–40.

state, as a centre both of moral and spiritual freedom and of memories and personality traits formed in relation to this world.'[27] Hick compares this phase to the classic Buddhist *Bardo* state in-between embodiments of our basic nature as empirical selves.

This 'bridging period' represents a modified form of dualism in several ways. In the first place, advocates such as Stephen Davis, Paul Badham, Peter Geach, John Hick and (more cautiously) Richard Swinburne[28] do not envisage the soul as an enduring and unchanging substance only superficially connected to the body. Hick refers to it as a 'basic dispositional structure' or a moral and spiritual 'character',[29] Davis as 'in part the constellation of those human activities that would typically be classified as "mental"' and 'just about everything that makes up what we call person-ality'.[30] Similarly Richard Swinburne identifies a 'structure' of the soul, which is a system of beliefs and desires that motivate the person.[31] This soul is in deep interaction with the body, and while Swinburne defends the idea of a soul as having mental 'substance', he certainly does not think that it is unchanging; having evolved to the state in which it is now, it works 'in interaction with the rhythms of the brain' and its consciousness is 'guaranteed by the functioning of the brain currently connected with it'.[32]

Despite this interactionism, advocates of a disembodied soul maintain that it is logically possible for the soul to continue to exist without the brain, and believe that persons could be identifiable to themselves and others in this state through the single criterion of memory.[33] They remember who they are, and other souls confirm it or remember it for them. However, some advocates (such as Davis and Swinburne) modify

---

[27] Hick, 'A Possible Conception of Life After Death', p. 195.

[28] Unlike the others cited, Richard Swinburne leaves open the possibility that an omnipotent God *might* find another way to 'light up' the soul than by 'plugging it' into a new body and brain after a period of inert activity; see Swinburne, *The Evolution of the Soul* (Oxford, Clarendon Press, 1986), pp. 307–11.

[29] Ibid., p. 193.

[30] Davis, 'The Resurrection of the Dead', p. 124.

[31] Swinburne, *The Evolution of the Soul*, p. 262.

[32] Ibid., pp. 29–31, 298ff. Paul Badham similarly advocates 'interactionist dualism', in 'God, the Soul and the Future Life', in Davis (ed.) *Death and Afterlife*, pp. 48–50; also, Paul Badham and Linda Badham, *Immortality or Extinction?* (London: SPCK, 2nd edn, 1984), ch. 6.

[33] Davis, 'The Resurrection of the Dead', pp. 138–40; Swinburne, *The Evolution of the Soul*, pp. 162ff, 310.

traditional dualism further by arguing that the high degree of soul–brain interaction means that the soul's remaining in being without the body must depend entirely on the act and power of God. Swinburne concludes that while it cannot be shown that there is a naturally *necessary* connection between soul and body, it also cannot be shown that the soul is naturally immortal.[34]

Yet a further, and fundamental, modification of dualism in this approach is the temporary nature of the soul's disembodiment. The human person is usually diagnosed as being incomplete without a body, which is granted in the resurrection from the dead.[35] In Aquinas' form of this argument, the soul is restless until its desire to be united with the body is fulfilled. While Augustine had maintained that this desire, until satisfied, will actually hold the soul back from its full enjoyment of the vision of God,[36] Aquinas hesitates to say that the redeemed soul is imperfect, or lacks any perfection necessary for complete blessedness as this would somehow make the judgement passed by God upon the soul at death incomplete. He therefore proposes that the resurrection adds an incidental kind of perfection, which affects the soul's well-being (*bene esse*) but not its essential being.[37] The modern problem of continuity of identity is here entangled in the more traditional problem of two judgements, about which we can see that Aquinas shows some embarrassment. As Christian thinkers had increasingly developed a personal eschatology in which the soul is judged and either rewarded or condemned at the point of death, this seemed to make the public eschatology of the Last Judgement redundant. As Simon Tugwell puts it neatly, 'By the end of the twelfth century, then, it was clear that there was one judgement too many'.[38] One way of dealing with this apocalyptic conundrum was to stress the incomplete and provisional nature of an intermediate disembodied state.

We should note that Hick has a different reason for stressing the provisional nature of the disembodied state of the soul: persons need resurrection, not to complete them once and for all, but to allow them a further period for growth and development on their way to final union

---

[34] Swinburne, *The Evolution of the Soul*, pp. 305–8, cf. pp. 191–7.

[35] This is stressed by Peter Geach, *God and the Soul* (London: Routledge & Kegan Paul, 1969), pp. 25–8.

[36] Augustine, *De Genesi ad litteram* (Commentary on Genesis), 12.35.

[37] Aquinas, *Summa Theologiae*, 1a2ae.4.5; cf. 3a.59. All references are to the Blackfriars Edition of the *Summa Theologiae* (London: Eyre & Spottiswoode, 1964–81).

[38] Simon Tugwell, *Human Immortality and the Redemption of Death* (London: Darton, Longman and Todd, 1990), p. 131.

with God in the eschaton proper. Hick suggests that there will be a number
of embodiments, each separated by the *Bardo*-like state of the soul; 'the
formation of new empirical selves will go on as long as they are needed for
the development of the deeper self or soul.'[39] The final state of the soul is
an undifferentiated communion with the divine life in which the self is
effectively absorbed. This would answer to Parfit's desire for the loss of self
in the Other but, as I have already indicated, I intend to propose an
eschatology in which there is loss of egoism without total loss of individual
identity; this fits better, I suggest, with God's creative project of moving
out from unity into diversity in the first place.

The Person and the Finality of Death

The scheme of two judgements with an interim disembodied state is a
widespread solution to an eschatological puzzle in Christian thought.
However, I believe it to be quite unsatisfactory. To begin with, philosophical objections can be levelled against a temporarily disembodied state in
the same way as they are brought against a more thorough-going view of
an immortal soul, and here I briefly mention two. There is the problem of
how souls without bodies could communicate with each other in such an
existence, even if only temporary, and there is the problem of the
unreliability of memory as the single available criterion for personal
identity.

Of course, attempts can be made to answer these objections. With regard
to the first, we might apply the argument of H. H. Price that disembodied
souls could be aware of each other's existence telepathically, could create
an environment which was mind-dependent and could have the same kind
of perceptions of it as we have of dream worlds.[40] While unsatisfactory as a
final state of affairs (though Price proposed it as a total and not a provisional
answer), it might be urged as tolerable as an interim kind of existence.
With regard to the criterion of memory for identification, Davis argues

---

[39]   Hick, 'A Possible Conception of Life After Death', p. 194; cf. *Death and Eternal
Life*, pp. 414–22.

[40]   H. H. Price, 'Survival and the Idea of "Another World"', in John Donnelly (ed.),
Language, Metaphysics and Death (New York: Fordham University Press, 1978),
pp. 176–95. H. D. Lewis has extended these ideas in *The Self and Immortality* (London:
Macmillan, 1973), ch. 8, and *Persons and Life After Death* (London: Macmillan, 1978),
pp. 86–91.

that in a community of disembodied persons, memories could be checked against each other. Moreover, he claims that the fallibility of memory means only that it cannot be *evidence* for personal identity, not that it cannot be a criterion.[41] Here perhaps too we could add the view of Peter Geach that *temporarily* disembodied minds could differentiate between each other because they could recognize the capacity in each to be final reunited with a particular body.[42]

Here I do not wish to enter in any detail into these arguments, because they do not seem to me to be the decisive ones. The real objection to a continuation of the soul in a disembodied state is that it does not take death seriously. No less than the view of an immortal soul, it fails to reckon with the impact of death upon the whole human person that we cannot escape in listening to the witness of such tragedies as *King Lear*. Only an entering of the nothingness of death and a throwing of ourselves in trust upon God to justify us in the face of this utter destruction can accord with our experience of death's finality, a boundary that has the power to give shape to life. This is fundamentally the witness of scripture to death as the last enemy, a good thing corrupted. It is what the Apostle Paul has in mind when he equates the final conquest of death only with the moment of resurrection from the dead at the *parousia* of Jesus Christ. Nor does merely 'conditional' immortality of the soul, in which the soul survives death because of a special divine act rather than by its own immortal powers, take death sufficiently seriously. If a temporary disembodiment of the soul is proposed as a solution to the problem of continuing identity beyond death, this can only mean that God sustains the soul in being through the event of dying, so that death does not touch it. But the witness of scripture, of experience, of feeling, of biology and of the great tragedies is that there is no thread of survival, no lifeline through death. In the face of this total end to body and 'soul', the only hope can be in re-creation.

Indeed, without the impact of death it is hard to find any real difference between conditional immortality (which many of the Church Fathers accepted) and resurrection with a 'spiritual body'. As Maurice Wiles argues,[43] the more we stress the different nature of this future body from our present material bodies on the one hand, and the action of God in giving life to the soul beyond death on the other, the closer these two

---

[41] Davis, 'The Resurrection of the Dead', pp. 137–9.

[42] Geach, *God and the Soul*, pp. 23–28.

[43] Maurice Wiles, *The Remaking of Christian Doctrine* (London, SCM Press, 1974), pp. 128–32.

models drift together. The boundaries between them become still more blurred when we postulate an intermediate state of a disembodied soul. The point of the image of resurrection is that there is an action of God to *overcome* the fact of death, not to avoid it. The early Church Fathers knew this, despite their assumptions about the soul, as they thought of physical death as a sharing in the death of Christ, as a 'dying in his passion',[44] and so attaining eternal life as resurrection. This means, of course, that we still have the problem of the preserving of identity to solve, and I intend to offer some suggestions before the end of this chapter.

Taking this radical view of death also means that dualism and reductionism are not the only two alternatives for understanding the nature of the human person, even in their modified versions. We can think of the person as being more than the body, and even more than a collection of mental and physical events, and yet still being *inseparable* from the body. There is a tendency among philosophers of religion to think that showing the difference of the 'soul' from the body also demonstrates its capacity to survive in a disembodied state. H. D. Lewis, for example, points to an immediate self-experience of being *differentiated* from our bodies: 'everyone knows himself to be the being that he is in just being so'.[45] But while this immediate experience may enable us to know that the 'I' is a distinct self with thoughts, feelings and actions which is not reducible to the body, it does not establish (as he thinks) that the self is potentially disembodied. Paul Badham's argument that the spiritual experience of God does not come to us through the senses and neural pathways is an attack upon person–brain identity, but it does not in itself establish (as he thinks) that this openness to God that we may well call 'soul' can exist *without* the body.[46] Similarly, Richard Swinburne cleverly provides an argument against the reduction of the personality to 'nothing but' the brain, by appealing to the example of a 'split-brain' state often used by other philosophers to establish precisely the opposite (a person–brain identity). The discussion centres on the fact that, if we were to transplant the two hemispheres of a divided brain into two different bodies, we could not predict how personality would be attached to them; Swinburne argues that

---

[44]   Simon Tugwell demonstrates this well with regard to Ignatius' views on death: see *Human Immortality*, pp. 97–100.

[45]   H. D. Lewis, 'Immortality and Deism' in Stuart Brown (ed.), *Reason and Religion* (Ithaca, New York: Cornell University Press, 1977), p. 289; cf. Lewis, *Persons and Life After Death*, p. 86.

[46]   Badham, 'God, the Soul and the Future Life', pp. 43–4.

this shows that 'knowledge of bodies will not suffice to give knowledge of persons'.[47] But this does not in itself lead us to the conclusion that persons can exist without bodies.

It is consistent with the finality of death to conceive of the person as 'more than' the body, and as a 'centred' self distinct in some ways from it and its experiences, without ever being separable from it. I suspect that this is what Parfit would call a 'deep fact', but it is not the kind of deep fact which would have been recognized by Plato or Descartes. If this personalness is to have any future beyond death, God must remake it together with something analogous to the body. However, there is much more to say about the nature of a person than this self-identity. Several dimensions have been missing in our discussion so far, which has largely been driven by the kind of discourse favoured by philosophers. To open up another aspect we shall turn from the scenarios of 'teletransporters' to the exploration of human relationships in the 'science fiction' of Doris Lessing.

Survival and Relationships: Doris Lessing's *The Memoirs of a Survivor*

Lessing's novel *The Memoirs of a Survivor* (1974) marked a turn of direction in her writing towards a 'science fiction' genre, already foreshadowed in her earlier *Briefing for a Descent into Hell*, and later to be explored explicitly in the *Canopus in Argos: Archives* series of novels (from 1979 onwards). *Memoirs* is very much about the nature of personal identity and, at least by implication, about life beyond death.

The narrator of *Memoirs* is an elderly woman living in a block of flats in an unnamed city at a time of increasing breakdown of society; it is sometime in the future, dated 'after the Age of Affluence'. From her window she watches things fall apart in what, from her present vantage point, she remembers as 'the protracted unease and tension before the end'.[48] As organized society collapses, gangs of mainly young people take to a street life, huddling together for self-defence, looting and killing, and gathering on street corners to attract followers before travelling away like migrating tribes in search of a better life somewhere else. While observing this outer, public decay of life, the narrator has discovered an inner world; from time to time the wall of her living room dissolves to allow her to

---

47 Swinburne, *The Evolution of the Soul*, pp. 147ff.
48 Doris Lessing, *The Memoirs of a Survivor* (London: Picador, 1976), p. 7.

enter a mysterious set of rooms behind it, in which time also dissolves. The rooms are of two kinds. There is an endless series of rooms empty of people in which the narrator can clean, decorate and set in order the chaos that is strewn around; there are also rooms that she calls 'the personal realm', in which she views a series of scenes where a small and helpless child suffers from the lack of love of an accusing parent, never living up to her mother's expectations, always being passed over in favour of the baby boy on whom all attention is lavished. The narrator, looking back on that time, does not expect the two worlds of her hidden inner space and the outer social space to join together:

> And this is my difficulty in describing that time: looking back now it is as if two ways of life, two lives, two worlds lay side by side and closely connected. But then, one life excluded the other, and I did not expect the two worlds ever to link up. (p. 25)

Into this situation comes Emily, a child of about twelve unexpectedly brought into her care by a stranger, who demands: 'Look after her, she is your responsibility'. The story then traces the next three years or so in which Emily grows into a beautiful young woman, falls in love with one of the gang leaders, Gerald, and becomes his favourite (though not exclusive) partner. With Gerald, who has a touching concern for the homeless young children roaming the streets, she forms a commune in a deserted house to care for them. Her life is stretched between the flat to which she still retreats for sanctuary, and the constant demands made on her by Gerald and the commune, as the structure of society around continues to disintegrate into savagery.

The novel charts, as Jeanne Murray Walker puts it, 'the breakdown of social exchange'.[49] It is a comprehensive statement of a loss of integration; against the background of the external breakdown between authority and the masses, and the internal breakdown between the unhappy child and its parents 'behind the wall', new relationships are formed that have some promise but which are also sadly fragmented. There are the relationships between the narrator and Emily, between lovers (Emily and Gerald), between members of the collective, between female friends (Emily and June, an even younger child who becomes Gerald's next sexual favourite)

---

[49]   Jeanne Murray Walker, 'Memory and Culture within the Individual: The Breakdown of Social Exchange in *Memoirs of a Survivor*', in Carey Kaplan and Ellen C. Rose (eds.), *Doris Lessing: The Alchemy of Survival* (Ohio University Press, 1988), pp. 93–113.

and between Emily and 'her animal'. The latter, Hugo, is a bizarre misshapen beast, half-dog and half-cat, utterly devoted to Emily whom she neglects as she gets involved in the life of the street and the commune. It is clear that the only hope of survival, of salvation, is in the integration and mutual reciprocity which seems increasingly elusive.

The need for integration is both social and psychological. Some critics have suggested that Emily and the narrator are in fact simply two sides of the same personality, the activist side which is involved in social relationships, and the reflective side which is absorbed in individual memories.[50] There is a mysterious overlap between the identity of these two, as they are portrayed as painfully and sympathetically forming a social bond. There is an ambiguity here at the heart of the narrative. Emily is a teenager in her own right, and she is evidently to be identified with the unhappy young child in the scenes behind the wall; her initial polished brightness of manner has obviously been adopted to hide her emotions and to please her elders, in response to the attitude of her mother. But on the other hand, the narrator views the scenes of Emily's childhood in rooms that are furnished according to the vintage of the narrator's own youth; the last scene assimilates her thoroughly to the narrator, showing her at the age of fourteen, wearing a dress of the narrator's period, designed to make her into an object of sexual provocation in a scene of which Emily could never have been a part (pp. 164–6). I suggest, however, that since these are memoirs they are written from the perspective of the 'end', and the narrator is evidently now living a more inter-personal kind of existence ('we tell each other over and over again the particularities of the events we shared . . .', p. 7); we are not presented here with a Jungian divided personality, but a kind of corporate personality which is present earlier in potential and now fulfilled.

As the critic Frank Kermode suggests generally, a novel is organized into a whole from the sense of its ending, and events here move towards the end-point of a breaking down of the wall between the hidden world and actuality. In external society, Gerald – with mixed motives of a desire for power and a genuine desire to help – had invited the most barbaric group of young children into his commune, a group in whom all the elementary constraints of society against killing and cannibalism had broken down. They had broken up the house and the community, and now threaten the life of the narrator, Emily and Gerald himself. At this critical moment, the

[50] See Roberta Rubenstein, The *Novelistic Vision of Doris Lessing: Breaking the Forms of Consciousness* (Urbana: University of Illinois Press, 1979), pp. 223–7.

wall dissolves and all walk through into a new world, guided by the presiding Presence of the realm, 'the one person I had been looking for all this time . . .':

> Beside her, then, as she turned to walk on and away and ahead while the world folded itself up around her, was Emily, and beside Emily was Hugo, and lingering after them, Gerald. Emily, yes, but quite beyond herself, transmuted, and in another key, and the yellow beast Hugo fitted her new self: a splendid animal, handsome, all kindly dignity and command, he walked beside her and her hand was on his neck. Both walked quickly behind that One who went ahead showing them the way out of this collapsed little world into a new order of world altogether. Both, just for an instant, turned their faces as they passed that other threshold. They smiled . . . seeing those faces Gerald was drawn after them, but still he hesitated in a fearful conflict, looking back and around, while the brilliant fragments whirled around him. And then, at the very last moment, they came, his children came running, clinging to his hands and his clothes, and they all followed quickly on after the others as the last walls dissolved. (p. 190)

Leading up to this eschatological moment, the narrative explicitly reconfigures time through the device of the two sets of rooms behind the wall and their relation to what is going in in the outside world. In the 'personal' scenes, where the child is being imprisoned within emotions of guilt, 'nothing could happen but what what one saw happening . . . above all time was a strict, unalterable law' measured by the ticking of the nursery clock (pp. 40–41). But in the other rooms, no matter how devasted or dirty they were, however much needing restoration and repair, there was 'a freedom, a feeling of possibility. Yes, that was it, the space and the knowledge of alternative action'. The past has fixed Emily and the narrator into a chain of 'necessity' (p. 139), and behind them is also bound the crying child whom the narrator never finds but who is presumed to be Emily's mother. Yet in the present, there are creative tasks to be done, whether in the empty rooms behind the wall or out on the streets, and the narrator soon notices the link between the damage done by the gangs of marauders outside and the devastations of the rooms behind the wall. Here there is also a future which is open, for when rooms are redecorated they are never revisited (p. 60). But how to organize past, present and future into a whole? It is not enough to understand how the present is bound by the psychological chains of the past, to understand why Emily works to please others and assuage her guilt, and how despite all her efforts the authority she exerts over the small children becomes an echo of the tyranny of her own mother.

As Northrop Frye puts it, the narrative also expresses the *desired* world, through 'apocalyptic' symbols which include both the world of human work and the world of nature. Two major images of integration which we are offered in the course of the narrative, and which appear again at the end, are respectively the making of a patterned carpet, and a garden. In her explorations behind the wall the narrator comes upon a hexagonal room in which there is a carpet with an intricate design; but it seems dull and lifeless in itself, its colours only 'potential', until the many people who are in the room select pieces of multicoloured fabric and lay them down on top of the carpet to match the pattern underneath. As a piece fits the carpet it glows and comes to life, and the narrator notes that 'there was no competition here, only the soberest and most loving cooperation' (p. 73). Another time the narrator strays beyond the house into a fruitful garden, and it gives her an indescribable feeling of comfort and security to discover that beneath this garden there is another one occupying exactly the same space, with a network of water channels around each bed of vegetables or flowers; as she returns to the higher garden she hears the water running everywhere there too, although she had not noticed it before. She reflects on 'Gardens beneath gardens, gardens above gardens: the food-giving surfaces of the earth, doubled, trebled, endless – the plenty of it, the richness, the generosity . . .' (p. 141).

The sociality depicted in the making of the carpet is not a commercial matter of competition and exchange, or the kind of exact equivalence valued by Lear and his daughters in Shakespeare's play.[51] The patterns within existence only come to life in a generous mutuality between persons, in which the successful matching of a piece of material is met by 'a congratulatory glance from one of the others'; this is the kind of generosity that nature shows in the plural gardens, an 'excess' over exact need, which Lear has to learn to recognize. The fact that plenitude comes from *shared* existence is also implied in the garden scene, since while in the under-garden she asks the gardener (though, in an echo of Mary and the 'gardener' in the Fourth Gospel, without answer)[52] for news of 'the person whose presence was so strong in this place' (p. 142). The vision of integration is centred upon this presence, and she expects any moment to turn her head and see 'a strong, soft presence, an intimate, whose face

[51] See above, pp. 55–7.
[52] John 20: 15.

would be known to me, had always been known to me . . .' She is familiar
with it because she is part of this corporate personality, as she reflects earlier
on: '. . . how very many must have lived here, multitudes, yet all had been
subdued to the one Presence who was the air they breathed – though they
did not know it, was the Whole they were miniscule parts of . . .'
(pp. 90–91).

What is happening at the end? To what does this refer? A 'realist'
critique of the novel would want to know whether they have died,
whether it is implied that the barbarian children have finally murdered
Emily, the narrator and Gerald while they lay asleep, whether they are
meant to have entered another sub-space in the universe. A Jungian
critique would find the end to symbolize the final unifying of the narrator's
personality. The end is open, refusing closure to any one conceptual
scheme. But following Ricoeur, we may say that the novel together with
its ending refers to a 'possible world', and as we are drawn into that world
with the narrator, Emily and Gerald, we find ourselves more intensely
members of one another, part of a whole in the Presence which is the
guide and guardian of the spiritual realm. We cannot exclude some
reference to life beyond death from the text, but the text is not aiming to
give us information about such a world but to enable us to 'refigure' our
lives, and to take action to contribute to a desired future.

Corporate Resurrection

The 'eschatological' vision which compels and influences in Lessing's novel
is that of a more inter-personal life, a non-competitive sharing in one
another. This is the dimension which is missing in the discussions of
immortality, resurrection and identity among the philosophers with whom
we began. A reading of *The Memoirs of a Survivor* should thus move the
theologian towards a view of resurrection which takes this dimension
seriously, and there is plenty of basis in the New Testament from which to
do so.

The model for the Christian hope of resurrection is the resurrection of
Jesus Christ, and what has often been underplayed in considering the New
Testament account of this event is the way that the risen Christ leads an
intensely corporate and inter-personal life. Paul's daring identification of
the Church with the 'body' of Christ (e.g. 1 Corinthians 12:27) has been
weakened over the years into a dead metaphor. To call a community of
people the 'body' of someone is to make an arresting and even shocking

claim, and Paul does not hesitate to identify the members of the Church with the glorified body of the risen and ascended Christ. Paul's underlying conception, as John Robinson puts it, 'is not of a supra-personal collective, but of a specific personal organism.'[53] The term 'body of Christ' is used in three ways in Paul's writings – for the singular resurrection body of Jesus of Nazareth, for the eucharistic bread, and for the whole Church – and these meanings intertwine. Paul's supplementary metaphor that Christ is the 'head' of his body makes clear that the transformed personality of the risen Christ cannot be reduced *without remainder* into the Church, as scholars such as John Robinson and L.S. Thornton tend to imply;[54] an individual identity remains, and this is significant when we apply the metaphor of resurrection to our own future hope. But there is still a profound overlap between the risen body of Christ and the bodies of his followers, as Paul in 1 Corinthians 6:13–20 urges that the person who is joined to the Lord is 'one spirit' or one spiritual body with him. Robinson asks how Paul made the leap from *'feeding'* on the body of the Lord in the eucharist to *becoming* the body, and suggests that we should find the creative moment in Paul's encounter with the risen Christ, with the revelation that the Church he was trying to stamp out was no other than Jesus Christ himself: 'Saul, Saul, why do you persecute *me*?' (Acts 26:14).[55]

Paul's argument is that the single resurrection body of Jesus Christ can include diversity without ceasing to be a unity. This builds on the Old Testament insight that the one can *represent* the many, as with the Isaianic Servant of the Lord, or the Danielic Son of Man; there is also the general background of a kind of 'corporate personality'[56] in Hebrew social life, where the sense of *relationship* within it is so strong that there appears to be a fluidity of identity between the individual and the group. But Paul goes much further than this. The hope that our body will become a

---

[53]   J. A. T. Robinson, *The Body. A Study in Pauline Theology* (London: SCM Press, 1953), p. 51.

[54]   L. S. Thornton, *The Common Life in the Body of Christ* (Westminster: Dacre Press, 1944), p. 298: 'there is only one organism of the new creation'; cf. Robinson, *The Body*, p. 79n1.

[55]   Robinson, *The Body*, p. 58.

[56]   See H. Wheeler Robinson, *Inspiration and Revelation in the Old Testament* (Oxford: Clarendon Press, 1946), pp. 70–1, 264f. Robinson's over-reliance on the theories of L. Lévy-Bruhl about 'primitive mentality' has been rightly criticized recently (see J. W. Rogerson, 'The Hebrew Conception of Corporate Personality: A Re-Examination', *Journal of Theological Studies* 31 (1970), pp. 1–16), but the basic dynamic of 'corporate personality' seems sound.

'spiritual body' in resurrection from the dead is entirely dependent upon our being part of the particular spiritual body of Christ. From baptism we participate in the resurrection body of Christ, but our body (*soma*) still carries the nature of 'sin and death' until we share in the renewal of the whole creation. We cannot 'put on' the body of resurrection until the lordship of Christ has been established and manifest in the whole cosmos at the moment called the *parousia* – the coming of Christ to open appearance as Lord. 'The resurrection body signifies the solidarity of the re-created universe in Christ' (Robinson),[57] just as the 'body' at present signifies the Church, where the glory of Christ is recognized already. If our theology of resurrection is centred upon Christ then there can be no separate resurrection bodies *existing on their own*; we shall be inseparable from the inclusive resurrection body of Christ which has cosmic scope. Inseparability need not, however mean indistinguishability; the continuing identity of Christ himself, in whom it is possible to identify the 'Lord of the Spirit' with the human Jesus of Nazareth, the resurrected Christ with the crucified Jesus (though not simply to equate them), assures us that solidarity need not undermine some individuality. Why all individuality should not be absorbed into a greater Whole we shall see further in a moment.

The hope of a more intense corporate existence is a challenge to present actuality. It is disturbing to Christian believers who would like eternal life to be simply the same as their present life but with all the inconveniences and pains removed. Hope in a new future cannot simply be a projection of the present. It has continuity with the present, since we experience some kind of inter-personal life already in the *koinonia* of the body of Christ, but it has discontinuity as this sharing of life and consciousness will be deepened into unpredictable forms. It also disturbs those who want their ego to be preserved on the grounds that this is the thing of most value to them; in this way, resurrection in the body of Christ contradicts egocentricity no less than does Parfit's loss of the self into a series of experiences.

Such a hope requires a cosmic context for it to be realized, and here theology brings a critique to Lessing's account. The escape of her characters 'behind the wall' runs the risk of sheer escapism. Whatever she intends the ending to mean, the two worlds of the inner life and outer society have been brought together only in the world of the *inner* consciousness, leaving society to its self-destructive fate. The Christian hope

---

[57] Robinson, *The Body*, p. 79.

of resurrection concerns the renewal of the outer, physical environment as well as the release of consciousness into a wider life. This also means that there is a universal bringing of truth to light portrayed in the symbol of eschatological 'judgement',[58] which cannot take place at the moment of the death of an individual; consequently, the traditional issue of 'two judgements' does not arise.

A picture of the inter-personal nature of resurrection leads us to a different kind of solution to the problem of identity, which issues from the troublesome gap between death and resurrection. In the face of the impact of death, putting an end to the whole person as far as *our* capacity to survive is concerned, the only hope for continuing identity is in God. The doctrine of justification by faith throws us upon God for our salvation and not upon our abilities; the finality of death makes clear that only God can justify us and preserve who we are. If our existence comes to an end at death, and we hope in God to recreate us together with the renewal of the whole cosmos, the only possibility of our being the same person is in God, and not in ourselves. *God* alone is the link between the old person and the new. This is not merely a question of not daring to dissent when God declares who we are in the resurrection, as Simon Tugwell rather humorously suggests: 'something must have gone very wrong if I disagree with my creator about who I am – Maybe hell is like that.'[59] Tugwell is basing everything here in the divine will: if the creator *intends* me to be 'I' then I just am. But evidently he senses some weakness in this view, since he adds something like the survival of a soul to strengthen his argument: 'there is something there even after death which can be judged by God'. The point, I suggest, is that we can trust that 'I' will be the same person with the same life story, not just because God *identifies* us but because God has preserved our *identity* within God's own self.

Derek Parfit concludes that a person reproduced through a scanner replicator would not be the same as the original, since the cause of personal continuity would be different from the usual one. The differences between God and a 'scanner-replicator' as the cause of personality are many (if not infinite), but most relevant to the issue is that we only exist *now* as a person because we exist in God. According to the Christian vision of the Trinity we share already in the inter-personal life of God as Father, Son and Holy Spirit; God makes room for us in the divine communion of relationships, and in recreating us God will 'conform us to the image of his Son, Jesus

---

[58] See below, pp. 189, 193, 195–6.
[59] Tugwell, *Human Immortality*, p. 162.

Christ'[60] – that is, our identity will be even more deeply bound up with the resurrection Body of Christ than it is at present. Unlike the scanner-replicator, we will be remade by the one who *is* involved here and now in the making of our personal identity.

We may use an analogy and say that when we have died God will 'remember' us, and from this memory will recreate us. But memory is hardly an adequate term; to be remembered by God is a quantum leap forward from being in the memory banks of a scanner, or to be remembered by a fellow finite being. To be remembered by God would be nothing less than being alive in God. We can give no rational or literal description of this state (though in a later chapter I am going to employ some insights from process theology to create an image for it), since if we *could* conceptualize it, it would no longer challenge present reality and we would cease to depend on God alone for justification. The radical sense of trust required in the face of this unknown corresponds to the existential sense of loss felt in bereavement, even by those with a strong faith. There is no survival capsule of a soul on which we can rely; the familiar has been left behind and we are left only with trust that God will preserve the identity of the loved person, and recreate him or her in a new body and environment that will be the 'same' and yet not the same, that will be unforeseeable in its newness of relationships and yet faithful to the relationships that have been in the past.

This experience of anxious trust is vividly expressed by the Apostle Paul in 2 Corinthians 5. He realizes that he is likely to die before the *parousia* of Christ, and so his longing to have his resurrection body put straight over his present earthly body ('not that we would be unclothed, but that we would be further clothed', v.4) is going to be frustrated. He fervently desires this immediate entrance into the new creation because he shrinks from the alternative of being stripped 'naked', that is dying without as yet receiving his spiritual body; he describes this promised body as 'a building from God, a house not made with hands, eternal in the heavens' (v.1), and I do not think we need exclude either the individual or corporate dimensions from this picture of a heavenly Temple.[61] Some commentators have found in Paul's reference to being 'unclothed' and 'naked' evidence

---

[60]   Rom. 8:29; cf. Phil. 3:21, 2 Cor. 3:18.

[61]   Robinson, *The Body*, p. 78ff takes the 'temple' as a corporate image, while Witherington takes it as individualistic: Ben Witherington, *Jesus, Paul and the End of the World. A Comparative Study in New Testament Eschatology* (Exeter: Paternoster, 1992), p. 205.

that he believed in an interim period in which the soul exists in a disembodied form, so combining Greek notions of the soul with Hebrew ideas of resurrection.[62] But the feeling of the passage is quite against this. Paul makes no reference to the soul, and finds being 'unclothed' a deeply undesirable state, where in the thought of both Plato and Philo the soul longs to rid itself of the weight of the body and be naked.[63] Here we may draw a parallel with the image of the seed in 1 Corinthians 15, where the seed is described as 'naked', and is then said to die before being given a body. As in *King Lear*, being unclothed is a negative image, not an 'apocalyptic image' (Frye) of eternal life and a desired existence;[64] this is accentuated by the frequent New Testament image of salvation as being newly clothed. Thus we may conclude that, like the image of sleep which Paul uses elsewhere, being 'naked' is not meant to describe the interim existence, but is an image for the non-being with which death confronts us. In the face of this threat, all Paul can do is throw himself in trust upon God to maintain his identity until the day of judgement comes (v.10), saying simply that it is better 'to be at home with the Lord' (v.8), without specifying what being 'in God' might mean.

The Identity of the Self:
Lessing's *The Making of the Representative for Planet 8*

Thus, giving weight to the corporate dimension of the resurrection opens up prospects of maintaining identity where a merely individualistic kind of survival puts it in doubt. But there is always the suspicion that in a high degree of inter-personal existence individual identity will be absorbed into the Whole,[65] and we can conveniently study these aspects of the relation

---

[62] For a review of the secondary literature, see Ralph Martin, *Word Biblical Commentary. 2 Corinthians* (Waco: Word Books, 1986), pp. 97–116. While Martin himself thinks that Paul has an interim state in view, he comes close to my argument when he insists that this reference 'simply reveals Paul's desire to avoid nakedness' (p. 107).

[63] See e.g. Plato, *Cratylus* 403b, *Gorgias* 524, *Phaedo* 67DE; Philo, *Legum Allegoria* 2.57–9.

[64] See above, pp. 20, 60–2.

[65] Colin Gunton offers a theological study of this danger in human society, but not in reference to the idea of resurrection: see Gunton, *The One, the Three and the Many. God, Creation and the Culture of Modernity* (Cambridge: Cambridge University Press, 1993), pp. 41–73.

between the One and the many in Lessing's *The Making of the Representative for Planet 8*.[66]

The novel begins, as does *Memoirs*, with the narrator looking back to a past time and sharing memories with others: 'You ask how the Canopean Agents seemed to us in the times of The Ice'. The significance of the 'us' in this opening sentence unfolds as the narrative progresses, since this story presents – as the title itself indicates – a more explicit description of the corporate nature of personality than is to be found in any of Lessing's books. Planet 8 has been colonized by the superior spiritual civilization named Canopus, and its inhabitants are guided by visits from the Canopean emissary Johor. The story charts the gradual death of this warm and pleasant planet through an unforseen onset of terrible cold, and it records the fulfilling of the promise made by Canopus that 'all' the inhabitants would be transferred to another planet. The intention had been to relocate them on Shikasta (earth), but this is frustrated as Shikasta is seduced by the evil Empire of Shammat and falls out of harmony ('the lock') with Canopus. Nevertheless, 'Canopus *does* keep its word . . . in one way if not in another' (p. 73). The promise is to be fulfilled unexpectedly, as the inhabitants gradually come to look on their hopes that 'One day Canopus will come and save us . . .' as childish expectations. They realize that apocalypse for their planet is not after all going to be marked by the landing of Canopean space ships to air-lift millions of them to another home.

The key to the story lies in the nature of the 'representatives' of the people. Certain persons are chosen to lead others by representing them, and they choose their name according to the function that comes naturally to them: representatives include Marl (keeper and breeder of herds), Klin (maker of fruits and guradian of orchards), Alsi (keeper of flocks), Masson (maker of housing), Pedug (teacher of children), Bratch (maker of medicines and healer) and – the narrator of the story – Doeg (maker of memories and teller of tales). It is in the nature of representatives to have a shifting and inclusive identity, and as we read the story we are not sure whether the individual we were meeting earlier on is the same as the one we are meeting now. The representatives not only represent many people in themselves, but several bear the same name and are treated as a single Representative: for example, 'At that time Masson was very many, because of having to get the wall built' (p. 75); 'three figures came staggering towards us out of the gloom . . . these were Marl' (p. 147). Moreover, in

---

[66]   Doris Lessing. *Canopus in Argos: Archives. The Making of the Representative for Planet 8* (London/New York: Granada, 1983 [1982]).

achieving a consensus of agreement among the people, 'a Representative who felt a change was needed would step back into the mass, or someone who felt entitled or equipped would step up into the Representative group' (p. 103). Not only do the Representatives merge in and out of the whole people, but they do not keep fixed social roles, and can share functions: 'my aid was needed. I was to become Bratch for a time, as Alsi had become Doeg . . .' (p. 129). Any one of the Representatives can represent the others (p. 77). The nature of the Representative, it is understood, can find new expression in other kinds of existence: when all the herds have finally frozen to death, 'Marl could not cease to be, since Marl was needed. But here, with us, on our cold planet, Marl was not' (p. 150).

Doeg comes to understand that the inclusive and comprehensive identity of the Representative is possible because at root all beings are made up of a 'dance' of molecules and atoms, and 'the spaces between [the] core, and the oscillations are so vast, so vast' (p. 91). This does not reduce the importance of the body which seems 'thick and heavy' in comparison with the dance of light at the heart of the self, since everything in the universe is a kind of substance, even thought. But the spaces in the dance allow for others to share in the existence of any one individual, and as the Representatives work to encourage people to fight their lethargy and to achieve the seemingly futile task of staying alive for as long as possible, they find that they are being changed; something is happening to them 'in the unimaginably vast spaces between the particles of the particles of the electrons and neutrons and protons – between the particles that danced and flowed and vibrated' (p. 136). Johor early on had challenged Doeg: 'Representative Doeg, whom do you represent? And what are you?' Doeg had come to admit to Johor that 'this precious thing, what I hold on to when I say: *I am here, Doeg*. . . this little feeling, *here I am*, the feeling of me . . . is not mine at all, but is shared, it must be . . .' (p. 111).

So it gradually dawns upon Representative Doeg and upon the reader that the promise of Canopus is to be fulfilled through the making of a single Representative for the whole planet, who is Doeg and yet who carries all the other identities with him. Nor is this corporate Being to survive in a conventional sense and leave by a space craft; this shared existence which is Doeg, teller of tales, and yet many in one, is to be released through death into a wider life. Doeg describes how the Representatives together make a final forced march towards the pole of the planet, and as they all die on the way they are transformed into a single consciousness, without losing the individual 'flavours' of personality and differences of functions. If they had lost what they had been, they were

'still something . . . patterns of matter, matter of a kind, since everything is
– webs of matter or substance or something tangible . . .' In the spaces of
the dance there is room for all, room too for Johor from Canopus who
had come to share their final agony with them – 'Johor with us and of us,
the Representative of Canopus part of the Representative of Planet 8':

> The Representative swept on and up, like a shoal of fishes or a flock of birds;
> one, but a conglomerate of individuals – each with its little thoughts and
> feelings, but these shared with the others, tides of thought, of feeling, moving
> in and out and around, making the several one. (p. 159)

> As we swept on there we felt beside us, and in us, and with us, the frozen
> and dead populations that lay buried under the snows . . . what these had
> been, our peoples, our *selves* – were with us then, were us, had become us –
> could not be anything but us, their representatives . . . There we left that
> planet, and came to where we are now. We, the Representative, many and
> one, came here, where Canopus tends and guards and instructs. (p. 161)

This novel is the most extensive expression of a shared consciousness
and a corporate identity that Lessing has undertaken, and it has been
greeted with some horror by critics who applauded her earlier novels of
feminist and political realism. Carey Kaplan charges Lessing of looking
'resolutely backwards into Britain's imperialist past, Lessing's Rhodesian
cradle, for models of ideal behaviour and of obedient resignation to superior
beings from a higher civilization'.[67] In place of the individual's calling the
power structures into question as in the earlier novels, the stubborn self is
now to be aligned to a cosmic 'Necessity', and the superior Canopus
colonizes with the benign intention of bringing everyone into harmony
with it. Kaplan concludes that while Lessing could never be racist, she has
become 'ageist'; with advancing age she has given up hope on the human
scale, and has become resigned to the long-term Necessity of cosmic
rhythms. This Necessity includes the death of Planet 8 that life may spring
elsewhere.

Lorna Sage adds the interesting observation that the 'we' of shared
consciousness has in fact become the mechanism by which the imperial
power imposes its will. The 'we' is the voice of the colonized; agents like
Johor persuade their subjects into saying 'we' and in this way to yield
consent to a hierarchy. She brings an interesting 'deconstructive' critique,

---

[67]   Carey Kaplan, 'Britain's Imperialist Past in Doris Lessing's Futurist Fiction', in C.
Kaplan and E. Rose (eds.), *Doris Lessing*, p. 149.

pointing out that the text which Doeg is writing for the Canopus archives attempts to suppress 'difference'.[68] While Canopus apparently respects cultural diversity by incarnating its agents as historic individuals, in fact there is one meta-code to which all the group codes are assimilated. She reflects on Lessing's own desire as an author to be a representative, to be articulate on behalf of all those who are inarticulate;[69] but the authorial 'we' can be as authoritative as the more traditional 'I'.

These criticisms seem to me to be only partly fair. While Canopus is a superior civilization, it is also subject to the Necessity; it cannot 'transcend its boundaries' (p. 79) and through agents like Johor it feels the pain of being limited in the help it can give. Moreover, the sense of the individual within the whole is never lost, as the above quotations should make clear; there is a precious individual 'core' to the dance of molecules. But for all that, there is a deep sense of fatalism in these science fiction novels, or resignation to the cosmic Necessity which is above and beyond Canopus as much as its colonies. As early as *The Memoirs of a Survivor*, when the narrator reflects on her feelings about the 'Presence' that pervades the realm behind the wall, she concludes that the many individuals who are parts of the Whole do not know that 'their living and their dying [was] as little their personal choice or wanting as the fates and fortunes of molecules in a leaf are theirs' (p. 91).

I agree with Lorna Sage that a narrative that *attempts* to deny difference (although it can in fact never be suppressed) cannot open hope to us. Here literary criticism and theology come together, for if Lessing's novels urge the theologian to take a deeper inter-personal life and sharing of consciousness more seriously, the theologian has a perspective to offer on how this can avoid subjection to mere Necessity. We notice that the Canopean agent Johor shares in the corporate resurrection body of Planet 8 in a sympathy that touches his very being, but Lessing does not dare to suggest that this might be true of the Necessity itself. If the Ultimate Reality of the universe were personal, and freely chose to enter into our existence in a mutual participation, then such a God *would* be involved in suffering, and would be open to being affected by our actions and decisions. Using the language of classical theism, we could say that God would be 'Necessity' or 'Necessary Being' only in the sense of owing existence to nothing outside God's own self; we are not required to draw the classical conclusion

---

[68] Lorna Sage, 'Lessing and Atopia' in Kaplan and Rose (eds.), *Doris Lessing*, pp. 166–7.
[69] Lorna Sage, *Doris Lessing* (London/New York: Methuen, 1983), pp. 45ff.

that God also cannot be changed or affected by anything contingent.[70] The traditional term 'Necessary Being' may still be useful as long as it indicates self-existence, but not when it is extended to include self-sufficiency, as this would deny that God has the freedom to allow others to enhance the divine life. A God with this freedom and this desire will never bind creation in the chains of necessity, and can be trusted to maintain our identity.

The Making of the Person

A more intense inter-personal existence in resurrection need not, then, mean loss of freedom within a cosmic whole. Neither need it mean loss of all individuality. We have seen that the corporate dimension of being embodied 'in God' makes it possible to affirm the continuity of identity of a person between present life and future resurrection; I now want to maintain that this identity can be understood in a stronger sense of personal uniqueness than is allowed for in Lessing's vision of the dead millions enclosed in the Representative.

Here we need to take a view of the nature of personhood as we know it at present, and I suggest that the inseparability of the person from his or her relations with others does not undermine the reality of being a distinct subject. To have a centre of personality that organizes one's experience and activities does not imply the existence of a substantial 'core' of being which pre-exists relationships, or to which relationships are subsequently added. Rather we can conceive, as Alistair McFadyen puts it, of 'individuals formed through social processes, their identities *sedimented from* histories of significant relation.'[71] We become truly ourselves when we are truly for others. Persons are 'called' into being through inter-personal ('I–thou') relationships; to be open to others, or to be 'for' others, precisely constitutes the 'spirit of communication'[72] which is the self.

Persons only exist in relationship, but the distinct centre of each person is assured for at least three further reasons, which we can envisage enduring through eternity. First, there is the ethical responsibility we have to 'resist' the claims of others as well as to respond to them; it does not enhance

---

[70]   Further on this, see below pp. 173–5.
[71]   Alistair I. McFadyen, *The Call to Personhood. A Christian Theory of the Individual in Social Relationships* (Cambridge: Cambridge University Press, 1990), p. 72. My italics.
[72]   Ibid., p. 151.

personhood in society, for example, if we always capitulate to the oppressive demands of a dictator. Being for others may require resistance, as it requires being open to the way that others resist us. McFadyen lays some stress on the ethics of mutual 'resistance',[73] apparently developing the idea from a hint in Dietrich Bonhoeffer's *Ethics*. He also learns from Bonhoeffer the fact that this resistance is grounded in the call to be conformed, not to others, but to the Christ who is present in and with others:[74] 'Centredness and resistance are to be in conformity to Christ and directed in a genuine orientation on God and others'.[75] This leads us to an understanding of resurrection life where corporate existence is not simply a merging of individuals into a sum total, but a deeper incorporation into 'the Body of Christ'.

Now, there is clearly no place in a perfected eternal state for *distorted* demands of others, and so no need for resistance of this kind, but here Bonhoeffer's more neutral earlier idea of a community as a 'conflict of wills' may be helpful. The other who meets us is a 'boundary' to our subjecthood, 'activating a will with which the other will comes into conflict, as an I for a Thou'.[76] As long as eternal life is marked by growth and development (as I will argue later that it must be), then there will always be the need to accept or resist the claim of others upon us, acting in accord with the divine will or purpose embodied in Christ. We can surely envisage something corresponding to a 'creative conflict', or creative tension without the destructiveness we experience at present. John Macquarrie's description of 'a commonwealth of free *responsible* beings united in love' seems apt here as a description of 'the great end'.[77]

Indeed, Macquarrie here points to a second ground for the continuing of 'some kind of individual identity'. The 'commonwealth' which he envisions is not an undifferentiated unity, but a 'richer and more fully diversified unity' which is being built up as God's creative project. He rightly points out that God's purpose in creation is the making of finite beings who can imitate their creator in the power of letting others be, and it would be a defeat if these individual existents were simply to vanish into

[73] Ibid., p. 162ff.
[74] See e.g. Dietrich Bonhoeffer, *Ethics*, ed. E. Bethge, transl. N. Horton Smith (London: SCM Press, 1971), p. 232.
[75] McFadyen, *Call to Personhood*, p. 152.
[76] Dietrich Bonhoeffer, *Sanctorum Communio. A Dogmatic Inquiry into the Sociology of the Church* (London: Collins, 1963), pp. 31–33.
[77] John Macquarrie, *Principles of Christian Theology* (London: SCM Press, 1977), p. 360.

a whole. God has moved out from unity into diversity, through the risk and struggle of creation, and consummation cannot be a mere return to simple unity. With Macquarrie we must affirm that 'the highest love is not the drive towards union, but rather letting-be'.

This takes us to a third ground of personal uniqueness in relationship, which is the nature of love itself. As Eberhard Jüngel expresses it, 'lovers are always alien to themselves and yet, in coming close to each other, they come close to themselves in a new way'.[78] We always become more truly ourselves as we give ourselves away in love, for – in the words of the Gospel text – 'he who loses his life . . . will gain it'. This is the pattern of the divine love itself, for as God opens God's own self in love to the creation, accepting finite beings into the fellowship of triune life through 'the body of Christ', God is becoming self-related in new ways. Thus God fulfills God's own being (eros) through the pouring of Self out in sacrificial love (agape). To find ourselves anew as a mysterious by-product of losing ourselves has nothing to do with selfishness, which would be a matter of setting self-realization as a goal. In reply then to Parfit's question as to why we should be concerned about self-identity at all, we should say that we hope for a preserving of personal uniqueness not because our egos are so important that they must remain; rather, it would be a denial of the love of others, who have made us what we are, if the results of their love were to be absorbed into a cosmic whole. At the same time, the nature of love and of God's creative purpose means that we hope for the relationships in which we live to become deeper and more intense than we experience them at present.

Finally, I should admit that throughout this chapter I have avoided giving any verdict myself on the case of the teletransporter. Would the person who 'arrived' be the same as the one who 'left'? I could take refuge in the politician's defence, the refusal to discuss a hypothesis, as it is totally unlikely that in the forseeable future such a machine could be built. But I will venture a conclusion. I judge that this case falls into the same class as putative split-brain operations, and that (in line with Swinburne's argument) we should say that the very fact we cannot predict the outcome shows that there is no simple physical basis for human personality. So, if it turned out that identity was maintained, then God would

---

[78] Eberhard Jüngel, God as the Mystery of the World. On the Foundation of the Theology of the Crucified One in the Dispute Between Theism and Atheism, transl. D. Guder (Edinburgh: T. & T. Clark, 1983), p. 318.

be no less involved in making this happen than God is with our day-to-day identity at present. If the result were a loss of identity in this life, we could trust in the God of new creation that this need not be the end of the story.

Chapter Five

THE ETERNAL MOMENT

Literature is full of complaints about time. It is 'the devourer of everything' (Ovid) and 'out of joint' (Shakespeare's *Hamlet*); W.H. Auden laments that

> Time and fevers burn away
> Individual beauty from
> Thoughtful children . . .[1]

It seems that the problem of time is not just that human life never has enough of it, but that in some way the personality is broken by its passing. Augustine observes that as time flows through the present moment from expectation of the future to memory of the past, it gives 'extension' to the mind (*distentio animi*);[2] but he deliberately uses a word (*distentio*) whose verbal stem also means 'to divide' or 'to distract'.

   The philosopher Heidegger has pointed out that the experience of time fragments us because we fail to bring our future and our past into harmony with our present.[3] We can readily see the truth of this: we are trapped in the past in nostalgia, or in regret, or we try to blank it out in guilt; we refuse to face the future because we fear it or we try to escape into it in wish fulfilment dreams. Paul Ricoeur, as I noted in the second chapter, claims that an orientation to eternity, as Augustine proposes, will be more effective in achieving unification of the person than will a fixation upon

---

[1] W. H. Auden, 'Lullaby', in W. H. Auden, *Collected Shorter Poems 1927–1957* (London: Faber and Faber, 1969), p. 107.

[2] Augustine, *Confessions*, XI.26. For discussion of *distentio*, see Paul Ricoeur, *Time and Narrative*, vol. 1, transl. K. McLaughlin and D. Pellauer (Chicago: University of Chicago Press, 1984), pp. 5–30.

[3] Heidegger, *Being and Time*, transl. J. Macquarrie and E. Robinson (Oxford: Basil Blackwell, 1973), pp. 236–7, 279–80, 458–63.

death, as Heidegger himself believed. Writers and theologians have in fact often appealed to the experience of an 'eternal moment' which breaks into time and overcomes it, and as well as exploring further the predicaments of time, we shall follow up this idea to see what light it throws on the nature of eternity itself.

The Problem of Fragmentation by Time: T. S. Eliot's 'Ash Wednesday'

In his poem 'Ash Wednesday',[4] T.S. Eliot probes the dis-ease in time that arises from failing to integrate our past, present and future. The vehicle he uses is a meditation upon repentance, as indicated by the title. (Eliot had become a Christian believer shortly before he wrote it.) In penitence we bring confession for the past and resolve to live a holy life in the future: penitence should then link the three modes of time into one. In penitence we tell a story about our lives that reconfigures time, that enables us to face the end and to open up hope. A poem about repentance therefore brings narrative and images together in an intense way.

In offering penitence, Eliot discovers the problems that we have about making the past a basis for the future. That is, he evokes our experience of finding a very narrow line between contrition for the past and a regret that still traps us within it. There is also a knife-edge distinction between detachment from past failures or past glories, and a cynical indifference to them. The poem begins then with a mind awake, aware of its past power and strength:

> Because I do not hope to turn again
> Because I do not hope
> Because I do not hope to turn
> Desiring this man's gift and that man's scope
> I no longer strive to strive towards such things
> (Why should the agèd eagle stretch its wings?)
> Why should I mourn
> The vanished power of the usual reign?

Here is a painful blend of indifference and yet bitter regret. There is an effort to be whole in the present:

---

[4]   T. S. Eliot, 'Ash Wednesday', in *The Complete Poems and Plays of T. S. Eliot* (London: Faber and Faber, 1969), pp. 87–95.

> Because I cannot hope to turn again
> Consequently I rejoice, having to construct something
> Upon which to rejoice.

But in fact the poet finds he is in the state of mind where the almost unbearable sense of what *was* troubles the present and prevents hope for the future:

> And pray to God to have mercy upon us
> And I pray that I may forget
> These matters that with myself I too much discuss
> Too much explain.

So he makes the prayer that is to run throughout the poem: 'Teach us to care and not to care/ Teach us to sit still'. To care and not to care . . . that is, taking acount of the past in thankfulness and confession, yet not trapped by it. One attempt to feel what this might be like is provided in the second section of the poem, where the poet has a vision of his personality as a heap of dry bones left over after three white leopards have gorged themselves upon his more digestible parts.

> . . . And God said
> Shall these bones live? Shall these
> Bones live?

Eliot is echoing the vision of Ezekiel in the valley of dry bones, which has become in Christian tradition a classical image for resurrection (Ezekiel 37); but he uses the image in an unexpected way. These bones are content to lie there and shine brightly; they lie by the side of a lady who is meditating in peace, a 'Lady of silences' who is 'torn and most whole', a 'Rose of memory/ Rose of forgetfulness'; she knows how to remember and yet also how to forget the past, a time of 'love unsatisfied' and 'the greater torment of love satisfied'. There is the hint that her story may show how time can be integrated and the past be made whole with the present, and inspired by her presence, the bones also seem to have achieved peace with the past. They refuse to listen to the wind of resurrection ('prophesy to the wind . . . for only/ the wind will listen'):

> Under a juniper-tree the bones sang, scattered and shining
> We are glad to be scattered, we did little good to each other,

Under a tree in the cool of the day, with the blessing of sand,
Forgetting themselves and each other . . .

The bones seem to have come to terms with the past; yet we know that
they are still bones, 'in the quiet of the desert'. There may be peace with
the past, but no harmony with the future. After this moment of trying the
mood of resignation, the next section of the poem shows that even the
past cannot be coped with quite so easily. It evokes once again the horror
of past memories which return to haunt, as well as the memories that
return to distract with self-indulgence:

> The broadbacked figure drest in blue and green
> Enchanted the maytime with an antique flute.
> Brown hair is sweet, brown hair over the mouth blown,
> Lilac and brown hair . . .

In the fourth section the Lady, who is of course Mary, returns. The idyllic
memory of the girl who walked with him years ago, 'going in white and
blue, Mary's colour' evokes the greater Lady who walks between the years
and who urges him in silence (a bird actually sings the message): 'Redeem
the time, redeem the dream'. She has memories both of joy and sorrow, the
birth and the death of her Son, but she is in harmony with time because she
made assent to the message of the annunciation. Mary is remembered in
Christian tradition as the 'handmaid of the Lord' who said yes to the purpose
of God: she 'bent her head and signed but spoke no word' and yet she gave
birth to the Word. Out of silence came the word. There is a hint here to the
resolution that Eliot is to find in the *Four Quartets*, and he suggests it again in
the fifth section of the 'Ash Wednesday' series:

> And the light shone in darkness and
> Against the Word the unstilled world still whirled
> About the centre of the silent Word.

It appears that the Lady is a powerful image of peace and harmony
because of her silence, her orientation to eternity which is motionless and
silent in contrast to the busy and noisy world. But there is no more than a
hint. The final section begins with a restatement of the dilemma:

> Although I do not hope to turn again
> Although I do not hope
> Although I do not hope to turn

> Wavering between the profit and the loss
> In this brief transit where the dreams cross
> The dreamcrossed twilight between birth and dying

The poet, as one who lives in 'the time of tension between dying and birth', prays in his predicament:

> Teach us to care and not to care
> Teach us to sit still
> Even among these rocks,
> Our peace in His will.

Suiting the theme of the breaking of the personality in time, the whole poem has the mood of memory, as fragments and images from the past are taken up in free association. The critic Helen Gardner comments:

> The figures in *Ash Wednesday* are not persons; they are like figures seen for a moment through the window of a swiftly moving train, where an attitude or gesture catches our attention and is then gone forever, but remains to haunt the memory.[5]

That poetic technique of a memory at work in a mood of reverie, catching the fleeting moment and preserving it, is exactly the narrative method used by the novelist Virginia Woolf. Pioneering the prose style often dubbed 'stream of consciousness', her narrative describes inner moods, responses and reactions to external events rather than the objective events themselves. She portrays the impressions produced by events, so that – for example – the death of Mrs Ramsay in *To the Lighthouse* is alluded to obliquely:

> [Mr Ramsay stumbling along a passage stretched his arms out one dark morning, but, Mrs Ramsay having died rather suddenly the night before, he stretched his arms out. They remained empty.][6]

The death is bracketed off from the inner life which is in the foreground, and is referred to as Mr Ramsay's experience of touching nothing. Earlier Mrs Ramsay had been described impressionistically by the painter Lillian Briscoe as a purple triangle, casting a shadow on the steps as she sat knitting

---

[5]   Helen Gardner, *The Art of T. S. Eliot* (London: Faber and Faber, 1968), p. 100.
[6]   Virginia Woolf, *To the Lighthouse* (Harmondsworth: Penguin Books, 1964), pp. 146–7.

in the holiday house. So the memory rescues fragments from the flux of life and sorts them into some kind of order. Time is reconfigured in the narrative, as space is reconfigured in a painting. Just as this technique is related in Eliot's poetry to the problem of the fragmented experience of time, in Woolf it is related to another dimension of the same problem.

The Problem of Isolation in Time:
Virginia Woolf's *Mrs. Dalloway*

The problem with time, as Virginia Woolf conceives it, is how to reconcile the time of the individual consciousness, or inner time, with the public time of history, or outer time. The personality is fragmented through this split. Even if a reconfiguring of time into harmony can be achieved within the mind, this still has to relate to the outer flux of time in which the person is dislocated between past, present and future. Since the outer world is made up of other people, this also means a bringing of an individual's time into relation with *others'* inner time. The consciousness can be isolated from the outer world *and* from the consciousnesses of others who inhabit it. This dual problem of isolation is treated in Woolf's equivalent to 'Ash Wednesday', the novel *Mrs. Dalloway* (1925). It is exposed, for example, in a little scene where Clarissa stands at the window of her house in Westminster, looking across the street at an elderly woman in her own room. Both hear the sound of Big Ben striking; both are involved in the same external scheme of time, so it seems as if the old woman 'were attached to that sound, that string'; yet each has her inner time-scale, her inner room of memory: '. . . here was one room, there another. Did religion solve that, or love?'[7]

This vignette focuses a more pervasive isolation of consciousness and inner time-scales in the book, between the awarenesses of Clarissa Dalloway and her social circle on the one hand, and Septimus and Lucrezia Smith on the other. Clarissa spends the day preparing for a dinner party in the evening and musing on her memories of the past, including her broken love affair long ago with Peter Walsh; Septimus Smith spends the day wracked by memories of the horrific death of a comrade in the First World War, descending deeper into madness and finally committing suicide. There is a gulf between their inner lives, until we are given a hint of healing at the very end, but throughout the narrative outer events are

---

[7]   Virginia Woolf, *Mrs. Dalloway* (London: Panther/Granada 1976), p. 114.

shared between the characters. Peter Walsh sits on one park bench remembering the 'awful' moment of parting from Clarissa, while opposite him on another bench Rezia Smith is remembering the 'tortured' moments of her marriage to Septimus (pp. 58–9). We move between their consciousnesses again as they both listen to the 'ageless song' of an old woman in the street, singing of the ancient May day and eternal spring, 'remembering how once she had walked in May, where the sea flows now, with whom it did not matter' (p. 73). Woven through all these impressions, punctuating the flow of the day, is the public time which is marked by the striking of Big Ben and other clocks in Westminster.

In his book *Time and Narrative*, Paul Ricoeur admires the way that Woolf refigures time in her narrative through these devices. Fundamentally there is the reaction that all the characters have to the sound of Big Ben, beginning with the response of Clarissa to the strokes: 'First a warning, musical; then the hour, irrevocable. The leaden circles dissolved in the air' (p. 6). This ominous public announcement of time prompts the twofold pull of the narrative which shapes inner time; as Ricoeur puts it, 'the day advances, pulled ahead by the arrow of desire and expectation shot off at the beginning of the narrative (the evening's party to be given by Mrs. Dalloway) and pulled back by the incessant retreat into memory'.[8] This refiguration produces several different fictive experiences of time in the minds of the characters. Septimus is totally unable to bring his inner world into any coordination with public or monumental time, and is broken up by it: '"I will tell you the time", said Septimus, very slowly, very drowsily, smiling mysteriously at the dead man in the grey suit. As he sat smiling, the quarter struck . . .' (p. 64). The specialist he consults, Sir William Bradshaw, has conformed himself totally to public time, urging 'proportion' upon his patients; consequently he has lost all human sympathy. The clocks of Harley Street by which he lives 'nibbled at the June day, counselled submission, upheld authority, and pointed out in chorus the supreme advantages of a sense of proportion' (p. 91). Only Clarissa is to offer a hint of a resolution by responding to the chimes of Big Ben at the end of the day with a resolution to live courageously.

However, I suggest that the result of all this is to create in the reader a sense of time which is mainly problematic. This is an 'Ash Wednesday' novel. In it the 'possible worlds' created by the configured narrative produce no unambiguous feeling of hope. Ricoeur is, to be sure, more

---

[8]   Ricoeur, *Time and Narrative*, vol. 2, transl. K. McLaughlin and D. Pellauer (Chicago: University of Chicago Press, 1984), p. 108.

hesitant about underwriting Septimus's vision of eternity than is the critic John Graham. In his study, Graham greets with enthusiasm Septimus's revelation, sitting in Regent's Park, that 'first, there is a unifying reality hidden in the phenomena of time which gives them pattern and significance, and second, that the pattern is eternal because there is no death.'[9] Ricoeur, though more cautiously, nevertheless compares this with Augustine's orientation of time towards eternity, and suggests that it is Clarissa's inheriting of Septimus's vision of eternity that gives her courage to live and to scorn death.[10] But we must not forget that Septimus is mad, even if at times he appears like Nietzsche's madman, telling the unwelcome truth in the light of the harrowing experiences of war.[11] His message that 'there is no death' takes the form of the illusion that his dead comrade Evans keeps on confronting him and speaking to him. He cannot relate his vision to the outer world of things as they actually are, including (I suggest) the reality of death.

At the climax of the novel, the inner worlds of Clarissa and Septimus interact as the appalling Sir William announces the suicide of his patient at her party. In some way Septimus's consciousness enters hers, and she is encouraged by recollecting his favourite line from Shakespeare (a lament for the dead in *Cymbeline*): 'fear no more the heat of the sun'. In a replay of the earlier scene of the two rooms, Clarissa again notices the old woman in her house across the street:

> The clock began striking. The young man had killed himself; but she did not pity him; with the clock striking the hour, one, two, three, she did not pity him, with all this going on. There! the old lady had put out her light! The whole house was dark now with this thing going on, she repeated, and the words came to her, Fear no more the heat of the sun. She must go back to them. But what an extraordinary night! She felt very like him . . . (p. 165)

She has gained the courage to 'go back to them', to meet others and to take part in public life. She will go back to her party, one of her famous parties which she had earlier compared to a kind of eucharist, an 'offering'

[9] John Graham, 'Time in the Novels of Virginia Woolf', in Jacqueline Latham (ed.), *Critics on Virginia Woolf* (London: George Allen & Unwin, 1970), p. 30. He is referring to the scene in *Mrs Dalloway*, p. 24.

[10] Ricoeur, *Time and Narrative*, Vol. 2, pp. 109–110, cf. p. 101.

[11] In direct contradiction of Nietzsche's madman in *The Joyful Wisdom*, however, he cries: 'there is a God' (*Mrs. Dalloway*, p. 23).

to life (p. 109), bringing together those who lived individual existences, scattered all over London. Here then is a hint of a transfigured existence in the face of which Peter feels 'terror . . . ecstasy . . . extraordinary excitement' as he meets her in the last line of the novel: 'For there she was'; there is a hint of a sharing of consciousness and an eternity which can overcome the threat of death – but it is only a hint. The madness of Septimus forbids any simple closure to the narrative.

Certainly, the problematic rift between inner and outer time is still prominent in Woolf's next novel, *To the Lighthouse* (1927). A central section called 'Time passes' bridges a long gap of time between one holiday taken by the Ramsay family in their vacation house by the sea, and a later one. In the first holiday, the children are all quite young; by the time of the second, two of them have died, one in war and the other in childbirth, and the mother is also dead. In the first holiday there had been a projected expedition to row to a lighthouse, which had to be abandoned because of the weather; in the second, the father and two remaining children (now young adults) make the journey at last. The passing of time during this bridge section is described almost entirely through inner impressions; the effect of the changing seasons, as they wreak havoc upon the holiday house, is made an image for the impact of outer life upon the human consciousness. As summer comes, for example, an interlude between the marriage and death of Prue Ramsay,

> . . . there came to the wakeful, the hopeful, walking the beach, stirring the pool, imaginations of the strangest kind – of flesh turned to atoms which drove before the wind, of stars flashing in their hearts, of cliff, sea, cloud, and sky brought purposefully together to assemble outwardly the scattered parts of the vision within. In those mirrors, the minds of men, in those pools of uneasy water, in which clouds for ever turn and shadows form, dreams persisted . . .[12]

But in the outer world, outside these inner pools of reflection and memory, the First World War has been happening. This is the sole reference to it:

> [A shell exploded. Twenty or thirty young men were blown up in France, among them Andrew Ramsay, whose death, mercifully, was instantaneous.][13]

---

[12]   Woolf, *To the Lighthouse*, p. 150.
[13]   Ibid., p. 152.

To retreat into inner moods is one way of escaping the flux of time, and so the predicament of being broken through its flow from past to future, but finally the inner history has to be related to the outer, if the personality is to remain whole.

Eliot and the Timeless Moment: *Four Quartets*

So we return to Eliot, who had set out his version of the problem of time in 'Ash Wednesday', and ventures to present a resolution in *Four Quartets*. He had diagnosed the problem as being the fragmentation of the personality through the passing of time, its brokenness between past, present and future. In *Four Quartets* he reaches towards a unifying of time into a whole, and finds his focus in the nature and function of words; for Eliot, words are the subject of poetry as well as its medium. First, in 'Burnt Norton', he reflects upon the fact that words are subject to decay and to fragmentation of meaning through the passing of time, but he suggests that they can be preserved by being placed in a *pattern* in a poem. Words are held in their meaning against the ravages of time by being related to other words, and in being so they somehow unify time itself. Words in a pattern can weave time itself together.

> Words move, music moves
> Only in time; but that which is only living
> Can only die. Words, after speech, reach
> Into the silence. Only by the form, the pattern,
> Can words or music reach
> The stillness, as a Chinese jar still
> Moves perpetually in its stillness.
> Not the stillness of the violin, while the note lasts,
> Not that only, but the co-existence,
> Or say that the end precedes the beginning,
> And the end and the beginning were always there
> Before the beginning and after the end.
> And all is always now . . .

There is the cautious feeling after the idea that words fixed in a pattern might be the means to 'redeem time', that this might be the key to the unifying of time in an eternal 'now', in a 'co-existence' of end and beginning, in 'one end, which is always present'. But there is a problem with words if we hope they will achieve this:

> . . . Words strain,
> Crack and sometimes break, under the burden,
> Under the tension, slip, slide, perish,
> Decay with imprecision, will not stay in place,
> Will not stay still.[14]

This might be taken as a debate between structuralism ('the form, the pattern') and deconstruction ('words decay with imprecision'), except that – as we shall see – Eliot finds all meaning centred upon a 'transcendental signified'. Above all he is speaking of his experience as a poet.

In the second poem, 'East Coker', Eliot explores some of the ways in which words can unify time, as a meeting place in the present for past and future. Words reach out towards the future, because as soon as we have succeeded in expressing something in words, when we have 'got the better of words', then we want to use words in a different way to express our idea or our feelings better. What we want to express is not static; it has developed further just because we have framed the words for it, and so we need to re-use words to catch up:

> . . . And so each venture
> Is a new beginning, a raid on the inarticulate
> With shabby equipment always deteriorating[15]

At the same time, this achievement is only a recovery of what has already been discovered in the past by the great poets whom 'one cannot hope/ To emulate'. There is only 'the fight to recover what has been lost/ And found and lost again and again'. Finding it does not simply mean repeating it; it is recovery, reminting and above all, re-vision of the old in new contexts. Eliot understands a major part of the poet's task as being the reviving of past words and phrases, giving new life through new contexts of meaning. Eliot has often been criticized for stuffing his poems full of quotations from past authors; so he does, but it is deliberate; the poet redeems the past in the present and allows it to provoke a new future in what he calls 'an easy commerce of the old and new'. Theory and practice combine in the beginning of 'Burnt Norton', evoking memories of 'the door into the rose-garden' that has appeared in so many pieces of past literature from the *Roman de la Rose* to *Alice's Adventures in Wonderland*.

---

[14]   Eliot, 'Burnt Norton', V; *Complete Poems and Plays*, p. 175.
[15]   Eliot, 'East Coker', V, p. 182.

Our failures to open the door need not trap us in the past in regretful speculation for an unrealized future:

> What might have been and what has been
> Point to one end, which is always present.
> Footfalls echo in the memory
> Down the passage which we did not take
> Towards the door we never opened
> Into the rose-garden . . .

Yet the first two poems have a pervasive note of doubt and weariness. Can words really be fixed in a pattern and unify the flow of time 'at the still point of the turning world'?

> . . . My words echo
> Thus, in your mind.
> But to what purpose
> Disturbing the dust on a bowl of rose-leaves
> I do not know.[16]

In the fourth poem, 'Little Gidding', Eliot brings together the two ideas of words held in a pattern and words as a meeting place for past, present and future, combining them in a new insight. When a sentence is in the right place in a poem, then it can overcome the tyranny of sequence and flux in time, for the whole pattern of the poem can be grasped in that sentence alone. The shape of the whole can be comprehended in its entirety at any one of its moments. If a phrase is right, 'where every word is at home/ Taking its place to support the others' with 'the complete consort dancing together', then every phrase is in itself 'an end and a beginning / Every poem an epitaph'. Within the configuration of the time–flow of the poem, a phrase is a timeless moment. Now Eliot goes on to tell us that the place of a *word* in a poem is a symbol of *events* in time; any one event can disclose the whole pattern of human history; a single moment can become 'timeless' in the sense that we can grasp within it the whole shape of past, present and future. Like a phrase or a sentence in a poem, a moment in life can be 'an end and a beginning'. It can lead to a significant death which gives life to those who come afterwards: 'we are born with the dead'.

---

[16]   Eliot, 'Burnt Norton', I, p. 171.

> Every phrase and every sentence is an end and a beginning,
> Every poem an epitaph. And any action
> Is a step to the block, to the fire, down the sea's throat
> Or to an illegible stone . . .
> The moment of the rose and the moment of the yew-tree
> Are of equal duration . . .

But for Eliot there is more than an *analogy* between the word in a poem and the timeless moment in life. They are integrated through Christ, the Word of God. The eternal Word has been made incarnate in the flux of time; so it is the words of the Christian story, the tongues of prayer, the embodying of Christian values in the great images of the faith, that can give this sense of wholeness and pattern. To live by the Word and by the witness of words to the Word means that any moment can become 'the intersection of the timeless moment' with time which gives a glimpse of eternity. We can, if only partially, begin to know the unifying of our time. Especially we can look back to the moments in the past in Christian tradition where there have been experienced such moments where time has been overcome:

> . . . A people without history
> Is not redeemed from time, for history is a pattern
> Of timeless moments. So, while the light fails
> On a winter's afternoon, in a secluded chapel,
> History is now and England.[17]

The chapel is at Little Gidding. To sense the tradition of Christian worship where the timeless moment has been often known, to 'kneel/ Where prayer has been valid' is to be assured of the wholeness of the pattern despite our sense of brokenness in time; it is to know that 'what we call the beginning is often the end' and 'the end is where we start from'.

> . . . the communication
> Of the dead is tongued with fire beyond the language of the living.
> Here, the intersection of the timeless moment
> Is England and nowhere. Never and always.[18]

The Word of Christ, known in prayer which is 'more/ Than an order of words', transcends the flux of time and opens a vision of eternity. It takes

---

[17]   Eliot, 'Little Gidding', V, p. 197.
[18]   Eliot, 'Little Gidding', I, p. 192.

us beyond fragments to the whole, and well-placed words in a poem can suggest nothing less than this Word Itself.

Eternity as Simultaneity?

In Eliot's portrayal of the relation of the person to time, two basic beliefs therefore emerge. First, Eliot assumes that eternity is timeless, and second he believes that the broken self will be healed through an intersection of this timelessness with human life. In describing events in the timeless moment as of 'equal duration', he seems on first sight to agree with Boethius' classic definition of God's eternal nature as being 'the whole and perfect possession *all at once* of an endless life' (*interminabilis vitae tota simul et perfecta possessio*).[19] According to Boethius' thought – building on Plotinus and Augustine before him – past, present and future are one simultaneous point in the eternity in which God exists. As Augustine confesses, 'Your years stand all at once (*simul stant*), because they stand'.[20] The passing of time as we know it in the mundane world is the moving image of this unmoving reality: 'Except for the point, the still point,/ There would be no dance'.[21] For Eliot, the unifying of our selves, fragmented through time, has happened objectively with the coming of eternity into history with the incarnation of Christ, and this goes on happening subjectively in our acts of prayer and contemplation. But actually

> . . . to apprehend
> The point of intersection of the timeless
> With time, is an occupation for the saint – [22]

and most of us have to make do with 'hints and guesses', 'the unattended/ Moment, the moment in and out of time'.

In all this, the influence of Augustine seems strong. The human mind, according to Augustine, makes the future present through expectation, the present present through sight, and the past present through remembrance. Thus, within the thinking subject, there is a kind of simultaneity within the flow of time; though it is fragmentary, it is an image of the

---

[19]   Boethius, *De Consolatione Philosophiae*, 5.6.
[20]   Augustine, *Confessions*, XI.13.
[21]   Eliot, 'Burnt Norton', II, p. 173.
[22]   Eliot, 'The Dry Salvages', V, pp. 189–90.

simultaneity of God's present in eternity and so timeless eternity itself participates in the present moment.[23] However, despite the powerful influence of Augustine on the concept of time in Western culture, we ought not to assume that Eliot is simply reflecting it in his image of the 'intersection of the timeless moment'. For Augustine, the fact that the simultaneity within the mind is only partial is itself the cause of the brokenness of the self in time, and we are only released from this pain of the present by a contemplation of eternity beyond time. With the claim 'in my end is my beginning' Eliot takes a more positive view of integration of time here and now through the impact of eternity upon it. His 'equal duration' may owe something to the 'pure duration' of Henri Bergson,[24] who suggested that our experience of time was less that of moments in strict succession than a vision of many sequences at once, rather like a film montage (or indeed the technique of Virginia Woolf's novels). Anyway, as we shall see further, there is much to be said for Nathan Scott's listing of Eliot among those writers of the twentieth century (also including Brecht, O'Casey, Joyce Carey, Camus and Auden) who take time seriously rather than attempting to abolish it.[25]

Another version of the 'eternal moment' which is not simply constrained by Augustine's thought was that of the so-called 'dialectical theologians' in the 1920s, with Karl Barth prominent among them. In his momentous commentary on *The Epistle to the Romans*, Barth speaks of the breaking of the eternal moment into time when a person is faced with a call by God's Word to a decision about ultimate values here and now: 'this is the secret of time which is made known in the 'Moment' of revelation, in that eternal Moment which always is . . .'[26] In a moment between past and future, between the times, 'eternity is now' (*nunc aeternam*), and all earthly time is defined and transformed by this presence of eternity. While for Barth the hearers of God's word are called to a radical decision about *God's* direct claim on human life, Rudolph Bultmann stresses the demand for a decision to understand *human existence* in the light of the New Testament

---

[23] Augustine, *Confessions*, XI.11, 13, 14,17.
[24] Henri Bergson, *Time and Free Will*, transl. F. L. Pogson (London: Allen & Unwin, 1912), pp. 23–8.
[25] Nathan Scott, *The Broken Center. Studies in the Theological Horizon of Modern Literature* (New Haven: Yale University Press, 1966), p. 76.
[26] Karl Barth, *The Epistle to the Romans*, transl. from the 6th edn by E. C. Hoskyns (Oxford: Oxford University Press, 1933), p. 497.

kerygma.[27] But for both, the striking of human life by the eternal moment is truly eschatological; the 'end of history' is not a future event, but happens here and now at the frontier where time meets eternity in the self-disclosure of the eternal God. While Barth retains a belief in the future coming of Christ, the *parousia* is essentially what happens 'between the times', since the presence of Christ through the word is the 'turning point' of every time.[28]

This exhaustion of eschatology into the 'eternal moment' does not, I believe, either take history seriously or satisfy the demands of justice for the wrongs of historical actions to be righted. However, our immediate concern is with the nature of our experience of the eternal moment itself, and Jürgen Moltmann is surely right to find at least a limited value in the idea of a 'kairotic' moment as witnessing to the intensity or depth of eternity as marked by fulfilment and 'absolute presentness'.[29] But we notice that its impact does not depend upon a view of eternity as 'simultaneous', or even strictly timeless. Although Barth later does use the language of simultaneity, what matters is the *otherness* of eternity from human time, its incomparability,[30] in order to be able to qualify time and take up time into it. By contrast with the classical approach to time and eternity, recent theology and philosophy of religion has in fact been challenging any view of a timeless state of eternity, and has been denying that the relation between time and eternity should be envisaged as a radical antinomy. Reasons for this have been drawn both from a doctrine of God and from eschatology.

With regard first to God's own nature, Richard Swinburne has stressed that to make the affirmation that God acts, doing 'now this, now that', requires a temporal kind of existence; acts such as choosing, loving, punishing and forgiving all involve time and states of change. It is, maintains Swinburne, only coherent to say that God acts if this is true 'at this or that time or at all times'.[31] This logical argument from the concept of an act itself is directed by Nelson Pike towards creation in particular; there is, he maintains, an inconsistency between notions of timelessness and

[27] See e.g. Rudolph Bultmann, *History and Eschatology* (Edinburgh: Edinburgh University Press, 1957), pp. 155ff.

[28] Barth, *Romans*, p. 501.

[29] Jürgen Moltmann, *The Coming of God*, transl. M. Kohl (London: SCM Press, 1996), p. 289.

[30] Barth, *Romans*, p. 498.

[31] Richard Swinburne, *The Coherence of Theism* (Oxford: Clarendon Press, 1977), p. 221.

omnipotence, as a timeless being cannot bring states of affairs about, and so we cannot think of a God who exists outside time as sustaining or preserving a temporally extended universe.[32]

Karl Barth, in his *Church Dogmatics*, brings an objection against a timeless God founded more in the Christian idea of revelation. He does not bluntly draw the conclusion that a God who has become incarnate in time must for that reason be temporal in God's own self. Rather, if God has graciously entered human time in the incarnation, then he has revealed that he already 'has time for us';[33] since it must be really God in himself who has time for us (as God discloses the truth about himself), time must be important eternally for God. We can even say, 'God *is* time for us'.[34] Moreover, in his self-unveiling God has revealed himself as triune, existing in three modes of being characterized by relationship; he is not static, but living in the interweaving movements of begetting, being begotten and proceeding. Any concept of eternity must do justice to the 'event' character of this threefold repetition in the being of God. God's very being is revealed as a dynamic act, and this 'happening' cannot *exclude* time, but be a basis and 'prototype' for *our* time and history. Barth thus concludes that eternity is an 'eminent' or 'authentic' temporality which affirms, fulfils and judges our time.[35] Time, we may say, is eternally in God as the potential for God's coming into our history. God's repetition of himself makes space eternally within himself for time, so that 'God has time, because and as he has eternity.'[36]

If we ask why Boethius developed his influential concept of a 'simultaneous' eternity, it seems that this was not only because of Platonic presuppositions about the timeless and unmoving world of Being as the only ground of our world of becoming, though he certainly inherited these assumptions. It was primarily in order to solve the problem of divine foreknowledge and human freedom. His argument went that God can infallibly know all our future actions, and yet those actions still be freely chosen by us, if God sees these real choices as eternally present rather than foreknowing them.[37] Philosophers of religion are divided as to whether

[32]   Nelson Pike, *God and Timelessness* (London: Routledge & Kegan Paul, 1970), pp. 97–119.

[33]   Barth, *Church Dogmatics* transl. and ed. G. W. Bromiley and T. F. Torrance (Edinburgh: T. & T. Clark, 1936–77), I/2, pp. 45ff.

[34]   Barth, *Church Dogmatics*, II/1, p. 611f.

[35]   Barth, *Church Dogmatics*, III/2, pp. 437, 526; II/1, p. 617.

[36]   Barth, *Church Dogmatics*, II/1, p. 611.

[37]   Boethius, *De Consolatione Philosophiae*, 5.4.

this would in fact preserve human freedom, but Swinburne makes the point that even if it does, it destroys *God's* freedom. Such a God would have to be absolutely immutable, and unless God is mutable in some sense we can hardly affirm his freedom in acting, responding to human beings in relationship, being affected by them or having purposes and fulfilling them. Above all, as I myself argue elsewhere,[38] it is not possible to speak of God's suffering with the world unless God changes from one state to another. Immutability and timelessness mutually reinforce each other, as Aquinas argued.[39] But, as Swinburne again suggests, the perfection of God can consist 'not in his being in a certain static condition, but in his being in a certain process of change. Only Neo-Platonic dogma would lead us to suppose otherwise.'[40]

The dogma he no doubt has in mind is the Platonic dictum that God cannot change, because one who becomes more perfect could not have been God before, and one who becomes less perfect is not God any longer. But this envisages 'perfection' as a fixed maximum of being and value, whereas we can envisage God as the ever-new source of new possibilities for the world and thus for God's own self. With the process theologians, we can make a distinction between 'perfection' and 'completion' in God; Charles Hartshorne, for example, helpfully speaks of God's 'relative perfection' in being both perfectly related to all the reality there is at any one moment, and yet also having a perfection relative to that particular moment in history.[41] Thus God can be conceived as 'perfect', that is perfectly related to each stage of creation and history, and yet still having a completion that lies ahead. God, we may say, has a 'perfect incompletion', and while the process theologians root this in God's ability always to be self-surpassing, we may also trace it to God's own free resolve to allow created beings to contribute to God's project and God's satisfaction. So John Macquarrie writes also of perfection not being a static 'end-state' for

[38] Paul S. Fiddes, *The Creative Suffering of God* (Oxford: Clarendon Press, 1988), pp. 49–57.

[39] Aquinas, *Summa Theologiae*, 1a.10.1.

[40] Swinburne, *Coherence of Theism*, p. 215. Against Swinburne, Paul Helm, *Eternal God* (Oxford: Clarendon Press, 1988), p. 171ff, maintains that a timeless God can be free as long as freedom does not entail being 'unpredictably interactive' with his creation. But divine suffering, as I argue, requires exactly this unpredictability: *Creative Suffering of God*, pp. 59–63.

[41] Charles Hartshorne, *The Divine Relativity. A Social Conception of God* (New Haven: Yale University Press, 1976 [1948]), pp. 79–82.

God: 'This does not rule out the idea of ever higher grades of perfection and goodness as the context is widened.'[42]

We can thus keep the attribute 'immutable' if we understand this as a moral stability, in which God is unchanging in faithfulness to God's character and promises. Pike also proposes that we can retain 'immutable' if we understand it not as an attribute in itself, but as a qualifier for all other attributes of God – for example that God is immutably omnipresent. This, he concludes, is nearer to the biblical tradition and portrays a God who is more worthy of worship.[43]

To affirm that God is in some sense mutable and temporal has, of course, consequences for a belief in the omniscience of God, and in particular for God's knowledge of the future (which is our particular concern in this study). I am going to urge in the next chapter that a belief in God's omniscience is satisfied by God's 'knowing all there is to be known', which does not mean a detailed knowledge of the future or of human free actions. Meanwhile, we should observe with Anthony Kenny that there is actually a conflict between the attributes of timelessness and omniscience as traditionally conceived; if God knows events in a simultaneous moment, then God does not know events in the way that we in the world know them (as a sequence in time), and thus there appears to be something we know that God cannot.[44] This conclusion has led some philosophers to enquire in an ironic manner, 'Does God know what time of day it is?'[45]

If God's possession of eternity is not to be understood as timelessness, how then is it to be conceived? Both Swinburne and Pike propose that it is to be understood as indefinite extension 'backwards and forwards'. It means that 'God has always existed and . . . will go on existing for ever' (Swinburne), or that the life of God has 'unending duration' (Pike).[46] This is thoroughly consistent with the early Old Testament ascription 'God of ages' (*'el 'ōlām*) which envisages God as existing in the remotest past, and the later affirmation that God is 'from everlasting to everlasting' (*mē-'ōlām ad 'ōlām*) which envisages God as existing in unending time, unlimited by either the beginning or end of the world. 'God of ages' was translated in

[42]   John Macquarrie, *Principles of Christian Theology* (London: SCM Press, 1977), p. 209.
[43]   Pike, *God and Timelessness*, p. 179.
[44]   Anthony Kenny, *The God of the Philosophers* (Oxford: Clarendon Press, 1979), pp. 38–42.
[45]   See N. Kretzmann, 'Omniscience and Immutability', *Journal of Philosophy*, 63 (1966), pp. 509–21.
[46]   Swinburne, *Coherence of Theism*, p. 211, cf. Swinburne, *The Christian God*, (Oxford, Clarendon Press, 1994), pp. 137–44; Pike, *God and Timelessness*, p. 184.

the Septuagint as 'the eternal God' (*ho aionios theos*) and so appears in the
New Testament at Romans 16:26. The Hebrew idiom is still clearly
apparent in the title 'king of the ages' in 1 Timothy 1:17. Neither in Old
or New Testament is eternity thus placed in anithesis to time; that God
exists 'from everlasting to everlasting' means that God exists prior to,
through and after time as we measure it.

However, I suggest that we should add an essential dimension to this
portrayal of God as being 'backwardly and forwardly eternal' (Swinburne),
that is an eminent *participation* of God in time, transcending any experience
of finite beings. To understand what this participation might mean, we
need to take a short detour through views of time in modern physics.
Special Relativity theory as developed by Einstein informs us that time can
no longer be thought of as a single 'receptacle' into which all things and
events can be put, as Newton had once envisaged 'absolute time'. Physical
entities in the universe have different time-scales, since time as well as
space is relative and 'malleable', able to stretch and shrink according to the
observer's motion, the speed of light being the only constant factor. So
there are likely to be as many time-scales in the universe as there are space-
frames. This in turn means that to accommodate the different 'here and
nows' of all the places in the universe, events and moments may be
conceived as being laid out 'all at once' like a landscape, or what the
physicist Paul Davies calls a 'timescape'. Space is not just a metaphor for
time; space and time form a unified 'fourth dimension' or continuum, and
in accord with this image, Einstein pronounced that 'the distinction
between past, present and future is only an illusion, even if a stubborn
one.'[47]

On first sight it might be thought that this modern view of time works
against my argument. As Paul Davies suggests, it seems to correspond to
the traditional view of eternity as simultaneity, and of God's own vision of
temporal events as simultaneous.[48] The inevitable corollary is that there can
be no free will; what will happen in the future is already 'somewhere out
there'. However, we should note two important qualifications. First, while
the theory of relativity works well in application to the universe on a large
scale, small-scale exploration of sub-atomic particles through quantum
mechanics shows a basic indeterminacy in the way they behave, and this
may well indicate a sequential view of time. As yet there is no comprehen-

[47]   Cited in Paul Davies, *About Time. Einstein's Unfinished Revolution* (London: Viking,
1995), p. 70.
[48]   Ibid., p. 72.

sive theory of time which unites the perceptions of relativity and quantum theory,[49] and so we cannot conclude that time is simply simultaneous in four-dimensional space-time. All we can say is that a theory of simultaneity works well for *certain* purposes of physics. This is a point I intend to follow up further when considering the 'arrow of time' in a later chapter.

Second, and significantly for our present concern, even the Special Theory of Relativity makes clear that as far as participants in time are concerned, there can be no common 'now' between two time-frames. It is not possible for someone to witness the 'nows' of someone else in another time-scale since instantaneous communication is not possible; among other reasons, the theory assumes that no material object can exceed the speed of light, so simultaneity itself must be relative to the observer. This leads the theologian Wolfhart Pannenberg to propose that, unlike finite beings, God is the supreme observer who 'does not need light to know things', so that God's eternity is 'simultaneous with all events in the strict sense'.[50] All events, whether in the past, present or future of whatever time-frame are present to God, and embraced in a divine eternal present. But relativity theory need not be pressed in this way into the service of supporting a simultaneous eternity. Instead, the relation of God to multiple time-systems may be envisaged as an unsurpassable participation, taking the journey of time seriously in each as God indwells each.

We might say that God can relate to all time-scales because God can participate in them all concurrently, moving at the same moment along their individual time-paths, where we are limited to our own.[51] God then is the supreme traveller in the 'timescape' of the universe. Just as Karl Barth maintains that God can enter our time on the grounds of being already a triune 'event' which makes space for our history within the divine communion of life, so we can say that God makes room for *all* the histories there are in the universe (or in many universes). God can 'intermesh' with them all just because God has an eminent temporality. This points us to a vision of eternity which is about *integration* of time through participation, rather than either simultaneity or extension of time. Discussion of this must wait for our return to a reading of Eliot, but we should notice that when Einstein speaks of the distinction between past, present and future as an

---

[49]   See Roger Penrose, in Stephen Hawking and Roger Penrose, *The Nature of Space and Time* (Princeton: Princeton University Press, 1996), pp. 61–2.
[50]   Wolfhart Pannenberg, *Systematic Theology*, vol. 2, transl. G. Bromiley (Edinburgh: T. & T. Clark, 1994), p. 93.
[51]   I have already suggested this in *The Creative Suffering of God*, pp. 98–9.

'illusion', he means an absolute separation in which only the present is regarded as real; a spatial view of time does not eliminate the *direction* of time as being orientated towards the future, and in fact confirms it.

We have seen that the issue of how a strictly timeless God could act in a contingent world has been one significant motivation for questioning a timeless eternity. A second reason is the related one of eschatology itself: if the eternal is to be envisaged as *entering* time at the eschaton, rather than simply being the object of contemplation from within time (as with Augustine), then how could a timeless eternity interact with time? How could two such incompatible realities conjoin so that one can transform the other? How, in an eschaton, can there be 'a point of intersection of the timeless/ With time'? It seems that for time to be swallowed up in eternity, or be clothed by it (2 Cor. 5:4), there must be some continuity between them. The force of this problem has been admitted by those who want to argue for a non-temporal eternity, either in the form of simultaneity or in the apophatic mode of dissociating God's eternity from any concept of time. They have therefore had resource to the notion that created beings do not enter the 'absolute eternity' in which God exists in God's self, but are given a 'relative eternity' or 'quasi-eternity'.

One form of this argument takes a traditional view that God's eternity is simultaneity, but admits that finite beings need some kind of experience of successiveness, a before and after, in order to remain persons characterized by a sense of discovery and development. So F. von Hügel proposes that: 'the sense of Time, in the most fully eternalized of human spirits, would be so durational as almost to lapse into Simultaneity'.[52] We note a sense of regret in this approach, as if it would be better to enjoy complete timelessness, but that it cannot unfortunately be attained even in the most advanced souls. More recently, Simon Tugwell also reflects this minimalist concession to time, by allowing a special kind of time in the case of the bodies of the resurrected, while ascribing timelessness to their souls.[53] He is tentative in putting forward this solution of an *aevum* for bodies, but can see no other way of envisaging an eternity which is generally characterized by immobility but in which bodies (as Aquinas observed) need time in which to move.

A second form of quasi-eternity has been developed by Jürgen Molt-mann. While he denies any temporality to God's own eternity, he cannot

[52]   Friedrich von Hügel, *Eternal Life* (Edinburgh: T. & T. Clark, 1913), p. 391.
[53]   Simon Tugwell, *Human Immortality and the Redemption of Death* (London: Darton, Longman and Todd, 1990), pp. 167–8.

regard it as being timeless simultaneity, since no images connected with time – positive or negative – can be ascribed to God's essence. Created beings cannot share directly in this eternity, and thus in preparation for creation, God forms a 'relative eternity' or 'aeon' (cf. *aevum*) which mediates between the eternity of God and the time of the world.[54] It is this 'aeonic time', according to Moltmann, into which the created universe will be assumed at the last day. Thus the eschatological moment corresponds to the primordial moment; the exit of time from eternity at the beginning is matched by the exit from time into eternity at the end. This intermediate aeonic time is characterized by 'cyclicity', 'reversibility' and 'simultaneity'. I intend to postpone – to chapter 7 – an examination of the first and second aspects, which in Moltmann's view reflect both the cyclical rhythms of nature and the cyclical movements of the Trinity. Here our concern is with the concept of simultaneity, which Moltmann treats rather ambivalently as being both a special kind of time ('eternal time') and as putting an end to time altogether. In practice, the second view prevails, as Moltmann regards aeonic time as corresponding to the eternity of God, so that it is not only unending but 'without before and after', and life within it is 'without growth'.[55] It is this relative eternity, and not God's 'absolute eternity' that Moltmann sees as being reflected in the present moment of the thinking subject, as Augustine describes it. That is, there is a 'relative simultaneity' of past, present and future in the mind through the force of memory and expectation, which here and now anticipates relative eternity (simultaneity) and the resurrection from the dead.

Though I wish to oppose any view of 'simultaneity' as an image for eternity, it is important to understand why Moltmann prefers it. In the first place, he is anxious that every moment in earthly time should be open to redemption in eternity. Everything must be brought back in the moment of final reconciliation and nothing must be lost. He finds an articulation of this in 'simultaneity': the Last Day of general resurrection must, he thinks, be simultaneous with every day in human history (it is the 'Day of days'), and thereafter every moment of a person's past life should be exposed to the transformative power of eternity.

> The linear time of evolution will be carried into a unique and then final eschatological cycle: into the return of all the pasts in the eternal aeon of the

---

[54] Moltmann, *The Way of Jesus Christ*, transl. M. Kohl (London: SCM Press, 1990), pp. 328–31; Moltmann, *The Coming of God*, pp. 290–2.
[55] Moltmann, *The Coming of God*, p. 282, *The Way of Jesus Christ*, p. 331.

new creation of all things. Eschatological future is to be understood *diachron-ically*: it is simultaneous to all the times, and in being so it represents eternity for all things.[56]

However, it is by no means self-evident that a 'diachronicity', in which every phase of life and history is to be touched by the resurrection, is the same as simultaneity. In fact, it could be argued that simultaneity precisely fails to take history seriously, abolishing the 'before and after' that makes events what they are. Nevertheless, any alternative vision must be able to express the potential for redemption of every moment. It must also reflect Moltmann's second concern, which is even more strongly expressed by Tugwell, that we should take the *end* of history seriously. Tugwell, as we have already seen, points out that there can be no meaningful story without an ending to which it moves; for him this is the moment of death which, because eternity is timeless, is for the dead (though not for those still living in history) identical with the day of judgement and resurrection.[57] Molt-mann does not envisage simultaneity beginning until the Last Day, which lies ahead in public time for the dead and the living alike. But for both thinkers, a movement into simultaneity at some point seems to put an end effectively to our present kind of existence, characterized as it is by succession. Death cannot, as we have already seen in reflecting on tragedies such as *King Lear*, be a merely smooth point of transition from one phase to another.

Despite the weight of these concerns, the theory of simultaneity cannot do justice to a third consideration which stands against timelessness, in addition to the two factors already reviewed, namely, an adequate doctrine of God and the nature of the eschatological event. Some form of time is needed in eternity, we have already seen, for both God and the eschaton to enter the time of human history. But it is also needed for any concept of growth and development of created persons beyond death. Recent thought in theology and philosophy of religion has turned against the concept of a static perfection in eternity in favour of a more dynamic account. Given that persons have the nature of existing in a state of becoming, which means holding identity through time, it is hardly coher-ent to envisage anything like personal life as continuing without such experiences as setting and fulfilling aims, adventuring into unknown areas and increasing in awareness and satisfaction. Eternity, as it has often been

---

56   Moltmann, *The Way of Jesus Christ*, p. 303.
57   Tugwell, *Human Immortality*, pp. 158–60, 164–7.

remarked, would be tedious if there were nothing new to be achieved and only hymns to be sung. Even Aristotle, who excluded becoming from blessedness, still regarded the blessed life not as a condition but an activity.[58]

To this reflection on the nature of persons should be added the demand of theodicy, for lives that have had no proper chance of development to fulfill their potential for flourishing. There is the young child who is full of curiosity about life and dies of cancer; there is the young man who has many intellectual and personal gifts, yet falls victim to schizophrenia and takes his own life before he has left his teenage years; there is the young woman who has just entered upon the experience of being a mother when she is killed in an accident. Moltmann feels the demand for justice here, and urges that eternal life must 'give the broken and impaired . . . space and time and strength to live the life which they were intended for'.[59] This account is either inconsistent with his envisaging of 'aeonic time' as being simultaneous, or he must understand it in terms of an instantaneous completion. Yet the awarding of a static perfection to such as those I have mentioned above would be no just compensation for missing the particular pleasures of growth, the excitement of process and the journey of exploration.

Development is compatible with perfection in human destiny in the same way as perfection can be coherent with future completion in God. As John Macquarrie puts it, 'the goal of a human existence cannot be static, but . . . must be an expanding perfection within the continually expanding perfections of Being.'[60] But does this vision of an increasing perfection undermine the seriousness of death? We recall that the need for a sense of an ending to the human story seemed a strong argument for those who conceive eternity as timeless. It would indeed be persuasive if the development being imagined for eternity were a merely evolutionary progression from this life onwards. But it is possible to conceive of a radical transformation, a 'quantum-shift' to a different environment in a new creation, which still leaves room for adventure. For instance, in our present human condition moral development is not possible without a moral struggle between good and evil alternatives, but this does not logically entail that there cannot be other contexts in which moral development might take a different form. A.E. Taylor suggested many years ago that the essential character of moral life, that of 'aspiration', will remain as long as there

---

[58]   Aristotle, *Nichomachean Ethics*, 1176a–b.
[59]   Moltmann, *The Coming of God*, p. 118.
[60]   Macquarrie, *Principles of Christian Theology*, p. 361.

remains a distinction between God and finite beings, regardless of the presence or absence of evil. Even if persons were so transfigured that everyone practised mutual love, there would still be 'the whole work of embodying the love of each for all in the detail of life'.[61] There would be much to discover about the 'manifestation' of goodness, and so a journey *within* the good even if not towards the good.

A view of the end of human earthly life and history as decisive transformation leading to further journeys of exploration does, in fact, meet the need for an integration of closure and openness in the ending of any story. Simultaneity and timelessness tips the balance too far towards closure, and perhaps threatens the meaning of 'new creation' altogether.

The Healing of Time

In the light of our review of the claiming of time for eternity by theology, must we conclude that there is a conflict between the theologians and Eliot's poetic vision of the 'timeless moment'? The contrast, as I have already hinted, is not as straightforward as this. If we allow Eliot's images to make their own impact, we shall find a deep-laid ambiguity, a refusal to be conformed to any neat system of thought, which points beyond itself to a possible resolution of the problem with time that he identifies.

In the first place, doubts about the redemption of time through an 'eternal present' persist. There is the puzzling beginning to 'Burnt Norton'. What can Eliot mean by the assertion that: 'If all time is eternally present / All time is unredeemable'? This could reflect Augustine's insight that the mere fact that all time is a mode of the present (the future-present, the present-present and the past-present) is not sufficient to redeem our experience of it. According to Augustine, while time is measured by its flowing through the present moment of the mind so that 'all time is present' (the direction of flow being from the anticipated future to the remembered past), the result is only to leave the self in tension and brokenness. This would make sense if Eliot had written simply 'if all time is present', but *eternally* present' casts doubt on Augustine's hope that the way we are redeemed from this predicament is by a contemplation of eternity. Morris Weitz suggests that Eliot is developing a contrast between *time* as present and the *end* as present, the 'end' being understood as the

---

[61]   A. E. Taylor, *The Faith of a Moralist*, vol. 1 (London: Macmillan, 1930), pp. 400, 406.

telos (end, goal of history), which is Christ.[62] As Eliot writes a few lines later:

> What might have been and what has been
> Point to one end, which is always present.

So we are redeemed not by the simultaneity of time in the present moment, but by the presence of the goal of time. Yet this seems an over-subtle exegesis, and would again make more sense if the word 'eternally' were missing. It is possible that Eliot is here not referring to an Augustinian view of the present at all, and is instead registering a sense of despair if time were to be viewed as an eternal *recurrence*, reflecting 'the myth of the eternal return' or the cyclical view of history propounded by Vico. But if this is what he means by all time's being present, the way it is expressed also communicates a sense of unease at *any* view of an eternal present. It does emphasize the need to be realistic about the losses of the past and the uncertainty of the future ('footfalls echo in the memory/ Down the passage which we did not take'). So Eliot declares:

> But only in time can the moment in the rose-garden . . .
> Be remembered; involved with past and future.
> Only through time time is conquered.[63]

I suggest then that these images point to a different kind of unifying of time in the present moment than a mere simultaneity, undermining the Platonic-Augustinian view of timelessness that still stands there on the surface.

This ambiguity is deepened by the weight that Eliot gives to death as an enemy. 'Dry Salvages' shows that death is to be taken seriously, and this is done by appeal to a flux of time that seems Vicoesque or Heraclitean in its rhythms. The contrivances of human clocks are mocked by the recurring movements of the tides, 'the ground swell that is and was from the beginning', and by the rhythm of death itself:

> There is no end of it, the voiceless wailing,
> No end to the withering of withered flowers,
> To the movement of pain that is painless and motionless,

---

[62] Morris Weitz, 'T. S. Eliot: Time as a Mode of Salvation', in Bernard Bergonzi (ed.), *T. S. Eliot, Four Quartets. A Casebook* (London; Macmillan, 1969), pp. 146–9.
[63] Eliot, 'Burnt Norton', II, p. 173.

> To the drift of the sea and the drifting wreckage,
> The bone's prayer to Death its God.[64]

Pain here is 'motionless' only in the Heraclitean sense of an eternal return to the same human agony, which 'abides . . . /Like the river with its cargo of dead negroes, cows and chicken coops'. Eliot actually quotes Heraclitus in the phrase, 'the way up is the way down, the way forward is the way back',[65] but he does not draw the Stoic conclusion that we must simply accept the passing moment; time itself does not heal, for 'the patient is no longer here'. Eliot seems to be evoking the rhythm of the tides of life and death, not to put forward a theory about time and history but to act as a counterbalance to a view of a 'simultaneity' which is too easily attained. There is a tension between different views of time in Eliot; while reaching towards the 'timeless moment', we must not forget that time the preserver is also time the destroyer.

So, within this tension, Eliot points to another way of conceiving the unifying of time – that of love. I agree with Nathan Scott here that Eliot is not commending an annihilation of time, but 'an existential discipline whose goal is moral, not metaphysical'.[66] Redeeming the time is not a matter of exploring 'the womb, or tomb, or dreams . . .'; it is

> . . . an occupation for the saint –
> No occupation either, but something given
> And taken, in a lifetime's death in love,
> Ardour and selflessness and self-surrender.[67]

The intersection of the timeless moment does not result in a detachment from the happenings of historical time, or from involvement in human society. It does invite a loss of self, a loss of self-centred preoccupation with the past and the future so that we can hear the command 'Fare forward, travellers!'.[68] So, as Eliot comforts us in 'East Coker', 'if we do well, we shall/ Die of the absolute paternal care'.[69] Love calls us to die to self, and so to adventure:

[64]   Eliot, 'The Dry Salvages', II, p. 186.
[65]   Ibid., III, p. 187.
[66]   Scott, *The Broken Center*, p. 70.
[67]   Eliot, 'The Dry Salvages', V, p. 190.
[68]   Ibid., III, p. 188.
[69]   Eliot, 'East Coker', IV, p. 181.

> With the drawing of this Love and the voice of this Calling
> We shall not cease from exploration
> And the end of all our exploring
> Will be to arrive where we started
> And know the place for the first time.

In love we find that there is a unifying of past, present and future which cannot be reduced either to a theory of an eternal return (for we shall know the place for the first time) or the simultaneity of a fixed moment, frozen in eternity (there *is* exploration). So Love is:

> A condition of complete simplicity
> (Costing not less than everything)[70]

I suggest, then, that despite his language of a 'timeless moment', and despite his inheritance of the traditional view that eternity is timeless, Eliot is reaching towards a view of eternity that is not a mere abolition of time. Employing a term used in passing by Karl Barth, we may call it a 'healing' of time.[71]

There are theologians, Barth among them, who have used the language of 'simultaneity' while insisting that this is not a total absence of time. Pannenberg, notably, has attempted to draw a contrast between ideas of simultaneity in Augustine and Boethius; he argues that while Augustine's 'eternal present' assumes the Platonic tradition of opposing time to eternity (and so, in Pannenberg's view, only hints at simultaneity), Boethius follows Plotinus in conceiving eternity as the simultaneous presence of the *totality* of time.[72] Boethian simultaneity, claims Pannenberg, is not strictly timelessness but the embrace or 'concurring' of the whole past, present and future in an 'undivided present'.[73] It is this totality of time in eternity which is the ontological basis for the separation out of the tenses of time in the course of history.

Other theologians, too, appear to wish to keep the language of both time and simultaneity. John Macquarrie refers to the 'reconciling' of time

---

[70]   Eliot, 'Little Gidding', V, p. 197.

[71]   Barth, *Church Dogmatics*, II/1, pp. 617–8.

[72]   Wolfhart Pannenberg, *Systematic Theology*, vol. 1, transl. G. Bromiley (Edinburgh: T. & T. Clark, 1991), pp. 402–4.

[73]   Wolfhart Pannenberg, *What is Man?* Transl. D. A. Priebe (Philadelphia: Fortress Press, 1970), pp. 74–6, and Pannenberg, *Systematic Theology*, vol. 2, p. 92.

as the 'simultaneity of [God's] universal experience'[74] even while he is thinking of the integrating of the past into a real future 'with expanding horizons'. Karl Barth criticizes any attempt to develop a notion of eternity in opposition to time as we know it generally in human life, since this is 'lost time' and so problematic; the timelessness of classical metaphysics is a kind of idolatry, a mere projection of human fallibility, where we should rather be attending to what we can learn from the 'time of revelation' which God gives to us.[75] But for all that, he still commends the Boethian formula of a simultaneity between beginning, middle and end.[76]

Unlike these theologians, in my discussion so far I have been taking the common-sense course of treating simultaneity as one form of timelessness, as it appears to be meaningless to speak of time without any kind of succession, any 'before and after'. This is not a mere matter of terminology; in a later chapter we shall see the consequence, for human personality, if we do follow Pannenberg's view of eternity as a simultaneous experience of time.[77] We can surely agree that eternity is the wholeness of time in the sense of overcoming the *division* and *separation* between past, present and future; but I suggest that the metaphor of the 'healing' of time retains a *distinction* between time's phases in a way that simultaneity cannot. We might think of God's eternity as a relation to time in which there is indeed succession (a 'before and after'), but in which God's being is not fragmented by time's passing, as ours is; instead, God would be always integrating past, present and future within perfect love. As Eliot does, we need to take love seriously in a discussion of time, as 'a condition of complete simplicity'. We might conceive of a God for whom the past is still open to transforming vision, and which is being brought (as John Macquarrie puts it)[78] 'into an ever widening reconciling context' as 'the horizons of time and history continually expand' into the future. Time would feel very different if it were being continually harmonized in the self rather than breaking the self.

In fact, if we think carefully about the experiences we have which we tend to call 'timeless moments' or 'epiphanies of eternity', we find that they have this quality not of dissolving time but 'healing' it. We are absorbed in a piece of music or in reading a piece of poetry, and we do not notice that an hour has slipped by. But though we may call this a

---

[74] John Macquarrie, *Christian Hope* (London and Oxford: Mowbrays, 1978), p. 118.
[75] Barth, *Church Dogmatics*, I/2, p. 45.
[76] Barth, *Church Dogmatics*, II/1, pp. 608–10.
[77] See below, pp. 212–15.
[78] Macquarrie, *Principles of Christian Theology*, p. 361.

timeless moment, it is not strictly so. It is not even a 'relative simultaneity'. The whole effect of the music or the poetry depends upon a sequence of time in rhythm, repetition and variation. We have not escaped from time but experienced a new relation to it. The same is true for the composer, even if – as Mozart is supposed to have recounted – he saw the notes of a piece 'as if they were all at once'.[79]

As modern relativity theory tells us, time is characterized by its relations – to space, to velocity, to the observer – rather than being something absolute. Our hope of sharing God's eternity would then be the hope of participating, at least to some extent, in God's own unbroken relation to the multiple time-paths of creation. Perhaps this is what Barth is reaching after with his term 'pure duration', wanting to affirm that the *kind* of distinctions we know between past, present and future are overcome in eternity; but such 'duration' is bound to be at odds with his approval of 'simultaneity'.

The image of the *parousia*, as Moltmann stresses, is about the 'coming' of Christ as Lord to history, and to be complete this coming must be related to every phase of time. Moltmann (and in his own way, Tugwell) tries to express this comprehensive 'coming' with an appeal to eternity as simultaneous, but we have seen the tangles he gets into here. Rather, we can conceive of the healing of time, the transforming of memories and hopes in a way that will be a supreme act of justice.

Woolf and the Symbols of Eternity:
To the Lighthouse and Between the Acts

Woolf's novel, *Mrs. Dalloway*, exposes the problem of time as being most sharp in the difference between inner time (the time of memory) and outer time (the sequence of events in history). This includes the dilemma of the isolation of individual consciousnesses from each other, each locked apparently in its own inner time-scale and its own inner overcoming of the tyranny of time. Caught in the split between inner and outer time, the personality fragments. In her novel *To the Lighthouse* she seeks to solve the problem in an apparently similar way to Eliot, by an appeal to the timeless moment, a glimpse of eternity that transcends both inner and outer time. But unlike Eliot, she has no religious basis for this, no rooting of the

[79] Recounted in Josiah Royce, *The Spirit of Modern Philosophy* (Boston: Houghton Mifflin, 3rd edn, 1892), p. 457.

intersection of eternity with time in the incarnation; she has a mystical *hope* that such a timeless moment is there and can be symbolized in art. It is a secular reliance upon the power of the symbol, parallel to Eliot's religious confidence in the Word, that takes Woolf one stage on from the hints about eternity in *Mrs. Dalloway*.

The lighthouse is such a symbol, and the journey to the lighthouse is symbolic of the unifying of the fragmented human personality. Such symbols, embodied in a narrative, give confidence that the timeless moment is there, and bring us into glancing contact with it. The lighthouse stands firm and unchanging amid the pounding of the waves, yet it cannot be separated from the rhythm of the seas. It unites the movement of time and the stillness of eternity. Mrs Ramsay, in the first part of the novel, is the most self-integrated of the characters, and she finds in the lighthouse an objective assurance of stability that is peculiarly her own. She has discovered that one does not find rest in concentrating upon oneself and one's own needs, but in being drawn out of the personal self by something other, something beyond the self:

> . . . and there rose to her lips always some exclamation of triumph over life when things came together in this peace, this rest, this eternity; and pausing there she looked out to meet that stroke of the Lighthouse, the long steady stroke, the last of the three, which was her stroke . . . this thing, the long steady stroke, was her stroke. Often she found herself sitting and looking, sitting and looking, with her work in her hands until she became the thing she looked at – that light for example. And it would lift up on it some little phrase or other which had been lying in her mind like that – 'Children don't forget, children don't forget' – which she would repeat and begin adding to it, It will end, It will end, she said. (73–4)

That fragment of memory, 'Children don't forget' relates to an incident which had happened earlier. The children had badly wanted to make an expedition to the lighthouse but their father, Mr Ramsay, had refused to take them. He is a man wrapped up in his own concerns, full of self-pity, always demanding the emotional support of his wife. The reason for not going on the trip is a genuine one, the poor weather, but he does not notice the hurt it causes the children when he keeps rubbing in the fact that they will certainly be unable to go. As Mrs Ramsay puts the youngest child, James, to bed, she looks across the bay at 'one long steady stroke . . . the light of the Lighthouse' and she is sure that the child is thinking 'we are not going to the Lighthouse tomorrow', and she thinks, 'he will remember that all his life. No, she thought . . . children never forget. For this reason, it was so important what one said, and what one did, and it was a relief when they went to bed' (p. 72). Memories like this disrupt a life; the past plagues the present. While the lighthouse is a symbol of the eternal moment of stability and peace, failure to go to the lighthouse is a symbol of the isolation of individuals in their own time, their own memories, their own configuration of past, present and future.

In the third part of the book, after the passing of years and three deaths in the family, the father and two remaining children finally go 'to the Lighthouse'. They return to the holiday house, with Lily Briscoe the painter (now in middle age); they complete their journey, and Lily completes her picture that she had begun years before. Mr Ramsay has become even more self-pitying, dwelling upon the losses of his wife and children, more self-absorbed, more demanding of emotional support from the women around him, especially from Lily and from his daughter Cam. But as the boat nears the lighthouse, Mr Ramsay spontaneously praises the steering of his son James; all his life he has craved the pity and the praise of others, but now he offers a word of praise himself. He leaves his ego and the traps of past regret behind. He has reached the lighthouse.

> He rose and stood in the bow of the boat, very straight and tall, for all the world, James thought, as if he were saying, 'There is no God', and Cam thought, as if he were leaping into space, and they both rose to follow him as he sprang, lightly like a young man, holding his parcel, on to the rock.

> 'He must have reached it,' said Lily Briscoe aloud, feeling suddenly completely tired out . . .
> 'He has landed,' she said aloud, 'It is finished.' (p. 236)

At this very moment she turns quickly to her canvas and completes her picture:

> With a sudden intensity, as if she saw it clear for a second, she drew a line there, in the centre. It was done; it was finished. Yes, she thought, laying down her brush in extreme fatigue, I have had my vision. (p. 237)

She and Mr Ramsay have both now shared with Mrs Ramsay an intuition of eternity.[80] The stroke she makes recalls the lighthouse, and also

---

[80] Richard Bauckham, 'Time and Eternity', in Richard Bauckham (ed.), *God Will be All in All. The Eschatology of Jürgen Moltmann* (Edinburgh: T. & T. Clark, 1999), pp. 109–13, interestingly suggests that there is a difference between Mr and Mrs

Mrs Ramsay herself, for she has become the lighthouse in their memories. The surge of the waves of death have not been able to destroy the vision of stability which Mrs Ramsay had, and now is. At least, the narrative *affirms* that death has not been able to destroy 'this rest, this peace'. But Woolf allows a moment of doubt to slip in at the end; as Mr Ramsay prepares to leap onto the rock, his two children cannot share his inner feelings:

> He sat and looked at the island, and he might be thinking, We perished, each alone, or he might be thinking, I have reached it. I have found it, but he said nothing. (p. 236)

Through the thoughts of the various characters, Woolf is making the mystical assertion that somehow the timeless moment that heals the breaches in time is there, and can be represented in the symbolism of art. Yet she enters a caution; the impact of death is serious and final, and the eternal moment is vulnerable in the face of death to being an illusion. Mr. Ramsay might be thinking, 'We perished each alone', a quotation from William Cowper's despairing and depressive poem, 'The Castaway', whose next line Mr Ramsay often used to express his feelings: 'But I beneath a rougher sea' (p. 234).

The following novel, *The Waves* (1931) presents us with the same doubt about whether or not death triumphs over the vision of a timeless moment. The novel ends with the lonely venture of the individual against the flood-tide of death: ' ". . . Against you will I fling myself, unvanquished and unyielding, O Death!" *The waves broke on the shore.*'

In both these novels Woolf has been developing another notion, complementary to timelessness, of how the discord of the self in time might be healed. In face of the split between inner and outer time, she suggests that the only real time scheme is the inner one, the consciousness shaping time for itself, making a fictive experience of time. The mind can make the pattern that brings passing time into a whole and enables one to live courageously in a world of public time, but not the individual mind by itself. The earlier hints of shared consciousness in *Mrs. Dalloway* are now taken up fully in the idea that each individual must reach out into the consciousness of others to achieve the shaping and conquering of time within the inner life of humankind as a whole. *The Waves* is an experiment

---

Ramsay's vision of eternity: the former is diachronic, the latter synchronic. But he offers no critique of the image of eternity as timeless.

in this kind of shared consciousness, as we hear the thoughts of six minds, six friends, interweaving and interpenetrating because of their common love for a seventh friend, Percival. They live their lives through each other in 'this globe whose walls are made of Percival'[81] (though Percival himself never speaks in the book), and their communion persists through, and makes some sense of, the passing of time.

The special feature of this 'collective mind', which we have already seen appearing in the later novels of Doris Lessing which are also about corporate identity, is that it brings healing to the discordances of time. The narrative is punctuated by the breaking of waves on the shore throughout twenty-four hours from one dawn to another sunset, as it is marked in *Mrs. Dalloway* by the chiming of Big Ben. Here, however, the day is an image for an entire life-span and a sense of wholeness is achieved between this outer rhythm of nature and the inner reflections of the mind. Yet there is still the doubt about death and its destructive power. As darkness begins to lift with the new dawn, and the waves gather themselves together to fall on the shore, Bernard feels 'Yes, this is the eternal renewal, the incessant rise and fall and fall and rise again. And in me too the wave rises . . .' (p. 255). A little earlier he has been reflecting, '"Who am I?" I have been talking of Bernard, Neville, Jinny, Susan, Rhoda and Louis. Am I all of them? Am I one and distinct? I do not know' (p. 248); but now, with Percival and Rhoda dead and the group divided, he thinks 'I am alone now'. He determines to launch himself against death, though with the courage of Percival:

'. . . It is death against whom I ride with my spear couched and my hair flying back like a young man's, like Percival's, when he galloped in India. I strike spurs into my horse. Against you I will fling myself, unvanquished and unyielding, O Death!'

In this novel, configured in time by the rhythm of the day and the tides, we can find two modes of reaching beyond the brokenness of time which Nathan Scott notes as characteristic of our present century.[82] There is the Bergsonian 'pure duration' in the consciousness, the memory acting as a catalyst to integrate experiences from past and present into a stream of reflection, and there is the Vicoesque 'eternal renewal' of the natural cycle expressed in timeless myth. Woolf's novels bring before the theologian the

---

[81]   Virginia Woolf, *The Waves* (Harmondsworth: Penguin Books, 1964), p. 124.
[82]   Scott, *The Broken Center*, pp. 48–9.

need for a healing of time, but as death remains an unreconciled enemy they also prompt the theologian to suggest that Eliot (for all his playing with the concepts of timelessness) is right when he affirms that 'only through time is time redeemed'.

Woolf's last novel (only just completed before her suicide) is *Between the Acts* (1941), and here the attempt to heal the wounds of time through a sharing in the consciousness of others is most clearly worked out. The plot is simply the presentation of a historical pageant during one sleepy afternoon in the garden of a country house. The pageant celebrates public time, the life of the village through the centuries, but between the acts several human dramas are being worked out in the relationships of the people gathered there. In different ways, they are troubled by the disintegrating force of time. There are, for example, Giles Oliver and his wife Isa. Giles is a man of action, concerned with the external public sequence of events; he is disturbed by time past (when he had been a respectable stockbroker) and he is anxious about time future (the war is impending in Europe, and he can do nothing about it). His intense frustration leads him to be unfaithful to his wife in ways that can only be described as childish. She irritates him because she longs to avoid the burdens that passing time brings ('this year, last year, next year, never')[83] by escaping into an inner world of absolute knowledge and beauty, and she despises the outer life of action. So each oppresses the other with their absorption in their own time-scheme.

The pageant presents in successive acts the Elizabethan, Restoration and Victorian Ages. The portrayal is fairly chaotic, at times not even audible; the author and producer, Miss La Trobe, appears to be intending this effect, making the point that history has no pattern and is not leading us anywhere in particular. Outer time has no shape of its own, no wholeness, and yet the scenes evoke in the inner life of the players a sense of purpose and the overcoming of time: 'What a small part I've had to play, and yet you've made me feel I could play . . . Cleopatra' says an elderly lady (p. 107). The fourth and last act is assigned to the present day. The audience watch a tableau of a man and a woman rebuilding a ruined wall, and then out dance children carrying mirrors or some shiny objects that will reflect the members of the audience to themselves while the actors repeat fragments of speeches from all the previous acts. The audience is shocked, embarrassed at being forced to look at themselves, and offended

---

[83]   Virginia Woolf, *Between The Acts* (Harmondsworth: Penguin Books, 1972), pp. 19, 151.

that all they can see of themselves is parts of the their bodies, 'Here a nose, there a skirt . . . Now perhaps a face . . . Ourselves? But that's cruel . . . And only, too in parts . . . That's what's so distorted and upsetting . . .'. But then the voice of Miss La Trobe thunders through a megaphone:

> Look at ourselves, ladies and gentlemen! Then at the wall; and ask how's this wall, the great wall, which we call, perhaps miscall, civilization, to be built by (here the mirrors flicked and flashed) orts, scraps, and fragments like ourselves? . . . All you can see of yourselves is scraps, orts, and fragments? Well then, listen to the gramophone affirming . . . (p. 131)

After a hitch in which the wrong record is played, the tune began and 'like quicksilver sliding, filings magnetized, the distracted united . . . compelled from the ends of the horizon; recalled from the edge of appalling crevasses; they crashed; solved; united . . .' The notes of music and the separate minds of the audience converge, are 'all enlisted', precisely because they are divergent and in opposition. The sententious summary of the play's 'meaning' by the well-intending clergyman is that 'to me at least it was indicated that we are members one of another. Each is a part of the whole' (p. 133). Like all reductions of art to prose there is a certain truth in this, but Miss La Trobe refuses to offer an explanation for her play, and grits her teeth over this parsonic (and religious) conclusion, because no concept can exhaust the way in which consciousnesses merge. The analogy with music leaves open the way in which shared awarenesses can cope with the great breaches that time rends in life. The audience who see themselves in the mirrors, broken into fragments, have been spectators of the onward and chaotic march of outward history, but they can form a true history within themselves, though not alone. The work of art has presented the time of the external world in such a way that the spectators are driven to reconfigure time within, in a wholeness that comes from a harmony of minds. As Frye and Ricoeur would put it, the play has not been an *imitation* of history, but it is *creating* future history.

What is 'between the acts?' Is it the relationships and reflections of the members of the audience that go on between the acts of the play? Or is it the play which is performed between the acts of the drama of life? Or is it the book itself which inserts itself between the acts of the lives of the readers? All these are true, for the work of art is the catalyst that can enable us to arrange our inner time in communion with others, and so go on living in the outer world. As with the poetry of Eliot, Woolf's novels expose the urgent need for our awareness of time to be healed. According to Woolf, the symbols of art (the lighthouse, the pageant) allow us to enter an eternal world, timeless in 'pure duration', and also to enter a world in which consciousness is somehow shared.

But the theologian may observe that the possible worlds the novels create have the shadow of death at their heart, and that a timeless eternity (whether in this life or beyond) has no power to lift it. Writing within the boundaries of the Christian story, Eliot – unlike Woolf – has a model for bringing together an image of eternity with a sharing of consciousness in the participation of love. He can also hold open the way in which this overcomes the destructive nature of time, finding a focus in the Word which is the Christ in history rather than in any particular theory of temporality. In the impact of the 'moment' of eternity within time, everything does not depend upon timelessness and simultaneity. It depends upon the 'complete simplicity' of love. If the theologian is going to find a 'transcendental signifier' in the Word of the Christ, it must be surely be in the context of an eternity that takes time seriously and does not merely cancel it.

Chapter Six

EXPECTING THE
UNEXPECTED

It is likely that the parables of Jesus had a wide circulation in the early Church, and the strongest evidence for this exists in the case of the two little parables that appear paired together in Luke 12:35–40. The stories of the Watching Servants and the Unexpected Thief seem to have had a particular attraction for early Christians, and a wide usage.[1] It is not hard to see why this should be, as they speak to the situation of a community in which there were conflicting ideas and feelings about the *parousia* of Jesus Christ, his expected 'coming in glory' to the world of which he had been proclaimed Lord in his resurrection.

We would be unwise to succumb to the influential view of Albert Schweitzer and assume that there was a universal 'crisis' in the churches caused by the failure of Christ to make his appearance, and that this generated some revised eschatologies.[2] Rather, we may envisage a more diverse situation in which some members were indeed perplexed at the delay of what they had believed would be an imminent end, some had ceased carrying on their daily activities in the light of the coming event, some needed encouragement to go on believing in the hope of Christ's coming at all, and others had already adopted a more spiritualized or 'realized' eschatology. It also seems possible that many Christians took none of these more extreme positions, believing that an imminent *parousia* was *possible* but not *necessary*.

Some scholars, such as Ben Witherington in his study *Jesus, Paul and the End of the World,* find the two parables of Luke 12:35–40 to be strong

---

[1] Evidence for this is collected by Richard Bauckham in his *The Climax of Prophecy* (Edinburgh: T. & T. Clark, 1993), pp. 96–117.
[2] Albert Schweitzer, *The Mysticism of Paul the Apostle,* transl. W. Montgomery (London: A. & C. Black, 1931), pp. 52ff., p. 75ff, pp. 379–85.

evidence for this more moderate understanding, since they stress precisely the unexpected nature of the *parousia*. Witherington includes the Apostle Paul among the moderates, and finds Paul's appeal to the parable of the Thief in 1 Thessalonians 5:2 (a story which he assumes the recipients of his letter 'know well') to be evidence that he was prepared for any eventuality – either to be left still alive at the *parousia*, or to die beforehand. Paul's view, suggests Witherington, does not substantially alter throughout his ministry, from the early period of 1 Thessalonians 5 to the later point of 2 Corinthians 5. He regards the *parousia*, maintains Witherington, as an event that *may* happen at any moment, but which is not necessarily going to happen soon. The 'thief in the night' motif perfectly encapsulates 'how both Paul and Jesus convey an eschatological message involving *possible but not necessary* imminence of the end to inculcate moral earnestness and diligence in the believer'.[3]

Two Parables of Waiting

My concern here is not to adjudicate in the argument about the so-called 'delay' of the *parousia*, but rather to explore the effect of the parables as combining the expected with the unexpected. Their portrayal of the surprising character of what will certainly happen could, in fact, have a multi-purpose use according to different situations. It could calm perplexity and panic, or confirm a perpetual stance of watchfulness. There is an open-endedness about these parables which is produced in the first place by their being brought together into a pair as they appear in Luke:

> Let your loins be girded and your lamps burning, and be like men who are waiting for their master to come home from the marriage feast, so that they may open to him at once when he comes and knocks. Blessed are those servants whom the master finds awake when he comes; truly, I say to you, he will gird himself and have them sit at table, and he will come and serve them. If he comes in the second watch, or in the third, and finds them so, blessed are those servants! But know this, that if the householder had known at what hour the thief was coming, he would have been awake and would not have left his house to be broken into. You must also be ready; for the Son of man is coming at an hour you do not expect.[4]

---

3   Witherington, *Jesus, Paul and the End of the World* (Exeter: Paternoster, 1992), p. 47.
4   Luke 12:35–40, Revised Standard Version.

The pairing of the two stories makes them qualify each other, rather as pairs of contrary proverbs appear in the Wisdom literature,[5] and the result is to bring out the unexpectedness not only of the timing of the coming, but the unexpectedness of its *manner*. These are complementary pictures of a lord and a thief, and while they together express the dual aspects of blessing for those who are prepared and judgement for those who are unprepared, they also make clear that we are dealing with metaphor and not literal description. The coming home of the master from a marriage feast can be no less metaphorical than the breaking-in of the thief. The daring comparison of the Son of man with a burglar may have been too much for Paul, as the version in 1 Thessalonians 5 softens the personal analogy by comparing the coming of the thief with the the coming of 'the *day* of the Lord', though the risen Christ in Revelation 3:3 and 16:15 declares boldly that 'I am coming like a thief'! The rather impressionistic nature of the parables is underlined by the action of the master when he comes to his servants, and proceeds to serve a meal at the unlikely hour of midnight. The two other similar Gospel parables – the Faithful and Unfaithful Servants (which Luke proceeds to add in 12:42–48) and the Ten Virgins (Matt. 25:1–12) – are more realistic in their detail, though the point of unexpectedness and surprise remains.

It is noteworthy that it seems to be the Watching Servants and the Unexpected Thief that achieve a wider circulation than the other two parables, and that the tension between the two stories is kept. Where there is an allusion to the Thief, it is accompanied by the injunction to keep awake like the servants at night; thus, the motif of watching has already crept into Matthew's version of the Thief (Matt. 24:43) where it did not belong (if, as seems reasonable, we take Luke's version of the material in the 'Q' sayings-source as original here), and the setting of the scene at night, as in the situation of the servants, has been made explicit. Similarly, the 'keeping awake and watching' theme is to be found attached to the image of the Thief in 1 Thess. 5:2, 2 Pet. 3:10 (cf. 12, 14), Rev. 3:3, Rev. 16:15 (as well as later in Epiphanius, *Haereses* 69:44:1).[6] Moreover, the openness created by the reflection of the two stories upon each other seems to generate further development. In Revelation 3, the allusion to the Thief in verse 3 in the warning letter to Sardis, is followed in verse 20 by an allusion to the Watching Servants in

---

[5]   See e.g. Proverbs 17:27–28, 26:4–5.
[6]   Text in Bauckham, *The Climax of Prophecy*, p. 115.

the letter to Laodicea,[7] but now developed into a Eucharistic theme[8] and so employed for a coming of Christ to his church here and now in the crisis of worship as well as in the future: 'Behold, I stand at the door and knock; if anyone hears my voice and opens the door I will come in to him and eat with him [cf. Luke 12:37], and he with me.'

In Revelation 16:15 there is a novel expansion of the Thief saying into the benediction: 'Blessed is he who is awake, keeping his garments that he may not go naked. . . !' It is unlikely that the author means us to systematize this into a command to stay awake in order to guard our clothes from the possibility of theft, as the Revised English Bible rather absurdly suggests.[9] The point is rather that 'the man who stays awake, fully clothed [is] contrasted with the man who sleeps and will therefore be caught naked when surprised in the night'.[10] That is, having invoked the picture of the thief to suggest the sudden and unexpected nature of the *parousia*, the author has then left this picture to develop a variation on the complementary metaphor of the watching servants. The two stories, thrown together, open each other up for further meaning. I have not seen elsewhere the suggestion that Rev. 16:15 may also contain an allusion to Luke's introduction to the two parables in 12:35, 'Let your loins be girded [and your lamps burning]', though this would require a familiarity with the Gospel of Luke as well as with the 'Q' sayings-source from which the parables have come. The introductory saying in Luke pictures the Christian life as a pilgrimage, 'as a constant readiness to set out on new paths at uncertain times, or to have an unexpected encounter and act appropriately'.[11]

The parables thus urge an openness to the unexpected in the future. In their present redaction they reflect the fact that some space of time has elapsed after the resurrection of Jesus, whether or not this was felt as a troublesome delay to the expected *parousia*, needing to be explained. The reference to 'the second watch and the third' in Luke's version implies this, and Mark makes it explicit by giving four divisions of the night, and

---

[7] See Joachim Jeremias, *The Parables of Jesus*, transl. S. Hooke, Revised Edition (London: SCM Press, 1972), p. 55.

[8] See Paul Minear, *I Saw a New Earth: An Introduction to the Visions of the Apocalypse* (Washington: Corpus, 1968), pp. 57–8.

[9] But Austin Farrer, *The Revelation of St. John the Divine. Commentary on the English Text* (Oxford: Clarendon Press, 1964), p. 178, offers the same interpretation.

[10] Bauckham, *The Climax of Prophecy*, p. 105.

[11] Eduard Schweizer, *The Good News According to Luke*, transl. D. Green (London: SPCK, 1984), p. 213.

identifying the master in the story with Christ himself, enjoining his disciples, '*You* do not know when the master will come' (Mark 13:35). This would mean that in this case the Lukan source belongs to an earlier stratum than Mark. It is possible that Mark has made a collection of sayings in chapter 13 'precisely in order to dampen speculation about an imminent *parousia*',[12] but these various redactions do not rule out the possibility that a good deal of the material in an earlier form goes back to the expectations of Jesus himself. I do not think, however, that the evidence supports the view that Jesus *either* thought the end of the world was near, *or* that he taught anything as precise as that he would return to his disciples after a long and incalculable interval. Rather, these parables about 'being on the watch' show Jesus opening himself to a future which has a great deal of the unknown in it. He has a sure and certain hope that his Father will bring in the Kingdom fully and finally, but his prayer in Gethsemane ('if it be possible, let this cup pass from me') shows that he does not know how this will happen.

We may suppose that Jesus envisaged the crisis which his ministry had brought into Israel having critical consequences. The crisis could only increase. He could forsee a time of severe testing ahead for himself and his disciples, probably involving his death (for he must have known from the Old Testament that disturbing prophets often met their fate in Jerusalem). It seems that he believed that God his Father would vindicate his ministry, showing him to be right in his conflict with the religious authorities about God's free offer of forgiveness and acceptance to the outcasts. Whatever form that vindication would take, he seems to have believed that Israel as a whole was to meet an event of decisive judgement at God's hands. His eschatological language need not therefore refer to the end of the world; indeed, the precedent of the similar language used by the Old Testament prophets stands against this; we have already seen that Jeremiah, for example, could use cosmic images of the mountains quaking and the sky turning black (Jer. 4:23–27) to describe the onslaught of the Assyrian Army against Jerusalem. Jesus seems to have expected 'an end' in human history within God's purpose,[13] a turning point after which things would never be

---

[12] Witherington, *Jesus, Paul and the End of the World*, p. 43.

[13] This then is an alternative either to eschatology as the imminent end of the world (A. Schweitzer), or as *fully* realized in the present crisis of the breaking-in of the Kingdom (C. H. Dodd). The major proponent of this view has been G. B. Caird: see his *Language and Imagery of the Bible*, (London: Duckworth, 1980), pp. 255–60. There are some affinities with the proposal of James Alison that Jesus is 'subverting the

the same again, and he may even have used the Old Testament imagery of the glorifying of the Son of Man to describe this (Daniel 7:13).

The two parables of the Watching Servants and the Unexpected Thief thus commend an attitude of wakefulness in the face of coming events, and there was a need to keep awake precisely because the nature of these events *would* be unexpected and unpredictable. It would be like a master knocking at the door and calling for his servants unexpectedly, or like a thief breaking in. It is possible, then, that at least a version of the saying in Mark 13:32, which Mark has used to introduce the parable of the Watching Servants, may go back to Jesus himself: 'Of that day or hour no one knows, not even the angels in heaven, nor the Son, but only the Father.' It is unlikely that the early church would have invented a saying which attributes ignorance to Jesus, but more important, it fits in with the openness of Jesus to the unexpected ways in which his Father would fulfil his promises. Because the timing of the *parousia* is what interests Mark, this is what he concentrates upon, but the parables themselves open up a much wider area of the indeterminate and the unknown – not just the when but the how.

In the light of the actual events of the cross and resurrection of Jesus, the early Church came to believe that the vindication of Jesus and the open display of his lordship would take the form of his future coming in glory, a universal resurrection and the renewal of the whole cosmos, and it is this kind of expectation that the present versions of the two parables now imply. The opening chapters of the Book of Revelation show that such a development of eschatology may have been assisted by utterances of Christian prophets, giving pronouncements that were accepted as the words of the risen Christ spoken to his disciples through the Holy Spirit, and among them it seems was this new understanding of the parable of the Thief: 'Lo, *I* am coming like a thief!'. But, as I have all too briefly sketched it, I believe there to be a profound continuity between the hope of Jesus and the hopes of the early Church, and especially in an attitude of expectant waiting for the unexpected.

If the new creation is really new, then it cannot be described in the objectifying language of the old creation. If it could be contained within the concepts of the world as we know it, then it would cease to contradict the present and to protest against the *status quo*. The renewal of all things can only be portrayed in metaphor and image, but (as Janet Martin Soskice has argued in another context), metaphor can refer to an objective event without being a literal description of it.[14] We have already considered the need to be open to unknown and surprising elements in resurrection, and now we should notice that the idea of *parousia* itself has some openness in it. The term *parousia* itself does not mean a 'return' or a 'second' coming. As Moltmann has urged,[15] the notion of a 'second coming' is highly misleading, because it implies some kind of repetition of a first coming, and so merely projects a future event out of the experience of the past and the present. As *adventum*, it is not merely 'what will be' (*futurum*), but what is 'coming towards the present', bringing the end of history and new creation. It is not a 'second' coming of Christ, Moltmann suggests, but the 'completion of the way' of Jesus Christ; 'in his eschatological person he is perfected and is universally manifested in the glory of God'. He is now on the way to his glory, a journey marked by his ministry, cross and resurrection, and *parousia* means 'arrival' or 'presence'. *Parousia* indicates that the lordship of Christ, which is hidden to many at the moment, will come to full and open presence.

Thus, associated with *parousia* are words for 'appearing' (*apocalupsis* and *epiphaneia*), and yet the *parousia* of Christ according to the New Testament is not simply the 'unveiling' of a past salvation; the appearing of Christ in glory is a saving event, *completing* the history of Christ and opening the adventure of the new creation. The Apostle Paul thus prefers to *parousia* the Old Testament phrase 'The Day of the Lord', the day when God would manifest himself in judgement and blessing, and attributes it to Christ as 'The Day of Christ.'[16] As the Day puts an end to days of history and opens new days of eternity, Moltmann rightly insists that the course of events at the *parousia* cannot be narrated, as this would turn the future into the past. 'It can only be awaited', and is present in the mode of promise.[17]

The Reversal of Expectations

The openness to the future which Jesus urged in the original setting of the parables of the Waiting Servants and the Unexpected Thief is thus not

[14]   Janet Martin Soskice, *Metaphor and Religious Language* (Oxford: Clarendon Press, 1987), pp. 134–8.
[15]   Jürgen Moltmann, *The Way of Jesus Christ*, transl. M. Kohl (London: SCM Press, 1990), pp. 314–8.
[16]   See e.g. 1 Cor. 1:8, 5:5; Phil. 1:6, 2:16; 1 Thess. 5:2.
[17]   Moltmann, *The Way of Jesus Christ*, p. 320.

undermined when they are used as *parousia* parables. The expected event is still unexpected. That is, at the heart of the Christian story of the end is *peripeteia*, the literary trope (as identified by Aristotle) whereby a story comes to its expected end, but in an unexpected way. Without reversals and falsifications of expectations a story would lose its interest, but *peripeteia* only works because we want to reach an end, and we are confident the end will be reached. Frank Kermode makes two important observations about this trope which are relevant to our theme.[18] First, by upsetting the ordinary balance of our naïve expectations, *peripeteia* is 'finding something out for us, something *real*'. As we have already seen in *King Lear*, the death of Cordelia badly shakes all the expectations that have been aroused by her reconciliation with her father, but however terrible this is, 'it is a way of finding something out that we should, on our more conventional way to the end, have closed our eyes to'. Thus the unexpected form of the *parousia* is indeed an unveiling, an *apocalupsis*.

Second, Kermode suggests that the experience of *peripeteia* in all stories is parallel to the 'readjustment of expectations in regard to an end which is so notable a feature of naïve apocalyptic'. That is, Kermode supposes that early Christian eschatology *did* affirm the imminence of the end of the world, but that there was no crisis when the end failed to materialize because apocalyptic always 'adjusts' itself, finding reasons why the end has failed to come. There can be no dispute that this has happened in apocalyptic movements through the ages, as the falsifying of confidently made predictions of the end has not brought the movement to an end (we might instance the Adventist movements of the nineteenth century, still flourishing at the end of the twentieth century).[19] But I have been suggesting that there is a more internal *peripeteia* to early Christian eschatology, a blend of confident expectation and an openness about the nature of the expected events.

This momentum of Christian eschatology is illustrated in the very structure of the Book of Revelation. Since the exegesis of the Church Fathers (e.g. Tyconius, Augustine) it has been recognized that the narrative moves, not in a simple forward progression, but in a series of parallel episodes. After the seven letters in which Christ promises to come to visit

---

[18] Frank Kermode, *The Sense of an Ending* (Oxford: Oxford University Press, 1968), p. 18.
[19] For the 'resilience of the apocalyptic mentality', see Stephen D. O'Leary, *Arguing the Apocalypse. A Theory of Millennial Rhetoric* (New York: Oxford University Press, 1994), pp. 135–42.

his churches (chapters 1–3) and the initial vision of heaven (chapters 4–5) there are various sets of pictures which are presented as if they are in sequence, but which are parallel in significance. They all portray the attaining of victory over the forces of evil and chaos through the endurance (not the avoidance) of persecution, and with the ending of each set of pictures we think we are reaching the final scene of the drama; but the climax is constantly postponed; expectation is falsified.[20] The seventh seal is followed by silence, and then not by the end but by a series of seven trumpets. The seventh trumpet sounds, but the last trump ushers in not the last judgement (surprisingly) but a new scenario of the Dragon and the Beasts (perhaps containing seven unnumbered visions, 12:1–15:4); this episode reaches a climax with the appearing of the Son of Man (14:14–16), but this too is followed by a new series of woes, by the seven bowls. The seventh bowl marks the battle of Armageddon but this is not, after all, the last battle we had expected; it is followed by a three-chapter account of the pride and the fall of Babylon (17–19), a thinly disguised reference to the Roman Empire. With the fall of 'the great whore' there is a shout of triumph and the Word of God rides forth from heaven on a white horse (19:11); but this also is not the expected end, for there follows a one-thousand year reign of Christ and his saints, at the conclusion of which Satan is loosed once more. With the overthrow of Satan and the coming of the New Jerusalem there is a making of new heavens and new earth, and we may presume we have arrived at the end at last. But, as the literary critics Northrop Frye and Jacques Derrida have both pointed out,[21] there is a final surprise: there is an invitation to something further – to 'come' and drink the water of life (22:17).

This continual postponing of the end, a multiple *peripeteia*, has several effects. It creates the impression that this often-repeated shape of events – crisis, judgement and vindication – can be found in every age; there will always be opposition to God and victory through the cross. It heightens the effect of the final climax when it comes, the renewing of heaven and earth (chs. 21–2), and so increases confidence that the purpose of God will

---

[20]   This is stressed by H. H. Rowley, *The Relevance of Apocalyptic*. New and revised edition (London: Lutterworth, 1963), p. 142. Elisabeth Schüssler Fiorenza, *The Book of Revelation – Justice and Judgement* (Philadelphia: Fortress Press, 1985), pp. 171–87, suggests a non-linear shape to the book with interlocking of episodes.

[21]   Jacques Derrida, 'Of an Apocalyptic Tone Newly Adopted in Philosophy' transl. J. Leavey, in H. Coward and T. Foshay (eds), *Derrida and Negative Theology* (Albany: State University of New York Press, 1992), pp. 63–4; Northrop Frye, *The Great Code*, (London: Ark Paperbacks, 1983), p. 137. See above, pp. 18, 35.

reach its fulfilment. But it also undermines any attempt at programming the end, and opens up a plurality of meanings for the 'coming of Christ'. The building and then the puncturing of expectations cuts across the typical apocalyptic move from a coded portrayal of the present situation to actual future prediction; that is, it overlays the shift from the persecution of the present to the promise of the fall of Rome and the coming of the new creation. So it stresses the element of the surprising and the unpredictable about the future, in accord with the cry of the risen Christ, 'Behold! I come like a thief in the night'.

If it is characteristic of Christian eschatology to expect the surprising, to be confident of a future which is not predestined but open, this has implications for the nature of God and human freedom. It raises questions about the omniscience of God, and about God's ability to fulfil divine purposes. But I want to move on to these issues with the help of a literary comparison.

Two Plays of Waiting: Samuel Beckett's Waiting for Godot and Endgame

Alongside these two 'parousia parables' of the New Testament we may place two short plays of Samuel Beckett, which are also about waiting for the end to come, though in these plays the end never does arrive. In Beckett's world, there is no parousia, no eschaton, no end to any story or to any sequence of action, but only the endless successiveness of time and the indeterminacy of place. Even death never comes, though it is often desired. The interest for the theologian in entering this imaginative world is not simply that of finding a contrast with Christian eschatology; as we shall see, there is something about the nature of waiting being expressed here which is important for the development of an eschatology (though Beckett might have been surprised to hear this). Alongside the parables of the waiting servants and the watchful householder we may therefore place Waiting for Godot in which the master never returns to the servants, and Endgame, in which neither the thief nor anyone else breaks in to the house, as there is no one left outside.

I do not intend to suggest that Waiting for Godot can be simply interpreted as Waiting for God (though the association has proved too strong a temptation for the title-makers of a recent British television sitcom, set in a retirement home). The Godot for whom the two tramps Estragon and Vladimir are waiting by the side of the road each evening, and who always

postpones his arrival, may stand for any object of expectation that we desire
to give shape and meaning to the world around us. In the terminology of
the postmodernist critics, Godot is a cipher for any 'grand metanarrative',
including the kind of controlling effect over existence that Heidegger
ascribes to death. In fact, *God* is no more explicitly mentioned in the play
than a *dog*, the dog of Vladimir's song which occupies the mid-point of the
play at the start of the second of the two acts.[22] The song tells the story of
a dog who is killed by a cook, and whose tombstone carries the account of
his death, so that the end of the song leads back into the beginning and is
a never-ending circle. One critic has ingeniously pointed out that Godot
backwards nearly spells 'Tod-dog', so meaning (if *Tod* is read as a German
word) 'death-dog'.[23] However significant this might be, the death of the
dog in the song is continuously postponed as it begins again with the dog
alive and stealing from the kitchen. The circularity of the song sums up the
circularity of the play, which denies any ending (and perhaps also recalls
the state of the tramps – as Estragon at least is beaten each day by someone
or other). Act II ends with the lines:

> VLADIMIR: Well? Shall we go?
> ESTRAGON: Yes, let's go.

and the stage direction reads: *They do not move.* This circles back into
Estragon's opening line to Act I 'Nothing to be done', reflecting a verbal
routine in the play repeated several times wholly or in part:

> ESTRAGON: Let's go.
> VLADIMIR: We can't.
> ESTRAGON: Why not?
> VLADIMIR: We're waiting for Godot.
> ESTRAGON: Ah! (*Pause. Despairing.*) What'll we do, what'll we do!
> VLADIMIR: There's nothing we can do.   (p. 68)

We receive the full impact of this circular repetition at the end of the
play, but Act II has already been repeating in a varied form the action of
Act I, so even as it progresses this is felt to be a play 'in which nothing

[22]   Samuel Beckett, *Waiting for Godot* (London: Faber and Faber, 2nd edn 1965 [1956]),
pp. 57–8.
[23]   James L. Calderwood, 'Ways of waiting in *Waiting for Godot*', *Modern Drama*, 29
(1986), pp. 370–1.

happens – twice'.[24] Moreover, Act I sets up an *anticipation* of future repetition in the two events that occur to break the monotony of waiting. When Pozzo and Lucky appear for the first time in Act I, Pozzo as an imperious, pompous figure driving his slave Lucky along the road before him with a whip and a rope, the tramps greet them as exotic strangers. But when they have left, Vladimir comments 'Haven't they changed?' and insists 'We know them, I tell you. You forget everything' (p. 48). We do not take this completely seriously, as Estragon understands 'haven't they changed?' as a conversational cliché and responds, 'That's the idea, let's make a little conversation', so that we suspect this to be another of the games they play to while away the time. But the idea has been sown in our minds that this scene may have been played out before, despite (or because of) Vladimir's musing, 'Unless they're not the same . . .'. The idea is strengthened when in Act II Estragon has an extremely hazy memory about the arrival of Pozzo and Lucky the day before, and even maintains against the evidence of our eyes, 'I tell you, we weren't here yesterday. Another of your nightmares' (p. 66). When Pozzo and Lucky re-appear they are indeed 'not the same': the formerly tyrannical Pozzo is blind and pitiful, and Lucky is dumb. The effect is either to re-view their appearance in Act I as an anticipation of the repeat in Act II, or as one of a series of repetitions. Since the play circles back on itself, ready to be repeated the next night in the theatre, it is indeed true that the Pozzo and Lucky of Act I have 'changed' since their last manifestation in Act II.

The second 'happening' (or rather, non-happening) in Act I is the coming of the messenger boy at the end to announce that 'Mr. Godot told me to tell you he won't come this evening but surely tomorrow' (p. 50). Vladimir says, 'I've seen you before, haven't I? It wasn't you came yesterday?' while the boy insists that this is his first time of coming (to which Vladimir responds 'words, words'). When the boy re-appears at the end of Act II with the same message (p. 91), Vladimir again claims to recognize him and the boy again denies it; Vladimir attempts to adjust to reality by suggesting that perhaps it was the boy's brother who came the day before, to which the boy responds 'I don't know'. The circularity of the structure of the play, end linking to beginning, Pozzo, Lucky and the boy re-appearing not only in the second Act but in a proleptic way in the first, creates the sense of a total lack of goal or end.

24   Vivian Mercier, 'The Uneventful Event', *Irish Times*, 18 February 1956, p. 6.

However, as Steven Connor perceptively points out,[25] the repetition in Beckett's plays is not only circular; it also takes the form of a 'series repetition' in which an event is repeated 'with decrease'. In this play, Pozzo and Lucky have sadly deteriorated when they re-appear; Pozzo has lost all his bombastic confidence and Lucky cannot think when he cannot speak. This serial kind of repetition might offer a sense of working towards some conclusion, except that Beckett constantly undermines any expectation that the process of 'coming to an end' will ever *reach* the end. This is particularly marked in *Endgame*, which shows both a circular and a series form of repetition, but in which the series form predominates.

Endgame has a one-act structure, so that it cannot use the device of continuous back and forward reflection between the two acts typical of a Beckett play, but the end still circles back to the beginning in a similar way to *Waiting for Godot*. At the close of the play Hamm settles back in his wheelchair and places his handkerchief over his face, calling it affectionately 'old stancher', ready to remove it with the very same words when the play begins again at the next performance. The opening words of his servant Clov underline the failure of the end to come: 'Finished, it's finished, *nearly* finished, it must be nearly finished'.[26] But it is always only *nearly* finished, despite Hamm's despairing cry 'It's time it ended' (p. 12) and his question 'Do you not think this has gone on long enough?' (p. 33). When Hamm asks Clov: 'Have you not had enough?' and Clov replies 'I always had', Hamm concludes gloomily 'then there's no reason for it to change'. The sense that it is always 'nearly finished' is created by series repetition, in which there is a constant diminishing without ever reaching vanishing point. In a repeated routine, Hamm asks for things or inquires about them, only to be told by Clov that there are 'no more': in succession we learn that there are no more bicycle-wheels (p. 15), no more pap (p. 15), no more nature (p. 16), no more tide (41), no more rugs (p. 44), no more pain killers (p. 46) and finally no more coffins (p. 49); Hamm has added, on the way, that there are no more sugar-plums (p. 38) and no more navigators (43):

> CLOV: [*Imploringly.*] Let's stop playing!
> HAMM: Never! [*Pause.*] Put me in my coffin.

[25] Steven Connor, *Samuel Beckett. Repetition, Theory and Text* (Oxford: Oxford University Press, 1988), pp. 118–25.

[26] Samuel Beckett. *Endgame. A Play in One Act followed by Act Without Words* (London: Faber and Faber, 1964 [1958]), p. 12.

CLOV: There are no more coffins.
HAMM: Then let it end!   (p. 49)

But the end is constantly postponed. We are in a universe winding down in increasing entropic disorder, or a creation coming undone; but it is always endgame and never end. The play is set in a bare room, or perhaps a shelter, with two small windows high up in the wall. Confined in this space are Hamm – blind, pitiless, imperious and in a wheelchair – his servant Clov, and his aged parents Nell and Nagg whose legs have been amputated and who are apparently housed in two dustbins. One window looks out onto land, and one onto sea, but all is empty and featureless; looking out, Clov describes the scene successively as 'corpsed, all gone, lead, zero, grey'. While in the Genesis account of creation the sea was separated from the land, here in a reversal of creation land and sea are merged into one greyness so that there is no crack of light between.[27] We recall the watery apocalypse of *King Lear* where Lear out in the storm 'bids the wind blow the earth into the sea'.[28] There has evidently been a cosmic catastrophe, an apocalypse, perhaps a nuclear war, but still the end is deferred.

The end would be to leave this sheltered space, Hamm through death and Clov by leaving his master; but neither have achieved their goal by the end of the play. The series of inner repetitions in the play, described by Beckett himself as 'full of echoes, [where] everything answers itself',[29] charts a movement of deterioration ('we breathe, we change'). But this movement is not like a line intersecting the circle, but rather as if the circle itself were shrinking inwards; it is as if the four walls of the refuge were contracting yet the room never reaching the point of disappearance. Hamm is a compulsive story teller, but he never reaches the end of the interminable tale which, Clov remarks acidly, 'you've been telling yourself all your . . . days' (p. 40).

CLOV: Do you see how it goes on.
HAMM: More or less.
CLOV: Will it not soon be the end?
HAMM: I'm afraid it will.
CLOV: Pah! You'll make up another   (p. 41).

---

[27]   See Charles Lyons, 'Beckett's *Endgame*: An Anti-Myth of Creation', *Modern Drama*, 7 (1964), pp. 204–9.
[28]   Shakespeare, *King Lear*, III.1.15.
[29]   Quoted in Connor, *Samuel Beckett*, p. 122.

In a world where the awaited end never comes, all we can do is tell stories and play games. The tramps in *Waiting for Godot* are self-conscious games players, almost all language games, drawing the attention of the audience to their playing with a nod and a wink:

> VLADIMIR: Charming evening we're having.
> ESTRAGON: Unforgettable.
> VLADIMIR: And it's not over.
> ESTRAGON: Apparently not.
> VLADIMIR: It's only beginning.
> ESTRAGON: It's awful.
> VLADIMIR: Worse than the pantomime.   (pp. 34–5)

They play, for example, the game of abusing each other and making up ('how time flies when one has fun!', p. 76), the game of philosophical dispute ('that wasn't such a bad little canter', p. 65), a game with the boots ('we'll always find something to give us the impression we exist', p. 69), a game with the hats, and the game of pretending to be a tree ('let's do the tree', p. 72).   *Endgame* has a similarly self-conscious theatricality: the reference to chess is struck right at the beginning with Hamm's first words – 'Me to play' – and these are repeated at the beginning of his last speech, which is a soliloquy practised for effect: 'You cried for night; it falls: now cry in darkness. [*Pause*] Nicely put, that.' Calling for Clov and receiving no reply, he does not for one moment think Clov has finally left (though he stands at the door, dressed for travel, unmoving) and responds, 'Since that's the way we're playing it . . . [*he unfolds handkerchief*] let's play it that way . . .'. Hamm and Clov play the games of wheeling Hamm around the room, looking out of the window, talking to the toy dog with three legs – all punctuated by Hamm's constant refrain, 'we're getting on'. Jane Hale draws attention to the fact that, like chess pieces, the characters in *Endgame* have certain fixed rules of movement; Hamm, for example, can sit but not stand, while Clov can stand but not sit.[30]

According to established theory of social game-playing, games are used to create order in a world that appears chaotic and confused.[31] But the games in a Beckett play do not have the effect of producing structure,

[30]   Jane Alison Hale, '*Endgame*: "How are your eyes"', in Steven Connor (ed.), *Waiting for Godot* and *Endgame. Contemporary Critical Essays* (Basingstoke: Macmillan, 1992), pp. 83–4.
[31]   See J. Huizinga, *Homo Ludens. A Study of the Play-Element in Culture* (London: Routledge, 1988).

whatever the hopes of the characters themselves; they are not an indirect way of creating a metanarrative, an over-arching discourse which will configure time (in Ricoeur's phrase) or give an explanation to existence. Rather, the games witness to the futility of waiting for a 'not yet'. When Clov asks, 'do you believe in the life to come?' Hamm replies, 'Mine was always that' (p. 35); since life is always 'to come' but never does, the games leave the impression of being mere time-fillers. In the context of endless time, the games soften the agony of waiting for the great event that never comes ('that passed the time . . . It would have passed in any case . . . Yes, but not so rapidly', *Waiting for Godot*, p. 48). The tramps in *Waiting for Godot* are constantly asking, 'what do we do now?'. Vladimir greets the re-appearance of Pozzo and Lucky with enormous relief that something has happened to help pass the time: 'Reinforcements at last! . . . We were beginning to weaken. Now we're sure to see the evening out' (p. 77). For a moment it seems that in his enthusiasm he will break free of waiting, and make something more of the events of the present:

> We are no longer alone, waiting for the night, waiting for Godot, waiting for . . . waiting. All evening we have struggled, unassisted. Now it's over. It's already tomorrow . . .
> Time flows again already. The sun will set, the moon will rise, and we away . . . from here.

But almost immediately he relapses into the old routine. When Estragon urges 'let's go':

> VLADIMIR: We can't.
> ESTRAGON: Why not?
> VLADIMIR: We're waiting for Godot.

The repetitive structure of these plays, nullifying the sense of goal and direction, and the use of games simply to fill time, together stress the futility of waiting for something to happen. The immediate theological response, comparing these two plays with the two parables of Jesus, might be to draw a simple contrast. The servants and the householder in the *parousia* parables are also waiting for a coming, but the form of the narrative encourages us to expect that this is not a waiting in vain. Christian hope seems completely opposed to the hopelessness of Beckett's world. But as Christian theologians enter the living-space of these plays, they should pay careful attention to the *reasons why* the waiting is so futile. Christian eschatology has a good deal to learn here, since there is a kind of waiting for the future which *is* futile from a theological perspective, and the plays of Beckett can help us in defining it.

The Futility of Waiting: (a) Waiting for the 'Not Yet'

In the first place, we notice that Beckett portrays a waiting for a future event which is merely 'not yet', for something that has 'not yet' happened. Hamm and Clov have not yet reached the end expected, and the future in these plays is merely that which is not yet realized. This mode of waiting, as Beckett depicts it, has an effect on both the present and the future. With regard to the present, any sense of meaning in the here and now is totally undermined. Existence is a mere waiting for something else, and is thus an emptiness that has to be filled up with games.

Hamm in *Endgame* uses the image (borrowed, probably from Sextus Empiricus) of grains of millet pattering down but never making a heap – 'and all life long you wait for that to mount up to a life' (p. 45). He reflects that 'I was never there . . . Absent, always. It all happened without me' (p. 47). The tramps in *Waiting for Godot* similarly want to be reassured of their existence, to find some game that 'will give us the impression we exist' (p. 69); the only message that Vladimir has to send to Godot by way of the boy is 'tell him you saw us', to which he immediately adds, 'You did see us, didn't you?' (p. 52). The second time round, the boy declines to say yes.

Waiting for what is 'not yet' cannot constitute existence, being there (*Dasein*, in Heidegger's terminology). It is a non-activity, to which even death cannot bring any sense of ending; this is why in Beckett's world, death is included (and is perhaps predominant) among the things that do not come. Waiting for a 'not yet' to arrive becomes stultifying and paralysing, taking away any motive for action; a constant refrain in *Waiting for Godot* is 'nothing to be done.'

On the other hand, waiting for what is 'not yet' also undermines the future. A future which is merely 'not yet' is merely 'not the present'. That is, we are thinking of the future only in terms of what we know here and now: it is *not* that, *not* actuality as we are familiar with it. A future like this simply reverses the present, or extends it beyond what we can know, and so we project the future out of the present. In the terminology of the theologian Jürgen Moltmann, this is a future which we can *calculate*, rather than a future we *desire*. It is a future we can predict from computer models, or from the extrapolation of curves on a graph.[32] We know what the future will be like; it is just 'not yet'.

So we notice that Beckett's characters have fixed ideas about what they are waiting for, and when and where to wait. *Godot* is a mysterious figure, but the tramps are convinced that if they have the right time and the right place he ought to show up. Vladimir says:

> What we are doing here, *that* is the question. And we are blessed in this, that we happen to know the answer. Yes, in this immense confusion one thing alone is clear. We are waiting for Godot to come –
> . . . We have kept our appointment, and that's an end to that. We are not saints, but we have kept our appointment. How many people can boast as much? (p. 80)

Estragon replies, 'Billions' and Vladimir responds, 'You may be right'. But with their fixation upon the appointment, they are not open to the surprising and the unexpected.

What can the critic or interpreter build on this exposure of the futility of waiting for what is 'not yet'? Beckett evidently lends himself to a postmodern development, and a good deal of recent criticism has taken this direction. Jeffrey Nealon, for example, finds Beckett's plays to be an attack on modernism with its ideologies and Grand Narratives which claim to interpret the world. The plays are not a modernist lament for the *loss* of meaning in our present age; rather they show an '*excess* of meaning and possibility' which is brought about by the liberating notion of play.[33] In *Waiting for Godot*, suggests Nealon, Beckett shows us that Estragon and Vladimir are 'trapped by their modernist nostalgia for legitimation in Godot'. The legitimation is there already in the language games themselves which decentre the self and break the old structures of thinking. As Lyotard writes in *The Postmodern Condition*, 'language games are the minimum relation required for society to exist'.[34] Utterances form a social bond, but not through any agreed-upon pattern of significance (against theories about the ordering function of games); in the to and fro of communication, participants are 'changing games from one utterance to the next: questions,

---

[32] Jürgen Moltmann, *The Future of Creation*, transl. M. Kohl (London: SCM Press, 1979), pp. 55–6.

[33] Jeffrey Nealon, 'Samuel Beckett and the Postmodern: Language Games, Play and *Waiting for Godot*', in Connor (ed.) *Waiting for Godot* and *Endgame*, p. 51.

[34] Jean-François Lyotard, *The Postmodern Condition*, transl. G. Bennington (Manchester: Manchester University Press, 1984), p. 15.

requests, assertions, and narratives are launched pell–mell into battle'.[35] Estragon and Vladimir already have this conflictual relationship, and the mistake they make – suggests Nealon – is in looking beyond it for some kind of metaphysical system, or transcendental signified: Godot. Instead of waiting in despair for a deferred hope, they could be deferring meaning joyously to the future, celebrating 'the beauty of the way and the goodness of wayfarers' (*Waiting for Godot*, p. 16). Nealon appeals to points in the play where the tramps seem to be on the verge of a 'postmodern breakthrough'. They are, he suggests for example, on the right track when Vladimir says, 'This is getting really insignificant' and Estragon replies, 'Not enough' (p. 68). They nearly achieve the 'deconstructive breakthrough' when towards the end of the play, having been disappointed for the second time by Godot's non-appearance, Estragon toys with the idea of 'dropping' Godot and going 'far away from here'; but Vladimir replies 'he'd punish us', despite claiming at the beginning of the play that they were not 'tied to Godot': 'What an idea!', he had exclaimed,' No question of it. (*Pause*) For the moment' (p. 21). A significant pause indeed. To Nealon's examples, we could add the relief with which Vladimir greets the second arrival of Pozzo and Lucky, and the temporary forgetting of Godot in the game of the moment: 'Now it's over. It's already tomorrow . . . Time flows again already' (p. 77).

It is hard to find quite the same potential for joyous communion in play in the exchanges of Hamm and Clov; when Hamm wonders 'We're not beginning to . . . to . . . mean something? . . . To think perhaps it won't all have been for nothing!' (p. 27), the mood seems different from Vladimir's bouncy 'this is getting really insignificant!'. The stress in *Endgame* is more on the lack of a metanarrative (though this is not, to be sure, regretted) than a positive rejoicing in 'excess of meaning'. Nevertheless, Beckett's plays do lend themselves to this kind of postmodern interpretation; it is one way of building on his portrayal of the futility of waiting for the 'not yet'. But it is not illegitimate for the Christian theologian to bring a different perspective to the plays and to move in a different direction.

Waiting for a Possible Future

Beckett's two tramps are not open to the unexpected. They know what they are waiting for. We feel the waiting to be a futile exercise, and this is

[35]   Ibid., p. 17.

at least partly because they are anticipating merely a 'not yet', only an extension of the present. But here is a remarkable difference with the two parables of waiting that Jesus tells. They emphasize that the time and the manner of what is expected is quite unpredictable. They cannot be booked in a diary, as a projection from the present date. The servants do not know when the master will knock, or when the burglar will break in. There are also open questions, as the use of metaphor makes clear, about what this will be like. The effect is to create a real future and a real present. The servants are engaged in a holy activity and not a hopeless waiting.

The future in Jesus' stories is the future in which the Master comes, which is much more than a 'not yet'. It is a commonplace of scholarly commentary on the Parables of the Kingdom, among which are numbered our two parables of waiting, to say that in their Gospel redactions they express a tension between an 'already' and a 'not yet'. Much exegesis proceeds along the line that the Kingdom has 'already' broken in with the ministry of Jesus in which the poor are given good news and the sick are healed, but the Kingdom has 'not yet' come in its fulness.[36] While this contrast expresses a truth, Moltmann rightly objects that it tends to transpose eschatology into time, in which history and the last things lie along the same temporal line, and the end is included in a series among other events. Rather, if eschatology is about the transforming of creation rather than merely interrupting it, then God's future is not just *futurum*, but *adventus*; it is defined by the coming of God, so that we can say 'God's being is in coming'.[37] This is the desirable rather than the predictable future.

Eberhard Jüngel, as we have already seen, puts this in terms of a contrast between actuality and possibility.[38] His point is that eschatology is about more than a 'not yet'; it is about *possibility*, and there is an 'ontological priority' of possibility over actuality. What we expect from God is possibility, and God has revealed what is possible in the resurrection of Jesus from the dead. The possibilities for new creation in God challenge the actual tendencies of the present, or its potentials; they break in from

---

[36] Oscar Cullmann, *Christ and Time*, 3rd edn, transl. F. V. Filson (London: SCM Press, 1962), pp. 83–90; cf. W.G. Kümmel, *Promise and Fulfilment. The Eschatological Message of Jesus*, transl. D. Barton (London: SCM Press, 1961), pp. 146–55; J. Jeremias, *The Parables of Jesus*, revised edn, transl. S. H. Hooke (London: SCM Press, 1963), pp. 151–60.

[37] Jürgen Moltmann, *The Coming of God*, transl. M. Kohl (London: SCM Press, 1996), pp. 12–12, 23.

[38] See above, pp. 48–9.

the future. If we think of possibility as mere *potential*, we are really simply subordinating it to actuality again, for the potential is the 'not yet' made actual. We look forward not to what is merely 'not yet' actual, but to what God makes possible.

We are not characters in a Beckett play waiting for what is not yet to happen. We are players in God's drama, expecting new possibilities to break in from God's future. In the final redaction of the 'parables of waiting' this refers to the eschaton, the last Day, but we may take the hint from their earlier use that there are many comings in the course of history, disturbing the present, and making us see that what we thought was our potential is not the whole story. We expect the coming of the Master, yet we are ready for the unexpected too.

But in what sense then can we think of the possibilities that God opens to created beings and which constitute the desirable future?[39] In the first place, we may be sure that God in God's own self from all eternity envisages possibilities for the world to which we are blind. This is a classical view, but I believe we should take issue with one aspect of it. Aquinas maintained that all possibilities that are in God must be actualized at once; this is what is meant by naming God as 'pure act' (*actus purus*). Aquinas needed to say this because he thought there could be no change in God, no moving *from* possibility to actuality as there is with us. Such a movement would mean a change from one state of being to another.[40] But the consequence of the view of God as *actus purus* is that eternity must be conceived as simultaneity (past, present and future in one instant flash), and we have seen the problems with this in the previous chapter. The 'process' thinkers have made the significant contribution of *distinguishing* between God's grasp of possibilities and actualities:

> He is the Whole in every categorial sense, all actuality in one individual actuality, and all possibility in one individual potentiality. This relatively simple idea was apparently too complex for most of our ancestors to hit upon.[41]

[39]   In what follows I draw on chapter IV of my earlier book, *The Creative Suffering of God* (Oxford: Clarendon Press, 1988), though placing the concepts there in a new context.

[40]   Aquinas, *Summa Theologiae*, 1a.2.3; 1a.3.1; cf. 1a.9.1–2.

[41]   Charles Hartshorne, *A Natural Theology for our Time* (La Salle, Illinois: Open Court, 1967), pp. 20–21.

If the possibilities in God are inexhaustible then they cannot all be actualized anyway, because some will be alternatives, excluding each other. So with A. N. Whitehead we may affirm that God has the freedom to choose among the myriad possibilities that God envisions within God's own self, offering aims from among them to be to be actualized in the world.[42]

But we should surely go on to add a second understanding of possibility in God, that God can also conceive *new possibilities* from the divine imagination as the creative work proceeds. As Keith Ward suggests, this can be conceived as a kind of divine desire, in which God continually aims to 'realize new and imaginative forms of beauty and intellectual complexity', limited only by 'God's character as wise, good and loving'.[43] Such freedom in God means that the end of all things must have the kind of openness that our two gospel parables point us towards. The end will have a surprising quality to it because, as one Old Testament scholar puts it, 'God fulfils his promises in unexpected ways'.[44] This accords with the Hebrew story of the self-revelation of God to Moses, in which 'I am what (or who) I am' (Exodus 3:14) is not a claim to unchanging being but carries the dynamic sense that 'I will be what I will be', or 'I am there for you, wherever it may be'.[45] Similarly, the Old Testament prophets present the oracles of God as relating to the future not in the mode of exact prediction, but as promise. The later prophets claim that the words of earlier prophets have been fulfilled in ways that their predecessors never envisaged or intended, and this reuse of earlier oracles is especially marked in apocalyptic. The writers of Daniel, for example, pick up the promise of God through Jeremiah that the dominion of Babylon would only last for seventy years, and interpret this as meaning seven groups of seventy (490 years) which brings readers to their own day; now, they believe, the national degradation which had continued despite their return from exile long ago would finally come to an end with a new act of glorification by

---

[42]   A. N. Whitehead, *Process and Reality* (New York: Macmillan, 1929, repr. 1938), pp. 69–73.

[43]   Keith Ward, *Religion and Creation* (Oxford: Clarendon Press, 1996), pp. 185–6, *Rational Theology and the Creativity of God* (Oxford: Blackwell, 1982), p. 154.

[44]   Walther Zimmerli, 'Promise and Fulfilment', in C. Westermann (ed.), *Essays on Old Testament Interpretation*, transl. J. L. Mays (London: SCM Press, 1963), p. 107.

[45]   See Brevard Childs, *Exodus: Introduction and Commentary* (London: SCM Press, 1974), pp. 65–70.

God.[46] The picture of God this assumes is not one who has a blueprint for the future, but one whose promises are elastic enough to be adapted.

In making promise rather than prediction, God thus leaves room for the new and the yet unknown, but we must ask whether this space *only* comes from the possibilities in God's own creativity. To take the love of God seriously implies that God allows those who are loved to make a contribution to the mutual relationship, and so to share in his creative project. As soon as love is understood to be more than a 'doing good' to the other, and to involve mutuality and passions, space must be made for genuine human response to the purpose of God. The reality of human freedom also points, of course, in the same direction. So we may envisage a third kind of possibility which constitutes the future: new possibilities are not only conceived by God in the divine mind, but emerge from the *interaction between the creator and the created.* This latter insight is stressed by the process thinker Charles Hartshorne, who protests against his mentor Whitehead that all possibilities cannot envisaged eternally (as 'eternal objects' in the Primordial Nature of God); unless many are emergent from the process we have no real freedom.[47]

Appealing to the analogy of an artist, Hartshorne thus denies that the exact colours used by an artist have to be stored eternally in God's mind: '. . . the blue, the red, why may these not emerge for the first time in some individual's experience?'[48] A particular tinge of pigment is not 'something haunting reality from all eternity', just begging to be actualized somewhere. Hartshorne thus proposes that the 'abstract essence' of God can be conceived as the unchanging ground of all possibility, like someone's character that endures through all changes of experience; out of this 'power of possibility' God sets boundaries and limits for *particular* possibilities to come to birth in the world and to be actualized in due time. These particulars are in turn received into the contingent nature of God's being, into God's 'concrete states of experience', to be harmonized there and to contribute to God's own richness of being. Like any person, ahead of time 'the painter knows roughly what he can do. But that he can do just this which he subsequently does, not even deity can know until it is done . . .'[49]

---

[46]   Daniel 9:24–7; cf. Jer. 25:11ff., 29:10. See Norman Porteous, *Daniel. A Commentary* (London: SCM Press, 1965), pp. 133–41.

[47]   Charles Hartshorne, *Creative Synthesis and Philosophic Method* (London: SCM Press, 1970), p. 58.

[48]   Ibid., p. 63; cf. Hartshorne, *Man's Vision of God and the Logic of Theism* (Hamden: Archon Books, repr. 1964), pp. 247–8.

[49]   Hartshorne, *Creative Synthesis*, p. 65.

Extending Harthorne's analogy, we can imagine the painter beginning a work with a vision of what he or she wants to portray, but then finding that the materials themselves – the texture of the canvas, the swirling density of the oils, the impact made by the brush-strokes, the way that colour and shape actually look when laid on a flat surface rather than simply conceived in abstract – all these make their own contribution. So the potter has to take account of the pliancy of the clay, the carpenter the grain of the wood, the sculptor the lines of resistance in the marble. Adapting a phrase from W.H. Vanstone, we may say that 'the activity of creating includes the passivity of waiting – of waiting upon one's work-manship to see what emerges from it'.[50] It is not only the creatures who wait for the end, but God.

But this does not mean that we have to follow Hartshorne in attributing to God's eternal vision only a very general grasp of possibilities. While we may agree that God cannot envisage *all* the possibilities that will emerge from partnership with the creation, I have been arguing that God must have the creative freedom to envisage *some* particular possibilities, and unless God can do so the divine activity in the world will be severely limited. I commend the process insight that God acts by offering persuasion rather than coercion, and that this influence has to be met by cooperative response from created beings before God's aims can be actualized; but unless God is able to offer *particular* aims and possibilities the initiative from God's side will be severely restricted. Without this initiative, God can offer no guidance, inspiration, challenge and consolation in the midst of the actual experiences of life, joyful and painful. In the terms of Old Testament faith, when Yahweh's unfaithful people have broken the covenant he would have no means of offering a specific new beginning,[51] but would only be able to present 'more of the same'.

This process becomes even clearer when we move from the analogy of the artist to a more relational analogy such as that of the theatre director. Here Timothy Gorringe, in his account of divine providence, has made effective use of the experience of the director Peter Brook as recorded in his book *The Open Space*.[52] Gorringe first draws from Brook the perception

---

[50]   William H. Vanstone, *Love's Endeavour, Love's Expense* (London: Darton, Longman and Todd, 1977), p. 33, also, *The Stature of Waiting* (London: Darton, Longman and Todd, 1982), pp. 89–94.

[51]   See e.g. Hosea 2:14–20; Isa. 43:16–20.

[52]   Peter Brook, *The Open Space* (Harmondsworth: Penguin, 1972); Timothy J. Gorringe, *God's Theatre. A Theology of Providence* (London: SCM Press, 1991), pp. 77–82.

that if the drama was not to be 'deadly theatre', the director had to allow the actors to contribute, as the rehearsals went on, to his vision of the play; he remarks that there was a particular rhythm to be found and a particular actor to find it, and this demanded that the actors should find their own inner resources. But second, Gorringe notes Brook's experience that the director could not simply stand back from the play. The idea that a company or actor can do without leadership he describes as a 'wretched fallacy'. Without manipulation, in mutual exploration between director and actor, 'the director must look for where the actor is messing up his own right urges – and here he must help the actor to see and overcome his own obstacles. All this is a dialogue and a dance between director and player'.[53]

Gorringe, of course, draws the implications for God as theatre director, suggesting that the dialogue between director and player is prayer. In terms of our own discussion about the nature of possibility, this also offers an illuminating perspective on the disagreement between Ricoeur, Jüngel and Moltmann that we have noted in earlier chapters, where Ricoeur alone of the three detects some basis for *all* possibilities in human life itself.[54] If he were using this analogy, Jüngel would tell us that the human drama needs the kind of possibility that springs *entirely* from the mind of the Theatre Director, which is more than a potential in the actor, more than a mere 'not yet'. There can be no true conclusion for the play or the dance unless there is this kind of possibility that strikes from beyond, from the God of the future. Yet, following the image of the theatre suggests that this transcendent possibility should interact with the potential that Ricoeur observes, the possibility that lies in the resources of the actor, or in Brook's words in the 'particular rhythm' that belongs to 'a particular actor'.[55]

I suggest that these two kinds of possibility need not remain yoked as sheer paradox, though there will always be a mystery of cocreativity in the divine–human drama. Ricoeur points out (in contrast to Northrop Frye) that the possible world that emerges from human imagination is not already present as a fixed archetype in the human spirit; it *emerges* newly from the fecundity of possibility itself in human life. Focusing on the conditions of this emergence, we may affirm with Jüngel and Moltmann that everything

[53]   Cited in Gorringe, *God's Theatre*, p. 80.
[54]   See above, pp. 45–9, 72–5.
[55]   Hans Urs Von Balthasar suggests something similar: *Theo-Drama. Theological Dramatic Theory. Prolegomena*, transl. G. Harrison (San Francisco: Ignatius Press, 1988), pp. 252–7.

depends on the God of possibility. In the first place this means that the new possibilities of God's future have a power which works back into the present, as hope for the new creation sets the old creation in a new light. The word of promise uttered in the resurrection of Jesus seizes the imagination and enables it to envisage the future in new ways, leading to actions of resistance and renewal which create 'anticipations' of the Kingdom here and now. The forming of these anticipations of peace and justice in the midst of history has increasingly been the theme of Jürgen Moltmann's recent eschatology, though based on hints in his earlier *Theology of Hope*.[56] So, 'the future-made-present creates new conditions for possibilities in history'.[57] But, considering the nature of 'possibility' as we have explored it, we should also discern another meaning for human dependence on divine possibility.

What the word of promise quickens is surely an already existing potential of the imagination for picturing alternative visions of the future. While the promise exceeds what is merely 'not yet' it also transforms it. We need not, however, presume that the dreaming of these 'real-possibles' (Bloch) is a purely human function. The basic forward orientation of the human spirit, its overflowing quality of 'not yet', the 'particular rhythm' of the human actors, need not be seen as a purely autonomous state; this itself may be seen as the result of being open to a continuous presence of God in creation, so that persons are what they are because (as Karl Rahner puts it)[58] they are the recipients of God's self-gift. The key term in the 'not yet' of human life would thus be not 'autonomy', but the 'theonomy' coined by Paul Tillich.[59] In the following chapters we shall be exploring a trinitarian model for thinking of this continual engagement of God with the world. God, we can say, is ceaselessly calling out possibilities from *within* history and from *within* the present, that interact with the surprising possibilities God holds for the future, and which weave their own rhythm into the dance.

This vision of cocreativity between divine persuasion and human response, seeing particular possibilities *for God* emerging from the world,

56 Jürgen Moltmann, *The Spirit of Life. A Universal Affirmation*, transl. M. Kohl (London: SCM Press, 1992), pp. 153–5; *The Coming of God*, pp. 22–3; cf. *Theology of Hope*, transl. J. Leitch (London: SCM Press, 1967), pp. 34–5.

57 Moltmann, *The Coming of God*, p. 22.

58 Karl Rahner, *Foundations of Christian Faith*, transl. W. Dych (London: Darton, Longman and Todd, 1978), pp. 127–33.

59 Paul Tillich, *Systematic Theology* (Welwyn: James Nisbet & Co., 1968), vol. 1, pp. 92–5.

will be contested strongly by a more classical Christian theism. According, for example, to a neo-Thomist like E. L. Mascall, the glory we give to God augments only his 'accidental' glory and not his 'essential' glory. We cannot make the divine Being richer in any way, and so the world is strictly 'useless' to God.[60] R. E. Creel makes the similar distinction that God's creatures can enrich God's being 'extensively' but not 'intensively'; that is, he suggests that our response to God can affect the 'texture' or 'flavour' of the divine life, but not the depth of its bliss or satisfaction.[61] The issue in the end, I believe, is not simply the philosophical one of distinguishing between possibility and actuality in God. It is a conviction about the nature of God's project in creation. Is it simply God's purpose to create a world out of a generous desire to do good to someone (i.e. anyone), or is it also God's desire to be satisfied by fellowship with personal beings who can, in love, make their own contribution to the relationship?

The former view appeals to the belief that the world must have its explanation in a 'necessary being' who is totally self-sufficient. The latter (which I adopt) distinguishes both between self-existence and self-sufficiency, and between perfection and completion. That is, a God who depends upon nothing outside God's own self for existence (is self-existent, having *aseity*) may still, out of pure free will, become dependent upon others for enrichment of the divine life. The Creator who is perfect in the sense of having no deficiency at any stage of relationship with creation, may still *choose* to be in need and to be completed by those who are created.[62] This appeal to the freedom of God, which is an appeal to the richness of possibilities in God, takes issue with process thought as well as classical theism, since in the process metaphysic God has no choice about dependence upon the world; there it is a matter of the 'creative advance', while I am advocating the grounding of inter-dependence within God's primal will.

We expect an end which is open, a coming of Christ to his glory which is certain and yet surprising. This challenges the view of a monarchial God whose power is shown in determining the lives of creatures. It suggests a

[60]   E. L. Mascall, *He Who Is. A Study in Traditional Theism* (London: Longmans, Green & Co., 1945, repr. 1958), p. 110ff.

[61]   Richard E. Creel, *Divine Impassibility* (Cambridge: Cambridge University Press, 1986), pp. 145–6.

[62]   See Fiddes, *The Creative Suffering of God*, pp. 63–70. Vincent Brümmer, *The Model of Love* (Cambridge: Cambridge University Press, 1993), p. 237, commends and adopts my approach; Keith Ward, in *Religion and Creation*, pp. 177–9 finds problems with it.

vulnerable God, whose power is shown in loving persuasion and not coercion. But then, waiting would surely be a futile exercise if the future had been completely fixed in advance by an 'unmoving' God. In this case, why bother to wait or watch at all? There is then, a second reason why a life spent in waiting can be experienced as empty and meaningless, and this also is portrayed in Beckett's plays. While waiting is felt to be futile if the future is simply the 'not yet', it also feels futile if the future is thought to be programmed.

The Futility of Waiting: (b) A Programmed Future

'Godot' is probably not meant to be God. But Beckett does present a God-like figure on the stage – at least a God of traditional omnipotence. The tramps have just about exhausted their repertoire of games in Act I when something happens on the dusty road. Pozzo arrives, whom they at first mistake for Godot. He is an imperious, dominating figure, half circus manager and half theatrical impressario. Cracking a whip, he drives his servant Lucky in front of him on a rope, a shambling figure weighted down with all Pozzo's baggage – cases, stool, coat and a picnic basket.

Pozzo has all the pretensions of the God of traditional metaphysics. He expects the others to know his name, and claims the open road as 'my land'. He greets them mockingly as 'Of the same species as myself . . . Made in God's image!', adding 'I cannot go for long without the society of my likes even when the likeness is an imperfect one' (pp. 23–4). He is the creator-impressario, a theatre director who absolutely controls his actors, and in particular the hapless Lucky whom he jerks around on his rope.

Religion, which has often pictured God as a despot like this, has also vainly tried to maintain that his human servants are somehow free. This is now satirized, as Pozzo complains of being misused by his servant, and the others join in belabouring Lucky for his supposed sins: 'How dare you! It's abominable! Such a good master! Crucify him like that! . . .' (p. 34) When Estragon finally asks why Lucky never puts any of the bags down on the ground, though it is obviously an agonizing effort to hold them, Pozzo replies:

> Why he doesn't make himself comfortable? Let's try and get it clear. Has he not the right to? Certainly he has. It follows that he doesn't want to. There's reasoning for you. And why doesn't he want to? . . .
> He wants to impress me, so that I'll keep him. (p. 31)

Pozzo's name probably refers to the omnipotence of God, as Pozzo sounds like the Latin verb *posse*, to be able, or to have the power to do something. Pozzo has all the power, all the ability, and he exploits it mercilessly. Finally Lucky, who has been silent all the while, is commanded to 'think' and gives vent to a ranting speech which sounds full of nonsense and yet is a long criticism of the traditional God of all power:

> Given the existence as uttered forth in the public works of Puncher and Wattmann of a personal God quaquaquaqua with white beard quaquaquaqua outside time without extension who from the heights of divine apathia divine athambia divine aphasia loves us dearly with some exceptions for reasons unknown but time will tell and suffers like the divine Miranda with those who for reasons unknown but time will tell are plunged in torment plunged in fire . . . it is established what many deny that . . . man in Possy of Testew and Cunard that man in Essy that man in short that man in brief in spite of the strides of alimentation and defecation is seen to waste and pine waste and pine . . . (p. 43)

This 'think', as Jeffrey Nealon points out, 'is directed against all Grand Narratives of Western metaphysics'.[63] Nealon suggests that the speech is deconstructive in exposing the limits of all language and thought by its 'trans-reasonable content'; the tramps, he judges, are themselves on the verge of a Lucky-like postmodern breakthrough but they cannot think beyond the limits of the 'Godot' meta-system. However, the discourse is in fact quite coherent in its riddling way.

Although human beings, according to Lucky are 'Essy-in-Possy' or *esse in posse* – that is, beings with potential – in the face of an impassible and timeless God they waste and pine, they 'shrink and dwindle'; they can have no 'possy', no possibilities. They simply decline. Nor does it help to suggest that, like Miranda in *The Tempest* weeping for the seafarers (supposedly) drowned by her father Prospero, Christ sympathizes with human suffering which God his Father has caused 'for reasons unknown'. In this case all eschatology must be reduced to the vain and vague hope of 'but time will tell'. The tramps throw themselves on Lucky in horror and try to stop him speaking (by taking his hat off), as they see themselves only too well as those who waste and pine, who have no *posse*, no future.

Waiting is futile if there is a Pozzo-God around. But Beckett in fact does not think there is, though many do. In Act II Pozzo appears again, sadly changed. He is a wreck of his former self, blind, no longer omniscient

63   Nealon, 'Samuel Beckett and the Postmodern', p. 48.

(he used to have 'wonderful, wonderful, sight'). Lucky is dumb. The God of traditional metaphysics is dead to the modern mind. He may have power, but he has no real possibilities. But instead of a Pozzo leading his servants on a rope, I have been advocating the concept of a God who always makes new possibilities, working humbly in partnership with us. Such a God makes waiting worthwhile, since such a God has a real future. But what does this mean for the traditional attributes of omniscience and omnipotence? Can God *know everything* if the end is not totally fixed in advance? Can God be omniscient if the end is not determined, but is open both to God's creative freedom and to the results of human response? Clearly, in this case, God cannot know the future – at least in any detail. But does this mean that God is the pathetic Pozzo-God of Act II, of whom it can be said, 'the blind have no notion of time' (p. 86)?

It does not mean, I suggest, that we have to abandon the attribute of omniscience. Rather, we should follow a good number of modern philosophers of religion (including H. P. Owen, Richard Swinburne and Keith Ward) in defining omniscience in the sense that 'God knows everything there is to be known'.[64] God knows all the actualities and all the possibilities that there are, but does not know possibility *as* actuality until it is actualized in the world. God cannot know the details of the future because these events have not yet come into being through God's own creativity and the cocreative response of the world; they are just not there *to be known*, and so not knowing them cannot limit divine omniscience.

It is not merely, as some process thinkers suggest,[65] that God knows all possibilities but does not know *which* of them are going to be actualized. This says both too much and too little at the same time. It says too much, because there are some possibilities (as I have suggested above) which God cannot know since they have not yet been conceived, whether by the Creator or by the creatures. As the cocreative project of God and the world progresses, some possibilities have not yet emerged; when they have,

---

[64] See, for similar accounts but with some differences, H. P. Owen, *Concepts of Deity* (London: Macmillan, 1971), pp. 30–33; Richard Swinburne, *The Coherence of Theism* (Oxford: Clarendon Press, 1977), pp. 175–8, cf. Swinburne, *The Christian God* (Oxford: Clarendon Press, 1994), pp. 130–4; Ward, *Religion and Creation*, pp. 275–7.

[65] That is, those essentially following Whitehead rather than his pupil Hartshorne; for an attempt to apply this vision of God's omniscience to the postmodern challenge to theism, see David R. Griffin, 'Postmodern Theology and A/theology', in David R. Griffin, William A. Beardslee, Joe Holland, *Varieties of Postmodern Theology* (Albany: SUNY Press, 1989), pp. 40–51.

and before they are actualized, God will know them as the One who is related to everything that exists.

But the view that 'God does not know which possibilities are going to be actualized' also says too little. It presents God as working 'blind' like Beckett's Pozzo, having no idea what tomorrow will bring. God must know, *in general outline*, that the possibility for new creation will be actualized. As I have argued elsewhere, we can conceive of God as knowing the boundaries of all possibilities, while not knowing particular possibilities until they emerge.[66] So God knows the future in a way that we do not. God knows the general outline of possibilities for the universe, as we do not; God is related to all reality, as we are not; God knows the particular possibilities that are present within the world *here and now* as we know them not; and most of all, God knows the power of divine persuasive love to bring about godly purposes. So God, who freely chooses to walk the path of time, will walk it in a different way from us, with an infinitely greater hope and certainty, though there will still be something open about the future, even for God.

We should, then, be a little cautious in speaking about creation as a 'risk' for God. This is often put in a romantic way, without considering the implications. W. H. Vanstone, for example, proposes that God's love must involve being prepared for a *total* tragedy, for the possible outcome that '*all* has been given in vain.'[67] But as we consider the hope of God for the future, we can only think of God's embarking upon creation with what might be called 'a limited risk' rather than a 'total risk'. The end is in one sense certain, but the route to the end, and thus the character of the end, has an openness about it that stems from human freedom. The goal of God is the making of personalities in relationship with others and with God's own self, and this is not a 'product' that can be made on an assembly line, as if there were a standard model of a personality. When we are concerned with persons, the route to the end shapes the content of the end; the road is marked by decisions about acts and values which make us what we are and shall be. I want to consider the consequences of this for a view of final salvation in the next chapter, but here I want to urge the nature of God's vision of the end – as both certain in fact and open in content. There is room then for tragedy as well as triumph in God's victory over evil and suffering.

If love is in fact the strongest power in the universe, on which Christian believers take a wager, then a God who works through persuasive love

[66]   Fiddes, *The Creative Suffering of God*, pp. 97–8.
[67]   Vanstone, *Love's Endeavour, Love's Expense*, p. 77.

must succeed in bringing about a new creation with reconciliation at its heart. Yet what is reconciled may be less than it might have been. While persons will not lack anything in their beatific vision of God, the God who feels and values the worth of every life will also (as Hartshorne puts it), be open 'to the tragedy of unfulfilled desire'.[68] We can suggest that God may see, as finite persons will not, that some possibilities have not been actualized, some potentials have not been fulfilled. The possible tragedy is not that evil will be taken eternally into the being of God, but that there will be an absence of some good that might have been produced. God's suffering is thus more than that of the 'divine Miranda' in Lucky's speech; God is passible in being affected by the *way* that possibilities are actualized in the world, and by the *failure* to actualize them.

Christian hope is to expect the unexpected. This is the mood of the two Lukan parables; *peripeteia* is at the heart of the Christian story, a coming of the expected end in a quite unexpected way. But the *peripeteia* is thorough-going; it makes the end what it is, an endgame that shapes the whole game. Beckett, we notice, also relies upon an interruption of expectations as a playwright. As Kermode suggests, he depends upon an awareness in his audience of the Christian story of the ordering of creation and history in order to disturb us with a vision of the world which is in perpetual transition 'from one condition of misery to another' with no end in sight; the signs of order and form are there, but 'they are resources not to be believed in, cheques which will bounce'.[69]

In general, the major reversal of expectation is the failure of the end to come. In particular, within each of the two plays we have been considering, there is a moment that forbids closure. Two powerful symbols appear, one in each play. In *Waiting for Godot* there is the tree, the bare tree on which the tramps threaten to hang themselves, and which bursts into a moderate four or five leaves overnight. In *Endgame* there is the boy who suddenly appears in view of the window, sitting on a rock when we had thought the landscape was lifeless ('corpsed, all gone'). In the original French version the boy is related to the story of the resurrection of Jesus, as the stone he sits on is compared to the one rolled away from the tomb. The function of these two symbols is mainly to prevent closure, as the presence of leaves on the tree make us uncertain about time and place, and uncertainty about the future of the boy leaves any end to Hamm's story

---

[68]   Hartshorne, *Man's Vision of God*, p. 294; see my *The Creative Suffering of God*, pp. 105–6.
[69]   Kermode, *The Sense of an Ending*, p. 115.

open: 'if he exists he'll die there or come here' (p. 50). Perhaps this is why Hamm forbids Clov to kill the boy, although Clov identifies him as a 'potential procreator', and Hamm has previously insisted that even a flea should be killed, in case 'humanity might start from there all over again!' (p. 27).

The symbols of tree and boy are not obvious signs of hope. They resist ending, and so they contribute to Beckett's general project of upsetting any expectation for the final consummation of all things. But at the same time, by resisting closure they cannot avoid opening possibility; they cannot be tamed, bursting out of their confines, giving a hint of a movement towards a goal. The Christian story itself holds to an end which is both certain and open, a fulfilment resisting closure, and so (I dare to suggest) is more radical than Becket in its disturbing of expectations in the midst of expectancy.

Chapter Seven

THE ARROW OF TIME

The One-way Flight of the Arrow

The image of time as an arrow has long been used to express the remorseless nature of time's onward movement. In our personal span of life, once the arrow has been loosed from the bow-string at birth it flies point forward until it hits the target of death; as John Wesley confesses, 'I am a Creature of a Day, passing thro' Life, as an Arrow thro' the Air'.[1] The world-weary narrator of Martin Amis's novel, *London Fields*, reflects that 'death is packed with information. At last you find out the direction time's taking. Time's arrow'.[2] The metaphor thus depicts what seems to be the irreversible and unidirectional quality of time. On the scale of history, the Judaeo-Christian tradition has insisted on this linear view of time, with the arrow flying from creation to the Last Judgement.

More recently the metaphor has been used in scientific discussion, and especially in mechanics, to describe the phenomenon that many physical processes seem to have an inbuilt unidirectionality. There is, notably, the one-way flow of heat from hot to cold. Scientists are intrigued and puzzled by several riddles which are connected with this phenomenon, and we shall have occasion to refer to them as this chapter proceeds. An immediate mystery concerns the very origin of this unidirectionality, since Newton's concept of a flow of 'absolute time' has now been discounted, and the basic laws of physics seem to be symmetric in time. The direction of the arrow is exemplified by the Second Law of Thermodynamics, namely that entropy, or the degree of disorder within a closed system, always tends to increase. This implies that the whole cosmos is hitched to a universal

[1] John Wesley, *Collected Sermons*, Vol. I (London: 1769), Preface, p. vi.
[2] Martin Amis, *London Fields* (London: Penguin Books, 1990), p. 432.

principle of degeneration, running downhill towards chaos. In line with the movement of heat from hot to cold states, one possible destination for a universe locked on the path of increasing entropy would be 'heat death'; all the nuclear fuel of the hot stars would be used up and there would be a low-temperature equilibrium, a freeze beyond the ice age in which no present organic life could exist.

Not only individual human life, but the whole universe, appears to be on target for death. Yet the relation between the 'arrow of time' and the Second Law of Thermodynamics is ambivalent; increasing entropy is an important example of the arrow's directionality, but its *source* cannot be found there, as in some states a gas can be shown to be likely to return to its initial state of entropy over long periods of time.[3] Scientists are inclined to say, cautiously, that the mysterious origin of time's arrow can be traced in some way to the large-scale behaviour of the cosmos, in its expansion from the point of a 'Big Bang' of released energy; in some way the arrow is 'intimately connected with the issue of the origin and possible end of the universe'.[4]

In referring to the 'arrow' of time in scientific discourse, I am using the term in the neutral sense of an indicator of the *direction* of time. As an arrow on a weather vane indicates the direction of the wind, so the 'arrow' of time indicates the direction of flow of such processes as heat transfer. As I have already mentioned in my earlier discussion of 'simultaneity', according to relativity theory where space-time is a four-dimensional 'block', time itself does not literally 'flow' and so the arrow is not a moving point. Past, present and future are laid out all at once as if on a cosmic landscape. I have also already noted, however, that quantum theory suggests that this account of time is only one aspect of the story,[5] and that we ought not to be dogmatic in asserting that time does not *actually* flow; to this I intend to return towards the end of this chapter. Our subjective experience of time is certainly that time passes and the arrow moves from one moment to another towards death.

Literature shows a desire to escape this remorseless movement of time's

---

[3]   This was shown as early as the last century by the experiments of Henri Poincaré: see Paul Davies, *About Time* (London: Viking, 1995), pp. 37–8.

[4]   Davies, *About Time*, p. 282. Stephen Hawking, for example, makes this connection in *A Brief History of Time* (London: Bantam Press, 1988), pp. 145–53.

[5]   The physicist William Unruh concludes that 'the exact nature of time, of dynamics and change, still has to be elucidated': 'Time, Gravity and Quantum Mechanics' in Steven Savitt (ed.), *Time's Arrows Today. Recent Physical and Philosophical Work on the Direction of Time* (Cambridge: Cambridge University Press, 1995), pp. 23–65.

arrow. Novelists in particular have experimented with other approaches to time than the strictly linear. We have already explored the 'montage' or 'overlaying' technique, akin to the cinematic 'cutting' of film, which is characteristic of the novels of Virginia Woolf, and which aspires towards a simultaneity of an 'eternal moment'. Another device is that of *circularity* of structure and theme, demonstrated by such novels as James Joyce's *Finnegans Wake* and Flann O'Brien's *The Third Policeman*. There is a kind of *reversal* associated with circularity, as the end of the cycle returns to the beginning and events are relived, but a more strict reversal in the form of living backwards has also been tried, for example in the popular science fiction television series *Red Dwarf*,[6] and in the more serious *Time's Arrow* by Martin Amis.

In this chapter I shall be considering the use of circularity and reversal in these and other novels, and bringing them into dialogue with theological arguments about eschatology. Significantly for this dialogue, the motivation for the development of these novelistic devices has not simply been a frustration with the arrow of time and a desire to escape the threat of death through alternative visions. Recently it has been driven by a postmodern concern to deconstruct the patterns of history; in reaction against the 'novel of realism' which largely accepted the linear conventions of history-writing, novelists have adopted structures which challenge any sense of direction in history and which undermine patterns of cause and effect. As Alison Lee proposes in her study of realism and the postmodern novel,[7] some writers wish to show that all meaning in history is imposed through the use of language, that history is nothing other than construct and discourse. Graham Swift, for instance, has his narrator in *Waterland* (a history teacher) tell us that he began his historical enquiries in search of an 'Explanation', but forty years later concluded 'that history is a yarn'; circularity is one of the techniques the novel itself uses to rub in the lesson that history could yield up no 'Grand Narrative', no 'filler of vaccuums', and no 'dispeller of fears of the dark'.[8]

Ironically, while the intention of circularity and reversal in the novel may be to disperse meaning by refusing to provide an ending, the result may in fact be to emphasize closure. Unless handled carefully, there is little

---

[6]   Episode 'Backwards', screened BBC2, 14 November 1989; written by Rob Grant and Doug Naylor. Cf. Grant Naylor, *Better than Life*, Part Four, in *Red Dwarf Omnibus* (Harmondsworth: Penguin Books, 1992), pp. 542–553.

[7]   Alison Lee, *Realism and Power* (London: Routledge, 1990), pp. 24–8.

[8]   Graham Swift, *Waterland* (London:Pan/Picador, 1984), p. 53.

more closed than a circle. Theological versions of circularity and reversal
may fall into the same trap, as they attempt to show the transfiguration of
time's arrow in eternity, and to this we should be alert in our aim to find
a balance between closure and openness in Christian eschatology. In
chapter 5 I discussed some of the problems connected with the idea of a
simultaneous moment of eternity. Jürgen Moltmann's description of the
relative eternity which is promised to finite beings associates with simultaneity the further images of circularity and reversal of time:

> Aeonic time can be thought of as a time corresponding to the eternity of
> God: a time without beginning or end, without before and after. The figure,
> or configuration, of time that corresponds to the one, unending eternity is
> *cyclical* time, which has no end. It represents the reversible, symmetrical,
> unending and hence timeless form of time.[9]

With this heavenly time Moltmann contrasts the arrow of earthly time,
which is 'the time-hand, the pointer . . . the course of this time is not
circular; it has an irreversible trend'. The question, however, is how
adequate the images of circularity and reversibility might be for expressing
the eternity which is the final context of earthly time and which touches it
here and now. In quest of an answer, we shall first explore the implications
of reversal.

The Arrow Moves Backwards:
Martin Amis's *Time's Arrow*

Martin Amis's novel, *Time's Arrow*, provides a test-case for the possibilities
of reversal for exploring the meaning – or lack of meaning – of a human
life. The novel is not apparently about life after death, but tells the story of
a man's life as running backwards in time, like rewinding a film, from
death in old age in America ('I moved forward, out of the blackest
sleep . . .') to birth in Germany ('we brang, we putten').[10] Unlike the
arrow of time in Amis's novel *London Fields*, this one is flying point
backwards, cleft forward. We gather as the story proceeds that in the
original run forward of his life, the central character was a war criminal, a

---

[9] Jürgen Moltmann, *The Coming of God*, transl. M. Kohl (London: SCM Press, 1960,
p. 282.
[10] Martin Amis, *Time's Arrow* (Harmondsworth: Penguin Books, 1992), pp. 11, 173.

young doctor in the concentration camp at Auschwitz-Birkenau responsible for human experimentation and extermination. He has escaped under a false name to America, where it seems he has tried to atone for his crimes by working conscientiously for the remainder of his life as a doctor in various hospitals, aiming to be a healer in place of his former atrocities. His final name, the name with which the backwards story begins is Tod Friendly ('Friendly Death'), while his earliest with which it ends is Odilo Unverdorben ('uncorrupted').

The narrative device of temporal inversion allows for a good deal of straightforward, knockabout humour. People walk backwards, they vomit out their food, babies want their nappies to be filled up with 'shit from the trash' (p. 91), letters arrive from rubbish bins or are created out of fire, taxi drivers pay their passengers, prostitutes give money to their clients and people are healed through fighting each other. (Similar vaudeville jokes appear in an episode of *Red Dwarf* screened in 1989, when the characters arrive on earth through a 'time-hole' and find the inhabitants living backwards).[11] The narrator has an ambiguous relationship with Tod, sometimes appearing to be an alien intelligence inhabiting his body and observing him, and sometimes more closely identified with him, perhaps as his conscience; of his experience in this strange world he comments:

> I know I live on a fierce and magical planet, which shreds or surrenders rain or even flings it off in whipstroke after whipstroke . . . which with a single shrug of its tectonic plates can erect a city in half an hour. Creation . . . is easy, is quick. (p. 23)

But the main effect of the narrative technique on the reader is not comedy; it is a sense of *judgement* on human life in general, and especially on this one life. In general, running the film of human existence backwards produces an ironic critique of our society and its priorities. The process of eating as vomiting (the narrator calls restaurants 'vomitoriums') and the returning of the resultant food to the supermarkets for cash (p. 19) raises questions about conspicious consumption. The returning of cars to their component parts raises issues of conservation (p. 27). The beginning of nourishment from the sucking up of excrement into the body from the sewers underlines the sheer finitude and materiality of human existence: 'All life . . . all sustenance, all meaning (and a good deal of money) issues from a single household appliance: the toilet handle' (p. 18). There is a

---

[11]   See note 6 above.

Swiftian delight in the scatological here which punctures all human pretensions.

Since the film of life is running in reverse, broken love affairs begin with a moment of hate and often a slap or a shove, followed by 'everything on the first date . . . Instant invasion. Instant invasion and lordship. An hour or two here, max, is all it takes' (p. 59). The relationship ends with a gradual withdrawal, 'they will start to recede, irreversibly, fading from me, with the lightest of kisses, the briefest squeeze of the hand', until the woman has no memory of Tod whatsoever (p. 61). This ironic reversal exposes the truth of many relationships, embodying male acts of power ('invasion') and the transience of human love, 'this human talent for forgetting' (p. 89). It is also a judgement on Tod in particular, who is obviously unable to sustain any permanent relationships.

An even more specific judgement relates to Tod's career as a doctor in America, where a reversal of the film of life means that the hospitals in which he works are experienced by the narrator as places of unremitting mutilation and destruction. Tod's work as a doctor means stuffing tumours into breasts and stomachs, inserting rusty nails and glass into wounds, attaching a 'farcically mangled leg' to a thigh, making babies disappear into women's bodies or forcing embryos into wombs. As patients 'leave' his consulting room, the narrator observes wryly, 'they certainly don't look too cheerful on their way out' (p. 35). Depicting the practice of medicine as the violation of bodies makes the point that Tod cannot expiate his offences in the concentration camp by his own efforts, without genuine repentance, which he never manifests. The reader perceives that driven by guilt, all his attempts at healing will be in vain.

When the film winds back remorselessly to the period of Tod's activities as a concentration camp doctor, Auschwitz is of course experienced by the inner narrator as a place of healing. For the first time the narrator approves unreservedly of Tod's actions, which he interprets as creation and resurrection. Reversing the process of extermination means that the purpose of the camps is to bring Jews to life, raising them out of the graves and forming them into living beings out of the flames. Reversing the process of experimentation means that mangled people have parts of their bodies restored to them, wasted flesh is made good through lethal injections into the heart: 'Creation is easy. Also ugly . . . Our preternatural purpose? To dream a race. To make a people from the weather. From thunder and from lightning. With gas, with electricity, with shit, with fire' (p. 128).

Because we already know of the evil of the events, through this process of ironic reversal they become, if possible, even more horrifying as they are viewed from a new angle. As the narrator comments, entering Auschwitz and seeing the piles of ordure, 'now human shit is out in the open, we'll get a chance to find out what this stuff can really do' (p. 125). Like Jonathan Swift's *Modest Proposal*, the quiet, understated and reasonable tone underlines the terror. The gold, for instance, which is 'placed' in the prisoners' teeth comes mostly 'direct from the *Reichsbank*. But every German present, even the humblest, gave willingly of his own store . . .' (p. 130) and Tod – now Odilo – more than any. Families are 're-united' on the selection ramp when 'their hands and eyes would plead for one another under our indulgent gaze' (p. 132). It is an achievement of Amis's novelistic technique that there is judgement upon human life whether what lies behind the ironic presentation is designed to be constructive or destructive. The particular judgement of Tod/Odilo also leads to a more general one on certain trends in modern medicine, as the narrator reflects near the end that whether a doctor is apparently taking human beings apart or putting them together, 'of course, you shouldn't be doing any of this kind of thing with human beings' (p. 156).

Judgement, then, is the most obvious result of reversal, judgement particular and universal, judgement on the individual and society. There is also just a hint of the possibility of redemption, though none appears in the American period of attempted atonement. Despite the narrator's pleasure in Odilo's supposed acts of healing in Auschwitz, when the narrative voice and the subject of the story are most identified, a note of compassion still creeps in, especially for children. The narrator ventures to criticize one aspect of the process of 'creating' and resurrecting Jewish people, that they were made to wait too long for their families to be 're-united'. What finally concerns the narrator in Odilo's consciousness are 'questions of time: certain durations', for there is always suffering in the moving of time's arrow:

> The Jews were made to wait too long in summer meadows, under racing skies, where families were often united by procedures that involved too much suspense, with children running this way and that and stopping still with their hands raised like claws, searching, and babies on the ground every few yards in shawls, crying, with no parents readily available, for much too long . . . (p. 172)

For the truth of what is going on – terrible separation – this has to be read forwards, but compassion still emerges in the backward movement; there may then just be a grain of truth in the narrator's conclusion on his reliving of Auschwitz, that 'there was redemption' (p. 156). But any redemption in Odilo that there might be cannot be earned through the attempted self-atonement of Tod.

Much more prominent than redemption is the sense of lack of meaning that emerges from the backward journey, as the narrative device deconstructs the patterns and metanarratives that might be imposed on reality. In the American period the inner narrator constantly admits he is baffled to find any point in the peculiar events around him and asks 'Where am I heading?' (p. 14); it is only when he enters Auschwitz that (with what irony!) he announces 'The world is going to start making sense . . .' (p. 124). In the use of this device of reversal we can find typical marks of a postmodern narrative. Basic polarities and binary oppositions – of good and evil, destruction and construction, life and death, crime and expiation – are subverted. The narrator is dissociated from both the author and the autobiographical character, so that the sense of a 'self' anterior to the text is displaced. Above all, history is treated not as a series of objective events but as a form of discourse or text, created by language.

One reason for applying the fuzzy label 'postmodern' to a novel is when it uses the *form* of history, appealing to events that belong to what we are accustomed to regard as history writing, but at the same time seeks to subvert it.[12] This kind of novel appears to be referential, incorporating events from 'documentary' history, but undermining the very possibilities of reference. The motivation is to expose the fictional aspect of history-writing itself, the bringing of interpretation to events in the service of some ideology or other. In *Time's Arrow* the making of history into discourse could be said to be a healthy attack on all 'revisionist' histories of the Holocaust, which deny it happened or try to reduce its extent; as we have seen, it also questions received interpretations of progress in the capitalist Western world since the Holocaust. But deconstruction is, by its nature, difficult to limit, and the hostile reviews which greeted this novel on its publication expressed the feeling that playing linguistic games with the Holocaust had undermined the actual suffering of the victims. If all interpretations of history are to be made relative, then moral lessons cannot be drawn from the Holocaust, and it ceases to be a warning to our common humanity.

Amis is not in fact a total relativist (and nor of course are other postmodern writers and critics, including Derrida); the Swiftian irony depends upon some 'realist' assumptions – that readers will have a more or

---

[12]   See Brian McHale, *Postmodernist Fiction* (London: Routledge, 1989), pp. 89–96.

less similar response to the 'history' portrayed, and will find at least *some* common values. But the danger of losing any sense of meaning and truth in history lurks in the book, and tends to be exacerbated by the ending, when the device of reversal becomes that of circularity. At the very moment of birth the arrow changes direction to move forwards, dragging the narrator with it.

> When Odilo closes his eyes I see an arrow fly – but wrongly. Point-first. Oh no, but then . . . We're away once more, over the field. Odilo Unverdorben and his eager heart. And I within, who came at the wrong time – either too soon, or after it was all too late. (p. 173)

We have the impression that once arrived at the point of death there is no reason why the arrow should not reverse again. Nor are we now at all sure which direction can be called forwards and which backwards ('I see an arrow fly – but wrongly. Point-first.'). Time is always 'the wrong time'. We recall that, at the mock railway station in Treblinka, a painted facade in two dimensions erected to reassure the Jews that there was an onward journey, there is no dimension of time. The clock has painted hands, and the narrator reflects that 'time had no arrow, not here . . . A place without depth. And a place without time' (p. 151). Yet 'time [is] the human dimension, which makes us what we are' (p. 76). An arrow which continually reverses, on a circular track, no longer has direction to 'make us what we are'. The ending of the book, which refuses to end, thus points not so much towards openness but ironically towards closure.

In working towards a Christian eschatology, theologians are hardly likely to incorporate a literal reversal of time, such as Amis ingeniously depicts, into their vision of eternity. If the image of 'reversibility' is used, it cannot mean this, the fast-reverse button of a celestial video machine. But the novel does indicate that a *new relation to time* can expose the truth of situations and characters. It can throw a new light on the decisions and motives of both individuals and society, and can subvert ideologies that hide the truth in the name of making meaning. To re-experience events of the life once lived from a new temporal perspective, released from the one-way arrow of time, might well bring both judgement and redemption for those experiencing the exposure of judgement.

Also, however, the novel demonstrates that images of reversal and circularity can fail to take history seriously. There is a danger of playing games with events that, with their 'before and after', have been the occasion of moral and physical struggle for their participants, and in which they may have triumphed or failed miserably. If the effects of time can be reversed, it cannot be at the expense of history, taking cheaply the reality of decisions made. The transformations of eternity must surely not immediately transpose the most sadistic doctor of Auschwitz ('Uncle Pepi') into a benign healer.

The Counter-movement to Evolution

One theologian, Jürgen Moltmann, has offered a vivid account of the reversal of history on the Last Day:

> What has to be called eschatological is the movement of *redemption*, which runs counter to evolution. If we want to put it in temporal terms: this is a movement which runs from the future to the past, not from the past to the future. It is the divine tempest of the new creation, which sweeps out of God's future over history's fields of the dead, waking and gathering every last created being. The raising of the dead, the gathering of the victims and the seeking of the lost bring a redemption of the world which no evolution can ever achieve.[13]

Though Moltmann immediately joins this concept of reversal with that of circularity (in which 'evolution' becomes 're-volution' and is 'carried into a unique and then final eschatological cycle'), we may focus for a moment on the image of 'counter-movement'. It is clearly not to be taken literally, in an Amis-like way, but it does seek to express the reversal of all negative outcomes in individual lives and world history. Like the notion of simultaneity, redemption must touch every moment of every life. In particular, God's Day of Justice will bring redemption to the *victims* of the forward movement of time's arrow which has been embodied in the process of evolution.

Here Moltmann is complementing the picture of *Christus Evolutor* with *Christus Redemptor*. Teilhard de Chardin has offered a vision of the cosmic Christ, immersed into the process of the world's development and beckoning it forward to its completion.[14] The Christ of cross and resurrection

---

[13]   Jürgen Moltmann, *The Way of Jesus Christ*, transl. M. Kohl (London: SCM Press, 1990), p. 303.
[14]   Pierre Teilhard de Chardin, 'Christ the Evolver', in Teilhard, *Christianity and Evolution*, transl. René Hague (New York: Harcourt, Brace, Jovanovich, 1971), pp. 138–50; cf *Le Milieu Divin*, Eng. transl. (London: Collins, 1960), pp. 84–8, 111–15.

is the beginning of a phase in which the whole cosmos will be drawn into the life of God ('divinized'), and so Christ is the driving force of an evolution that is characterized by costly sacrifice. This is an eschatological vision because Teilhard finds the origin of this momentum forwards in *the future*, as coming from the God who is always 'ahead of us' and pulling us towards the fullness of divine being. Moltmann, however, draws attention to those who have fallen victim to the forward movement of biological and social evolution, who have made the sacrifice of themselves and their potential or had it thrust upon them. Every point of progress has been marked by its victims, and in God's aim for history none of these must be lost. So Moltmann formulates the complementary image of *Christus Redemptor*; only resurrection can deal with the victims, as Christ returns as it were through time to pick up those who have fallen by the way. The 'messianic extensity' of Christ 'pervades the times of creation to their furthest origins'.[15]

Now, this theological picture of evolution and its victims relates interestingly to a further scientific puzzle about the arrow of time. The riddle concerns the direction of the arrow: is it pointing towards progress or degeneration? This is not a question, we note, about the *temporal* direction of the arrow, but about its orientation to a *goal*. We have seen that the physicists' picture of the arrow is an irreversible movement towards increasing entropy, and so towards disorder and chaos. But the biologists' picture of the arrow, focused in evolution, is a movement in nature towards greater complexity and so towards the increase of order. The question is whether these two tendencies can be reconciled, and one scientific answer is to subordinate degeneration to progress. As Ilya Prigogine, among others, proposes,[16] an advancement towards greater organizational complexity might be seen as a universal tendency, based in spontaneous self-organization in nature; increasing entropy would then be envisaged as a mere by-product of the process, a price to be paid for achieving order out of chaos, but not the dominant tendency.

Paul Davies has appealed to this view in considering possible ends to the cosmos. If, as he inclines to think, the more likely end is that of 'heat-death' (i.e. a uniform coldness) rather than a 'big crunch' (i.e. the collapse of the expanding universe back on itself), then the tendency towards self-

---

[15] Moltmann, *The Way of Jesus Christ*, p. 304.
[16] Ilya Prigogine and I. Stengers, *Order out of Chaos* (London: Heinemann, 1984), p. 153f; cf. Peter Coveney and Roger Highfield, *The Arrow of Time* (London: HarperCollins/Flamingo, 1991), pp. 183–95, 222–4.

organization may offer some slight hope for the survival of life. If the movement of the arrow towards complexity is the more powerful tendency, then it may be possible for our descendants to outwit the loss of energy in heat-death by increasing their organization of life without squandering dwindling resources.[17] He admits, however, that the prospect of 'bizarre science-fiction creatures eking out an existence against odds that become forever stacked higher against them' is one that fills him with mixed feelings.

A conversation between science and theology over these issues is bound to be illuminating. Both disciplines are intrigued by the two orientations within the arrow of time, towards dissolution on the one hand and towards increasing complexity on the other. It is open to the theologian to offer an alternative to the theory that all depends on self-organization, a proposal based in the creator rather than the created. Wolfhart Pannenberg places this phenomenon in the context of his vision of eternity as wholeness of time.[18] God's future is the 'force-field' of the possible, and takes precedence over the present separation of time as the whole always transcends its parts. The Spirit of God expresses itself in creation with the dynamic of this future, and so increasing entropy can only be parasitic on the openness of creation to what is new. The 'possibility field' of the future, he suggests, constitutes all events in the flow of time, and this is why there is space for the rise of new structures through increasing complexity. Entropy, then, is subordinate not to the self-organization of entities, but to an openness to the future created by the Holy Spirit.

These are ideas to which I intend to return, but they confirm that there is room here for dialogue (if not 'convergence') with science and its data. Dialogue also clarifies a fundamental difference between the 'end' in science and in theology. While science is absorbed in explaining the balance between the progress of evolution and the 'price paid' in the coinage of entropy, Christian eschatology is concerned with the redemption of the victims, as Moltmann makes clear. Visions of the end are not about the ingenuity of some organisms in surviving against the odds, but about the fulfilling of the potential of all, including those who are too weak to survive biological or social change.

Further, the difference between the scenarios of science and theology

---

[17]   Paul Davies, *The Last Three Minutes. Conjectures about the Ultimate Fate of the Universe* (London: Weidenfeld & Nicolson, 1994), pp. 117–18.
[18]   Wolfhart Pannenberg, *Systematic Theology*, vol. 2, transl. G. Bromiley (Edinburgh: T. & T. Clark, 1994), pp. 93–100.

should warn us against any synchronization of the end of the cosmos as predicted by science, and the 'Day of the Lord' as imagined by biblical prophets. The 'end', in scientific terms seems to be more about the movement of the universe's mass into a new phase, under the same laws of physics but now probably unhospitable to organic life, than about transformation to 'new creation'. The alternative end to 'heat death', a contraction of the universe into itself, is linked by some scientists to a literal reversal of the thermodynamic arrow of time and the creation of 'anti-worlds'.[19] Such a time-symmetric evolution was once – but is no longer – espoused by Stephen Hawking, whose description of what it would be like bears some resemblance to the picture painted by Amis: 'Cups would mend themselves and jump back on the table. People would get younger, not older, as the universe got smaller again'.[20] The living backwards of an already lived life would not, of course, come into play as there could be no causality or communication between beings in oppositely time-directed phases of the universe; but the uncertainty at the end of Amis's novel as to which way the arrow is pointing would certainly obtain. 'In a time-symmetric universe words like "expanding" and "future" can be interchanged with "contracting" and "past"'.[21] Any place that 'reversibility' has in a Christian eschatology is not, however, about an endless oscillation of movement in time, but about hope for the finding of what has been lost.

The idea of reversibility, as we have explored it in literary and scientific forms, appears unsuitable for an image of eternity when taken at all exactly. However, as used by Moltmann, it seems to be a metaphorical way of denying that decisions made and consequences incurred in this life are final. It seems to be about inverting the destiny of those who have been discarded on the onward march of time, in line with the Gospel text that 'the last shall be first'. It seems to be an affirmation that judgement, not as the awarding of prizes and punishments but as bringing the truth to light, is a sign of hope not merely for some but for all. In short, anything is open to change. If the language of a great reversal can express this, then it may be a useful symbol after all.

But if the coming of the Day of the Lord gathers up all created persons in this way, must this be a vision of universal salvation? If so, does this take

[19]   Notably advocated by the astrophysicist Thomas Gold; see Davies, *About Time*, pp. 220–1.
[20]   Stephen Hawking and Roger Penrose, *The Nature of Space and Time* (Princeton: Princeton University Press, 1996), p. 101.
[21]   Davies, *About Time*, p. 228.

seriously the freedom of created persons to be independent of God if they so wish, and does it give worth to decisions made in the struggle of life? Discussion of these issues has unfortunately often been marred by failing to make a basic distinction between two sorts of universalism, which we might call 'dogmatic' and 'hopeful'.

The first asserts that all created persons will *inevitably* be brought into the salvation of life with God in eternity. This doctrine may be based on one or more of the following considerations: that the soul, being created from God, has a natural inclination to return to its origin;[22] that for any created beings to remain in rebellion against their creator would be a defeat of the power of God's love;[23] that for created persons to have the power of choosing or declining their own salvation would be to make them into God themselves;[24] and that the representative nature of Christ's atonement means that all humanity must be included within it (unless one were to take Calvin's view of an atonement limited to an elect few). This kind of universalism is in accord with the strand of thinking in the New Testament that finds expression in texts picturing the redemption of the whole cosmos (e.g. Col. 1:19–20; 1 Cor. 15:22, 28; Rom. 5:18, 11:33–6; Phil. 2:10–11). If those who hold this view want to give weight to all biblical witness on the subject, they will understand the other group of texts, which describe a destiny of separation from God (e.g. Matt. 7:13f, 25:31–46; Mark 9:45–8; Luke 16:23; John 3:36), as referring to an experience of 'hell' in this life before death, or to the experience of forsakenness which Christ suffered vicariously on the cross, or to a fate which *would* have befallen humanity but for the work of Christ.

The second kind of universalism is a hopeful one. It believes that it is *possible* for all created persons from the beginning of time to enter into the communion of God's triune life, and it hopes that this will indeed happen.[25] This hope has secure foundations in the power of God's love to draw all persons into response, and since this love is embodied eternally in the cross

---

[22] See e.g. John Hick, *Death and Eternal Life* (London: Collins, 1976), pp. 250–9.

[23] See e.g. John A. T. Robinson, *In the End God* (London: SCM Press, 1950), chs. 10–11.

[24] See e.g. Jürgen Moltmann, 'The Logic of Hell' in Bauckham (ed.), *God will be All in All* (Edinburgh: T & T Clark, 1999), p. 45.

[25] 'Hopeful universalists' seem reluctant to identify themselves clearly, but probably include Karl Rahner and Karl Barth: see Rahner, 'The Hermeneutics of Eschatology' in *Theological Investigations* IV, transl. K. Smith (London: Darton, Longman and Todd, 1974), pp. 336–41; see Karl Barth, *Church Dogmatics*, transl. and ed. G. W. Bromiley and T. F. Torrance (Edinburgh: T & T Clark, 1936–77), IV/3.1, pp. 476–8.

and resurrection of Jesus all salvation is inseparable from these Gospel events. But this view still leaves open the terrible possibility that some created persons may go on insisting on separation from God for eternity, preferring the satisfaction of being enclosed in themselves rather than opening themselves to the challenge and healing of divine love. Those who think like this understand biblical texts about hell as depicting, metaphorically, the possibility of this self-chosen state, though in fact 'hell may be empty'. Opinions will differ as to whether persons choosing an eternity of self-satisfaction will eventually fall beneath the 'lower limit of being' (as John Macquarrie puts it),[26] and drift into non-being altogether; this would then come under the heading of what is often called 'conditional immortality'. Perhaps the most satisfactory literary depiction of such a hopeful universalism is C. S. Lewis's fable *The Great Divorce*, affirming that 'No soul that seriously and constantly desires joy will ever miss it'.[27]

Some image of eternity close to the second option has the advantage of taking seriously the freedom God has granted to creation. It also allows to God the humility of being willing to be rejected; it adds another dimension to the tragedy within the victory of love for which I have already argued (chapter 6), in considering God's eternal vision of potentials that have not been actualized. The point of a 'hopeful universalism' is to take seriously both the questing love of God and the need for the free co-operation of responsible creatures, and so there needs to be scope for these factors to be worked out and for hope to be fully realized. There must be a realistic context where it is *possible* for God's desire 'that all human beings should find salvation and come to know the truth' (1 Tim. 2:4) to be fulfilled, and the space between the bounds of birth and death does not seem sufficient. There must then be limitless opportunities for God to offer love in the divine quest for reconciliation, and for created beings to respond. This space for hope fits in with the 'dynamic' view of eternal life we have already explored, suggesting a 'kind of continuum through which the [person] may move, perhaps from the near-annihilation of sin to the closest union with God'.[28]

Such a context, for which the most appropriate images are resurrection and new creation, initiated by a judgement which brings the whole truth to light, takes seriously the need for justice which we have seen to be

---

[26] John Macquarrie, *Principles of Christian Theology* (London: SCM Press, 1977), pp. 366–7.

[27] C.S. Lewis, *The Great Divorce. A Dream* (London: Bles, 1945), p. 67.

[28] Macquarrie, *Principles of Christian Theology*, p. 367.

implied by Amis's novel. While it is true that oppressors need to be liberated from the power of oppression no less than their victims, it is not so clear that the path of liberation should be the same. A dogmatic universalism tends towards a view of instantaneous transformation of the most wicked villain through the moment of judgement, painful though it will be to face the truth. It fits with a view of eternity as the simultaneity of time, where no future development is possible or needed. A hopeful universalism leaves scope for a longer process of self-understanding, repentance and growth into perfection, and this requires a model of eternal life where there is some kind of time and becoming.

In my view, this is the most coherent picture of human destiny available if we are to hope for eternal life at all, and take a wager on the power of love in the universe. Martin Amis's experiment with time's arrow leaves us uncomfortable about any instant 'reversal' of a destroyer into a healer. The irony in his fable prompts us to protest. To say that eternity contains 'a great reversal' means that the effects of all life-despoiling actions can be transformed, with their actors; it does not promise this will be an easy journey. Such a vision of eternity does take decisions in this life seriously, and even hints that some decisions will make future response to the divine offer of love difficult and resistance more intransigent.[29] But the images of resurrection, new creation and the healing of time promise that there will be a new context for response, and possibilities for change which life before death could not provide.

Cycles of Torment and Renewal

If eternal life offers all created persons a journey 'farther up and farther in' (in C. S. Lewis's words from the last of the *Chronicles of Narnia*),[30] does the image of circularity or 'cyclical existence' offer a useful way of articulating it? Amis's novel and Moltmann's theology connect the images of reversal and circularity, and it is to the latter that we now turn our attention.

In many cultures the ritual celebration of cyclical rhythms of life has been regarded as a way of escaping the remorseless movement of time towards death. Any discussion of this topic is necessarily endebted to the studies of Mircea Eliade, who popularized the idea of 'the myth of the

---

[29] William Golding depicts this kind of state in his novel, *Pincher Martin* (London: Faber and Faber, 1956).

[30] C. S. Lewis, *The Last Battle* (London: Bodley Head, 1956), ch. 15.

eternal return', observing that natural cycles such as the lunar rhythm appeared to ancient peoples to interrupt the linear flow of time and to annul its irreversibility: 'Everything begins over again at its commencement every instant . . . Time has no final influence upon their existence, since it is itself constantly regenerated.'[31] Time could be regenerated through New Year Festivals and periodic purificatory rites; repetition in which there was 'nothing new under the sun' need not be felt as a frustrating lack of novelty, but as a reaching back to an archetypal moment in which there could be a deliverance from what seemed a meaningless progression from day to day.

The Jewish and Christian traditions of faith have, in principle, advocated a linear view of history, with the arrow of time flying from first creation to new creation rather than looping back to a primordial paradise. The pattern of promise and fulfilment assumes that there is something genuinely new about the future, something not contained in the past or present. But the situation is more complicated than any simple opposition of linear to cyclical time, such as was advocated for instance by Oscar Cullmann.[32] There is a place in Israelite faith for the celebration of the cyclical rhythms of nature in the annual festivals of Spring (Passover) and Autumn (New Year), and in the weekly Sabbath; to these Christian worship has added the mid-winter solstice (Christmas). Compared with other ancient Near Eastern religions, Israelite faith introduced a remarkable degree of historical remembrance into the rituals that celebrated cosmic renewal; the dramatic events of the emigration of Israel from Egypt and the establishing of Jerusalem as David's royal city merge, for instance, with the primordial defeat of the waters of chaos at creation and Yahweh's continual mastery of the waters that surround the earth.[33] So Israel's encounters with Yahweh on the linear road of history blended with her encounter with Yahweh in the repeated blessings of the harvest. But the circular rhythms are still there, especially in the weekly sabbath, and their significance should not be underplayed.

Although cyclical patterns might give people the sense of touching a 'land beyond time', this does not mean that eternity itself was necessarily

---

[31] Mircea Eliade, *The Myth of the Eternal Return*, transl. W. R. Trask (Routledge, London, 1955), pp. 3, 5, 89–90.

[32] Oscar Cullmann, *Christ and Time*, transl. F. V. Filson (London: SCM Press, 1962), pp. 51–60. The linear–circular contrast has been notably criticized by James Barr, *Biblical Words for Time* (London: SCM Press, 2nd edn, 1969).

[33] See e.g. Psalm 46:1–10, 68:7–10, 89:3–10, 114:1–8, 135:6–9, 136:6–15.

conceived as cyclical in nature. Eliade's own study suggests that the cyclical rituals were seen in many ancient religions as repeating certain archetypal actions performed by the gods at the beginning of all things; repetition actualized the mythical moment when the formative act or gesture was revealed. Moreover, we should not forget that for most of the Old Testament period Israel had no concept of eternal life at all. In our time science has given us a new circular rhythm of nature, as some cosmologists have argued for a universe of repeated expansions and contractions (with accompanying reversals of time), but this is rarely associated with a cyclic view of eternity.

However, in some cultures the natural cycles of growth, decay and regeneration *have* been seen as reflecting an eternal cyclical movement of the soul. Notably there is the Hindu belief in the reincarnation of the self or soul (*jiva*) through a round of rebirths (*samsara*) in a mixture of this world and other worlds. In the *vishishtadvaita* stream of Vedantic philosophy this is conceived as a purposeless cycle, simply expressing the superabundance and playfulness of divine life; in the *advaita* version of Vedantic thought the *samsara* is a purposeful evolution of the soul to true self-consciousness through a process of purgation. In both approaches the cycle of rebirths is shaped by the law of *karma*, reward or retribution for deeds done in previous lives, and in both there is hope of release (*moksha*, liberation) from the cycle through enlightenment.[34] In the mainstream Christian tradition reincarnation has had no place, and the Roman Catholic doctrine of purgatory has reserved concepts of progress and purgation to saved souls who are already on their way to heaven. As a result, images of circularity in the religious and literary imagination have been most frequently applied to the experience of the damned in hell. A cyclic form of afterlife has been usually presented as a horrifying prospect, an endless repetition of physical and mental pain driven by the engine of guilt.

Flann O'Brien's novel *The Third Policeman*[35] presents such a negative image of circular experience, in a comic allegory which cannot hide its hopelessness. The unnamed main character, who narrates the story, conspires with a friend, John Divney, to murder an elderly neighbour and steal his black cash box. The heinousness of this crime is not mitigated by his motive, which is to fund his obsessive scholarly research on an obscure and (it becomes increasingly evident) absurd amateur scientist and philosopher,

[34]   See Hick, *Death and Eternal Life*, pp. 311ff.
[35]   Flann O'Brien (i.e. Brian O'Nolan), *The Third Policeman* (London: Picador, 1974 [1967]).

named de Selby. Going to retrieve the cash box from where Divney has hidden it, the narrator finds himself suddenly propelled into a surreal landscape of rural Ireland, presided over by a three-man village police force. The main preoccupation of the Sergeant and his two constables, who seem to have been transplanted from the world of *Alice in Wonderland*, is to trace missing bicycles. They also steal them in the first place, to slow up the process of the metamorphosis of owner into bicycle through the transfer of atoms from flesh to metal through the impact caused by rough roads. This is the only kind of change that seems possible in this world, as the narrator remains as self-centred and self-preoccupied at the end of the story as at the beginning. We discover towards the end that the narrator was killed by Divney, his coconspirator, as he was searching for the box, and has been dead and in hell all the time. He manages to return to his house and appear to Divney, who dies of fright and joins him on the road as once again he arrives at the same hilarious police station, to be greeted by the same enquiry; 'Is it about a bicycle?'. The last two paragraphs exactly repeat the description of his arrival the first time, so it is clear that he has entirely forgotten the first cycle of events, which it seems will be repeated eternally. The circular movement of a bicycle ('cycle') wheel is the presiding motif of this country. As the author writes elsewhere, 'Hell goes round and round. In shape it is circular and by nature it is interminable, repetitive and very nearly unbearable'.[36]

This landscape of hell provides a number of object lessons on the subject of repetitive infinity, among them a diminutive, intricately carved chest made by one of the policemen (probably a recapitulation of the victim's cash box). The narrator recognizes it to be an article of great beauty, but his reaction changes from admiration to increasing horror as he discovers that it contains more and more identical chests nesting inside each other, reducing to invisibility and beyond. 'At that point,' he comments, 'I became afraid. What he was doing was no longer wonderful but terrible'.[37] He is, regrettably, less afraid of another example of interminable repetition, his own scholarly footnotes on de Selby, which become more elaborate as his subject becomes more ludicrous. This is clearly a version of hell especially designed for academics.

In this allegory of eternity, a sort of Pilgrim's Non-Progress, the circularity is caused by guilt. O'Brien's fellow Irishman James Joyce offers another comic vision of circular experience in his incomparably greater

---

[36] Ibid., publishers' note, p. 173.
[37] Ibid., p. 64.

novel *Finnegans Wake*,[38] where the cycles are once again driven by guilt, but where there is a joyous celebration of life despite it. Here the structural device of circularity is not applied to life after death, but to the movement of history. Joyce, like other twentieth-century novelists, has been influenced by the cyclical theory of history formulated by the eighteenth-century philosopher Giovanni Battista Vico, in his *Scienza Nuova* (1725). Vico envisaged a continual repetition of four periods: a theocratic age, an aristocratic age, a democratic age, and a transition back to the beginning again, a *ricorso*. His version of the 'eternal return' has no eschatology, no fulfilment, but it is also not a totally hopeless vision as the cycles are not envisaged as being identical in content, unlike the Stoic *palingenesia*. This relative openness is significant for Joyce's adoption of his basic scheme.

Joyce's feast of language, each scrap stuffed with overlapping plays on words and multiple cross-references, takes shape in four Vicoesque sections. There is first the age of the Colossal Hero, typified by the gigantic demigod Finn MacCool, the man-mountain on which Dublin is founded; then comes the patriarchy of a human ruler, followed by a so-called 'people's state' led by the son of the former patriarch who debases his father's aims; finally there is the *ricorso*. The final paragraphs are the meditations of Anna Livia, eternal woman, as she flows to the sea in the form of the River Liffey:

> Gulls. Far calls. Coming, far! End here. Us then. Finn, again! Lps. The keys to. Given! A way a lone a last a loved a long the

The last sentence, without full stop, runs back into the beginning of the first sentence of the book which is the only one without an initial capital letter:

> riverrun, past Eve and Adam's, from swerve of shore to bend of bay, brings us by a commodius vicus of recirculation back to Howth Castle and Environs.

The structure of this vast and sprawling book thus exemplifies its theory in a circular return, a 'vicus [= Vico] of recirculation'. Over the four ages there are imposed two other patterns, which constantly weave together and give the book its amazing complexity. There is first the traditional Irish ballad of 'Finnegan's Wake', which tells the tale of the fall of a

---

[38]   James Joyce, *Finnegans Wake* (London: Faber and Faber, 3rd edn repr. 1971 [1939]).

drunken builder from his ladder and his revival (wake) by the riot and noise of his friends at his 'wake' (i.e. burial party). This Finn/Finnegan appears in some guise as the main character in the four ages (e.g. Finn MacCool in the first, the master-builder of Dublin), and it is his 'fall', typical of the fall of the whole of humanity in Adam, that causes the turn of the wheel at each age. Joyce's version of Vico thus has the cycle driven by human guilt and the desire for resurrection from it.

The second pattern is the dream of one Humphrey Chimpden Earwicker (HCE) who is the keeper of a pub in Chapelizod, a suburb of Dublin, as he is lying in a drunken sleep next to his wife, Anna. It is he, in fact, who is dreaming the four ages, and he and his family appear as the main characters in them; he, for example, plays the part of the hero in the first age (Finnegan/Finn) and the patriarch in the second; his son Shaun supplants him in the third. His wife, Anna, is the eternal woman-river, Anna Livia Plurabelle (ALP), consort of the man-mountain Finn MacCool, and she flows as a rhythm of natural life through the sequence of the ages back to the beginning. HCE too has his own 'fall'; he has sexual desire for his daughter, Isabel, and was involved in some mysterious but scandalous incident with her and another girl in Phoenix Park. On the very first page, this fall – of Adam ['oldparr'], Finnegan, HCE, Humpty Dumpty, Charles Stewart Parnell, the finances of Wall Street ['wallstrait'] and everyone – appears in its usual form of a 100-letter word:

> The fall (bababadalgharaghtakamminarronnkonnbronntonnerronntuonnthunn-trovarrhounawnskawntoohoohoordenenthurnuk!) of a once wallstrait oldparr is retaled early in bed and later on life down through all Christian minstrelsy. The great fall of the offwall entailed at such short notice the pftjschute of Finnegan, erse solid man, that the humptyhillhead of humself promptly sends an unquiring one well to the west in quest of his tumptytumtoes: and their upturnpike pointandplace is at the knock out in the park where oranges have been laid to rust upon the green since devlinsfirst loved livvy.

In the *ricorso* not only Finnegan/HCE wakes from his fall, but the whole world is called to awake to a new day, summoned by the last trump of the Hindu prayer 'Sandhyas, Sandhyas, Sandhyas', a prayer for time of change (p. 593). There is a new dawn of Christian Ireland, personified in St Kevin (identified with one of HCE's sons), and 'it's high tigh tigh' to dance with hope (p. 607). We remember that this is not an eschaton, but a return to the beginning, to the theocratic age of St Patrick's Ireland: the creative command *fiat lux* – 'let there be light!' – takes the form *Fuitfiat!* – 'It was;

let it happen!' (p. 613). However, the turn of the cycle which is promised
with such jubilation is not a weary repetition. In his fine study of Joyce,
the novelist Anthony Burgess points to the significance of one phrase in a
letter from Anna which is read out aloud in this new dawn:

> . . . it is thanks, beloved, to Adam, our former first Finnlatter and our
> grocerest churcher . . . for his beautiful crossmess parzel. (p. 619)

Burgess, surely rightly, interprets 'crossmess parzel' as a mixture of
'Christmas parcel' and 'crossword puzzle'; this is what life is.[39] To this we
should add the echoes of 'cross'and 'mess', for it is the 'mess' of human life
that calls for the cross, and indeed for 'Christmas' itself. Our inheritance
from Adam is not only the fall and consequent guilt which drives the
restless cycle onwards; it is life as a beautiful 'crossmess parzel' to be joyfully
unwrapped. So the reader also moves with Anna from the end to the
beginning, with the hope of unpacking the parcel/puzzle in new ways
each time. As Burgess remarks: 'when Anna Livia promises the keys, she
seems to fulfil that promise ('Given!'), for a new lucidity seems to shine
through the zoetrope . . . we are beginning to understand'.[40]

I have not attempted in these comments to capture the richness of this
massive and baffling work. I have aimed only to summarize sufficiently to
make clear that while this novel attempts to escape from time's arrow into
a cyclic scheme, both within the inner psyche and in outer history, the
repetition has at least a relative openness to the new. While it might be
called a precursor of the postmodern in exemplifying the creation of reality
by language, it does not deconstruct history. Words certainly draw their
meaning from their '*différence*' from each other, but they are assumed to
have external reference, though this is an exceedingly multiple reference.
Joyce shares the modernist view that if reality is fragmented and re-arranged
drastically enough, the greater truth will shine through. The question then
is this: can we take the kind of confidence and exuberance in the rhythms
of nature exemplified in *Finnegans Wake*, and relate it to a hope of eternal
life? Can we discern a kind of circularity which does not, unlike the vision
of hell in *The Third Policeman*, shut down all possibility of the new?

The problem is that *eternal* cycles of events, even if they do not have a
hellish quality of lack of meaning, are difficult to distinguish from stasis.

---

[39]   Anthony Burgess, *Here Comes Everybody. An Introduction to James Joyce for the Ordinary
Reader* (London: Faber and Faber, 1965), p. 261.
[40]   Ibid., p. 263.

Thomas Mann, in *The Magic Mountain* (1924) had already made Hans Castorp reflect that if the motion by which one measures time is circular, 'it might equally well be described as rest, as cessation of movement – for the there repeats itself constantly in the here, the past in the present'.[41] A chapter in Julian Barnes's *A History of the World in 10½ Chapters*, entitled 'The Dream' makes this all too clear. The narrator begins, 'I dreamt that I woke up. It's the oldest dream of all, and I've just had it'.[42] He then proceeds to describe a heaven which provides him with all he had ever wished (sex, golf, shopping, the ideal breakfast and dinner, meeting famous people and 'not feeling bad'). The story deconstructs all narratives of the afterlife, since it appears that heaven can take whatever shape people imagine it to have; it is the supreme linguistic construct; it can, for instance, be either embodied or disembodied existence (though the modern preference, notes one 'attendant' is for having bodies). Even God and judgement exist for those who want them:

> That's the principle of Heaven, that you get what you want, what you expect. I know some people imagine it's different, that you get what you deserve, but that's never been the case. We have to disabuse them.[43]

The narrator, after many aeons has, however, exhausted all his desires; nothing much can be done with golf, for example, once one's handicap is down to 18. Continual sex and meeting famous people palls after millions of years, and even having sex *with* famous people comes to seem pretty arid. This is where an attendant mentions the possibility of 'dying off', and casually mentions that, in time, this option is chosen by everyone: 'there are bound to be a few surprises' she explains. 'Did you really want to be able to predict it all?'[44] But even this narrative is deconstructed, since after the narrator has chosen to die, the story ends: 'I dreamt that I woke up. It's the oldest dream of all, and I've just had it'. It seems that, like the nesting of boxes in *The Third Policeman*, there is an infinite circularity of waking from dream, and this means that there can never be anything new, even death.

It seems that the metaphor of circularity *can* express a relative renewal in

---

[41] Thomas Mann, *The Magic Mountain* (Harmondsworth: Penguin Books, 1960), p. 344.
[42] Julian Barnes, *A History of the World in 10½ Chapters* (London: Picador, 1990), p. 283.
[43] Ibid., p. 303.
[44] Ibid., p. 304.

the scope of finite life, yet extended to eternity it is incapable of expressing renewal and regeneration. But this is just where we need to take a more theological, or God-centred, approach. If our time is the time God has for us (as Karl Barth puts it), then whatever value there might be in our finite experiences of cyclical time must derive, not from time itself, but from God. That is, we should regard the rhythms of natural life, caught so exuberantly by Joyce, and the renewing rhythms of the liturgical calendar, as reflecting the rhythms of God's own being. They are truly a 'crossmess parzel'; not in the first place from Adam but from the triune God.

The symbol of the Trinity expresses not a society of three individual persons, but the communion of three movements or rhythms of being characterized by relationship. If we take relationship seriously and resist subordinating it to some kind of pre-existing essence or nature, then the *hypostases* or 'distinct identities' in God have their very being through their mutual self-distinction from each other[45] and their relation to each other. I intend to explore the relational nature of God further in the final chapter of this book, but for the moment we should notice that talk of God as Trinity is a language of *participation*, a symbol for being drawn into the life of God which is a communion. To confess God as Trinity is to share in relational movements of love like those between a Father and a Son, which are being continually opened up by a Spirit of newness towards each other and to the future.

Thus, our experience of circular rhythms in our present time-frame points us towards the inter-weaving and mutually indwelling movements of love in God, or what the early theologians called *perichoresis*.[46] While this concept of co-inherence was sometimes reduced to the more static concept of *circuminsessio* (a mutual 'sitting' of the persons in each other), the more dynamic sense is caught by the Latin *circumincessio*, a mutual 'moving' of each person in and through the other. Although these movements are not, of course, literally cyclic or circular, we might understand our experiences of cyclical rhythms as a pale shadow of divine *perichoresis*.

---

[45]   This is stressed by Wolfhart Pannenberg in his *Systematic Theology*, vol. 1, transl. G. Bromiley (Edinburgh: T & T Clark, 1991), pp. 308–12.

[46]   The verb *perichoreo* was first used in a trinitarian context by Pseudo-Cyril in the 6th century (*de Sacrosancta Trinitate*, p. 24), and the noun by John of Damascus (*de Fide Orth.* 1.14); but the verb *choreo* was used much earlier to express the way that the divine Persons 'filled', 'contained' and 'penetrated' each other by, for example, Hilary (*de Trinitate*, 9.69) and Cyril of Alexandria (*de Trinitate, Dial.* 3.467C).

The triune God thus makes space within the divine communion for created beings, a space wide enough for the whole of creation to dwell. Wolfhart Pannnberg emphasizes that the relation between time and eternity must be based in the being of God and not the nature of time; speaking of a 'trinitarian mediation' he appeals to the unity between the immanent Trinity (God within God's own relational life) and the economic Trinity (God present and active in the *oikonomia* of history and salvation). In the immanent Trinity there is a plurality of persons engaging in God's eternal grasp of time as a 'whole', and in the economic Trinity God participates in the life and temporality of a plurality of creatures; yet the two spheres of God's being are one.[47] Jürgen Moltmann uses the image of circularity more directly, as he envisions the mutual participation of God and creatures in the glorification of God in eternity. Having described the *perichoresis* of the divine persons as 'self-circling and self-reposing movements', and having noted that the symbol of circularity originates in 'the time of the natural cycles which regenerate life', he affirms that:

> Adoration and worship are the ways in which created beings participate in the eternal life and the eternal joy of God, and are *drawn into the circular movement of the divine relationships*.[48]

Moltmann is suggesting that cyclical rhythms in nature are symbolic both of the 'cosmic liturgy' of the new creation, and of the very being of the God who is being adored in the liturgy. The foundation for this correspondence he finds to be in God's gift of the Sabbath, which lies at the heart of our experience of cyclical time. In the old creation, he proposes, the Sabbath 'is the presence of God in the *time* of those he has created, or to put it more precisely, the dynamic presence of eternity in time, which links beginning and end, thus awakening remembrance and hope'.[49] In the new creation God will be fully present in the *space* of those who are created, in the unveiled *Shekinah* glory. In the sabbath day and its rhythm, creation thus holds within itself the promise of its consummation.

Moltmann's thought here is imaginative and provocative, but we notice that while he recognizes circularity to be only a 'temporal symbol' for eternity, he still uses it rather exactly to support a view of simultaneity,

---

[47]   Pannenberg, *Systematic Theology*, vol. 1, p. 407.
[48]   Jürgen Moltmann, *The Spirit of Life*, transl. M. Kohl (London: SCM Press, 1992), pp. 304–5.
[49]   Moltmann, *The Coming of God*, p. 266.

excluding any successiveness of 'before and after'. Just as we must sit light to the image of reversibility, so we must surely also to circularity. Reversibility points to the non-finality of life-despoiling events. So circularity points to *perichoresis*, or to the inter-weaving and inter-penetrating movements of love. Perhaps a more comprehensive symbol would be that of the divine *dance* (which Moltmann also mentions), which was used occasionally in the Middle Ages to picture the *perichoresis* of the Persons.[50] A dance includes circular movements, but cannot be restricted to them. In this dance the divine participants would not only move around each other but through each other, drawing in created beings to share in their ecstatic permeation of love. God, as it were, makes room for us among the steps of the dance, allowing us to experience the successiveness of past, present and future in a new harmony. In such a dance time comes to wholeness, not in 'simultaneity' but as a rhythm which no longer breaks the human dancers on its wheel.

Preservation and Retroaction

The relation between the present course of time and eternity can thus be conceived as the relation between two modes of engagement of created beings in the triune God: a participation during the course of earthly time with its linearity and cyclicity, and a participation in which our fragmentation by time is experienced as healed. This throws a good deal of light on the question of the continuity of identity of a person through death and resurrection that we considered in an earlier chapter, and we can explore this further through considering an interesting recent debate about 'objective immortality' in process theology.

According to the process vision of the relation between God and creation, God is 'dipolar': one aspect of God's being is deeply immersed into the flow of the world and time and the other is independent of the world and invulnerable to it. In God's world-related aspect, which A. N. Whitehead calls God's 'consequent nature' and which Charles Hartshorne

---

[50] The metaphor of the dance is assisted by a play on words: the verbal stem of *perichoresis* is *perichoreo*, to encompass; *perichoreuo* is to dance. For use of the metaphor, see Catherine M. LaCugna, *God for Us. The Trinity and Christian Life* (New York: HarperSanFrancisco, 1991), p. 271; Nicholas Lash, *Theology on the Way to Emmaus* (London: SCM Press, 1986), pp. 154–7.

calls his 'concrete states' of experience,[51] God is supremely influenced by the world; he is perfectly related to all the actuality there is, and receives the impact of all the actions, joys and tragedies of the world. In his world-independent aspect, which Whitehead calls 'primordial nature' and Hartshorne calls 'abstract essence' there is an infinite reservoir of possibility for the world which guides the process of continuous creation and provides for both stability and novelty.[52] The two formative thinkers I have mentioned in fact differ over the nature of this ground of possibility in God, or God's grasp of possibilities for the world. Whitehead thinks of God as having a perfect and eternal vision of all possible values whatever, which God views as 'eternal objects'. We might say, in a more modern analogy, that they are all contained in an eternal database. Hartshorne thinks of the abstract essence of God like a person's enduring character, so it is pure possibility itself; it is the open potential for definite possibilities that 'emerge' in interaction between God and the world in the concrete states of God's experience. In my previous discussion of future possibilities which we expect and for which we wait,[53] it will be seen that I have leaned more to Hartshorne's view in this respect.

In process thought, the dipolarity in God matches the dipolar nature of all 'actual entities' that constitute the world, and which have a mental and a physical pole. The basic building blocks of reality are understood to be momentary events of extremely brief duration, which grow to a peak of satisfaction and then perish, to be succeeded in the stream of life by other events. Through their mental pole these entities, or droplets of becoming, enjoy some kind of feeling appropriate to their level of existence. They have some freedom to create themselves, growing towards satisfaction through a process of 'concrescence' during which they prehend or grasp data of experience from many sources, including the entities that have preceded them.[54] Pre-eminent among these influences are God's aims and ideals, possibilities which will make for the greatest beauty and satisfaction. Momentary entities build up into 'societies' which are the large-scale objects in the world that we normally perceive. While the accumulation of

[51]   A. N. Whitehead, *Process and Reality* (New York: Macmillan 1938), pp. 46–7; Charles Hartshorne, *The Divine Relativity* (New Haven: Yale University Press, 1976), pp. 80–1.
[52]   Whitehead, *Process and Reality*, pp. 69–73; Hartshorne, *The Divine Relativity*, pp. 70ff., and *Creative Synthesis and Philosophic Method* (London: SCM Press, 1970), pp. 58ff.
[53]   See above, pp. 168-71.
[54]   Whitehead, *Process and Reality*, pp. 27–39, 163–6, 373–5.

the physical aspect of entities will result in inanimate objects (rocks and minerals, for example), a build-up of the mental aspect will enable the emergence of consciousness in persons.

My intention here is not to explore this complex world-view in detail. Those who do not want to adopt its metaphysics may still appreciate its basic model of the world as a living society, growing towards the aims God sets for it through a network of mutual influences, with God sharing in the suffering that is involved in its becoming. What is most relevant to our present discussion is its picture of the preservation of all moments of experience of entities, societies and persons in the consequent nature of God. No experience is ever lost to God, the sympathetic companion of the world; every event finds its fulfilment in God and, because it remains everlastingly in God's perception and experience, it can be said to have an 'objective immortality'.

Of objections that may be raised against this picture of eternal life, one can be quite quickly dealt with. It may be protested that this scheme makes evil experiences and acts as much everlastingly present in God as beautiful and good ones. This seems to give equal value to all events, and to turn God into an eternal victim of the universe, or a mere receptacle for its rubbish. But all versions of process thought insist on the *transformation* of experiences in the consequent nature of God; they are not simply preserved but transfigured, evil being overcome by the divine harmony whose origin lies in the primordial nature of God, or in God's 'abstract essence'. In some way, the possibilities in God's primordial nature are woven into his feeling of the world in his consequent nature; either God brings to these experiences the specific values which he envisages (Whitehead) or he brings the absolute potential for values in his essence which will make a difference to the summing up of the whole of reality (Hartshorne).[55] The defective part will be redeemed by the richness of the whole. There are in fact some strains in process explanations as to how world-dependent and world-independent dimensions in God *could* coalesce to effect this transformation,[56] and this is one reason in my view for preferring a trinitarian concept of God to a dipolar model. But we can surely approve the basic idea that if all experiences can be preserved in God, then they can also be transfigured, and evil need not triumph.

---

[55] Whitehead, *Process and Reality*, pp. 525, 531; Hartshorne, *The Logic of Perfection* (LaSalle, Illinois: Open Court, 1962), pp. 274–5, *Creative Synthesis and Philosophic Method*, pp. 238–42.

[56] See my *The Creative Suffering of God* (Oxford: Clarendon Press, 1988), pp. 125–35.

A second problem with 'objective immortality' occupies the centre of a recent debate among process thinkers themselves. As formulated in conventional process philosophy, God prehends the experiences of actual entities or of each momentary phase of experience of a person when they have 'perished' or come to an end. So there can be no conscious enjoyment of God by those who have created or endured the experiences. There is no 'subjective immortality'; the dead exist, as it were, in God's memory. But some process theologians have become convinced that this does not answer the demands of theodicy. There must be an eschatology in which God brings evil to an end, and this will only be achieved if every occasion of experience is everlastingly redeemed. The process theologian Marjorie Suchocki has argued that redemption for human beings at least cannot be meaningful unless it is subjectively experienced, except perhaps for those who have lived fortunate lives.[57] Another process theologian, David Griffin, willingly agrees: 'How can those who have never had a chance to actualize their potentialities, or for other reasons view their lives as failures, be cheered by the idea that their experiences will be everlastingly remembered?'.[58]

Suchocki's solution is to advocate the subjective immortality of all individual occasions of experience in God. The steps of her argument, which require some modification of Whitehead's thought, are threefold.[59] First, the 'satisfaction' of all entities at the end of their growth is a subjective state of enjoyment. They *feel* satisfied. Second, God alone can prehend that moment in its subjectivity as God preserves and transforms it, while finite entities are only influenced by prehending it objectively. That is, God feels what the entity is feeling, or what the person is feeling at the end of every fragmentary moment of experience. Third, every occasion then consciously experiences its own transformation in the consciousness of God. As part of the divine concrescence, 'it will feel its own immediacy and God's feeling of its immediacy as well'. It also will feel, through God, its relation to all other occasions, and will 'know experientially each destruction it has inflicted, and this is judgement';[60] since, however, it also experiences the harmony of the whole in God, judge-

---

[57]   Marjorie H. Suchocki, *The End of Evil. Process Eschatology in Historical Context* (Albany: State University of New York Press, 1988), p. 165.
[58]   David Ray Griffin, 'Marjorie Hewitt Suchocki, *The End of Evil*' (Review), *Process Studies*, 18 (1989), p. 58.
[59]   See Suchocki, *End of Evil*, successively pp. 88ff, 90ff, 102ff.
[60]   Ibid., pp. 102, 108.

ment will lead to transformation and peace. This, believes Suchocki, is equivalent to resurrection.

David Griffin brings a number of objections against this scenario regarding what God, according to the technicalities of process thought, can and cannot prehend. These need not delay us. What does concern us is his protest that this is necessarily a vision of the redemption of momentary experiences, not of 'enduring persons'. He calculates that if he has five occasions of experience every second and lives for 70 years he will have had over eleven billion momentary experiences in his lifetime, each one of which will enjoy subjective immortality in God. How is he related to the (so far) eight billion David Griffins, and how can their experiences now possibly concern him?[61] The problems of identity and identification remain even if, as Suchocki hints in her response,[62] momentary experiences could be somehow unified in God. There would still be a David Griffin living here and now, and a counterpart elsewhere at the same time.

Griffin's own solution is to return to a traditional idea of a soul that survives death. I suggest, however, that there is advantage in following Suchocki's first two stages of argument, while replacing the third. Her modified process account of an *objective* immortality gives us a model of the way that all our experiences, at every momentary stage, are being continuously valued and transformed by being brought into a whole in God. There is no need for a literal 'simultaneity' or 'reversal' or 'circulation' of time at the eschaton to touch every part of our lives. We are not just remembered by God when our lives are over, and neither does God have to return to our lives on the day of resurrection. Even as the arrow of time flies remorselessly forward, each moment of life is being assumed into God's life. So the Apostle Paul may be understood when he writes:

> Though our outer nature is wasting away, our inner nature is being renewed every day. For this slight momentary affliction is preparing for us an eternal weight of glory . . . (2 Corinthians 4:16–17)

While death brings an end to bodily-mental life, our experiences have been treasured in God, and already related through God to all other persons. Following Suchocki's affirmation of the 'subjective immediacy' of God to the feelings of all occasions (stage two of her argument), God can

---

[61]   Griffin, 'Suchocki', p. 62.
[62]   Marjorie Suchocki, 'Evil, Eschatology and God: Response to David Griffin', *Process Studies*, 18 (1989), p. 67–8.

be envisaged as living our life for us, and widening its horizons, giving it a place in a more inter-related life. Moreover, if we follow the version of process thought that envisages entities and societies as being influenced by prehending the consequent as well as the primordial nature of God, then God's persuasion of the world does not only flow from the aims and possibilities held in God. It also stems from the effect of our own experiences, transformed by God, upon those who come after. Through God we truly know the communion of saints.

But, of course, the proper objections of Suchocki and Griffin would not be answered if this were the whole story. In accord with my account of resurrection earlier, we may say that God's preserving and transforming of our life-experiences is the preparation for the resurrection of the whole person. The demand of theodicy for some kind of conscious eternal life will be met when God recreates persons on the basis of God's living their lives vicariously for them, now raising them to participate fully in the dance of God's triune relations. Judgement may be understood as a making manifest of the truth of our relations to all other persons, which has been hidden in our objective immortality in God.

In our present experience of the arrow of time, we participate as persons in the relational movements of the triune God by faith, not by sight. We *believe*, for instance, that in prayer we are sharing in some way in the movement of obedient response of the Son to the Father, that in our suffering we are sharing in the movement of forsakenness between Father and Son, and that in mission we are sharing in the movement in which the Father sends forth the Son into the world. We participate in the *perichoresis* of God here and now, but the linear effect of time often masks our sense of its reality. Nevertheless, the triune God receives our experience at every moment, created in and through the arrow of time, and makes it God's own. Then, in the circular movements of the liturgy and in the circular rhythms of nature we can catch just a glimpse, from time to time, of this *perichoresis*; in such moments we anticipate the fullness of our participation in God in eternity.

This concept of anticipation deserves fuller enquiry. As Wolfhart Pannenberg stresses, persons are only on the way to completion and so on the journey to their identity.[63] They possess their true 'selfhood' in openness to others, to God and to the future. Persons exist in the relationship between the present moment of the ego, which has the function of

[63] Wolfhart Pannenberg, *Anthropology in Theological Perspective*, transl. M. O'Connell (Edinburgh: T. & T. Clark, 1985), p. 238–42.

'centring' persons and their experiences, and the mysterious wholeness of the future which transcends the present just as the whole is always prior to the partial. A person's consciousness, which bridges time, is thus kept from disintegrating within time by its anticipation of the future; Pannenberg suggests, moreover, that it is a role of the Holy Spirit of God to hold the person open to this future, in this way constituting its very identity.[64] We may surely add, in accord with a view of interim 'objective immortality', that the same Spirit holds together the momentary experiences of a person in God, making a form or *Gestalt* which is always greater than the parts, and which is open for resurrection.

Now, these reflections on the nature of the person as determined by the wholeness of the future lead Pannenberg to a language of 'retroaction' which has some important links with our investigation of the metaphor of 'reversal'. If the end is the whole, events in the past cannot be regarded as frozen and static. They are open in meaning to a continually expanding horizon of interpretation as history proceeds. In opposition to a positivist view of history which attempts a scientific investigation of the 'bare event', Pannenberg asserts that event and meaning are inseparable, so that events can never be completed until meaning reaches its fullness in the end of all things.[65] He first developed this conviction from Christology, observing that what is revealed of Jesus in his resurrection must be true, backwards, of Jesus in his life and ministry: 'the resurrection event has retroactive power'.[66] The resurrected Jesus is the crucified Jesus; so the one who is revealed as Son of God and Lord in his resurrection from the dead must always have been the true Son. In rising from the dead Jesus reveals God fully, in the sense that he reveals God's purpose for all humanity to attain fellowship with God; so he must always have been 'one with the being of God'.[67] The resurrection of Jesus anticipates the end of all things, revealing ahead of time what is the nature of the 'whole' (i.e. fellowship in God) which transcends the present and makes its incompleteness clear.

This eschatology of meaning gives at least a partial validity to the postmodern project of questioning all settled interpretations of history, reflected in Amis's novel of reversal. Here the insights of Moltmann and

[64] Pannenberg, *Anthropology*, p. 525–8.
[65] See Pannenberg, 'On Historical and Theological Hermeneutic', in *Basic Questions in Theology*, Vol. 1, transl. G. Kehm (London: SCM Press, 1970), pp. 137–181.
[66] Wolfhart Pannenberg, *Jesus – God and Man*, transl. L. Wilkins and D. Priebe (London: SCM Press, 1968), pp. 135–8.
[67] Ibid., pp. 69, 127ff.

Pannenberg are surely complementary, although Moltmann has had a long-standing dispute with Pannenberg about the nature of the resurrection as 'anticipating' the future. The language of anticipation has seemed to Moltmann to be inadequate *on its own*; without the context of 'promise', he argues, it forecloses the future and especially the future of Jesus Christ.[68] He prefers then to speak of the resurrection as a 'promise event', revealing the 'coming God', and opening up a path to fulfilment which Jesus is treading on the way towards his *parousia*. But the concepts can be mutually supportive. Both the 'overplus' of promise beyond the present, and the anticipation of a future wholeness, can act as a challenge to ideologies which try to impose a total scheme on events for the sake of human power games.

In the establishing of the meaning of events from the end of history, we might expect Pannenberg to use the language of 'retrospection', but the paradigm of Christology leads him, as we have seen, to speak of a 'retroactive' force of the future on the past. Pannenberg affirms so strongly that the parts are made by the whole, that he sees 'anticipation' as an ontological category.[69] Things do not simply increase in meaning as history moves onwards, but they *are what they are* out of the whole-ness of the future. The force-field of future possibilities embodied in the Spirit of God can actually overcome the momentum of increasing entropy and open up new structures of life. It is a pity then that this perception is worked out in an understanding of eternal life that seems essentially static.

For when Pannenberg comes to consider what it means for a person to participate in God's wholeness, he understands it as the re-experiencing of one's past life from God's point of view. What was once experienced in the successiveness of time is now viewed from a new perspective, set in the context of the whole of history and comprehended in the eternal present of God in which there is no distinction between past, present and future. In this sense, asserts Pannenberg in an early account, 'eternity is the truth of time, which remains hidden in the flux of time'.[70] In his most

---

[68] Jürgen Moltmann, *Theology of Hope*, transl. J. Leitch (London: SCM Press, 1967), pp. 77–89; *The Crucified God*, transl. R. A. Wilson and J. Bowden (London: SCM Press, 1974), pp. 171–7. For Moltmann, the resurrection *creates* anticipations of the Kingdom.

[69] Wolfhart Pannenberg, *Metaphysics and the Idea of God*, transl. P. Clayton (Edinburgh: T. & T. Clark, 1990), pp. 95–6, 103–4.

[70] Wolfhart Pannnenberg, *What is Man? Contemporary Anthropology in Theological Perspective*, transl. D. Priebe (Philadelphia: Fortress Press, 1972), p. 74.

recent reflections Pannenberg remains essentially wedded to this idea, writing of the unifying of all the individual moments of our life's history into the simultaneity of 'God's eternal present, to be seen from the standpoint of the divine ordaining'.[71]

John Hick is probably unfair to dub this a theory of 'recapitulation',[72] since re-viewing one's life from God's perspective would open up possibilities and depths of experience that had been unknown before. It would not be a mere repetitive circularity such as depicted by Barnes's heaven or O'Brien's hellish countryside. Even the inhabitant of a shanty town in South Africa, or a child slave labourer in Asia dying early of disease, or 'hermit who has only participated minimally in the human community' (Hick) would have depths that the divine vision could unlock. So Pannenberg writes in his most recent theology of 'an element of compensation' within the transfiguration of life.[73] But Hick is surely right to protest that when earthly lives have been 'almost empty of moral, physical, aesthetic and intellectual good' justice calls for an experience with a quality of newness which is more than receiving the same life again, however much viewed as a whole and so transformed. Moreover, according to Pannenberg, the bringing of separate moments together into the eternal present will be experienced as the fire of judgement, since all existing contradictions and conflicts will come out as 'a shrill dissonance'. Those who have lived by the standard of Christ – whether or not Christian believers – will be purged into harmony by the fire, but in other cases 'nothing may remain'.[74] This is not then the kind of judgement which opens up the possibility of hope for all.

Pannenberg (and with him, similarly, Eberhard Jüngel)[75] has been brought to a vision of eternal destiny which fails to balance closure with openness because he conceives 'the whole' as a simultaneity of time in

[71] Wolfhart Pannenberg, *Systematic Theology*, Vol. 3, transl. G. Bromiley (Edinburgh: T. & T. Clark, 1998), p. 640, cf. p. 610.

[72] Hick, *Death and Eternal Life*, pp. 221–6. Pannenberg, *Systematic Theology*, vol. 3, p. 638, protests that Hick has misunderstood him because: (a) this simultaneity is not merely a matter of God's memory, as with Tillich and process thought, and (b) it can apply to all who have lived by the standard of Jesus, regardless of whether they are Christian believers. But this does not answer Hick's basic point about lack of any really new experience.

[73] Pannenberg, *Systematic Theology*, vol. 3, p. 639.

[74] Ibid., pp. 610, 620, *What is Man?*, p. 79.

[75] Eberhard Jüngel, *Death – the Riddle and the Mystery*, transl. I. and U. Nicol (Edinburgh: St. Andrew Press, 1975), pp. 121–2.

which there can be no real development, adventure or progress. He also assumes that the 'whole' as possessed and known by God is a kind of fixed maximum. God has perfect freedom in having no future outside himself, and no future that is different from his present.[76] But, as I have argued, we can understand the wholeness of time as a healing in which there is not a total loss of successiveness, and the wholeness of life as a perfection which is ever-expanding. Such a wholeness can still be the source of successive time as we know it in history; it can still transcend it and be 'retroactive' upon it.

Then we can envisage the Holy Spirit as not only holding created beings open to the future, but having the same role to play within the divine *perichoresis*. In accord with biblical images of quickening breath, life-giving water, refreshing wind, nurturing wings and cleansing fire, we can visualize the Spirit as a movement of love which distinguishes itself from the Father and the Son through always opening up the Father–Son relationship in new ways to new depths and to a new future. Part of this future, which God gives to God's self in the divine freedom of desire, will be the inclusion of created beings within the divine life. The Spirit holds God open for a future which will be 'retroactive' in God's self, making God what God is. There will be a real contribution of human steps to the divine dance.

The Eternal Dance

Physicists have found a further perplexity about the arrow of time; indeed Paul Davies regards it as the greatest puzzle of all. We have already had occasion to note that according to the special theory of relativity, space-time is a four dimensional 'block', in which events are 'strung out' along it in different places. In this view of the universe, the arrow of time does not literally 'move' at all, but is simply an indicator of the *direction* of physical processes. Why then does time appear to move or flow? Why does the arrow seem to fly? Why is there a 'glaring mismatch' between physical time and subjective or psychological time?[77]

Davies is not content to dismiss the flowing of time as a harmless illusion, as urged by philosophers such as D. C. Williams and J. C. Smart who

---

[76] Pannenberg, *Systematic Theology*, vol. 1, p. 410.

[77] Davies, *About Time*, pp. 272–5.

criticize the 'myth of passage'.[78] The uncertainty of the behaviour of particles at sub-atomic level, as explored in quantum physics, contradicts the determinacy which is implied by the loss of difference between past, present and future in Special Relativity theory. Moreover, quantum theory envisages multiple, overlapping states of reality. While this situation might be interpreted in terms of a total abolition of time, it can be argued that there is evidence for the passage of time in the 'collapse' of the many alternative possibilities for the cosmos into the single reality that the observer actually perceives.[79] As yet there is no satisfactory account that combines the insights of relativity and quantum theory, and so brings together various models of time, whether static or dynamic. Davies notes that several scientists have proposed that there must be some physical process that either makes time flow, or makes it appear to flow, but no satisfactory explanation has been found.[80] Roger Penrose has made some speculations in this direction, suggesting that the 'quantum' behaviour observed on the small scale of sub-atomic particles might be at work on the larger scale of the whole human brain, producing the distinctive nature of human consciousness.[81] This would account for our subjective impression that time flows, and might also contribute to a unified theory of time in which it could be shown that in some sense at least time does *actually* flow, even if not exactly in the way that it appears to progress in our conscious experience.

A theology of time and eternity should not presume to provide a scientific answer to these problems. But I suggest that the present state of

[78] D. C. Williams, 'The Myth of Passage', in *The Journal of Philosophy*, 48 (1951), pp. 457–72; followed by J. C. Smart, 'Time' in Paul Edwards (ed.), *Encyclopaedia of Philosophy*, vol. 8 (London: Macmillan, 1967). Alan Torrance appeals to this argument in order to advocate the view that the triune communion of God is 'simultaneously and omnipresently related to the totality of spatio-temporal reality': see Torrance, '*Creatio ex Nihilo* and the Spatio-Temporal Dimensions', in Colin Gunton (ed.), *The Doctrine of Creation* (Edinburgh: T. & T. Clark, 1997), pp. 93–103. I am arguing against such simultaneity.

[79] See Coveney and Highfield, *The Arrow of Time*, pp. 128–31. By contrast, Julian Barbour in *The End of Time* (London: Weidenfeld and Nicholson, 1999) argues that the many alternative states of reality in quantum theory indicate a disconnected and timeless agglomeration of instant 'nows'.

[80] Davies, *About Time*, pp. 277–8. Storrs McCall, 'Time Flow, Non-locality, and Measurement in Quantum Mechanics', in Savitt (ed.), *Time's Arrows Today*, argues that time flows if the spacetime structure has a certain 'branched' dynamic form.

[81] Roger Penrose, *The Emperor's New Mind. Concerning Computers, Minds, and the Laws of Physics* (Vintage, London, 1990), pp. 516–20, 574–8.

scientific discussion does not rule out the theological objections which I have been presenting to a view of time as purely simultaneous. Theology can also surely offer a complementary reason why we experience time as moving, a reason rooted in a doctrine of God. Our successive time, I have been suggesting, has its source in God's time, and so our sense of the moving of time derives from our participation in the movement of God, in the *perichoresis* of God's relational being which will be consummated in the eternal dance of the healing of time.

The Irish poet, W. B. Yeats, took the image of dance for the healing of memories. In his poem 'Byzantium' he imagines a country beyond historic time in which the soul can find regeneration, an ideal city in whose civilization art, religion and politics are unified. The imagery of the poem combines details of the culture of the historic Byzantium with Neoplatonic images of renewal, and the City stands both as an image of eternity beyond life and an ideal to be aspired to within life, perhaps in the new Republic of Ireland. The poem ends:

> Astraddle on the dolphin's mire and blood,
> Spirit after spirit! The smithies break the flood,
> The golden smithies of the Emperor!
> Marbles of the dancing floor
> Break bitter furies of complexity,
> Those images that yet
> Fresh images beget,
> That dolphin-torn, that gong-tormented sea.[82]

Following Neoplatonist imagery, souls ride on the backs of dolphins (a love-beast) across the sea of generation which is 'dolphin-torn', or split by passion, and 'gong-tormented' or oppressed by the fear of death. The chaotic mass of the sea is brought into order as it breaks against the golden walls of the celestial city, promising that the soul can be hammered into a unity or wholeness. This will happen as the marble of the dancing floor gradually brings the whirling feet of the dancers to stillness; that is, souls after death will have to repeat all the past events of their life, 'dreaming back' all the complex and bitter furies of experience, as if in the patterns of a dance. But stillness will not be the last word: now bitter memories have been healed, new images can be made and a new life lived. If the poem is read as a picture of after-death experience, then for Yeats this means

---

[82]   W. B. Yeats, *Collected Poems* (London: Macmillan, 2nd ed. repr. 1967), pp. 280–1.

reincarnation in another existence; if it is read as an aspiration in life, perhaps the spiritual city will be more readily built when the turmoils and troubled memories of youth are past.

Yeats has vividly caught the sense of renewal through a movement like that of dance (in the immediately preceding verse we have 'dying into a dance'). Yet 'stillness' remains a Platonic ideal, and new life is still troubled by passion and death ('That dolphin-torn, that gong-tormented sea'). It is not irrelevant that Yeats held an esoteric and hermetic view of history as cyclic, aligned to the phases of the moon.

Next to this poem we may place one by a fine modern Irish poet, Micheal O'Siadhail, who also has a vision of unifying faith, the arts and public life in what seems a 'fragile city'. In his poem 'Dance'[83] he begins by expressing his yearning for the formal dance of 'ritual, organic/ Patterns, circlings, the whorled dance'. In this dance there is also a healing, a 'stillness beyond the rhythm', but it comes through openness to others and through participation in relationships, so that 'I want to dance for ever'.

> Openness. Again and again to realign.
> Another face and the moves must begin
> Anew. And we unfold into our design.
> I want to dance for ever. A veil
> Shakes between now-ness and infinity.
> Touch of hands. Communal and frail.
> Our courtesies weave a fragile city.

[83] Micheal O'Siadhail, *A Fragile City* (Newcastle: Bloodaxe Books, 1995), p. 75.

Chapter Eight

A FULLER PRESENCE

The Desire for Presence

A contrast between the mutability of time and the constancy of eternity haunts the English poetry of the seventeenth century. Among the poets of that period, however, one wrote about eternity in the context not only of our desire for God, but of an eternal desire and 'want' (need) of God for fellowship with created persons.[1] For Thomas Traherne, therefore, eternity was not the dissolving of time, but the making of time possible:

> When first Eternity stoopt down to Nought
> And in the Earth its Likeness sought . . .[2]

It has been our continual theme that time must be understood theologically, as rooted in God. We are creatures of time because God has time for us, and so eternity makes time possible. Similarly, it is eschatology that makes endings possible. I have been suggesting that only a final end which combines openness and closure provides a horizon for the making of endings here and now.

We began this study with four critical views of the effect of an ending, and our discussion since then has explored the particular form these effects take when placed in the context of Christian eschatology, that is, a closure with openness at its heart. First, an end organizes the time of the story which leads up to it, giving it the shape of a whole (Kermode). From an eschatological perspective, this 'wholeness' reflects the nature of eternity,

---

[1] Thomas Traherne, 'The First Century', pp. 42–3, in *Traherne: Poems, Centuries and Three Thanksgivings*, ed. Anne Ridler (Oxford: Oxford University Press, 1966), p. 183.
[2] Traherne, *Poems*, p. 37.

but not as a 'timeless moment'; the wholeness which is hoped for is not a *simultaneity* of time but its healing, with room for development and adventure. This accords with a second aspect of the end, that it opens up possible new worlds (Ricoeur). From the viewpoint of an eschatology which is open, these possibilities are rooted both in God's creative imagination and in human potential; they flow from God's project, which is to include the contributions of created beings within the fulfilment of the divine purposes. This points to the truth within the third aspect of an end, stressed by 'deconstructionist' critics (for example, Derrida); an ending opens up meaning, always undermining authoritarian patterns of explanation and resisting the exclusion of the 'other'. The open-endedness of Christian eschatology disturbs structures of domination, while moving towards a closure which is a fulfilment of purpose.

An ending in a text also, fourthly, expresses desire (Frye). We have seen that an end which is the goal of hope is truly open, rather than merely based on an extension of the conditions of the present. If 'waiting' is not to be futile, it will be a waiting for an end which is more than 'not yet'. At the same time, this waiting is driven by *desire*. A future which is hoped for is 'desirable' rather than being 'predictable', and the desire for eternity is finally the desire for God. This is an aspect of the end that has perhaps received less attention up to this point in our study. Hope in eternal life is desire for fullness of divine presence, expressed in Christian tradition as the 'beatific vision', in biblical terms as the 'dwelling' of God with his people, and in rabbinic texts as the Shekinah-presence of God. The promise of God to Israel in exile in the sixth century BC, as recounted by Ezekiel, is that 'My dwelling place shall be with them; and I will be their God and they shall be my people. Then the nations will know that I the Lord sanctify Israel, when my sanctuary is among them forevermore' (Ezekiel 37:27–28). Reaching beyond national crisis and nationalistic expectations, the Apocalypse of John finds this promise fulfilled in a new heaven and new earth:

> 'See, the home of God is among mortals.
> He will dwell with them as their God;
> they will be his peoples,
> and God himself will be with them . . .'   (Revelation 21:3)

The desire for fullness of 'presence' can take the form of desire for fullness of the 'present', that is a simultaneity of the eternal moment. But this is a desire rooted in lack, in a longing for an 'eternal return' to recover a wholeness that supposedly lies in the past. This might take the historical form of nostalgia for a lost paradisial perfection, and it is in accord with this pattern that Northrop Frye (wrongly in my view)[3] locates the biblical images of desire in the regaining of paradise which was lost at the beginning of a supposedly 'U-shaped curve' of world history. Desire might also be interpreted psychologically as a yearning for a preconscious, prelinguistic or presexually aware state of existence in the womb or early infancy, Freud and Lacan being notable exponents of this sense of loss. By contrast, however, true Christian desire is rooted not in lack and retrospection, but in hope for a future which is anticipated in the present.

Human desire for fullness of presence takes symbolic form, I suggest, in the desire for a 'place' or a 'space' to be. Finally this is a desire for an eternal 'place', symbolized for instance in the new Jerusalem which John of Patmos is portraying as he celebrates the 'the dwelling of God among mortals'. But the desire for presence also drives two pictures of the future which fall short of the vision of eternity. These are the millennial reign of God on earth (based on such scriptural passages as Daniel 7, Ezekiel 37–8, Revelation 7, 20) and the secular image of Utopia. The first concentrates on a more immediate presence of *God*, and the second on a society in which *human beings* are more fully present to themselves and to the world around them, but the two are linked in illuminating ways. In this chapter I intend to focus on these symbols of penultimate forms of presence, and their context in the wider human quest to find a 'place to be'. In the final chapter I shall venture upon a vision of our final dwelling place in God, and I therefore ask the reader to take the two chapters together.

Millennium and Utopia

The millenarian dream that gripped Christian Europe in the Middle Ages and the Reformation could be interpreted in either a 'premillennial' or 'postmillennial' way, with varying kinds of divine presence within their scenarios. In the premillennial form, Christ himself was expected to return to earth before the millennium, to initiate a thousand year reign in which he would be physically present with his saints to rule the world in peace and justice, an empire which would end with the last judgement and eternal life. The present time was therefore felt to be a period of *transition* to the millennium in which one world age was ending and another

---

[3]   See above, pp. 17, 19–20.

beginning; the elect, such as the 'Fifth Monarchy Men' in Cromwell's England, were being called to purify themselves to prepare for the *parousia* of Christ as world-king.

A sense of living in the midst of transition also belonged to the post-millennial forms of expectation, in which the millennium would *end* with the *parousia* of Christ and the onset of eternity. Where the millennium was believed to be imminent, the new age, though without the direct presence of Christ, would still be marked by greater immediacy of the presence of God in the world. The most influential form of such expectation was Joachim of Fiore's scheme of the Third Age or 'Kingdom of the Spirit', soon to follow the Kingdoms of the Father and the Son, in which knowledge of God would be directly revealed in the heart. An even more radical version of Joachitism appeared in the 'Brethren of the Free Spirit', where the belief that every person would soon be an incarnation of the Spirit seems to have produced a kind of anarchistic community.[4]

The edges between these two forms of millenarianism were often blurred, though both were marked by what Norman Cohn has called 'a coherent social myth';[5] faced by disasters such as the Black Death, the masses of the new urban areas identified these as the Great Tribulation, turned to messianic leaders, demonized outsiders as the Antichrist and his followers, and fantasized about being part of the 'army of the saints'. Most germane to our present concern, however, was that the new age which was felt to be beginning was marked by a sense of *enlightenment*, a new nearness to both earthly and heavenly realities through seraphic visions and new intellectual powers. In its conflation of eschatological schemes of history, Joachite prophecy had identified the Christian millennium not only with the rabbinic seventh (sabbatical) age, but with the 'Golden Age' of Sybilline prophecy which Virgil had alluded to in his Fourth Eclogue. As Marjorie Reeves has pointed out, in the last decade of the fifteenth century the Christian Neoplatonists of Florence were announcing the dawn of a new Golden Age while at the same time they were assailed by fears of the advent of Antichrist.[6] Later, in seventeenth century England, Isaac

---

[4]   Norman Cohn, *The Pursuit of the Millennium. Revolutionary Millenarians and Mystical Anarchists of the Middle Ages* (London: Random House/Pimlico, repr. 1993), pp. 148–62.

[5]   Cohn, *Pursuit of the Millennium*, p. 88.

[6]   Marjorie Reeves, 'Pattern and Purpose in History in the Later Medieval and Renaissance Periods', in Malcolm Bull (ed.), *Apocalypse Theory* (Oxford: Blackwell, 1995), p. 100.

Newton saw increase in knowledge of the natural world as a providential
sign that the millennial reign of Christ was near, and considered that his
own discoveries in mathematics were decoding the secrets of the book of
nature and so hastening the coming of visible divine rule.[7]

In this hope for a new grasp of the world through an enlightened human
mind there lies an affinity with secular visions of Utopia. The social world
imagined in a Utopia provides a critique of the status quo in current
society, and disturbs existing structures with what Bloch has called a 'real-
possible'. Bloch contrasts this 'concrete Utopia', which explores real
alternatives to our present world, with the mere 'abstract Utopias' of
indulgent fantasy.[8] The Utopia is – literally – a 'No-Place' because it is a
'not-yet place'; according to Bloch, preconceptual insights in the mind
about what the world can be like – the 'not-yet conscious' – achieve
consciousness with the production of the picture of a Utopia. Thus the
'Utopia' (No-Place) is truly a 'Eutopia' (Good-Place), a play on words first
made by Sir Thomas More in his seminal account of the imaginary island
of Utopia (1516). A Utopia, then, pictures a place in which the self is fully
present to itself (knowing itself) and to its environment (being at home in
the world). At the same time, a Utopia expresses human *desire* for such a
place of well-being and harmony between individual, society and nature.
As Karl Mannheim puts it, a Utopia is the projection of human yearnings
into space, while millennial dreams project desire into time.[9] Utopias and
the millennium are both this-worldly, embodying our desires in a location
which belongs to our world and history. The overlap between them is
evident in modern fictional versions of Utopias which often portray the
Utopian period as beginning with the tribulations and woes which are
characteristic of the millennium, usually now a nuclear or ecological
disaster.

Utopias reshape our desires, directing them to life-enhancing goals, and
so Krishan Kumar is right to propose that the most interesting Utopias are
not simply blueprints and designs of a good society; they enable us to *feel*
what it is like to live in such a 'place' and create 'the texture of life there'.[10]

---

[7]   See Richard Popkin, 'Seventeenth-Century Millenarianism' in Bull (ed.), *Apocalypse Theory*, pp. 124–5.

[8]   Ernst Bloch, *The Principle of Hope*, vol. 1, transl. N. Plaice, S. Plaice and P. Knight (Oxford: Blackwell, 1986), pp. 142–50, 148–65.

[9]   Karl Mannheim, *Ideology and Utopia* (London: Kegan Paul, 1936), p. 36ff.

[10]   Krishan Kumar, 'Apocalypse, Millennium and Utopia Today', in Bull (ed.), *Apocalypse Theory*, pp. 213–14.

William Morris's *News from Nowhere* (1890), for example, has often been criticized for lacking detail about the workings of a future socialist society but, judges Kumar, it is 'shot through with what one might call the expressive or emotional structures of utopia'. It is a mark of our present age that, in the western world at least, we have a sense of apocalyptic doom without hope, so that it is difficult to express our desires. Western science fiction, for instance, has been more successful in depicting 'dystopias' than Utopias, leading to a critique from science fiction writers in Eastern Europe that American and British writers can only project the contradictions and social conflicts of present society onto imaginary space worlds.[11] A voice from the West, Michel Foucault,[12] doubts whether images of an alternative world can ever break free from the power-structures and manipulative relations of modern society, and so whether it is possible to depict a 'concrete Utopia' any longer.

This weakening of the ability to envision Utopia is an inheritance of Enlightenment belief that the millennium has already been reached, and at the same time it is a reaction against it. The confidence of the Enlightenment in human progress can in turn be seen as a secular version of what Jürgen Moltmann has diagnosed as 'historical millenarianism' within Christian tradition.[13] That is, a postmillennial form of future expectation lends itself to a transfer of the millennial reign of Christ into the present age. If the *parousia* of Christ will not happen until after the millennium, then it is possible to claim that we are in fact in the middle of the millennium here and now. In political terms, Christ is envisaged as ruling the world through an earthly representative, and this was an interpretation of eschatology which became orthodox in the Christian Church from the time of the foundation of the Christian Empire of Constantine. Eusebius, for example, celebrated Constantine as fulfilling the promise of Daniel 7:18 that 'the saints of the Most High shall receive the Kingdom', as messianic peace was achieved through the unity of the Roman Empire.[14] Correspondingly, the millennium could be identified with the age of the Church, as Augustine dated the beginning of the millennium (in his reckoning the sixth and final

[11]   There is a good account of this in John Griffiths, *Three Tomorrows. American, British and Soviet Science Fiction* (Macmillan, Basingstoke, 1980), pp. 100–109; he refers particularly to the Russian author Ivan Yefremov.
[12]   Michel Foucault, *Madness and Civilization. A History of Insanity in the Age of Reason*, transl. R. Howard (London: Tavistock Publications, 1967).
[13]   Jürgen Moltmann, *The Coming of God*, transl. M. Kohl (London: SCM Press, 1996), pp. 146ff, 192–4.
[14]   Eusebius, *Laus Constantani*, 3.

epoch of world history) from the day of ascension;[15] Christ was now envisaged as ruling through ecclesiastical authority, which claimed fullness of power to ordain priests and excommunicate heretics.

The official theology of the medieval Church accepted this Augustinian interpretation of history, and so its sense of 'transition' was not *into* a millennium but *from* it. Where the tribulation and messianic woes could be identified, they marked an intervening period of crisis before the world ended. In this scenario all that was left to hope for was the last judgement and eternity.[16] If the fullness of the presence of Christ on earth is experienced here and now in imperial and ecclesiastical rule, in Emperor and in Pope, this means that there is a suppression of any desire for fuller presence here on earth which might challenge the status quo. Visions of a coming millennium could not be tolerated, as was made clear in the persecution of the Anabaptists, among other millenarian sects.

In his account of this period, Moltmann regrets the swallowing up of the millennium into present history, since he believes that only a hope for a future *earthly* rule of Christ preceding the final entrance of eternity into time can satisfy the demand for justice for the oppressed. The righteousness of God, in his view, calls for a period in which human society is actually redeemed in time and history and the poor are given their rights. He is nostalgic for the 'premillennial' expectations of the Christian church before Constantine, which provided an eschatology for martyrs who resisted the ultimate demands of the powers of the state. Now, Moltmann is surely right to suspect the dangers of Christian imperialism, including the use of violence to support its mission, whenever a millennial presence of God is ascribed to present institutions. However, I suggest that the status quo can be subverted by a desire for new creation in a transformed universe without a literal earthly millennial rule of Christ. The language of millennium can be applied to the hope for eternal life itself, but the metaphors in which that life is envisaged have to be such as *will* unsettle the power structures of the present age, and this was not the case with the static images of perfection held in scholastic theology.

In the period of modernity, from the Enlightenment onwards, there has been a secularization of the 'historical' eschatology of Augustine and Eusebius. The modern world itself has been identified with the end-time,

---

[15] Augustine, *City of God*, 20.7–9.
[16] See Moltmann, *The Coming of God*, p. 156.

as a kind of millennium.[17] In his influential essay 'The Education of the Human Race' (1780), Lessing appealed to the Third Age of Joachim's scheme of history for the imminent dawning in his own day of the 'time of the perfecting' when people would live by the truths of reason, and would 'do right [just] because it *is* right'.[18] In such thinking, divine rule over the world was translated into the subjugation of the natural world by the rational human subject. The immediacy of the knowledge of God was translated into a direct access of the human mind to truth and a purified moral will, so that past cultural traditions were redundant. In his analysis of this millenarian mood, Moltmann makes the interesting suggestion that the rule of the redeemer was transferred in political terms to a nation with 'manifest destiny' to bring about a new world order, namely the young nation of the United States. In the 'great experiment' of American democracy, citizens were to make their own future without being hampered by the old traditions of Europe.[19]

In short, modernity was to achieve the desired fullness of presence of human beings to themselves, to their world, and to their God. While the religious language of the millennium was applied to this project, the final state envisaged was in fact closer to a Utopia, in that in a Utopia progress has come to an end. Both the Utopia and the millennium are characterized by an immediacy of knowledge, but the shape of the millennium is still forward-leaning; in its religious form it is penultimate to the coming of eternity. The secular millennium may be envisaged as culminating in a Utopia, as for instance in the 'sociocracy' of Auguste Comte[20] or Marx's (cautiously expressed) expectation of the 'true community of man'.[21] To the extent that society approaches perfection, any

---

[17] The thesis that the secular view of progress was a replacement or development of the Christian belief in the millennium has, however, been challenged by Hans Blumenberg, in *The Legitimacy of the Modern Age*, transl. R. Wallace (Cambridge, Mass.: Harvard University Press, 1985).

[18] Gotthold Lessing, 'The Education of the Human Race', paras. 85–9, in Henry Chadwick (ed. & transl.) *Lessing's Theological Writings* (London: A. & C. Black, 1956), pp. 96–7.

[19] Moltmann, *The Coming of God*, p. 173.

[20] Auguste Comte, *System of Positive Polity*, Vol. 4, Eng. transl. (London: Longmans, 1877).

[21] Karl Marx, *Early Writings*, Intr. L. Colletti (Harmondsworth: Penguin, 1975), p. 265. For the concept of Utopia in Marx, see Nicholas Lash, *A Matter of Hope. A Theologian's Reflections on the Thought of Karl Marx* (London: Darton, Longman and Todd, 1981), pp. 231–249.

change in its structure will represent a decline from the ideal. There is an irony here about the notion of Utopia that we shall have cause to return to: as an imaginative image of the 'not yet' it disturbs the status quo, but in so far as it depicts a society in rational equilibrium, it necessarily has a static quality.

The mood which has now overtaken the Western world is a reaction against the millenarian/Utopian vision of the Enlightenment and modernity. We are in a period marked – at least partly – by a 'postmodern' loss of the self, when the Cartesian subject which can make decisions and order its destiny has been replaced by a self which is 'an opaque product of variable roles and performances imposed upon it by the constraints of society and by its own inner drives or conflicts'.[22] With the loss of self has come a sense of loss of grasp of the world as a whole; we do not know how to name the world when it is no longer an object to be dominated by the self. This is a critique of fullness of presence, whether of the self, world or God. A different, but complementary, mood is one of weariness and disillusionment at the *success* of the modern project. So Francis Fukuyama asserts that we are at 'the end of history', in the sense that we are finally in an era without ideological alternatives for society; pluralist-capitalist democracy has triumphed everywhere, so that there can be no more revolutionary renewal but only a rather tedious process of gradual adaptation and reform.[23] Yet a third strand is a sense of imminent apocalyptic disaster, whether nuclear, ecological (especially global warming), economic ('meltdown' of world currencies), cybernetic (the 'millennium bug') or atronomical (asteroid collision). These strands necessarily overlap. Deconstruction of the self and world, for example, may use the rhetoric of nuclear apocalypse in order to destabilize discourse and reference.[24] Postmodernism may also be accused of regarding the world as a 'text' to be deconstructed because it has abandoned history to its 'end'

[22] Anthony Thiselton, *Interpreting God and the Postmodern Self* (Edinburgh: T. & T. Clark, 1995), p. 121.

[23] Francis Fukuyama, *The End of History and the Last Man* (London: Hamish Hamilton, 1992).

[24] See Derrida, 'No Apocalypse, Not Now', *Diacritics* 14/2 (1984), pp. 26–31; for the destabilizing effect of apocalyptic rhetoric and 'rhetoric of crisis' generally, see Derrida 'Of an Apocalyptic Tone', transl. J. Leavey, in H. Coward and T. Foshay (eds) *Derrida and Negative Theology* (Albany: State University of New York Press, 1992), pp. 30–8, and 'Cogito and the History of Madness', in *Writing and Difference*, transl. A. Bass (London: Routledge, 1978), pp. 37–9.

in the empire of multi-national corporations and a unitary consumer culture.[25]

For complex reasons, then, we seem to be in an age of 'judgement without a kingdom' (Moltmann)[26] or 'millenarianism without a utopian vision' (Kumar)[27] or 'transition without the millennium'. The author of the last phrase, Frank Kermode,[28] judges that for all this we are not very different from previous epochs. What is common is a sense of being in transition from one age to another, whatever cultural form this feeling of transition might take; he finds, for instance, remarkable similarities between the period of decadence at the end of the nineteenth century, and the postmodernism that marks the end of the twentieth. As we saw in the first chapter, he proposes that what we are finally awaiting through the experience of transition is our own deaths. Christian eschatology, however, wants to say more than this, to open up a future hope for the cosmos in the midst of transition. And desire has not been suppressed; even in postmodern critical thinking there are hints of transcendence (as we shall see), and fictional Utopias – though few – are still being written. The Christian claim is that an 'end' which is characterized by both openness and closure can offer hope in the face of apocalypse. What this might entail in terms of the fulfilment of desire for presence I intend to approach through reference to two fictional Utopias.

Fictional Images of Utopia: Aldous Huxley's *Island* and Ursula Le Guin's *The Dispossessed*

Aldous Huxley's depiction of a Utopian society in his last novel, *Island* (1962) is a mixture of an Enlightenment millennium and a Buddhist vision of 'the eternal now'. In fact these two strands combine genetically in the person of the paradisial island's leading wise man, the doctor Robert McPhail. His great-grandfather, a doctor from Scotland, had worked with the Raja of the time to recreate the community of Pala as an experiment in cooperative civilization, based on a combination of humanist-atheist and Mahayana Buddhist principles. The novel traces the impressions of a visitor

---

[25] See David Harvey, *The Condition of Postmodernity* (Oxford: Blackwell, 1990), pp. 115–118.

[26] Moltmann, *The Coming of God*, p. 227, cf. p. 217.

[27] Kumar, 'Apocalypse, Millennium and Utopia Today', p. 212.

[28] Frank Kermode, 'Waiting for the End', in Bull (ed.), *Apocalypse Theory*, pp. 25–63.

to the island, the cynical journalist Will Farnaby, who has arrived on a secret search for information about Pala's massive, unexploited oil resources. He has just come to appreciate the wisdom of their way of life, and with their help to understand himself and his failed marriage for the first time, when the island is annexed by invasion from the neighbouring fascist state on the mainland. Its totalitarian leader, Colonel Dipa, has made an alliance with the present boy Raja and his mother, the Rani, in order to turn the island into an industrial-consumer society like all others in the modern world.

When Farnaby stumbles injured onto Pala after an accident to his boat, the very first words he hears are 'attention!' and 'here and now boys!', repeatedly chanted by the thousands of mynah birds on the island.[29] Attention to the here and now is at the heart of the culture of the island, as Farnaby learns when he shares in the saying of 'grace' before meals, which consists in chewing the first mouthful of each course in silence, 'paying attention to the flavour of the food, to its consistency and temperature . . .' The point of this 'attention to the experience of something given, something you haven't invented', his host explains, is 'to make me more conscious of what the not-me is up to' (p. 225). But this is not attention to a transcendent personal God, whether Christian, Hindu, or one of the incarnations of the Buddha principle. Shortly after this meal, the children take their turn in operating mechanical scarecrows, which are life-sized, gorgeously clothed images of God the Father and the Future Buddha. As Farnaby's guide explains:

> 'It was the Old Raja's idea . . . he wanted to make the children understand that the gods are all home-made, and that it's we who pull their strings and so give them power to pull ours.' (p. 227)

Robert McPhail had earlier rejected transcendent authority, leaving behind the 'Wholly Other' deity of his strictly Calvinistic parents (p. 128). Divinity is immanent, 'here and now', expressed in such phrases as 'this is that' and 'pure Suchness'. But while the dancing scarecrows deconstruct transcendence, the immanent divinity is more than the individual; what is here and now is a corporate cosmic Mind to which each mind is to be open. The novel offers two images for this Mind, one Buddhist and the other Hindu in origin. First, the scarecrows prompt us to look up into the sky, and alert us to the void, a 'boundless and pregnant emptiness out of

---

[29]   Aldous Huxley, *Island* (London: HarperCollins/Flamingo, 1994), pp. 1–7.

which everything, the living and the inanimate, the puppet-makers and their divine marionettes, emerge into the universe we know . . .' (p. 228). Part of the Palanese culture is the use of an hallucinogenic drug to open the doors of perception to this empty space of the Buddha nature. Second, there is the image of the dancing Shiva, 'in other words their own Suchness visualized as God'. In a vivid scene in an ancient temple (itself a symbol of the divine void), the young people of the island are initiated at puberty into the use of the *moksha* medicine, and learn to identify themselves, their pleasures and pains, with the impartial dance of Shiva who fills the universe and 'dances in all worlds'. While the dancing scarecrows point to illusory divinity, the Shiva dances in every living thing, 'dancing everlastingly in the eternal now' (p. 189).

At the climax of the book, as the tanks of the military dictator rumble into Pala, Farnaby tries the hallucinogenic *moksha* for himself, and enters 'the timelessly present event, the Now'; in the light that envelops him 'its presence was his absence', and there is 'complete communication, but nothing communicated. Just an exchange of life'. Music playing is heard as: 'a Present Event with an infinite duration . . . there was a tempo, but not time. So what was there? Eternity' (pp. 306–7).

This mystical experience is presented as enabling Farnaby to pay attention to the here and now (p. 320), to himself as he really is, to the world around, and especially to Susila, the woman initiating him into this new awareness. In the society of Pala, its citizens learn to pay attention to each other and to the natural world, and so to live in a co-operative and harmonious way without the need for the usual centralized hierarchy of authority. Problems of individual and public health are tackled in a psychosomatic way, from every angle of physical, mental and spiritual life. Pala's inhabitants cultivate the earth sensitively, in a way that does not exploit its resources, and their spiritual adventures are matched by facing physical challenges in mountaineering. The tyranny of the small nuclear family has been replaced by 'Mutual Adoption Clubs' of twenty families grouped together, and population growth has been stabilized with the help both of modern contraceptives and a 'yoga of love'.

This Utopian existence has been achieved through a mixture of Eastern religion and the fruits of the Western Enlightenment, importing Western medicine, agricultural techniques, printing, the English language and with it a ready-made repertory of literature. As Anthony Burgess comments, 'they have read all the books that Huxley has read'.[30] When the mynah

---

[30] Anthony Burgess, *The Novel Now* (London: Faber and Faber, 1971), p. 42.

birds fly around crying the word *Karuna*, it clearly refers to 'enlightenment' both in the Buddhist and European sense.

This off-shore Utopia is to be destroyed by the crude, materialistic stupidity of the young Raja whose favourite reading is an American mail-order catalogue, coupled with the sentimental 'spiritual crusade' of his mother, who is besotted with a kind of spiritualism which embodies the worst aspects of a transcendent view of deity. Yet the reader comes to suspect that the real roots of destruction do not lie here. Huxley was worried that the novel was too philosophical, that 'the story has too much weight, in the way of ideas and reflections to carry'. It certainly does embody his 'perennial philosophy', including the induction of mystical experience through drugs, but as a good novel it also contains self-critical and deconstructive hints which make it more than a piece of propaganda for the good life. After writing the dystopia of *Brave New World* (1932), with its attack on test-tube eugenics, does Huxley really intend no hint of irony in the Palanese use of artificial insemination to 'improve the race' by breeding 'a better stock' and (theologically) to achieve 'a better karma' (p. 215)? Given his satire on the use of the happy-drug *soma* to control the population in *Brave New World*, is there no irony in the lauding of the *moksha* medicine as 'four hundred milligrammes of revelation' (p. 181)?

Whether or not the author *intends* to undermine his own Utopia, the reader is disturbed by a culture that insists so strongly on immediacy, on the instant accessibility of 'visionary and liberating experiences' (p. 195), and on attention almost exclusively to the present moment. What matters is 'getting on with the job' of 'practising all the yogas of increased awareness' (p. 271). The 'presence' of people to themselves and their environment is identified with the 'present', the overcoming of time in an 'eternal now'. This is a world from which not only the transcendence of God has been banished, but the transcendence of the future. It is a world without eschatology, without the motive to imagine alternative worlds, and so without perspective to criticize its own status quo, however admirable it is. Pala seeks to maintain its way of life in the modern age by self-sufficiency and by shutting out contamination, usually forbidding visitors to land on the island. The reader familiar with Shakespeare's *The Tempest* knows that life on such islands will inevitably come to an end, as Prospero needed to turn his face to the future, breaking the staff and drowning the book with which he had achieved control over the elements in his little island kingdom. The arrival of those who were outsiders and enemies on the shores of Prospero's island gave opportunity for reconciliation with the wider world which had treated him unjustly, and for setting sail into a hazardous new stage of existence.

Of course, we have no sympathy with the brutal invasion of the island of Pala by Colonel Dipa, driven by materialistic greed. Violence does not open up the future, and we agree with McPhail that an image of a dominating deity who predestines some of his creatures to destruction only encourages human violence. The stern Calvinistic father of the first Dr. McPhail had applied his theology of an 'infinitely offended Father' by beating his own children, prompting the speculative theory of the present Dr McPhail that 'wherever little boys and girls are systematically flagellated, the victims grow up to think of God as "Wholly Other"'. On the other hand, he proposes, 'wherever children are brought up without being subjected to physical violence, God is immanent' (p. 128). The story sets the theologian the task, therefore, of conceiving transcendence without oppression.

In many ways the world of Anarres in Ursula Le Guin's science fiction novel, *The Dispossessed. An Ambiguous Utopia* (1974), shares features with Huxley's Pala. This small planet houses an anarchistic society which relies on cooperation between its inhabitants through voluntary 'syndicates' rather than centralized authority. Like Pala there is an extended family arrangement, physical labour is willingly undertaken even by the intellectuals, food and housing is shared freely and there is no army. It has succeeded more radically than Pala in totally abolishing both money and the owning of property, both of which are still minimal in Huxley's world. It is also similar to Pala in shutting itself away from outsiders who might contaminate its way of life; the very first words of the novel are 'There was a wall' – a barrier which surrounds the rocket port where space freighters land from other planets for necessary trade, but whose crews are not permitted to stray outside the port area.

In other ways Anarres differs from Pala. The barren planet on which the inhabitants live lacks all charm of landscape, and the Annerestians have achieved their strong sense of solidarity by shared suffering in wresting a living from the unpromising earth. More profoundly, Le Guin is realistic in showing the defects of a society which regards itself – with some justice – as Utopian.[31] The main character, Shevek, comes to realize that a social conscience can oppress the individual conscience, and can subjugate each person's own need for fulfilment: 'we fear being outcast, being called lazy,

---

[31]   Le Guin has a particular strength in depicting 'semi-Utopias'; another good example is her novel *Always Coming Home* (London: Victor Gollancz, 1986).

dysfunctional, egoizing . . . we force a man outside the sphere of approval . . . we've built walls all around ourselves and we can't see them'.[32] Shevek, who is a brilliant physicist, himself suffers from the jealousy of a senior colleague in his institute who tries to suppress his revolutionary work on the nature of time. Shevek decides to leap the wall of Anarres by journeying to the neighbouring planet of Urras, a capitalist ('propertarian') society from which the settlers on Anarres had in fact fled to seek their freedom centuries before. Going there Shevek is condemned as a traitor by his own people, and does not know whether he will ever be able to return home; he is the truly 'dispossessed'.

He makes the journey between planets partly to gain freedom to work on his theory of time, which he does in the University on Urras where is he welcomed with honour. But his main motive is to try to bring harmony and understanding between two worlds, each of which he is convinced needs the other. His work in temporal physics comes to symbolize for him the need for symbiosis between societies, dealing as it does with two apparently irreconcilable theories. These, we discover, are nothing other than futuristic versions of the two models of time implied respectively by Special Relativity theory and by one interpretation of quantum theory as we have already surveyed them in this study: that is views of time as either 'simultaneous' or as 'flowing' in a linear sequence (pp. 186–91, 232–4). Shevek aims to develop a unified temporal theory that will integrate 'Simultaneity' and 'Sequency' theories, a feat that – as I have already observed – our present-day science has not achieved.

He succeeds, though comes to realize that his mission of reconciliation has been a failure, and that he has been effectively 'bought' by the Government of Urras so that it can possess his General Temporal Theory and use it for the instant transfer of matter across space. This will have commercial applications for space travel and military applications for weapons. Carrying his unwritten theory in his mind, he joins a rebellion of the working classes against the Government, and just escapes with his life, seeking temporary asylum with the ambassador from Terra (earth). He charges her to publish his equations widely as a gift to all civilizations; these cannot be used for transfer of matter but will enable instant *communication* – and so, hopefully, increased understanding – between planets separated by light-years of distance. The novel ends with his imminent return to Anarres, not knowing whether he will be accepted back, yet seeking also

[32] Ursula Le Guin, *The Dispossessed. An Ambiguous Utopia* (London: Panther/Granada, 1975), p. 273.

to introduce a visitor from another race into their society for the first time. They will walk through the wall together.

Like Pala, the way of life of Anarres reflects the 'simultaneity' model of time, even though Shevek's exposition of the abstract theory only gains grudging acceptance. As Shevek suggests to a musician who wants to call his rejected work *The Simultaneity Principle*, 'If you called it *The Joys of Solidarity*, would they hear it?' All energy is directed towards the present moment, and to mutual presence in cooperative activity, whether in the mines or mathematics. Any heritage of ideas from Urras or other planets is despised, and minds are not open to future relations with others, for fear that the tyrants they have defeated may interpret their action as saying 'the experiment has failed; come re-enslave us!' (p. 294). But Shevek is seeking to unify simultaneity with the flow of time, to 'work with time' in quest of joy and the 'completeness of being' (p. 276). As he explains to the Terran ambassador, who admires Anarres as a society that exemplifies virtues which lie as yet for Terrans in the future:

> You think Anarres is a future that cannot be reached, as your past cannot be changed. So there is nothing but the present, this Urras, the rich, real stable present, the moment now. And you think that is something which can be possessed! . . . Things change, change. You cannot have anything . . . and least of all can you have the present – unless you accept with it the past and the future. Not only the past but also the future, not only the future, but also the past! Because they are real: only their reality makes the present real . . . (p. 288)

Living imaginatively in the societies of Pala and Anarres, the theological reader begins to see some of the boundary lines for a Christian eschatology. Within history, any society needs an eschatology to challenge the *status quo* of its institutions and to open up the future to real alternatives. The desire for 'presence' – knowing oneself and being at home in the world – must not be confused with pure 'presentness'. Utopian dreams which make this confusion will undermine themselves, and have no power to liberate.

A recent writer on Utopias, Gorman Beauchamp, maintains indeed that progress and Utopia are always antithetical concepts.[33] If the point of a Utopia is that social life is perfectly adjusted in the present, then systemic change is neither desirable nor possible. Moreover, the immediacy of reason to all minds will result in a will to conformity, since if there is one

---

[33] Gorman Beauchamp, 'Changing Times in Utopia', *Philosophy and Literature*, 22 (1998), pp. 219–30.

'most reasonable' way of doing things, then there is no reason to vary it. Utopias, from Plato's *Republic* onwards, therefore present a uniformity in such matters as architecture, dress, city planning, and the raising of children. The supremely rational horses, the Houyhnhnms of Swift's satire on Utopia in Book IV of Gulliver's Travels (1726), cannot understand the notion of an opinion, 'or how a point could be disputable'.[34] Beauchamp examines one attempt to present a Utopia which escapes conformity, H. G. Wells's *A Modern Utopia* (1905); but despite Wells' assertion that a modern Utopia 'must not be static but kinetic, must shape not as a permanent state but as a hopeful stage', Beauchamp demonstrates that he reverts to describing a grey, homogeneous society. There cannot be a 'progressive Utopia'.[35]

Yet the image of Utopia persists, as Marianne de Koven remarks: 'Utopia in postmodernity is multiply defeated and discredited, yet it persists in the form not only of desire for elimination of domination, inequality and oppression but also of *desire for transcendence itself*.'[36] She observes that the Utopian imagination still survives in the form of a limited Utopia, a 'limited possible'.[37] This is not Wells's attempt to combine a full Utopian state with progressiveness, but 'an imagination of struggle for local, partial, always-ready compromised versions of the freedom, justice and equality that mark the utopian project'. This is surely what Anarres and Pala demonstrate, the former as an explicitly 'ambiguous Utopia', and the latter through its deconstruction and defeat. The image of the Utopia witnesses to the human desire for a 'place' or 'space' where there is fuller presence of persons to themselves and others, and a more immediate intuition of truth and universal access to reason. But the image of the *semi-Utopia* also shows the awareness that *full presence* and *total immediacy* would be as stifling as an eternal 'present'. The semi-Utopia, or limited Utopia is thus similar in nature to the 'millennium' in that it is penultimate and in transition.

For Christian eschatology, a question mark is bound to be placed therefore against the notion that in eternity we shall enjoy the full presence of God. Would this be the ultimate oppression, the supreme act of violence by the transcendent God of Dr McPhail's horrified imagination, leaving us with even less freedom than the social conscience of Anarres? We shall return to this question in our final chapter, when we have explored the

---

[34]   Jonathan Swift, *Gulliver's Travels* (Harmondsworth: Penguin Books, 1967), p. 315.
[35]   Beauchamp, 'Changing Times in Utopia', pp. 227–8.
[36]   Marianne de Koven, 'Utopia Limited: Post-Sixties and Postmodern American Fiction', *Modern Fiction Studies*, 41 (1995), p. 90; my italics.
[37]   Ibid., p. 91. Compare Bloch's 'real-possible'.

way that some contemporary philosophy and theology approaches the
issues of presence and transcendence.

The Critique of Full Presence

The 'Utopian' project of modernity can be portrayed in social terms as the
attempt to subjugate the natural world, with all its mysterious and threat-
ening aspects, to the control of the human consciousness. The human mind
is subject and the world its object, to be investigated and mastered. Now,
the same project can be described in philosophical terms as the total
equation of being with presence. It is proposed that to 'be' anything is to
be present and presentable to others; the more fully present something is
the more 'being-full' it is, and the greater the potential it has for control of
other beings. The human consciousness is directly present to itself (self-
conscious) and to the phenomena of the world, which have being because
they present themselves to the mind as sense-impressions.[38] This in turn
leads to a view of time which we have often had occasion to criticize in
this study: namely, that only the present is real, since the past is no longer
present and the future is not yet present.

Placing this ontology within a traditionally Christian perspective, God
can be seen as supreme Being because God is absolutely present, grounding
and validating the individual human consciousness and its own presence.
When this omnipresent Being is identified with self-causation and self-
determination (aseity), then the product is what Heidegger calls 'onto-
theological metaphysics', which he judged to have been brought to its peak
in Hegel. While Huxley in his novel *Island* firmly rejects the all-determin-
ing God of Calvin, it appears that his Utopia, which cultivates a sense of
immediate presence to the world, with its slogan 'here and now', is as
much marked by the project of the Enlightenment as by Buddhist ideas of
the eternal present.

It is the simple equation of being and presence that the 'postmodern'
mood attempts to overcome, replacing immediate, self-contained presence
with 'traces' of presence, whether of self or the world. It is important to
notice that key proponents of this deconstruction of full presence are not
denying presence altogether; they find 'a kind of constant flickering of

---

[38] Or, in phenomenology, because their 'essence' is directly and fully present/
presented to the mind: see Edmund Husserl, *Ideas: General Introduction to Pure Phenomenology*, transl. W. Boyce Gibson (London: Allen & Unwin, 1931).

presence and absence together',[39] or as Derrida puts it, 'Nothing is . . . anywhere ever simply present or absent. There are only, everywhere, differences and traces of traces'.[40] At the same time we shall see that in this deconstructive mood there is also an orientation towards a nameless 'place' that is a non-foundational origin of this flickering presence, as well as the source of all difference; it is an otherness that continually punctures attempts to establish either full presence or full absence. As Graham Ward discerns in the work of Derrida and others, this is 'an unstable, mysterious, ungrounding origin'.[41] It is a place or 'primordial space' (to use a theological metaphor) which cannot be reached, touched or established as a cause. To designate it we might re-employ the language of Utopia, but only in its sense of a place which is a 'Not-Place'; this space is not also a 'Good Place' in which one can actually dwell. By contrast, and anticipating the development of my thought in the next chapter, a Christian eschatology for today will try to think of God as our final dwelling-place, while learning from the postmodern attack on absolute presence.

The critique of 'presence' and the quest for a 'place' therefore go hand in hand, and this deserves some explanation and expansion. Heidegger had ventured to replace the metaphysics of presence with a new kind of ontology, based on the *difference* between Being and beings. Beings have their nature in *Dasein* – being there in the everyday world – and the experience of anxiety reveals to them that they have no secure grounding. To put it metaphorically, the manner of their 'arrival' in the world through Being is concealed. Being which gives itself to beings in an 'overwhelming' and 'unconcealed' way is nevertheless usually forgotten by beings who set out to establish their identity through such means of control as modern technology. The difference between Being and beings creates a kind of 'clearing' in space and time, a 'differential tension' (Ward's expression)[42] or an 'open region' (Heidegger) to which beings are exposed:

> The difference of Being and beings, as the differentiation of overwhelming and arrival, is the perdurance (*Austrag*) of the two in *unconcealing keeping in concealment*. Within this perdurance there prevails a clearing of what veils and

[39]   Terry Eagleton, *Literary Theory*, (Oxford: Blackwell, 1983), p. 128.

[40]   Jacques Derrida, *Positions*, transl. A. Bass (Chicago: University of Chicago Press, 1971), p. 26, cf. *Of Grammatology*, transl. G. C. Spivak (Baltimore and London: Johns Hopkins University Press, 1976), pp. 9ff, 143.

[41]   Graham Ward, *The Postmodern God. A Theological Reader* (Oxford: Blackwell, 1997), p. xxxiii.

[42]   Ibid., xxxii.

closes itself off – and this its prevalence bestows the being apart, and the being toward each other, of overwhelming and arrival.[43]

Being thus 'appears primordially in the light of concealing withdrawal'.[44] We cannot think Being itself, but we can think the difference and we can explore the space which is open to the transcendence 'beyond being' and in which Being itself has a hidden presence. For this 'between', Heidegger occasionally employs the term *khora* (or *khorismos*),[45] from the 'space' described in Plato's *Timaeus* which is neither being nor non-being, but a kind of interval between, in which the 'forms' were originally held.[46] 'The khora means the place' reflects Heidegger, and goes on to say that this poses the question of 'the wholly other place of Being',[47] the origin of the space we experience and which cannot be thought by metaphysics.

In his later work, Heidegger turned away from discussion of Being and more towards language as 'the abode of Being', as the context in which the ontological difference can be felt, so that human beings do not manipulate language when they speak, but speak when they respond to language itself. This track was followed by Derrida, in combining the ontological 'difference' in Heidegger with the semiotic 'difference' in Saussure's linguistics, according to which linguistic signs have their significance in their difference from each other.[48] The result is a denial of full presence, as no signifier can be immediately present to the signified. As we have already seen in chapter 2, within the network of differential signs in which we exist, all signifiers become the signified, so that meaning is dispersed. Signifiers cannot necessarily point to particular signified concepts. Negatively, there can only be a trace of the one in the other; positively, the trace is there and so the other is affirmed and not marginalized. Constructing a dialogue with Freud about the nature of the self, Derrida insists that all reference to a self must happen by way of detour through an other, and so presupposes an original self-effacement. Here then is a second

---

[43]   Martin Heidegger, *Identity and Difference*, transl. J. Stambaugh (New York: Harper and Row, 1974), p. 65.

[44]   Martin Heidegger, 'On the Essence of Truth', in David Krell (ed.), *Heidegger: Basic Writings* (London: Routledge & Kegan Paul, 1978), p. 140.

[45]   Martin Heidegger, *An Introduction to Metaphysics*, transl. R. Manheim (New Haven: Yale University Press, 1959), p. 66.

[46]   Plato, *Timaeus*, 50A–51B.

[47]   Martin Heidegger, *What is Called Thinking?* transl. J. Gray (New York: Harper and Row, 1968), pp. 245ff.

[48]   See above, pp. 31–3.

reason for denial of full presence: not only is there nothing more than a trace of presence, but the trace itself can be effaced or erased. The interplay between the self and the other both *makes* a trace and *erases* it: 'An unerasable trace is not a trace, it is a full presence, an immobile and uncorruptible substance, a son of God, a sign of parousia and not a seed, that is, a mortal germ.'[49]

Derrida picks up Heidegger's hint that the 'clearing' or space for the play of difference is itself a trace of something 'wholly other',[50] a place which it is impossible to speak about but which 'dictates an obligation by its very impossibility: *it is necessary* to speak of it . . .'.[51] In all his work Derrida is fascinated by the 'wholly other', which arrives to shock all horizons and prompts the crossing of all boundaries. Unlike the 'wholly other' in Emmanuel Levinas (to whom Derrida is indebted) this wholly other is essentially *within* the sign-network of language; there is an infinite alterity in the text since all signifieds are wholly other to other signs; yet this otherness points to the 'impossible possibility' of something outside and inside at the same time, and following Heidegger Derrida gives this 'singularity' the name of the *khora*. As John Caputo aptly summarizes it in his commentary on Derrida, talk about the *khora* is 'discourse about a desert, about a barren and naked place, a pure taking place, an empty place'.[52] It is a place which is no-place. In his essay, 'How to Avoid Speaking: Denials', Derrida denies that the *khora* is equivalent to the God of negative theology, despite the similarity that speaking about both is experienced as an 'impossible possibility'; his main reason is that the *khora* is not 'the giver of good gifts'. Indeed, one must refrain from saying that the *khora* gives anything at all, except perhaps that it 'gives place', as it receives all, but this is a gift 'without the least generosity', entailing neither debt nor exchange.

Yet the Totally Other is there (*il y a*), and it is necessary to speak about it, since it haunts the chain of signifiers (death as a powerful other reminds us constantly of it) and keeps open the promise at the heart of difference. This is a promise that any piece of writing can always be repeated with

---

[49] Derrida, *Writing and Difference*, p. 230.
[50] Derrida, 'How to Avoid Speaking: Denials', transl. K. Frieden, in H. Coward and T. Foshay (eds), *Derrida and Negative Theology* (Albany: State University of New York Press, 1992), p. 123.
[51] Ibid., p. 107.
[52] John Caputo, *The Prayers and Tears of Jacques Derrida. Religion without Religion* (Bloomington and Indianapolis: Indiana University Press, 1997), p. 37.

new meaning in forseen and unforseen contexts, and that it will retain its performative power to change lives when a reader 'choose[s] to have him or herself addressed there'.[53] Moreover, the promise reaches beyond even the web of language, undermining any distinction between the 'inside' and the 'outside'; it is always excessive, in a kind of 'quasi-transcendence' (Ward's term)[54] since it creates an open-ended *desire* for the primordial 'yes' to which 'we slowly, moving in circles around it, return'.[55] In this phrase Derrida reflects on the final 'yes' of Mollie Bloom in James Joyce's *Ulysses*, expressing a desire that cannot be confined; the project of deconstruction is to loosen and unlock rigid structures of meaning and authority, and – as Caputo discerns – 'above all to say yes, *oui, oui*, to something whose coming eye hath not seen nor ear heard'.[56] Derrida is thus not denying an outside to language, for 'the outside penetrates and thus determines the inside'.[57] What worries him about any theological designation of this outside, and particularly of the *khora*, is that it easily leads to a totalizing concept of presence which undermines the mediation of language. This danger he even finds in Heidegger's talk about the 'Voice of Being' which sounds out in the space of difference.[58]

The essay 'How to Avoid Speaking' thus offers another reason for denying full presence. If the being of something consists essentially in its presence, then there is a claim for immediate copresence with the other, and the *voice* or the spoken word will be the original presence from which written words are merely derivative. In a theological perspective, communion with the eternal mind will be an absolute subjectivity which grounds the inter-subjectivity of selves. God, on this reckoning, is 'the name and the element of that which makes possible an absolutely pure and absolutely self-present self-knowledge'.[59] But Derrida insists that all objects in the

53   Kevin Hart, 'Jacques Derrida: Introduction', in Ward (ed.), *The Postmodern God*, p. 163.
54   Graham Ward, *Barth, Derrida and the Language of Theology* (Cambridge: Cambridge University Press, 1995), p. 224.
55   Jacques Derrida, 'Ulysse Gramaphone: Deux Mots pour Joyce', repr. in Peggy Kamuf (ed), *Derrida Reader* (Hemel Hempstead: Harvester Wheatsheaf, 1991), p. 596.
56   Caputo, *Prayers and Tears of Jacques Derrida*, p. 18.
57   Jacques Derrida, *Limited Inc.*, ed. G. Graff, transl. S. Weber (Evanston: Northwestern University Press, 1988), pp. 152–3.
58   Jacques Derrida, *Memoirs of the Blind*, transl. P. Brault and M. Nauss (Chicago: University of Chicago Press), 1993, pp. 139–42; also 'How to Avoid Speaking', pp. 127–9, where Derrida concludes that for Heidegger, Being is God.
59   Derrida, *Of Grammatology*, p. 98; cf. pp. 279–80.

world can be inscribed in some kind of sign or mark (not necessarily a literal written text), and this mark can always be repeated in other contexts, with the promise that meaning may change and develop. Writing then interrupts the direct link between being and presence. Derrida takes the example of the *Mystical Theology* of Pseudo-Dionysius, which begins aptly with a prayer to God; because Dionysius is quoting his prayer for the benefit of his disciple, Timothy, by repetition his act of making the prayer falls short of immediate presence either to God or Timothy, and the writing 'stands in the space' of the turning aside of discourse from one addressee to another.[60] But even were the prayer uttered immediately, it could still be inscripted and repeated with consequent change of meaning. One cannot then approach God, concludes Derrida, by passing from language to silence, as the silence is marked by the *différance* embodied in the ambivalence of the prayer. Nor should *différance* itself be compared with the God of negative theology, for it is not a being which makes itself present. Like God it precedes creation, but in the form of a promise, which is not being but the *condition* of what is possible and impossible.[61]

Interwoven with all these reasons for the critique of pure presence, and in support of the breaking of complete identity between being and presence, is the concern about oppressiveness. The claim to immediacy of presence sanctions structures of power and authority, and the words spoken, especially if they present an explanation of the whole of reality (a 'meta-narrative'), are likely to be concealed ideologies. The suspicion that so-called absolute truths are in fact the product of a human will-to-power was inherited from Nietzsche (and notably expressed by Jean-François Lyotard). Even a gift, which in its giving challenges the usual structures of commercial exchange, is quickly absorbed by reception into the process of exchange and can become part of a power-game.[62] This is why Derrida criticizes Heidegger for retaining the personal language of 'self-giving' by Being,[63] even as Heidegger attempts to overcome 'onto-theological meta-physics', and why Derrida envisages the *khora* as giving place without making a gift. The theological concept of the self-revelation of God, while avoiding some of the traps of ideology contained in ideas of propositional revelation, still apparently falls under the shadow of this critique, and I shall return to this shortly in considering theological versions of hidden presence.

[60]   Derrida, 'How to Avoid Speaking', pp. 116–17.
[61]   Ibid., pp. 84–7.
[62]   See above, ch. 2, n.23.
[63]   Derrida, 'How to Avoid Speaking', pp. 124–5.

However, the denial of full presence, and the concepts of *différance* and the trace do not operate as a knock-down argument against the existence of God. Although Derrida confesses in a personal aside that 'I quite rightly pass as an atheist',[64] he actually leaves the question of God open, as recent theological commentators on Derrida have emphasized (notably Kevin Hart, John Caputo and Graham Ward). *Différance* does not settle the question one way or another; in fact, as Caputo puts it, 'it un-settles it', whether for the theist or atheist.[65] The *khora*, as a destabilizing, differentiating source is not to be described in either theological or atheological language, while traces of it operate as hints and promises of transcendence that puncture all systems built on complete immanence. The trace which undermines all pretensions to full presence also promises the possibility of some kind of presence. The 'margin of play of difference, of opening' forbids only that anything, including God, 'be present in and of itself, referring only to itself'.[66]

Moreover, the 'indestructible desire' (Derrida's phrase)[67] generated by *différance* and deconstruction is quite other than the will-to-power which Nietzsche saw as the motivation behind the textual nature of the world with its 'necessary fictions'.[68] As feminist postmodern thinkers such as Luce Irigaray and Julia Kristeva have developed the concept of *khora* as a womb-like, nurturing space of origin, they have resisted the Nietzschian association of desire with violence and have evoked a longing for presence which is characterized by relationships of love. Kristeva, for example, blending psychoanalysis with semiotics, understands the *khora* as the pre-linguistic receptacle of sub-conscious drives and archetypal relations with the mother and the father. The *chora* (as Kristeva transliterates Plato's term) 'precedes and underlies figuration and . . . is analogous only to vocal or kinetic rhythm'.[69] This is the space of the 'semiotic' which precedes linguistic symbols; it contains traces of an experience of a love which is prior to the Oedipal order of relations, and which can break through the signifiers of language, especially in religious experience. While the *chora* is thus envisaged as being deep in the self, it has a dimension of transcendence, because

---

[64] Quoted in Ward (ed.), *Postmodern God*, p. 166.
[65] Caputo, *Prayers and Tears of Jacques Derrida*, p. 13.
[66] Derrida, *Positions*, p. 26.
[67] Derrida, *Limited Inc.*, p. 116.
[68] See for example F. Nietzsche, *The Will to Power*, ed. and transl. Walter Kaufman (with R. J. Hollingdale) (London: Weidenfeld and Nicolson, 1968), aphorisms 480–1, 490–507.
[69] Julia Kristeva, *The Kristeva Reader*, ed. Toril Moi (Oxford: Blackwell, 1986), p. 94.

when its signs or traces subvert language they reach towards an 'Other' which is experienced as union with the divine. An example Kristeva offers of this leap is Augustine's image of faith in God as an infant sucking milk from its mother's breast, breaking open the usual order of symbols. Kristeva finds that the doctrine of the Trinity, as a highly articulated symbolic form of language reveals fundamental human desires and fantasies;[70] but presumably the symbols remain open to subversion by the traces of the fluid, maternal and rhythmic *chora*, a place 'constituted by movements'.[71] I hope to show later that it is the image of the triune God that may exactly point to the 'place that is not a place', and this is why it is the place in which we desire to dwell.

We have seen that thinkers who are critical of the old metaphysics of presence – including Heidegger, Derrida and Kristeva – nevertheless find themselves embarked, as Graham Ward puts it, on a 'journey towards another city, a new corporeality, a new spacing in which the other is housed, affirmed . . .'.[72] There is something eschatological about this, for it is not, of course, a journey back to the womb; there is a promise here that exceeds the kind of eschatology which consists in a continual openness of meaning through the play of difference, which we explored in an earlier chapter. But then, the logic of resisting closure means that while a future eschatology can be questioned, it cannot be struck out.

In contemporary fiction the quest for a 'place' of fuller presence which nevertheless gives room for freedom and difference is embodied in the 'limited Utopia', which has some affinity with the 'millennium' of religious imagination. In postmodern critical theory it takes the form of an unreachable and untouchable *khora*, a no-place which nevertheless leaves traces of its presence to provoke us and unsettle us from complacency.

Absence at the Heart of Existence

The force of these evocative ideas of the *khora* can be appreciated most clearly by contrast with the metaphors of spatiality which have been used to close the circle of immanence by some who have claimed the title of 'postmodern theologians'. In this they either deliberately or unwittingly

[70] Julia Kristeva, *In the Beginning was Love*, transl. A. Goldhammer (New York, Columbia University Press, 1987), pp. 42–4.
[71] Kristeva, *The Kristeva Reader*, p. 92.
[72] Ward, *Postmodern God*, p. xli.

take up the mantle of the modernist 'death of God' movement, insisting on a foundational *absence* without a flickering presence.

Don Cupitt, for example, denies that there is any 'outside' to our existence; we must embrace the material world of signs as the only truth we have. For Cupitt, reality is like the flat surface of a pond, and we are pond-skating flies who can only communicate horizontally, moving from one sign to another in their 'shimmering interplay'.[73] This is the only space there is, a 'Void' in which the 'dance of difference' takes place.[74] The metaphor of God evokes a dimension of mystery within human existence itself, 'blasting open' oppressive cultural and social codes.[75] If for Cupitt we are out in the middle of the surface of a pond, for Mark Taylor we are in the 'middest' of a maze. Taylor concentrates on the 'void' that opens up within the self when selfhood is placed under erasure as a trace rather than as full presence. Commenting on Beckett's *Endgame*, in which the end of the story is always deferred, Taylor judges that 'The very *search* for presence testifies to the absence of presence and the "presence" of absence'.[76] Rather than searching for a new presence – whether of the self or of God – that we think would be our salvation, we are to roam or 'err' in the maze of life, experiencing the newness of each moment and participating in the lives of others: this is the period of 'mazing grace' opened by the death of God and the disappearance of the self.[77]

While these a-theologians share the image of a 'void' with Derrida, there is no space of the wholly other that interacts with our space and disturbs the boundaries we draw, unsettling our conviction that we know what is inside and what is outside. Perhaps most interesting in his re-use of the metaphor of the void in this way is Thomas Altizer, since he sets it explicitly in the context of apocalypse. Like Taylor and Cupitt he accepts that in our age the self has become anonymous;[78] our experience is that we are facing an 'abyss' or 'unnameable void'.[79] Like Taylor and Cupitt he finds no other space of transcendent reality which interacts here and now

---

[73]   Don Cupitt, *Life Lines* (London: SCM Press, 1986), pp. 1–2.

[74]   Don Cupitt, *The Long-Legged Fly. A Theology of Language and Desire* (London: SCM Press, 1987), p. 107.

[75]   Ibid., pp. 61–2.

[76]   Mark C. Taylor, *Erring. A Postmodern A/Theology* (Chicago: University of Chicago Press, 1984), p. 72.

[77]   Ibid., pp. 98, 112–18, 168–9.

[78]   Thomas J. J. Altizer, *Genesis and Apocalypse* (Louisville, Ky.: Westminster/John Knox, 1990), p. 89.

[79]   Ibid., p. 180.

with the human void. However, rather than denying the presence of God, for Altizer the present situation in human life is the *result* of the full presence of God. Altizer asserts that the presence of God in the space of the world will still give room for human beings to face up to the reality of their void, because he affirms the *death* of God through this very presence.

This is a story of the death of God that has affinities both with the Christian story of God's self-emptying in creation and redemption, and with Hegel's story of the self-negation and so development of absolute Mind; it also ingeniously incorporates the Buddhist concept of the No-Self (which is not really a story) within the story. In all this, Altizer differs from other 'postmodern' theologians in beginning with the notion of total presence as the foundation for the absence which we now experience as characterizing existence.

To cut a long story short, Altizer envisages the divine act of creation as a negation of eternity; it is a self-negation of the eternal God which originates history and is consummated in the cross of Jesus. Eternity is an 'emptiness' and a 'silence' corresponding to the 'eternal now' in which there is no distinction between past, present and future, a state to which the self aspires in Mahayana Buddhism.[80] The self-naming of God as 'I am' in the act of creation results in a 'full and total presence' of God in time and space, which is thus both a perishing of the original eternity and a negation of the absolute transcendence of God.[81] The Voice of 'I am' 'empties the emptiness' of eternity,[82] in an act which gives birth to history and to a successiveness of irreversible moments. The negating of the void of eternity produces, however, a new kind of void or abyss, one marked by death. The self-naming of 'I am' is the self-naming of death because, in a history of irreversible events, each moment is marked by perishing and so by the death of the 'eternal now'.[83] This self-naming is also the 'birth of difference', since there is an otherness between eternity and creation comprehended within the self-alienation of the 'I am'; there is an otherness of the Voice from its hearers; and there is an otherness between past and future moments which are thereby brought into being.[84]

The event of creation thus begins a history of the self-negation of God,

---

[80] Ibid., pp. 32–6, 93ff. Altizer stresses that a 'plenitude' or 'pleroma' of eternity which is reversible and without 'difference' is the same as 'a pure emptiness' (p. 107).

[81] Ibid., pp. 36–40.

[82] Ibid., pp. 102–4.

[83] Ibid., pp. 47–9.

[84] Ibid., pp. 45–6, 51–3, 54–6.

a kenotic journey into death which is fully actualized in the cross of Jesus. According to Altizer, the crucifixion of the divine Word marks the end of the self-naming of God. In this abyss of death ('the death of death') there is a fulfilment of the total presence of 'I am' that was begun in creation, finally negating its 'otherness' from finite beings.[85] The Voice of 'I am' now continues in a new form of human consciousness, which experiences otherness and 'difference' in a division within itself, a dichotomy first expressed by the Apostle Paul in his distinction between the 'I' of sin and the 'I' of grace. This is the birth of the modern conscious 'subject' with its internal divisions and doubts, later to be articulated by Descartes and Hegel.[86]

For our present concerns, Altizer provides a revealing example of a philosophical theology of complete immanence. He understands 'apocalypse' to be any total reversal of a previous reality, any totally new beginning which negates a previous age.[87] His, then, is a kind of 'millennial' vision of continuous transition; the void of Apocalypse is really the empty space of Genesis. This is a Hegelian view of history as progress through continual negation, but Altizer differs from Hegel in that Absolute Spirit (God) does not return renewed to itself through its 'death' or exposure to its opposite, and through its incarnation in human consciousness. According to Altizer, through negation God 'dies into' the world, utterly perishing in assuming otherness. The death of God in the cross is the apocalypse from which is born the age of the modern human 'subject' which inherits the self-alienated centre of consciousness once found in the Voice of the 'I am'. 'Every trace of a truly and finally transcendent God has vanished, and this vanishing is the realization of a pure and total immanence'.[88] It is consistent with the apocalytic progress of history that in our time this void has in turn been replaced by an even darker void, as the thinking subject itself has 'necessarily' been negated. In 'an apocalyptic dissolution of the "I"', neither the interior subject nor its exterior world can any longer be named. We are in an apocalypse which is 'the deepest ending in history', which 'must necessarily void and erase every previous identity or naming of apocalypse . . .'.[89]

---

[85] Ibid., pp. 59–62.

[86] Ibid., pp. 79–84; Altizer, 'Apocalypticism and Modern Thinking', *Journal for Christian Theological Research* (CTRF@apu.edu), 2 (1997), §1–3.

[87] Altizer, 'Apocalypticism and Modern Thinking', §5.

[88] Ibid., §13.

[89] Altizer, *Genesis and Apocalypse*, p. 184.

According to Altizer, we can only affirm that this 'darkest of all nights' is a dawn because it is the apocalyptic principle of history that an end is always a beginning. There is no other hope except that 'the totality of dawning is inseparable from the totality of ending'.[90] Hope does not come from any interaction of our void with a primordial or eternal 'space', because in Altizer's view one is the complete negation of the other. Here Altizer takes account of the modern Western interest in the Buddhist concept of the loss or emptying of the self, which we have already noted in Derek Parfit's understanding of the person.[91] Altizer suggests that this interest certainly belongs to the general assault on the otherness of the self in our day and to the sense of an 'anonymous consciousness', but he is careful not to equate the Buddhist 'silence' with the present void in our culture. The absolute emptiness which the self desires in Mahayana Buddhism is an 'eternal now' in which past, present and future are simultaneous.[92] As in Huxley's vision of Utopia, the 'here and now' of the present moment is identified with a total moment which is the absence of time. In Altizer's view, this correctly describes eternity, but it was precisely this silence that was shattered once and for all by the Voice of 'I Am' and by the arrival of the total presence of God in creation. It was this original absence that was made absent, this emptiness that was emptied out in the actuality of creation, beginning a history of continuous self-negation that has arrived at the present void. The abyss into which we are plunged is a kind of consummation of the Buddhist vision of original silence, but a fulfilment through negation. In contrast to the lack of a future in the void of eternity, the future is real as a continuous series of apocalyptic voids, echoing the original 'I am'.

For Altizer, the result of the filling of our living space with the presence of God is not the subjugation of humanity, but the death of God. This is, I suggest, a consistent working out of the belief that eternity is an 'eternal now' of simultaneity. Like Moltmann and the other theologians we considered in chapter 5, Altizer asks how a God who enjoys the state of simultaneous eternity could enter time and history; but while their answer is to postulate a kind of 'semi-eternity' as a buffer state, his own answer is that it is only by total negation, the immersion of God into the body of the world without remnant, and the replacement of transcendence by immanence. This he imaginatively links with the 'postmodern' experience

---

[90]   Ibid., p. 179.
[91]   See ch. 4 above, pp. 81–4.
[92]   Altizer, *Genesis and Apocalypse*, pp. 88–99.

of the loss of self and the death of God. There is nothing of eternity that remains, and to try and get back behind the *kenosis* of God to recover it is sheer nostalgia; he pays Buddhism the compliment that, unlike Christian thought, it shows no hint of such longing for a return to Paradise.

Altizer's answer to the impasse of eternity and time seems to me to be more coherent than that of a 'semi-eternity', *if* our vision of eternity is indeed that of a simultaneity, empty of event. But my argument has been that we should envisage eternity as the *healing* of time, not time's absence, so that it is the very condition for our own experience of time. In this case the 'otherness' of God from God as expressed in the symbol of the relation between Father, Son and Spirit within the Trinity is the origin of all otherness in the world, but not of *estrangement*. As I have argued else-where,[93] otherness becomes alienation only with emergence of sin from the universe through its own free acts; something 'strange' confronts God, outside God's intentions in creation. Then indeed God encounters aliena-tion when plunged into the experience of death in the cross of Jesus, meeting and absorbing something which deeply disturbs the fellowship of divine life. But human history itself as created by God, in its nature as successive moments, will only be estranged from eternity if we understand eternity to be the abolition of time.

Altizer's theological writing is a kind of creative literature, a prose poem of repetition with variation, and he finds the deepest affinity not with other theologians but with poets and novelists. Among modern writers he especially values James Joyce, whose *Finnegans Wake* he understands to embody the dynamic of apocalyptic beginnings and endings in history, and to be a true successor to the cosmic epics of Milton and Blake. We have already briefly reviewed the pervasive motif of the fall in Joyce's work, and it is not surprising that Altizer finds it to be an image of the self-negation of God. The first 'fall' in traditional Christian imagination is the rebellion of Satan against God, and for Altizer this symbolizes the movement of alienation within God's own self. Satan is an image for God estranged from God, God envisaged as a purely abstract transcendence. This fall is matched by the willing 'fall' or descent of the Son into humiliation and death, a divine self-emptying that negates the negativity of Satan through an immersion into total 'eucharistic' presence in the body of the world. In annihilating Satan, Christ thus 'becomes' Satan in the 'apocalyptic Godhead of God'.[94]

---

93   Fiddes, *The Creative Suffering of God* (Oxford: Clarendon Press, 1988), ch. 8.
94   Altizer, *Genesis and Apocalypse*, p. 172; also pp. 163–8. Cf. earlier, Altizer, *The New*

Altizer finds the divine acceptance of death (as annihilation) to be evident throughout Joyce's epic, anticipated in a phrase written early on: 'I've a terrible errible lot todue todie todue tootorribleday'.[95] Through total death there is a new beginning, so that crucifixion *is* resurrection, expressed in the final affirmation 'Lff!' of Anna Livia Plurabelle, a 'Yes' to 'life' which is all in all: 'Lff! So soft this morning, ours. Yes.'[96]

Altizer's interpretation of *Finnegans Wake* fits within his view that eternity and time are a coincidence of opposites, and Joyce's universe is large enough to contain it. But if we do not begin with this presupposition, we are likely to read the *Wake* as about many versions of the fall of *humanity* into sin in the footfalls of Adam, our 'oldparr' as the first page of the book identifies him, in 'the fall . . . of a once wallstrait oldparr'. Adam is ancient father (old pa), ancestor of others who have fallen from grace such as Par-nell, and our 'par' whom we meet on an equal footing of guilt.[97] Neither Satan nor Christ easily fit this profile. The cyclic, Vicoesque view of history presented in the *Wake* which offers hope of continual renewal also seems to be at odds with Altizer's rejection of the 'eternal return'.

Altizer's poetic theology works out the consequences of a timeless eternity in a myth that embraces God, Satan, Christ and the whole of world history. There is no access from the void of existence to a primordial space of fecundity and fullness of life, since this was an emptiness that has itself been emptied. In this scenario, Altizer maintains that a total presence of God will be equivalent to 'a total absence or void'.[98] A simultaneous or recurrent eternity is 'empty' just because it is completely *full* of God in an undifferentiated way, in a 'pure nothingness of pure isness'. Altizer notes that in the Buddhist Nirvana which is full of the total compassion of the Buddha, 'nothing happens in enlightenment just as nothing happens in compassion'. This is 'a pleroma which is a full and total pleroma precisely in its emptiness'.[99] We may compare the apophatic Christian theology of Meister Eckhardt, in which God may be termed

---

Apocalypse. The Radical Christian Vision of William Blake (Michigan State University Press, 1967), pp. 104–7.

[95] Joyce, *Finnegans Wake* (London: Faber and Faber 1971), p. 381; see Altizer, *Genesis and Apocalypse*, p. 171.

[96] Joyce, *Finnegans Wake*, p. 628.

[97] See above, pp. 200–2.

[98] Altizer, *Genesis and Apocalypse*, pp. 179, 107.

[99] Ibid., pp. 97, 95.

'silence, emptiness, desert, nothingness'[100] because as pure intellect God is unified and simple in being.

By contrast, the void or abyss which Altizer identifies in history is not the same kind of void, as it negates the void of eternity. Here the presence of God is not a fullness without sequence of time, but a total immersion into time and history so that no transcendent identity remains over. Total divine presence in the world will result, according to Altizer, in an apocalypse in which we experience the absence of God. If God is omnipresent in the world in pure immanence, then what matters is attention to the 'here and now' (not to be confused with an eternal now). The kingdom of God is in the everyday detail of life, as illustrated in the parables of Jesus. 'God' is equivalent to the contingent world in its totality of presence. But this total presence remorselessly progresses through negation until not only is God absent but the self, and even the world, cannot be named any longer; this, according to Altizer, is the darkest apocalypse in which we are caught now, and in which we cannot even with Joyce's Molly Bloom and Anna Livia say 'yes' to the present moment. Our only hope is that saying 'no' is inseparable from yes, as darkness is a sign of the coming dawn and absence is only made possible by presence.

It seems that the 'flickering presence' of what lies beyond *our* network of linguistic signs in postmodern thinkers such as Derrida and Kristeva offers more hope in the void than the 'total presence' of Altizer's apocalypse or the pure absence of Taylor and Cupitt. The task for a Christian eschatology which maintains hope in a future new creation is thus not only to name the veiled presence as God, and to show that this kind of presence does not oppress or destroy the endless creativity of the inscription of signs or 'writing'. Altizer shows us that the challenge is also to name an eternity which is *full* of the presence of God while not being thereby an empty void in which all otherness of persons must vanish away.

Theological Versions of Hidden Presence

The quest for a place of fuller presence which does not dominate, or eliminate 'difference', takes form in the *khora* as a place which is unreachable and uninhabitable, but which leaves its traces. It takes form in Altizer's a-theology as our own living space in which God's total presence has

---

[100] Meister Eckhart, *The Essential Sermons, Commentaries, Treatises and Defence*, transl. and ed. E. Colledge and B. McGinn (London: SPCK, 1981), Sermon 9.

resulted in divine expiry; it is as if the presence of God can only give us room if God dies. But there are also theological versions of a hidden presence, in which God either is, or creates, a space in which there is a presence which is not stifling.

In the first place, the image of a void, or empty space, is employed by Jürgen Moltmann to describe the self-emptying of God in creation. Here Moltmann draws on the Jewish kabbalistic doctrine of a divine *zimsum*, or self-limitation, as expounded by Isaac Luria.[101] Altizer had also appealed to the image of *zimsum* as God's making a 'void' for creation through self-negation,[102] but found very different implications in it. For Moltmann, God 'withdraws himself from himself' in preparation for creation, contracting to make a primordial space in which there will be room for a finite world 'outside' God's own self. If God is to create 'from nothing', the argument runs, he must first provide such a *nihil* by limiting his omnipresence. Correspondingly, Moltmann maintains, in the eschatological moment God will reverse this self-restriction, 'de-restricting' his presence so that he will dwell fully in his creation, and be 'all in all' within it: 'The primordial time and the primordial space of creation will end when creation becomes the temple for God's eternal Shekinah'.[103]

Moltmann has been subjected to criticism for using this kabbalistic image of divine 'withdrawal' for creation, as it seems to promote the idea that space is not so much created as *vacated*, and so God is excluded from the world.[104] The image *in itself*, however, deconstructs the alternative of being either 'inside' or 'outside' God, as the space which is brought into being has both a distance – and so a freedom – from God, while remaining 'in' God at the same time. The point is not that space is a container, from one area of which God shrinks away, but that God withdraws from God's own exclusiveness of being, so that the room which is made for creation must still be within God. The metaphor thus expresses at once the inseparability of God from creation and God's ontological difference from it. The overtones of a 'womb' which the idea of a primordial space evokes also introduce a complementary feminine image of creation, to counterbalance

[101] Jürgen Moltmann, *God in Creation. An Ecological Doctrine of Creation* (London: SCM Press, 1985), pp. 86–8.
[102] Altizer, 'History as Apocalypse' in Altizer et al., *Deconstruction and Theology* (New York: Crossroad, 1982, pp. 148–9; here Altizer links the *zimsum* both with Derrida's 'groundless' *différance* and his own idea of presence-as-absence.
[103] Moltmann, *Coming of God*, p. 294
[104] See e.g. Alan Torrance, '*Creatio ex Nihilo* and the Spatio-temporal Dimensions', in Colin Gunton (ed.), *The Doctrine of Creation* (Edinburgh: T. & T. Clark, 1997), p. 90.

traditional masculine images of 'generation'. There are, however, still some
problems with the way that Moltmann himself uses the image, both for
creation and eschatology.

While the metaphor in itself does not imply God's general absence from
creation, Moltmann does in fact use it in this way. He maintains that while
creation is 'in' God, God is not essentially 'in' creation during the period
of history, but remains 'over against it', until the moment of new creation
when the universe will be filled with the presence of God in a *perichoresis*
or inter-penetration of divine and cosmic attributes.[105] Until the eschaton,
'Only God can be the space of the world, and the world cannot be God's
space'.[106] But in stating this contrast between time and eternity he naturally
finds it difficult to speak of the presence of God here and now. He cannot,
and does not, deny the 'indwellings' of God in the cosmos altogether, and
so conceives them as 'special presences' rather than being part of a 'general'
presence;[107] they are particular acts of self-humiliation, temporary or
fragmentary presences limited to a mode of suffering and patient waiting.
God is present in time in the form of the Sabbath, and present in space in
the form of the *Shekinah* of Ancient Israel and the incarnation of Christ.
That is, God is present in exile in the world, homeless and in the form of
suffering, awaiting redemption. This is a hidden presence, which Moltmann
equates with the experience of the 'hiding of the face of God' in the Old
Testament.

Moltmann has, I suggest, rightly found the potential within the metaphor
of 'space in God' for a hidden presence of God within created space. The
liberty of creatures depends upon this veiling of God's face; the distance
granted to creation through the primordial space gives room for freedom,
and only becomes deathly isolation through sin. But since Moltmann
assumes that the 'dwelling' of God in creation must mean a fullness of
presence in which God derestricts God's self and 'creation loses its place
outside God', he is necessarily ambiguous about the presence of God here
and now. The distinction between 'special' and 'general presence' means
that 'hidden presence' appears at times to be equivalent to real absence.
Moltmann seems, for instance, to approve the rabbinic view that the
Shekinah in history is to be differentiated in some way from God's own
being, so that in the new creation 'finally God and Shekinah become

---

[105]   Moltmann, *Coming of God*, p. 296.
[106]   Ibid., p. 302.
[107]   Ibid., p. 303.

one'.[108] This, as he recognizes, does not translate well into Christology, which requires a fuller indwelling of the divine glory.

Moltmann's scheme in which creation 'dwells' in God but God does not 'dwell' generally in creation is, perhaps, his way of dealing with the unhappy split between subject and object stemming from Enlightenment rationalism. When the very being of a conscious subject is understood to consist in its presence to objects in the world, and its capacity to make objects present through representing them in concepts and speech, then to desire the presence of God implies treating God as some kind of object we try to possess. Correspondingly, a God who is fully present to the world is the kind of subject who will overwhelm us forcibly as objects of his self-revelation. I suggest that affirming the hiddenness of God's presence does indeed prevent us from reducing God to an object of our knowing and desiring, but that hiddenness is quite compatible with the notion that God 'indwells' the world, both generally and continuously. Hiddenness also means that in humble self-effacement God does not dominate us but gives us our own time and space. Here Moltmann takes a similar line to Karl Barth, who affirms that God must be veiled in the very act of self-revelation. Without this veiling in *kenosis*, passion and humility, Barth declares that 'revelation would obviously be an act of violence'.[109]

According to Barth, the revealed God must be hidden because God makes himself an object of our knowledge by taking finite objects as a medium of self-disclosure. Objects in the world are unsuitable for the communication of the divine glory, because of the finitude and sinfulness of the world, and so 'the veil is thick'.[110] God is unexpectedly encountered in worldly objects, a meeting which is only made possible by God's self-identification with the worldly object of Christ's humanity. This is the true 'secularity' of the Word of God. Christ is the 'primary sacrament', and any sacramentality of the world derives from him and witnesses to him.[111] The mediated objectivity of God renders God vulnerable to rejection, and also protects human discourse. Verbal signs in themselves cannot either be bearers of transcendence or be subjected to transcendent presence; there is a crisis of representation here which brings Barth curiously close to Derrida. What is present is an absence of immediacy which would overwhelm the

---

[108]   Ibid., p. 307.
[109]   Barth, *Church Dogmatics*, transl. and ed. G. W. Bromiley and T. F. Torrance (Edinburgh: T. & T. Clark, 1936–77) 1/2, 36.
[110]   Barth, *Church Dogmatics*, 1/1, 165.
[111]   Barth, *Church Dogmatics*, II/1, 15–27, 49–54.

hearer of the Word; only the gift of divine grace can create an analogy between human speech signs and the reality of God, between The Word and the words.

It is well known that Barth's resistance to natural theology, stemming from his rejection of the 'culture-religion' of National Socialism in Germany, led him in his earlier work to restrict the scope of revelation to Christ, the Bible and the Church. In his later work, however, he follows through consistently the logic of his earlier thought that God is nevertheless free to take *any* worldly objects as media of self-revelation ('a flute concerto, a blossoming shrub, a dead dog . . .')[112] as long as they are understood as pointing to the primary sacrament of Christ, lesser lights deriving from the great Light.[113] There is much more scope in this thinking for a general presence of God in the world than in Moltmann's thought, for whom the world only becomes sacramental in the eschaton. However, we will surely only escape from the dualism of subject and object in our knowledge of God, and in our desire for God, if we lay stress on Barth's idea that revelation is a 'happening' or 'event' that takes place in the stage-setting of worldly objects, corresponding to the nature of the triune God as event: 'with regard to the being of God, the word "event" or "act" is final"'.[114] The last word about God is that God happens. Rather than following Barth's language of God's becoming 'objective' to us through revelation, or our being granted access to the 'primary objectivity' of God's own self-knowledge (which retains Hegelian overtones), we need to reach more radically towards the language of participation in this divine Event at which Barth hints.

Another theological version of divine hiddenness is provided by the Jewish thinker Emmanuel Levinas, who brings the welcome ethical emphasis that we encounter the transcendent in our infinite responsibility for the other person. He challenges the notion that the mind *makes* the world present through representing it accurately in thought and speech; when we attempt this, we simply make the 'the other' immanent within our own consciousness, and so expose it to a full presence which robs it of any enigmas or excesses.[115] Rather, the otherness of other persons *enters* our world on its own account; above all the infinite (God) turns our world

---

112   Barth, *Church Dogmatics*, I/1, 55.
113   Barth, *Church Dogmatics*, IV/3.1, 116–23.
114   Barth, *Church Dogmatics*, II/1, 263.
115   Emmanuel Levinas, *Otherwise Than Being, or, Beyond Essence*, transl. A. Lingis (Pittsburgh: Duquesne University Press, repr. 1998), pp. 51–9, 153–65.

inside out by coming into our world and causing a rupture in our powers of representation. The 'in-finite' may be understood as that which comes 'into the finite', and it breaks in through the face of our neighbour, calling us to limitless responsibility for the other person. Thus God is not an object of the powers of correlation of our mind, but *'comes* to mind'.[116]

There are evident affinities with Barth's thought here, except that all thought of divine objectivity is avoided, and there is an explicit universal-izing of encounter with the otherness of God in the face of all persons. 'A face is of itself a visitation and a transcendence.' This is a kind of hidden presence of the absolutely Other, though for Levinas what is present here and now is not strictly the infinite itself but a 'trace' of it, as Moses saw the back of the hidden God as he 'passed by' (Exodus 33:22–3):

> The absoluteness of the Other's presence . . . is not the simple presence in which in the last analysis things are also present. Their presence still belongs to the present of *my* life . . . But it is in the trace of the Other that a face shines . . . Someone has already passed.[117]

As beyond Being, God does not actually appear in time and space, but God's infinite reality comes into the finite to insert a 'space' in time, setting the stage for our encounter with other persons in whom can be found the trace of the wholly Other.[118] Levinas here stresses participation rather than 'observation': the 'God who passed' and left a trace of his passing is 'not the model of which the face would be an image. To be in the image of God does not mean to be an icon of God but *to find oneself in his trace*'.[119] The infinite, for instance, challenges the consciousness to a desire for the Other which is never satisfied, but God is not the *object* of desire; rather the desire called forth by the infinite is unsatisfiable because it is a desire for the non-desirable, that is the neighbour. So the metaphysical relation to God beyond Being is actualized in relation to a human person with concrete needs. Language is not a way of requiring the world to be present, and so unifying past and future into one present moment in the mind; it is

---

[116] Levinas, 'God and Philosophy' in *Of God who Comes to Mind*, transl. B. Bergo (Stanford: Stanford University Press, 1998), pp. 62–7 (cf. p. xv); Levinas, *Otherwise Than Being*, pp. 94–7, 184–5.

[117] Levinas, 'Meaning and Sense' in A. Peperzak, S. Critchely, R. Bernasconi (eds.), *Emmanuel Levinas. Basic Philosophical Writings* (Bloomington and Indianapolis: Indiana University Press, 1996), p. 63.

[118] Emmanuel Levinas, *Totality and Infinity*, transl. A. Lingis (Pittsburgh: Duquesne University Press, repr. 1969), p. 291: 'a curvature of inter-subjective space'.

[119] Levinas, 'Meaning and Sense', p. 64. Thus one participates only in God's trace.

the way we make ourselves available to others. A Christian theology will try to articulate a hidden presence of God in these relations, rather than an 'absent infinite' (Levinas), while keeping the stress on participation rather than objectification.

Yet another approach to the hiddenness of divine presence, and also to the problem of objectivity, is found within a much older theology, but one which has recently become of considerable interest to such thinkers as Derrida and Levinas. This is the negative way of ascent to God, or apophatic theology. It is characteristic of such thinkers as Meister Eckhart, the author of the *Cloud of Unknowing* and St John of the Cross to find a loss of distinction between the soul and God.[120] In an apophatic mood, the Lady Julian of Norwich also declares that 'I saw no difference between God and our essential being, it seemed to be all God'.[121] As Denys Turner has pointed out, this is not a simple affirmation that the soul *is* God, or that the soul has been totally *absorbed* into God, but that it is not possible to 'see' or 'name' the difference. 'From the fact that our language gives us no hold on the distinction between the created and the uncreated, it does not mean that there is no difference'.[122] There is certainly no language available for describing an 'experience' of our transformation in God, and the notion of a 'mystical experience' is – Turner urges – a modern one. The naming of the divine nature as an 'emptiness' or 'silence' or a 'desert place' thus overlaps with similar descriptions for the hidden ground of the self where there is a breakthrough into the ground of God. The 'detach-ment' commended by these writers is not an attempt to dig out or make a space in the soul for God to occupy; the space is already there and must be recovered from the 'infill' of attachments. Language can be used to *name* the place (but not the difference), and indeed an excess of language must be employed and then negated, until the point where language breaks down.

So far, as in Moltmann and Barth, God makes a space in God's own self where we can dwell. But these apophatic writers make clear – as the later theologians do not – that there is no way of objectifying this place as an 'object' of experience or knowledge or desire. The inability to name the

---

[120] See e.g. St John of the Cross, *Ascent of Mount Carmel* V.7, in *Collected Works*, ed. and transl. E. Allison Peers (London: Burns & Oates, 1964), p. 78.

[121] Julian of Norwich, *Revelations of Divine Love*, transl. E. Spearing (Harmondsworth: Penguin Books, 1998), ch. 54, p. 130.

[122] Denys Turner, *The Darkness of God. Negativity in Christian Mysticism* (Cambridge: Cambridge University Press, 1995), p. 161.

difference between the space in the human self and the space in God is probably why, as Turner argues, Meister Eckhart appears to claim that the way of detachment means an annihilation of any desire for God: 'So long as you have . . . a longing for God and eternity, then you are not poor'.[123] Turner suggests that Eckhart is not contesting all desire, but seeking to abandon the kind of desire that is possessiveness, and that treats God as an object of desire.

Since these writers stand in the Neoplatonist tradition, the inability to see the difference between God and the 'empty space' in the soul stems first from the incomparability of God with all beings, so that there is no point of comparison from which a distinction can be observed; it is too wide to be named. Second, there is a divine element in the human subject, the uncreated mind, which is inseparable from the uncreatedness of God. Third, God is named as 'emptiness' and 'nothingness' because God is absolutely 'simple' in being ('without parts') and enjoys a timeless eternity. There is no need for us to accept these philosophical explanations, and especially the last two, in order rightly to learn from apophatic theology that God's presence is hidden because God is so near to us that we cannot distance God as an object 'over against us'. This is not the 'total presence' of Altizer's thought, in which God ceases to exist, but an intimacy of presence such that we desire with the very desire of God. The notions of the simplicity of being and the timelessness of God, however, are not consistent with the 'complexity' of relations in a triune God and the healing of time that I have been arguing for.

These four theological accounts thus envisage the hiddenness of God as particular humble indwellings in creation (Moltmann), as a veiling in self-revelation mediated through worldly objects (Barth), as encounter with a moral challenge through traces of transcendence in the face of others (Levinas) and as a closeness that forbids any final identification as a distinct reality (apophatic theology). These correspond to a view of a 'space' or 'place' of divine presence as a space opened up for created beings within God (Moltmann), as the using of created places by God for staging the event of revelation (Barth), as the space opened up in relationships by the coming of the infinite into the finite (Levinas) and as the empty space in the ground of the soul (apophatic theology). At the same time, I suggest, these four versions of the hiddenness of God go a long way towards meeting the objection that an openness of human life and language to transcendence will result in human attempts to reduce God to an object,

[123] Cited in Turner, ibid., p. 179, cf. pp. 172–3.

or in domination by a supreme subject, or in validation of the subject–object split within human consciousness. The best insights of each of these four approaches, as I intend to show in the next chapter, are met by the idea of participation in the relationships of the triune God.

Yet the question of eschatology, the hope for a 'fuller presence' than we know here and now, remains. The symbols of this fuller presence are the millennium (penultimate) and eternity (final). But would not the fullness of presence in eternity cancel out all these perceptions of hidden presence? This problem seems most acute in Moltmann, who envisages the moment of eschatology as reversing the making of the primordial space, 'derestricting' the presence of God, and filling the created space with the divine glory. Moltmann insists that the final omnipresence of God will be a 'mutual indwelling of the world in God and God in the world', and not a dissolving of either the world or God into the other. But since creation has, according to Moltmann, been given 'freedom of movement' through the space conceded to it by God, the conclusion seems inevitable that when this space is 'lost',[124] freedom is also lost. This, of course, fits with a view of eternity as simultaneity, in which development through time is no longer possible. Imagining the feast of eternal joy over 'the open fullness of God', Moltmann asks pertinently, 'Redemption for what?' and answers that it will be a celebration by all creation of the plenitude of God; all created beings are 'destined to sing their hymns and songs of praise'.[125] To grasp the fullness of God, urges Moltmann, we must 'leave moral and ontological considerations behind, and . . . avail ourselves of aesthetic dimensions'. Satisfying in some ways though this vision is, it does not meet the demand for justice for the poor and oppressed and those for whom life has been restricted in its opportunities for human growth. Those whose vision of eternity is like Moltmann's, and who are also concerned for justice and the fulfilment of hope, must argue for a literal earthly millennium in which restitution is made, preceding the last day.[126]

---

[124]   Moltmann, *Coming of God*, pp. 306–8.

[125]   Ibid., p. 338.

[126]   In his suggestions of reasons why Moltmann opts for a millennium on earth, Richard Bauckham misses this point: see his 'The Millennium', in Bauckham (ed.), *God Will Be All in All* (Edinburgh: T. & T. Clark, 1999), pp. 136–43.

The Millennial Hope

Moltmann thus accepts the tradition of a millennial reign of Christ on earth. Since all eschatology must be Christological, concerning the 'way of Jesus Christ' to his glory, then the millennium will begin with the *parousia* of Christ and the resurrection of those who have been part of his ecclesial community. According to Moltmann this is the resurrection 'from' the dead which only believers share with Christ, and it does not merely *anticipate* the general resurrection 'of' the dead at the end of the millennium. The second resurrection, with the last judgement and a new heaven and a new earth, will be the *consequence* of the resurrection 'from the dead' and the millennial period.[127] That is, through the millennium which will be a messianic kingdom shared by Jews and Christians, there will be a gathering of all into the kingdom, ending with eternal life for all. With this picture Moltmann attempts to meet the problem of the 'two resurrections' that seems to be posed by a pre-millennial belief, resolving it through seeing the millennium as the final stage of the messianic mission of Christ, granting justice to those who have been despised by the powerful, and fulfilling the hopes of Israel. 'Without millenarian hope', he affirms, 'the Christian ethic of resistance and the consistent discipleship of Christ lose their most powerful motivation'.[128]

There is, however, an inevitable problem about time in this scenario. Moltmann declares that the millennium cannot be conceived in terms of 'literal, calendar time' since 'time is determined by what happens in it'.[129] The time of the messianic kingdom will not be the same as our present time, and may be regarded as 'fulfilled time in a victory of life'. Nevertheless, it is still a kind of time because eternity has not yet arrived to put an end (in Moltmann's view) to time. If, however, we do not hold a theory of simultaneous eternity, but a concept of the 'healing of time', then the justice of the 'fulfilled time' of the millennium can be transferred to the new creation. This is where there will be the possibilities of personal and social fulfilment that have been denied – or refused – in this life. Moreover, a literal millennium, initiated by the 'resurrection' of believers from the dead, is contradicted by the corporate and cosmic dimensions of resurrection I have argued for in an earlier chapter. Whatever reality the image of

[127]   Moltmann, *Coming of God*, pp. 195–7.
[128]   Ibid., Moltmann, p. 201.
[129]   Ibid., p. 200.

resurrection points towards, it cannot be an individual destiny but must be deeply involved with the renewal of the physical universe. There cannot be a resurrection dissociated from the new heavens and the new earth.

The millennium in Christian eschatology is an image for a fuller presence and greater immediacy of God in the world, exhibiting divine righteousness. Because it falls short of a 'fullness of presence' of eternity, it seems to make room for a co-working of God with humanity in bringing about God's final glorification. It is an image deeply rooted in the human mind, taking a secular form in the Utopia, which witnesses to a desire for a 'space' (a 'good place') where there is a fuller presence of the self to oneself and others. When there is a proper concern for human freedom, for continuing progress and for protest against uniformity, the secular image takes the form of a semi-Utopia, or an 'ambiguous Utopia'. Both millenniums and semi-Utopias look for the fulfilling of human hopes, but in a context where 'presence' remains at least to some extent hidden.

The millennium is therefore an image leaning two ways, back into history and forward into eternity. The Augustinian view that the millennium is the age of the Church has a truth in so far as we can hope for an increasing establishment of the justice and peace of God in history. There is nothing illusory in working for 'semi-Utopias', out of the human 'passion for the possible' and a vision of God's possibilities in new creation. In this sense we should always be expecting a fuller divine presence, and since it takes the hidden forms I have described – for example in the ethical demand of the neighbour (Levinas) – it cannot be used to validate structures of human authority or to inhibit change. But the image of the millennium, unlike the semi-Utopia, leans forward into eternity, when the demands for justice which cannot be satisfied within history will be fully met. It remains to be seen, in our final chapter, whether a vision of the 'dwelling of God among mortals' in eternity can retain the insights of the hidden presence of God. That it should, is expressed by a recent novel about the end of the world, Morris West's *The Clowns of God*.

In this novel, West expresses his desire for an eschaton which does not come violently, suppressing human freedom. In his story, a pope is forced to abdicate by the Roman Catholic hierarchy because he believes he has had a vision of the end of the world through nuclear war and the second coming of Christ. He believes that he has been been called by Christ to proclaim that the end will shortly happen, but agonizes about how he can announce it without shutting off hope, and without promoting the unhealthy growth of groups claiming to be the elect remnant. As we have seen, it is a basic theme of all apocalyptic movements that people believe themselves to be the chosen ones, the children of light, who will endure through the terrors of the last time and will be granted salvation in some form. The danger is that such groups employ violence to survive: 'It was a nightmare possibility' (thinks Jean-Marie's theologian friend, Mendelius) 'that the Parousia might be preceded by a vast and bloody crusade of the insiders against the outlanders'.[130]

The answer formulated by the former pope and now freelance prophet is to publish a series of letters to God, titled 'Last Letters from a Small Planet', and to present their author as 'Johnny the Clown', discussing the 'shutting down of the show' with the circus owner. The non-coercive form of this message achieves widespread discussion of the coming apocalypse without panic or fanaticism, and their content is in accord with their form:

> When a man becomes a clown he makes a free gift of himself to his audience. To endow them with the saving grace of laughter, he submits to be mocked, drenched, clouted, crossed in love. Your son made the same submission when He was crowned as a mock King, and the troops spat wine and water in his face . . . My hope is that when He comes again, He will still be human enough to shed a gentle clown's tears over the broken toys – that were once men and women.[131]

Significantly, the book ends not with the apocalypse itself but with a kind of millennium, an indeterminate pause before the end initiated by the arrival of Christ in a hidden form, his identity concealed as a Syrian speech therapist named 'Maran Atha' ('the Lord comes'!). In this interim period there will be an opportunity for national governments to resolve their enmities, and for small communities to be gathered together in preparation for the end, made up not of the rich and powerful but of the weak and despised, such as handicapped children – the 'Clowns of God'.

This fictional apocalypse expresses the desire for the final coming of God to the world to be an act, not of unilateral sovereignty, but of a humility no less than the *kenosis* shown in the incarnation and the cross.

---

[130]   Morris West, *The Clowns of God* (London: Hodder & Stoughton, 1981), p. 96.
[131]   Ibid., p. 316.

Chapter Nine

OUR ETERNAL
DWELLING PLACE

In the previous chapter we surveyed various approaches to the image of a transcendent 'space' which is not literally another country or another world in which God 'lives', but which interpenetrates *our* living space, bringing a constant challenge into what otherwise would be a self-enclosed existence. This is the space that postmodern critical thinkers such as Derrida and Kristeva are feeling after with their image of the *khora*, which apophatic theologians once named as the 'empty place' that is full of God, and which some contemporary a-theologians have transmuted into a void which is totally immanent in human existence. This is the space, I suggest, that writers of Utopias and visionaries of the millennium are seeking to reflect within history in their construction of 'no-place' which is a 'good place'.

If we affirm with Jürgen Moltman that 'the space of creation is its living-space in God', and that God has made room for those who are created 'by withdrawing himself and giving his creation space',[1] then this image implies that God already embraces or fills something corresponding to 'space' in God's own self. Only then can God 'give' space. However, contrary to Moltmann, the result must surely be a mutual indwelling of God and creation, each in the other's space throughout the whole span of history of the cosmos and not only in a future new creation. This is, after all, the logic of the kabbalistic metaphor of *zimsum*; if the kenotic withdrawal of God is from God's own self rather than from an external space that God occupies, then it must not only be true of the resulting space of creation that 'everything is in God' *but also* that God is present to everything.

This does not exclude, however, the hope that there will be a fuller kind of divine indwelling in the new creation than we know at present. It

[1] Jürgen Moltmann, *The Coming of God*, transl. M. Kohl (London: SCM Press, 1996), p. 299.

is this that prompts the question, raised several times in the last chapter, as to whether there can continue to be 'living space' for creation in an eschaton of God's final indwelling. If new creation is to be characterized by greater 'fullness of presence' than we know at present, will created beings be effectively absorbed and subjugated by this divine immediacy? We can only answer this question, I believe, by conceiving our 'living space in God' as a space between the interweaving relationships of the Trinity.

When we think of God as triune rather than as an undifferentiated Absolute, the image of 'withdrawal' can be conceived as a making room for us in the fellowship of the divine life, as a widening of communion so that we dwell in triune spaces. That is, our living space in God has been opened up in the midst of the 'spaces' that already subsist in God in the interplay of personal relationships. I want to suggest, however, that this in turn requires a far more radical identification of 'person' and 'relationship' than current trinitarian theology usually ventures upon; that is, using the coinage of traditional discussion, we need to take the idea of 'subsistent relations' much more seriously. As we shall see, only this will make sense of a present dwelling of God which can still become a fuller indwelling. Only this will allow us to think of eschatological fullness of presence as a non-dominating reality. Only this will allow us to conceive of an openness at the very heart of closure.

Participating in Triune Relationships

The idea that human persons are created to participate in the relational life of the triune God has become quite widespread in recent theology, owing a good deal to the recovery of the thought of the early Eastern Fathers of the Church. As the modern Orthodox theologian John of Pergamon (John Zizioulas) has summarized their vision of the divine *ousia*, 'Being is Communion'.[2] It has become well recognized that when the Fathers of East and West spoke about three 'persons' or 'hypostases' in God they understood them to be inseparable from their relationships with each other. Whereas in the tradition of both Plato and Aristotle to have relations with others was something additional to the real core of one's being (*hypostasis*), in the doctrine of the Trinity Christian thinkers took the revolutionary

[2] John Zizioulas, *Being as Communion. Studies in Personhood and the Church* (London: Darton, Longman and Todd, 1985), pp. 44–9.

step of affirming that the relationships between Father, Son and Spirit
belonged to the essential nature of God, and indeed defined it.

In our day, this vision of a God whose life is communion has been
rightly invoked to encourage a relational view of human life which reflects
the triune image, in family, Church and society. This approach is common
to Protestant,[3] Catholic[4] and Orthodox[5] theology, where the realization
has dawned – accompanied by some spirit of repentance for past failure –
that a basically non-triune concept of God as 'sole monarch of the universe'
has been appealed to in past ages by Church and state to validate the
totalitarian power of human representatives of such a heavenly ruler. By
contrast, an image of God living in communion will resist the reduction of
human persons to isolated and self-interested individuals. In response to the
challenge of the postmodern mood, it has also been suggested that the
image of a triune God provides a context for the human self which can
accommodate much of the reaction against the Cartesian subject. God is
not to be seen as a transcendent supra-subject grounding the human
conscious self in its perception and control of the world as an object. In
this case the death of God and the death of the self would indeed be
mutual fatalities. But rather, a triune God exists in self-giving relationships
which are characterized by a love that suffers even the desolation of death,
and which enable the human self to live in interactive relations with
others.[6]

However, for the image of a triune God to have these salutary effects on
our social and individual life, we need to reflect more closely on the
conceptual link between 'person' and 'relationship', and especially to
explore what it means to 'participate' in the divine communion. We may,
in fact, discern three stages in the integration of 'person' and 'relationship',
as exemplified in the thought of the Church Fathers. First, Athanasius

[3]   See e.g. Jürgen Moltmann, *The Trinity and the Kingdom of God*, transl. M. Kohl
(London: SCM Press, 1981), pp. 191–202, 212–9; Colin Gunton, *The One, the Three
and the Many* (Cambridge: Cambridge University Press, 1993), pp. 214–29.
[4]   See e.g. Leonardo Boff, *Trinity and Society*, transl. P. Burns (London: Burns & Oates,
1988), pp. 20–4; Catherine M. LaCugna, *God for Us. The Trinity and Christian Life*
(New York: HarperSanFrancisco, 1991), pp. 390–400.
[5]   John Zizioulas, *Being as Communion*, pp. 139–42; Gennadios Limouris, 'The Church
as Mystery and Sign in Relation to the Holy Trinity' in G. Limouris (ed.) *Church,
Kingdom, World* (Geneva: World Council of Churches, 1986), pp. 18–49.
[6]   See Anthony Thiselton, *Interpreting God and the Postmodern Self* (Edinburgh: T. & T.
Clark, 1995), pp. 154–63; cf. Brian Ingraffia, *Postmodern Theory and Biblical Theology*
(Cambridge: Cambridge University Press, 1995), pp. 225–241.

affirms that the persons in God are *distinguished* from each other only in their relations, and particularly in their relationship of origin to each other.[7] While they are one in divine *ousia*, explains Athanasius, the Father is 'other' (*heteros*) in that he alone begets the Son, the Son is 'other' in that he alone is begotten, and the Spirit is 'other' in that he alone 'proceeds' from the Father. This doctrine of relations was taken up by the Cappadocian Fathers, who seem to have taken it one stage further, at least in some of their writings: the divine persons are not only *distinct* from each other in their relations (which these theologians summarize as paternity, filiation and spiration), but are *constituted* in their being entirely by their relations.[8] The relationships of ecstatic, outward-going, love between the persons 'hypostasize' them, make them who and what they are.

We can certainly find this second stage in Augustine's assumption of Eastern trinitarian thought into Western theology. It is not quite so clear that a third stage is fully present, but Augustine is at least exploring the idea of what has come to be called 'subsistent relations' – not simply that relationships *distinguish* the persons and *form* the persons, but that they *are* the persons and the persons are no more or less than relationships. Although such an eminent Patristics scholar as J. N. D. Kelly asserts this to be Augustine's intention,[9] and Colin Gunton straightforwardly accuses him of what he considers to be a disastrous step in Western thinking,[10] it seems that Augustine is moving playfully and experimentally in this direction, without any clear basis on which to do so. He was dealing with the alternative presented to him by the Arians, that the persons of the Trinity must be distinguished either by substance (hence ending in tritheism) or accident (hence without the enduring nature of divinity); he replied that 'the names, Father and Son, do not refer to the substance but to the relation, and the relation is no accident'.[11] Although Kelly suggests that we should understand this in line with the belief of Porphyry and Plotinus that relations in themselves have real subsistence, it would be better to recognize that the statement 'the names refer to the relations' has the character of thought in process. Augustine is struggling to find a language to express

[7] Athanasius, *Contra Arianos*, 3.4–6; cf. 1.9, 39, 58.
[8] See e.g. Basil, *Contra Eunomium*, 2.22, 29; Gregory Nazianzen, *Oratio*, 23.8, 11; 29:2–3.
[9] J. N. D. Kelly, *Early Christian Doctrines* (London: A. & C. Black, 4th edn, 1968), pp. 274–5.
[10] Colin Gunton, *The Promise of Trinitarian Theology* (Edinburgh: T. & T. Clark, 1991), pp. 38–41.
[11] Augustine, *De Trinitate*, 5.6.

the revolutionary idea that God exists in the communion of 'paternity, filiation and gift', a concept that challenges both Platonism and Aristotelianism, and he admits that we only use the word person 'in order that we may not remain wholly silent when asked "three what?" '.[12]

It is usual for critics of Augustine to interpret his doctrine of relations in the light of his psychological analogies for the Trinity, and to see both as a suppression of the real identity of the *hypostases* in favour of the one *ousia*. He is thus seen as the chief architect of the Western 'modalistic' tendency of stressing the oneness of God at the expense of any real diversity of persons. Undoubtedly, his attempt to express complex personal reality in God suffered through his concentration on the human soul as an image of the Trinity, leaving the impression that he conceived of God as an absolute individual with three different faculties. However, it is significant for our own quest into the meaning of participation that he preferred the psychological analogy not merely of memory, understanding and will, but of our mind remembering *God*, understanding *God* and loving *God*.[13] Thus he associated the persons with our *involvement* in God.

I suggest that Augustine had taken an important step towards an idea that was, unfortunately, never developed properly in the West and was rejected in the East. Some of the experimental – and, indeed, participatory – nature of Augustine's thinking is lost when Aquinas finally takes the third step and formulates a doctrine of subsistent relations, since he grounds it in an Aristotelian view of the simplicity of the divine essence. Aquinas begins helpfully with *movements* or *actions* in God rather than with subjects, with the two processions of begetting and 'breathing forth', which therefore imply three unique relations (begets, is begotten, is breathed).[14] But Aquinas' logical reason for the subsistence or self-grounded existence of these relations as Father, Son and Spirit is that since the substance of God is simple in its unity, its relations and personal properties must be identical with it, and so they are real in the same way as the substance is real. They 'subsist' in the one substance of God. As Aquinas summarizes it, 'divine person signifies relation as something subsisting . . . relation is signified . . . as hypostasis'.[15] The Western tradition from Aquinas onwards thus bases the self-existence of the relationships in their identity with the one

[12]   Ibid., 7.11.
[13]   Ibid., 14.15–20.
[14]   According to Aquinas, there are four 'real relations' (*Summa Theologiae*, 1a.28.4) and three 'unique relations' (1a.30.2).
[15]   Aquinas, *Summa Theologiae*, 1a.29.4.

substance of God, and this will inevitably detract from three distinct identities (*hypostases*) in God.

We might, however, provide a very different reason for conceiving relations as being the ultimate reality in God. That is, focusing on relations rather than on personal agents who 'have' relations (or even those who are *constituted* by their relations) moves from an ontology of substance to one of event, from the static to the dynamic; correspondingly, talk of the triune God moves from being a language of observation to one of participation. Understanding the 'persons' of the Father, Son and Holy Spirit *as* relationships will enable us to avoid an application to God of the split between subject and object that has been a regrettable inheritance of Enlightenment rationalism.

Karl Barth provides an important key to this shift by placing the notion of 'subsistent relations' in the context of conceiving God's very nature as 'act'. As we have already noted, Barth affirms that 'With regard to the being of God, the word "event" or "act" is final'.[16] According to Barth, if God's self-revelation is a 'happening', then God must 'happen' in himself; in an eternal event of self-repetition, God is 'thrice the divine I', and eludes being objectified as either a numerically single 'I' or three individual 'I's.[17] Barth avoids using the term 'person' to denote what are thereby distinguished in God as Father, Son and Spirit, as he believes it to be irremediably bound up with modern notions of an individual self-consciousness and so undermining of the one Lordship of God.[18] His preference for 'mode (or way) of being' (*Seinsweise*) does however give some hostages to those who accuse him of presenting God as the absolute Subject of the Idealist heritage, reflexively diversifying himself.[19] While this is an unfair accusation, as it is clear that Barth conceives the 'ways of being' to be always defined by their relationships,[20] it would be better to take up his insight into the event character of God – and Aquinas's strategy of beginning with processions in God – by speaking of three '*movements* of being characterized by relationship', or more simply 'movements of relationship'. We can then build on the classical Western formula of 'three relationships subsisting in one being', perhaps

---

[16]   Karl Barth, *Church Dogmatics* transl. and ed. G. W. Bromiley and T. F. Torrance (Edinbugh: T. & T. Clark 1936–77), II/1, p. 263.

[17]   Barth, *Church Dogmatics*, I/1, p. 394.

[18]   Ibid., pp. 355–9.

[19]   See e.g. Moltmann, *Trinity and the Kingdom of God*, p. 142; LaCugna, *God for Us*, pp. 252–3.

[20]   Barth, *Church Dogmatics*, I/1, pp. 364–7.

reformulating it as 'three movements of relationship subsisting in one event'. Robert Jenson has a similar intention when he speaks of God as 'an event constituted in relations and personal in structure'.[21]

This concept of God as an event of relationships runs immediately into the criticism expressed by Jürgen Moltmann, that 'there are no persons without relations; but there are no relations without persons either'.[22] Of course, it is not possible to visualize, paint, or etch in stone or glass three interweaving 'relationships' without personal agents who exercise them, or three 'movements of being' characterized by their relations. But this has exactly the advantage of meeting the problems of what Nicholas Lash has dubbed 'spectatorial empiricism',[23] in which observation has been made the basic paradigm of knowing. In the latter case, knowledge takes the form of subjecting objects to the control of our consciousness, as things that can either be seen with the eyes or 'seen' (conceptualized) in the mind; correspondingly the task of language is to *represent* what has been perceived as accurately as possible. A relational doctrine of the Trinity makes clear that God cannot be known and spoken about in this way, and realizing this should then also open up other dimensions in our knowledge of the world around us. Speaking about God as 'an event of relationships' is not the language of a spectator, but the language of participation. This sort of talk only makes sense in terms of our *involvement* in the network of relationships in which God happens. While in his book on the Trinity Jürgen Moltmann portrays the divine persons as three subjects,[24] in an earlier book he himself speaks of God as 'the event of Golgotha' and to the question 'can one pray to an event? answered that one can 'pray in this event.'[25]

To refer to God as 'Father' thus does not mean to visualize, represent or objectify God as a father-figure, but to *address* God as Father, and so enter into a child–father relationship that is already there in God ahead of us. The language enables what Alan Torrance has aptly called 'doxological partici-pation'.[26] The New Testament portrays prayer as being *to* the Father, *through* the Son and *in* the Spirit. This means, I suggest, that we find our cry of

[21]   Robert W. Jenson, *The Triune Identity* (Philadelphia: Fortress Press, 1982), p. 161.

[22]   Moltmann, *Trinity and the Kingdom of God*, p. 172.

[23]   Nicholas Lash, *The Beginning and the End of Religion*, (Cambridge: Cambridge University Press, 1996), pp. 79–80.

[24]   Moltmann, *Trinity and the Kingdom of God*, p. 171.

[25]   Jürgen Moltmann, *The Crucified God*, transl. R. A. Wilson and J. Bowden (London: SCM Press, 1974), p. 247.

[26]   Alan Torrance, *Persons in Communion. Trinitarian Description and Human Participation* (Edinburgh: T. & T. Clark, 1996), pp. 307–9.

'Abba, Father' fitting into a movement like that of speech between a son and father; our response of 'yes' ('Amen') leans upon a filial 'yes' of humble obedience, glorifying the Father, a response which is already there.[27] At the same time, our self-offering is supported by a movement of self-giving like that of a father sending forth a son, a movement which in traditional language is named 'eternal generation' and 'temporal mission'. To pray in the event of Golgotha means that these movements of response and mission are undergirded by movements of suffering, like that of a forsaken son towards a father and a desolate father towards a lost son.

Dwelling in Triune Spaces

Thus we may identify distinct paternal and filial movements of relationship, or 'father-to-son' and 'son-to-father' movements of speech, empathy and action, in which we are invited to share. We are able to make these our own, moreover, through the complete identity of the eternal movement of sonship with human sonship in the person of Jesus Christ ('incarnation'), so that movements of human–divine communion are already present in God on which we can lean. We dwell in spaces that are already there for us, among the movements of love. While in describing these relationships I have followed the form of address that Jesus himself taught his disciples ('when you pray, say "Our Father"'), it should be readily apparent, however, that the basic pattern of these movements is giving and receiving in love, and so in appropriate circumstances it will also be right to use feminine images for the flow of relationships in which we are engaged – like those originating in a mother, for instance (cf. Isaiah 49:14–15), or like those characteristic of the response of a daughter. Nor are the patterns of relating into which we are caught up exhausted by metaphors drawn from human family life, as is made clear by the language of 'Holy Spirit' (Rom. 8:15–16, 26–7).

In the New Testament there is a special association of the Spirit with 'fellowship', but the nature of God as an event of relationships means that we cannot isolate the dynamic of communion to the Spirit alone; the whole network of relationships in the event of God is an 'open' space for human beings to be drawn into. The Western tradition of a self-sufficient Trinity closes the circle with the Spirit as bond of communion proceeding from Father and Son, and so the Spirit is also associated with unifying. This

---

[27] Cf. Rom. 8:34, 2 Cor. 1:20, Heb. 7:25.

is definitively expressed in the Hegelian definition of self-thinking Thought as Subject, Object and Process of Relating. But the pattern of movement of the Spirit in the world is the opening up of personal and social being, freeing us from structures of the present and turning us to future possibilities. If we accept that the economic activity of the Trinity at least *corresponds* to the immanent triune life of God, then we can discern an inner movement within the being of God which reflects the activity of the Spirit in history. The movement of 'spirit-ness' can be recognized as a continual opening up the hidden depths of relationship between Father and Son, a deepening and diversifying of communion that makes it apt to 'appropriate' fellowship to the Spirit, while not reserving the creating of fellowship entirely to this relationship. At the same time, this opening up of communion will mean an opening of God's own future, as I have already suggested in thinking about 'time's arrow' and its implications for God.

It is significant here that Scripture offers a range of impressionistic images for the Spirit – a breeze blowing gently, a gale uprooting everything in its path, a breath stirring in the body, oil trickling, fire warming and fire burning fiercely, water refreshing and flowing water in which we are immersed, wings beating and wings brooding.[28] We notice that these are all images of movement, and that they appear to be impersonal because they do not use the terms of human family and society. But they surely evoke another dimension of personality, reminding us that the personal relationships within God cannot be exhausted by filial and paternal characteristics. Speaking of the Spirit alerts us to not only to a particular aspect of *receiving* within God – being 'breathed forth' – but also an active movement of *giving*, in 'opening things up'.

An important contribution to the doctrine of the Trinity has been made recently by Alan Torrance in his study *Persons in Comunion*, where he puts a similar emphasis on 'participation' in God. Torrance stresses that the active self-giving of God as communion conditions our social existence, creating and commandeering our 'language games' in such a way that we can participate cognitively in the relations within God's own communion of life. There is thus both 'doxological participation' and 'semantic participation'. Talk of God as 'three persons' arises from this transforming of our language through the experience of God as communion. It is not a language of representation, as if it 'names' something which we have

---

[28] See e.g. Ezek. 37:9, Isa. 40:7, Gen. 2:7, Isa. 61:1, 4:4, 44:3, 1 Cor. 12:13, Acts 2:2–3, Luke 1:35, Gen. 1:2, Luke 3:22.

already thought, but it has 'performative' power and appropriateness; it enables us to participate in the 'movement' of God's relational life, and to develop our relations with each other. Torrance judges that Barth's language of 'ways of being' does not have the performative power to communicate the 'perichoretic and participative presence' of God, whereas the word 'person' does:

> Our judgement here is a contingent one – there is no 'absolute' need to use the term 'person' with respect to the members of the Trinity. But there is an absolute obligation, however, for our language games to participate as effectively as possible in the triune dynamic which claims them.[29]

Torrance suggests that while there is no 'common essence' between human and divine persons, there is suffient 'family resemblance' between the associations which the word 'person' evokes when used either of human beings or God, for it to be an effective means of enabling us to indwell God. We may agree that using the names 'Father, Son and Spirit' is indispensable for drawing us into the relational life of God, but I venture to suggest that Torrance has located the 'analogy of communion' in the wrong place when he finds it to lie between divine persons and human persons conceived as subjects of will, mind and action. By contrast, I suggest that the analogy or 'family resemblance' created by the gracious presence of God in human community must surely always lie between human *relations* and divine *relations*.

Like all analogies, there will be both continuities and discontinuities here, and the term 'person' will function in a different way because of the basic discontinuity between the created and the uncreated. However deep and empathetic the communion in human relationships, however much it releases the participants from self-sufficiency and isolation, since they are finite relationships there will still be 'persons' who are individual agents exercising the relationships. The appropriateness of the term 'person' in the divine communion is in pointing us, not to agents at the 'ends' of the relationships, but to the direction and flow of the relationships in which we find ourselves engaged.[30] To speak of the 'mission of the Father', for

---

[29]   Torrance, *Persons in Communion*, p. 335.

[30]   In my use of analogy here I am adopting the 'cautious theological realism' of Janet Martin Soskice, *Metaphor and Religious Language* (Oxford: Clarendon Press 1985), pp. 133–41; but unlike Soskice, I am only taking a 'critically realistic' view of personal relations in God, not of personal subjects in God.

instance, enables us to participate in a movement of sending like that of a father sending forth a son.

Other recent discussions of the Trinity have picked up the tradition of 'subsistent relations', stressing the ontological priority of relations in God, and insisting that the naming of persons as nouns is always derived from the verbal forms of 'processions' and 'missions' in God.[31] David Cunningham, for instance, affirms what he believes to be the insight of Aquinas that the persons 'are not endpoints between whom there are relations; they are, simply, relations'.[32] For all this, however, such studies portray the 'analogy of communion' as being an analogy between human and divine *persons*. Now, the human experience of participating in each other's thoughts and feelings, and of substituting for one another in individual and social actions, is indeed analogous to the divine *perichoresis* of persons. Examples can be drawn from mutual participation in family life, or from the mutual dwelling together of members in the church as the body of Christ, and especially from the most intimate interaction between a pregnant mother and the baby in the womb. The analogy is in the interweaving of relationships. But what we cannot do is to find the analogy in the *persons* participating, as if 'Father', 'Son' and 'Spirit' are like human persons sharing in community, but raised to the highest degree in their capacity for openness and intimacy.

To take this very common line is to reduce the being of God from 'communion' to 'community', and to remain – despite all intentions – under the shadow of a 'social doctrine of the Trinity'. It is to remain with the second stage of the link between relation and person, so that the divine persons are 'constituted' by their relations, only more fully than we are. It is to run the risk of treating the triune communion as a 'model' for human relationships to imitate rather than a reality which can only be apprehended by participation. In the end, we shall not escape from objectifying God, and we will fail to grasp a true epistemology of participation. The transcendent reality in which we are called to participate can be known as a 'perichoresis' of persons because it is like the complex relationship that results when finite persons participate in each other's lives, only in God it is a perfect inter-penetration and coinherence of love where ours is only

---

[31]   See e.g. David Cunningham, *These Three are One. The Practice of Trinitarian Theology* (Oxford: Blackwell, 1998), pp. 58–66; Jenson, *The Triune Identity*, pp. 122–30, 140–8; E. L. Mascall, *The Triune God. An Ecumenical Study* (Worthing: Churchman Publishing, 1986), pp. 11–23.

[32]   Cunningham, *These Three are One*, p. 62.

partial. The real analogy is between human *perichoresis* and divine *perichoresis*, not between the participants. This is why the metaphor of the dance[33] remains so effective for the eternal mutual indwelling and interacting of God. If the analogy is between the dancers, then indeed 'it is hard not to think of three people ... even if their dance is sufficiently elegant and harmonious so that they blur into one', as one critic observes.[34] But the analogy is with the movements and patterns of the dance itself, and these can move in and out of each other and occupy each other's space in a way that dancers cannot. Just a hint of this is caught in the popular hymn by Sydney Carter, 'Lord of the Dance', by the divine declaration: 'But I am the dance, and I still go on'.

My purpose here is not to develop a comprehensive doctrine of the Trinity, but to clarify what I mean when I refer to our present 'dwelling in triune spaces', and to our eschatological hope for fuller dwelling. The room that God makes for us within God's self is not a widening of a gap between individual subjects, but the harmonious opening up of spaces or intervals within the inter-weaving movements of giving and receiving. This is the 'withdrawal' that produces a void of 'nothingness' within God which gives creation a place to live, and the metaphor of intervals between movements draws out the intention of the kabbalistic image of *zimsum*, as it makes clear that there is no universal container, from a part of which God shrinks away. This space opened up for created beings is felt to be the 'nothing' or 'empty place' of apophatic theology, and the nameless *khora* of such thinkers as Heidegger, Derrida and Kristeva, because there are no 'infinite subjects' present making the relations and dominating finite participants. But this emptiness is at the same time a fullness, a *pleroma*, because the space is surrounded and inter-penetrated by active perichoretic movements of giving (sending, responding, and opening), and passive movements of receiving (being glorified, being sent and being breathed out). As Kristeva puts it in her version of the *khora*, it is 'analogous only to vocal or kinetic rhythm', and is a place 'constituted by movements.'[35]

We might find a limited parallel here with Heidegger's manner of signifying Being as the word *Sein* with a cross (X) through it; by this he apparently intends to indicate that the Being which is wholly other than beings is beyond all being, and therefore even the trace of Being should

---

[33] See above, pp. 206, 218.
[34] Cunningham, *These Three are One*, p. 180.
[35] Julia Kristeva, *The Kristeva Reader*, ed. Toril Moi (Oxford: Blackwell, 1986), pp. 94, 93; see above, pp. 242–3.

stand under erasure. Yet the middle-point of the cross also indicates a 'gathering point' from the 'fourfold earth and heavens', where beings encounter the self-giving of Being.[36] In reflection on Heidegger from a theological perspective, Jean-Luc Marion similarly inscribes the name of God as 'crossed by a cross, because he reveals himself by his placement on a cross', and so the gift or act of giving 'offers the only accessible trace of He who gives'.[37] I am proposing a fuller presence of God than this trace, in which the intersecting lines of the cross can stand for the place where movements of self-giving, ecstatic love inter-weave and inter-penetrate, so that we can truly dwell in God. We can find traces of this perichoresis in the intervals of 'difference' between human persons, and in the mutual participation that the difference between them makes possible. Indeed, these are contexts in which we are enabled to participate in the triune God, and which in turn that very participation can transform.

However, placing God under the sign of the cross/intersection makes clear that the presence of God in the world is hidden, as the glory of God is hidden in the humiliation of the cross. Self-disclosure means veiling for God, for reasons we have already considered,[38] to which we must now add the fundamental point that the presence of the triune God cannot be objectified or observed, but only *participated* in. It is hidden because it requires engagement. All the aspects of the hidden presence of God that we explored in the previous chapter are thus illuminated by the notion that we share in the movements of the divine relationships. While remaining opaque to the glory of God in their secularity, objects in the world become the means for drawing us into encounter with a self-relating and other-relating God (Barth), and the 'place' made between us by the ethical demand of our neighbour (Levinas) can become a 'trace' of the space which is opened for us in the infinitely Other.[39] Moreover, in the moment of being aligned with divine movements of relationship we cannot 'observe a difference' between the self and God (though of course one remains); as the negative theologians point out, God is not the *object* of desire but the one *in whom* we desire the good. God offers a movement of

[36] M. Heidegger, *The Question of Being*, transl. J. Wilde and W. Kluback (New Haven: College and University Press, 1956), pp. 81–3.

[37] Jean-Luc Marion, *God without Being*, transl. T. Carlson (Chicago: University of Chicago Press, 1991), pp. 71, 105.

[38] See above, pp. 257–8.

[39] Here I differ from Levinas, in proposing that the trace actually gives us access to the presence of God, whereas for Levinas we cannot participate in a God who is always absent, as having 'just passed by'.

desire in which we can share, and in leaning upon this movement it can be hard to disentangle – as the Lady Julian found – created from uncreated desire.

The subjective 'experience' of this presence and this dwelling in triune spaces will nevertheless not be homogeneous in all circumstances. As Alan Torrance points out, when God whose being is communion enters time and space this event creates structures of language ('language games') which shape the kind of community in which doxological and semantic participation in God becomes possible.[40] We may say that the gracious self-gift of God brings a society into being in which there are 'traces' of divine communion – in human relationships, in the sacraments and liturgy – and these provide us with the resources for finding ourselves in God. Our experience of divine presence will therefore vary according to the various contexts created by it, and this brings us to consider the eschatological hope of a new context in a new creation.

Particularity and Eschatology

When exploring what might be implied by the image of resurrection in a previous chapter, we were preoccupied with the puzzling question of the continuity of identity of the person who had died and been resurrected. We found that this question could only be properly resolved in the context of a vision of deeper and richer inter-relationships rather than the survival of the bare individual. We also saw that there are good reasons why some 'particularity' of identity should remain if we are to make sense of the diversity of creation and a loving God, and not least among these reasons are the need for justice for the oppressed and opportunity for those whose potential for growth has been stunted.

Particularity is not to be confused with individualism, as the particular nature of something is always established through relationality; its 'difference' from others is only discernible in its network of relationships with others. This particularity is what the medieval theologian Duns Scotus called the *haecceitas* or sheer 'thisness' of things, and the nineteenth century poet Gerard Manley Hopkins drew upon Scotus's concept as he continually celebrated the distinct forms, or 'inscapes' of everything created.[41] During

---

[40]   Torrance, *Persons in Communion*, pp. 341–6.
[41]   For Hopkins' debt to Scotus see *The Sermons and Devotional Writings of Gerard*

the period of his novitiate when he discovered Scotus, Hopkins wrote, 'when I took in any inscape of the sky or sea I thought of Scotus'.[42] Through the coinage 'inscape' Hopkins intended to denote that the myriad 'selves' of creation have an outer bodily shape (scape) which expresses a unique inner nature:

> Each mortal thing does one thing and the same:
> Deals out that being indoors each one dwells;
> Selves – goes itself; *myself* it speaks and spells,
> Crying *What I do is me: for that I came*.[43]

In this poem Hopkins observes that creatures reflect sunlight in different ways – 'As kingfishers catch fire, dragonflies draw flame' – that each stone makes its own kind of splash when thrown into a well, and that each bell in a peal makes its own ring, 'finds tongue to fling out broad its name'. This last illustration recalls another image Hopkins uses for inscapes – the particular place of musical notes in a scale; this, together with the image of colours in a spectrum makes clear that inscapes do not exist in isolation. There is communion between the selves of all creatures, including human personalities, and all inscapes have their particularity because they are upheld by the grace of the triune God. In expressing their particularity they are returning it in praise to the Father, through the presence of Christ in the world and the energy ('stress') of the Spirit. So the poem ends with a celebration of the response of human particular selves to God, participating in the joyful movement of response of the Son to the Father:

> . . . For Christ plays in ten thousand places,
> Lovely in limbs and lovely in eyes not his
> To the Father through the features of men's faces.

Hopkins' vision of the linking of created 'inscapes' to the communion of God's own life seems to embody the theology of participation I have been outlining. But it is precisely in this area of particularity that the greatest challenge to a doctrine of 'subsistent relations' might arise: would

---

Manley Hopkins, ed. Christopher Devlin (London: Oxford University Press, 1959), Appendix II.

[42] The Journals and Papers of Gerard Manley Hopkins, 2nd edn, ed. Humphrey House (London: Oxford University Press, 1959), p. 221 (19 July 1872).

[43] 'As kingfishers catch fire', in The Poems of Gerard Manley Hopkins, 4th edn, ed. W.H. Gardner and N.H. Mackenzie (London: Oxford University Press, 1967), p. 90.

the identification of person with relation in God actually undermine our grasp on the particularity which is God's purpose in creation? Perhaps the most powerful voice claiming that it does has been that of Colin Gunton in his studies on trinitarian theology, *The One, the Three and the Many* and *The Promise of Trinitarian Theology*.

Gunton is concerned with the loss of particularity in our present age, judging that the postmodern reaction against universals has not in fact led to a respect for the nature of particular persons and things in the world. Despite talk of 'difference' and 'otherness', the loss of transcendent universals has led to an indifferent pluralism in which everything is 'equally interesting'. In the now bygone period of modernity, the exaltation of the human will led to a loss of particularity as the body was subordinated to the abstract ideal of the mind. In the present reaction against modernity, a pluralism in which all cultural forms are treated as of equal value leads no less to a depressing homogeneity.[44] Gunton urges the need to recover a sense of the 'substance' of persons and things, by which he does not mean a kind of common, underlying substratum, but particular natures in all their relations with others and material embodiment. The idea of the Trinity generates a 'transcendental' concept of particularity (along with the concept of *perichoresis*) which should strengthen finite particulars to be themselves within their networks of relationships: that is, the Trinity is conceived as three particular realities (*hypostases*) related in one communion.[45]

The substantiality of God thus 'resides not in his abstract being, but in the concrete particulars that we call the divine persons and in [their] relations . . .'.[46] Gunton's complaint is that Western trinitarian thought has understood the substantiality of God to be a unity of being which underlies the three persons, and so has lost 'the particularity at the heart of God'. This is the source of the image of God as a changeless, unitary and arbitrary will against which there has been such a strong reaction in the modern age. But the dethroning of this divine substance has been accompanied by a loss of any sense of substance (i.e. material particularity) at all, and especially by the loss of a substantial self, as human persons have been reduced to mere bundles of relations and fragmentary moments of representation.

Thus far Gunton's analysis accords largely with the diagnosis of postmodernity in this present study, and usefully locates it *vis-à-vis* the history of

[44] Gunton, *The One, the Three and the Many*, pp. 41–5, 69–70.
[45] Ibid., pp. 188–204.
[46] Ibid., p. 191.

trinitarian thought. But Gunton also proposes that the loss of particularity in the concept of God was fostered by the *equation*, from Augustine onwards, of divine person with relationship, rather than the persons being *constituted* by their relationships.[47] The notion of 'subsistent relationships', in Gunton's view, thus loses a grasp on the particularity of the persons which 'tend to disappear into the all-embracing oneness of God'. This – he implies – encourages the modern insubstantial view of the human person.

I have already suggested that Aquinas's employment of the idea of 'subsistent relations' shows the very tendency Gunton criticizes. But in itself, understanding the divine persons as movements of relationships can be the context in which finite particulars are empowered to be what they are, in *their* relationships. The point is not that 'persons' in the Trinity are *models* for finite persons and human societies to imitate; talk of 'relationships' in God is not a language of observation but participation, and the analogy that arises is not between the divine persons-as-relationships and human *persons*, but between the divine and human *relationships* and the *perichoreses* or communions that result from these relations. The word *hypostasis* as chosen by the early Church Fathers for the divine 'persons', indicates particularity or distinctness of identity. A subsistent relationship in God is truly hypostatic, as a movement of relationship to and from a Father has an identity which is quite distinct from a relational movement to and from a Son, or from the relational movement of 'Spirit'. Human persons will be hypostatic in a different way, because they are and always will remain finite beings, but they can participate in the hypostatic reality of God and so discover who they are and what they are intended to be. Participating in the mission which is embodied in a relational movement like that from a father to a son (or a mother to a son, or father to daughter, or mother to daughter) will empower human persons to find their particular mission, given them by the will of God. This divine will, as Scotus and Hopkins make clear in their visions of *haecceitas* and *inscape*, is not a dominating and suppressing will, but a creative will which allows the diverse particulars to be themselves and to contribute (as I have argued) to their own shaping of their being.

The exploring of particularity is thus bound to be eschatological. If human persons were embodiments of some unchanging, ideal essence, as in the Platonist view of eternal forms, then time and space would ultimately be of no account. But particular beings, with their origin in the creative

47   See *The Promise of Trinitarian Theology*, pp. 38–42.

will of God for diversity, will not possess their nature fully formed from the beginning. They will achieve their particular identity through a cooperation of divine grace and human activity. There is, as we have seen, an openness within the gaining of this particularity; within the space opened out for them in the triune God, created beings are on a journey. Like the marches for liberation during the apartheid era in South Africa which often incorporated the movements of native African dancing, the divine dance is progressive, moving towards a goal.

The belonging together of particularity and a future goal is illustrated, though ironically, in an apocalyptic novel by Anthony Burgess, *The End of the World News*. The main plot line is the destruction of earth by a collision with a rogue asteroid, code-named Lynx. Just before the asteroid hits, a spaceship leaves earth with a few survivors, as an ark to carry human life and civilization to a new home and a new future. By command of its original, dictatorial leader (later overthrown) virtually all the music, art and literature of earth has been removed from the survival capsule. The new leader, though more enlightened, as a former professor of English and writer of science fiction, nevertheless welcomes this deprivation as clearing the ground for a truly new civilization, declaring that 'we have no past, but our future is limitless.' All that will be salvaged from earth's culture will be 'the game of skill or chance, based on the abstraction of number'.[48] The most important person on the ship is thus declared to be Dashiel Gropius, former gambler and casino operator – and, more than incidentally, the rebellious son of a Calvinistic evangelist named Calvin Gropius. The only particularities allowed will be abstract numbers; all else is dismissed as 'mere nostalgia'. There is something reminiscent here of the way that those who regard themselves as living in a millennial age seek to be liberated from a debt to the past, as we saw in the previous chapter. It is not a coincidence that the spaceship is named 'America'; the project is a new American Revolution, following a millennial catastrophe.

The authorial view is made rather clear as the space travellers are permitted for the last time to listen to the music of Mozart while they observe the world exploding beneath them. The author comments wrily that the music that poured out was 'the essence of human divinity or divine humanity made manifest through the gross accidents of bowed

---

[48]   Anthony Burgess, *The End of the World News. An Entertainment* (London: Hutchinson, 1982), p. 385.

catgut and blown reeds'.[49] These are the rhythms that carry them on their journey. When these 'accidents' or particularities are suppressed, the result is inevitable. The short epilogue that follows discloses that the story of Lynx is being told in a space classroom centuries afterwards to the descendants of the original survivors, who refuse to believe that they are on a journey anywhere. Talk of a world with ' – what do you call them, buildings, clouds, trees, those things with four legs and things with four wheels' is dismissed by the precocious youngsters as a myth. Their teacher asserts desperately, 'This is a journey. This ship was designed for getting somewhere. A place where we can plant trees, erect buildings, feel the wind blowing in our faces', but the children declare: 'Your generation talks about a journey. Our generation knows we're just *here*. We've always been here, right back to what they call the mists of myth . . . We'll always be here.'[50] The loss of the sense of *material* particularity has resulted in the loss of any sense of direction. All that is left is the *abstract* particularity of numbers, in games of bridge and chess.

The complex, fantastic structure of the novel makes the point in two further ways, since two more story-lines interweave with the story of the asteroid. The account of the crushing of earth by Lynx is merged with an account of the life of Sigmund Freud (in the form of a television script) and an account of the visit of Leon Trotsky to New York in 1917 (in the form of the libretto for a Broadway musical). These three stories are all about the end of history as humankind has known it: the impact of an asteroid is compared with the impact of Marx and Trotsky's doctrine of revolutionary history, and Freud's discovery of the role of the unconscious mind. All three cataclysmic events are 'millennial' in the sense of putting an end to the world as it had been. All three also lose their sense of direction, through losing a grasp on the reality of the particular. The large-scale, universal theories of Marx and Freud cannot cope with the particular details of Trotsky's love for Olga and the materialism of American workers, or the cultural differences between the Jewish practitioners of Vienna and the clinical Protestants of Zürich. By an improbable chain of events, the only pieces of past human culture to leave earth on the spaceship are censored videotapes of the television play about Freud and the Trotsky musical. The children of future ages can find no meaning in these presentations either, referring to the myths 'about the bad man called Fred

---

[49]   There is surely an echo here of Shakespeare's *Much Ado about Nothing*, II.3.57, remarking on the wonder that: 'sheep's guts should hale souls out of men's bodies . . .'.
[50]   Burgess, *End of the World News*, p. 388.

Fraud who kept people strapped to a couch and the good one called Trot Sky who wanted people to do what he did and run through space . . .'

Without a grasp on particularity, on substance rather than abstract universals, there can be no movement towards a goal. Conversely, taking particular persons and things seriously demands that we consider the completing of their natures. Alongside the openness of development there must therefore be a closure of fulfilment. But it cannot be a closure which cancels out particularity, or undermines the nature of divine *perichoresis*, which is inconceivable apart from some kind of time and space.[51] There can be no inter-weaving or inter-penetrating of relationships without something analogous to space for this to happen in, and time for it to happen. This evident fact was masked when perichoresis (*circumincessio*) was understood only as *circuminsessio*, a static occupation of each person by the other.

The eschatological closure can only then be understood as the decisive raising of creation onto a new level, a closure of the old for a new journey to begin. The old creation was marked by a divine indwelling which gave space through the hiddenness of God, and the fuller dwelling of God for which we hope must still be characterized by a participation which gives a place for development of particularity in relationship, for only this will bring praise to the creator who wills that there be diversity. As Alan Torrance suggests, we should thus reconstruct the notion of 'beatific vision' as 'beatific participation', since 'a properly theological concept of communion . . . precludes the element of detachment inherent within visualist metaphors and encourages a more dynamic, holistic and subject-involving concept of knowledge of God'.[52] It is odd, then, that Torrance also suggests that while 'God is not an object for our examination' during the period of alienation from God in human history, nevertheless new creation holds forth the promise of 'the realisation of humanity's epistemic powers at every level'.[53] If knowledge of God is participatory it can surely *never* become objective or a matter of 'purview'. This is why the fullness of presence of God is always empowering and never dominating. An element of hiddenness must remain.

Though the 'full presence' or 'full dwelling' of God can only be a metaphor, at least one way of understanding it is that the context for the participation of created persons in God will be qualitatively new. At

[51] So Gunton, rightly, comments in *The One, The Three and the Many*, p. 167.
[52] Torrance, *Persons in Communion*, p. 39, n73.
[53] Ibid., p. 40.

present, the event of God's communion of life conditions our sociality and its structures of language, enabling us to participate in the movements of communion that are already in God. If the sociality which God sustains and uses is transformed, then our cognition of participation in God will also be transformed. To offer some speculations based on previous chapters in this book, let us suppose that our relationships together are no longer disturbed by the alienation of sin and troubled by the threat of death; that there is a deeper degree of communal life between persons in the 'resurrection body' than in our present bodily life, and that this includes a greater empathy with our whole environment; that we no longer use language in an attempt to control and dominate our world, and that communication between persons breaks through to new levels of intuition and openness. This kind of sociality would be a context where participation in the movements of relationship in God would be enhanced to the point where we would be continuously aware of them, and consciously in tune with the movements of love between Father, Son and Spirit, rather than enjoying a fragmentary experience that strikes us only rarely now.

Then the promise that 'we shall know as we are known' would be fulfilled, and while we would still not be literally 'observing' God, the unobstructed interface between our love and the divine love could be expressed in the metaphor 'seeing the face of God'. Scripture does in fact offer an image for this transformed sociality; it is the new Jerusalem, or the eternal city.

The Eternal City

The 'place' to which we are journeying, the true living-space for human fellowship and culture, and the place in which God dwells in fullness, is depicted in the Apocalypse of John as the new Jerusalem (Rev. 21:1–22:5). The vision of the glorious City has the immediate function of stiffening resistance and endurance in the situation of persecution in John's time, standing as it does as an anti-symbol to Babylon, the image of earthly imperial rule. But the seer has plundered the resources of the Old Testament, especially the vision of the new temple in Ezekiel 47–8 and passages from Isaiah (e.g. 54:11–12; 61:3,10; 65:13–22) to provide a central symbol of the new creation which is the Christian's ultimate hope. Indeed, it expresses not only the final dwelling of God in creation, but *our dwelling in God*. As I have already remarked, we cannot visualize three movements of relationship in God, and this is a positive advantage in shifting us from a kind of knowledge based on observation to one which is participatory. But images can have a performative function in enabling us to engage in God, and the image of dwelling in this city provides such an image, evoking participation in God and remarkably escaping the kind of objectification we have been rejecting.

The symbol achieves this through deconstructing itself in the very process of describing the city in loving detail, so that it is literally a 'no-place' and yet a 'good place' to be. On first sight the city seems to conform to expectations in other apocalyptic texts: a reality which pre-exists in heaven, parallel to the process of earthly history, comes down to earth when the old order passes away. The heavenly Jerusalem, parallel to the earthly city, descends at the moment of the last judgement and the defeat of God's earthly enemies. Since God and his Christ, 'the Lamb', have their thrones in this heavenly city, they come to dwell among human beings, fulfilling the covenant promise of Ezekiel 37:27: 'My dwelling place shall be with them; and I will be their God, and they shall be my people'. Yet, no sooner do we have this clear, than the identity of the city begins to shift. It is not only that this city is also a kind of temple (Revelation 21:22), a paradisial garden (22:2) and perhaps the chariot-throne (*merkabah*) of God (22:1 cf. 4:2–8, Ezekiel 1:4–28). More startling, this city is also a person, the bride of the Lamb: 'And I saw the holy city, new Jerusalem, coming down out of heaven, prepared as a bride adorned for her husband' (21:2).

This is not merely a passing simile, for a few verses later the angel guide tells John, 'Come, I will show you the Bride, the wife of the Lamb' (21:9), and the Bride is herself shortly to speak ('The Spirit and the bride say, "Come"' [22:17]). In the repetitive structure of the vision, the bride has in fact already arrived for the marriage feast of the Lamb (19:7), and has appeared earlier in the guise of the woman wearing a crown of twelve stars (12:1), anti-symbol to the 'great harlot'. As Austin Farrer points out, the mother of 12:1 and the bride of 21:9 are complementary images 'of the same reality, the daughter of Zion, the congregation of God'.[54] It is not just, then, that God's people dwell in the city; the personal image communicates the sense that they dwell in a new sociality. They dwell in the Bride. To some extent the woman–city conflation is conventional, as cities would be (and still are) depicted in heraldry as a woman crowned with the battlements of the city; but even this metaphor is stretched as each

---

54   Farrer, *The Revelation of St. John the Divine* (Oxford: Clarendon Press, 1964), p. 215.

of the twelve gates of the city is depicted as constructed from a single pearl; the bride's crown is evidently still in the seer's mind.

Inhabiting a new human sociality in this city is at the very same time to dwell in God. It has been our theme that to speak of 'dwelling' in God is a participatory rather than an observational language, and the description of the city here resolutely refuses to objectify the divine presence; its aim is rather to draw the reader in to dwell there. The throne of God and the Lamb is mentioned as the source of the water of life (22:1), but it is not located anywhere; the city is effectively itself the throne. There is no palace, and no imperial household such as was described when the throne of God was in heaven (4:4–11). Nor is there a separate temple in this city where the presence of God might be localized, for the shekinah-glory of the immediate presence of God is pervasive throughout, and shines everywhere through the transparent building materials – crystal and fine gold. There are no barriers here between secular and sacred spheres of life. The reader might think that the dwelling of God is at least located in the city as a bounded object, but then this too is deconstructed by being depicted as a perfect cube (21:16). Taken literally, this would mean the city was 1,500 miles in height, and this clearly frustrates any attempt to make the city an object to the vision. The city is modelled on the cubic shape of the Holy of Holies, which was the central feature in Ezekiel's picture of the new temple (Ezekiel 41:4, cf. 1 Kings 6:20); here the space in which God dwells fills the whole cosmos, joining heaven to earth.

It is in accord with the merging of the city into the very presence of God, that the Bride is inseparable from (though of course not identical with) the Lamb. The coming of the City is presented as a parallel event to the coming of the Word of God (19:11–13), and the 'lamp' of the city is the Lamb. The conflation of images here is perhaps equivalent to the Pauline metaphor of the Church as the Body of Christ, expressing an overlap, but not a simple identity, between the risen body of Christ and the redeemed human community. The Pauline tradition had already portrayed this new humanity in Christ as a holy building or temple, with Christ as the chief corner-stone (Eph. 2:16, 20–22). In John's new Jerusalem, the first level of the foundations is made of jasper, which is also the general stuff of the walls above and the colour of the divine glory (Rev. 21:11–12, 18–19); the twelve precious stones evidently stand for the twelve tribes of Israel, jasper corresponding to Judah, the tribe from which the Messiah comes. Farrer concludes that 'Messiah is the chief corner-stone; it is by being founded on him that the whole city, or Church, acquires the substance and colour of the divine glory'.[55] Christ is the foundation in that it is the shape of his words and actions, his non-violent resistance to oppressive powers[56] and his offering of forgiveness, that is repeated and re-enacted within the community.

The poet William Blake, in a prophetic association of biblical images, explicitly brings together the Pauline image of the Body of Christ and the image of the city from John's Apocalypse. In particular the received image of the new Jerusalem comes into a remarkable interaction with the image of Blake's own city, London. At present London is 'blind & age-bent, begging thro' the streets/ Of Babylon, led by a child . . .'.[57] The city of human habitation is broken by squalor, and by injustices done to the poor by the industrial revolution; the minds of its citizens are shackled by the chains of legalism and unimaginative rationalism. Walking through the streets of the city, Blake traces 'marks of weakness, marks of woe' in every face:

> In every cry of every man,
> In every infant's cry of fear,
> In every voice, in every ban,
> The mind-forg'd manacles I hear.[58]

But the association of the city with the Body of Christ means that there is a hope for the resurrection of the city. Just as individuals come together into a city, so they come together into the corporate personality of Christ, 'the human form divine'. The new humanity, crucified with Christ and risen with him, is a holy city – '. . . the spiritual four-fold London eternal' – built through the imagination and forgiveness embodied in Christ. The city is 'fourfold' because it unifies the human faculties of reason, emotion, instincts and imagination which at present are scattered and isolated to the four points of the bodily and social compass. In the social harmony of this city (which Blake names Golgonooza, perhaps 'new Golgotha'), every particular thing is valued:

---

[55]   Ibid., p. 219.

[56]   In a subversion of images of violence, the Rider on the white horse of Revelation 19:11–16 wears a robe that is dipped in his own blood, and since the sharp sword issues from his mouth it is evidently a metaphor for the 'Word of God' (v. 13).

[57]   William Blake, *Jerusalem*, 84.11, in *Blake. Complete Writings*, ed. Geoffrey Keynes (London: Oxford University Press, 1966), p. 729.

[58]   'London', in *Blake. Complete Writings*, p. 216.

> For every thing exists & not one sigh nor smile nor tear,
> One hair nor particle of dust, not one can pass away.[59]

In the shifting identities of Blake's vision, the new Jerusalem is the Bride of the Lamb; but to dwell in this city is to dwell in the new humanity which is Christ himself.

In John's vision of the city too, the new sociality overcomes old divisions. The promise of Ezekiel that God will dwell among his elect people is universalized into the ringing declaration: 'Now is God's dwelling with human beings!'. The city's gates are open to all, bringing in 'the kingdoms and nations of the earth'; as G. B. Caird puts it vividly, 'the nations are the heathen, who had once been allowed to trample the holy city underfoot'.[60] Only that which is opposed to the character of God is excluded. One way of understanding the curious disparity between the height of the walls and vertical dimension of the city itself, the former being far lower, is that the walls and gates symbolize the Jewish and Christian peoples of God (12 gates = 12 tribes = 12 apostles) while the city itself is comprehensive of all peoples. In this new social context, there is a greater potential for awareness of the presence of God, so that it can be said that his servants 'see his face'; lest we take this visual image literally, however, it is immediately followed by another which demands to be taken metaphorically – 'and his name shall be on their foreheads' (Rev. 22:4).

This is all certainly a symbol for the fuller presence of God in the new creation, and the fact that there has been a decisive shift from old to new is made clear by the comment that 'there was no more sea' (21:1); the sea is a traditional Hebrew image (together with the wilderness) for the chaotic elements of the creation that seem to resist the divine purpose. There is a new context in the whole of creation that makes possible a fuller cognitive participation in God. But this does not mean that God is dwelling in creation for the first time. As Caird points out, this is a future which is anticipated in the present, for in a sense the city has always been descending into the world: 'The holy city is described as coming down out of heaven from God because this is the essential quality it already has in the anticipatory experience of the church'.[61] The descent of the city twice in

---

[59] *Jerusalem*, 13.66–14.1, in *Blake. Complete Writings*, p. 634.
[60] G. B. Caird, *Commentary on The Revelation of St. John the Divine* (London: Adam & Charles Black, 1966), p. 279.
[61] Ibid., p. 263.

the span of a few verses in chapter 21 is not, he suggests, an indication of poor editing or some complex timetable of the end, but a demonstration of the 'permanent characteristic of the city'.

The city continually descends because God constantly comes to dwell in the world. The 'dwelling' (*skene*) of God through the city (21:3) recalls the use of the Hebrew term *mishkān* (tent) in the Old Testament and rabbinic texts to indicate the divine presence. Based on the story of the 'tent of presence' in the wilderness wanderings, the 'tenting' of God became a reverent metaphor for the presence of God (e.g. Lev. 26:11, cf Ezek. 37:27) and later took the form of the *shekinah* in rabbinic texts. Notably this cluster of meanings is drawn upon in the Fourth Gospel, with the declaration about Christ that 'the word became flesh and dwelt ('tented') among us . . .' (John 1.14). The descent of the Holy City in the new creation does not then indicate a different *kind* of presence from the hidden and humble dwellings of the Shekinah within history. The difference is in the context, the new creation, but the indwelling of God throughout history can always be portrayed with the image of the city.

It is ironic that in the course of the history of the Christian Church, the image of the city has been used to validate worldly power, whether imperial or ecclesial. From time to time Rome or Byzantium (and even, recently, Moscow) have been symbols for the suppression of dissent and the imposing of uniformity. Their custodians have not allowed the status quo to be disturbed by visions and hopes of the future. They have had to be warned, by an Augustine or a Blake, that they are not the City of God. The city of John's apocalyptic vision is not a centre of dominating authority, and so it stands as an apt symbol for the 'promised end' of Christian eschatology. This city invites participation in a divine commun-ion of life, promising a fullness of presence that we cannot experience now, but not promising that we shall ever possess God as an object of our desire. There will remain a delightful, enticing hiddenness which elicits and requires engagement in the movements of love. Moreover, the city, unlike a temple, is an image of busy activity and creativity as well as fellowship. So the gates of this city are open, promising that there will be journeys to be made, adventures to be had, strangers to be welcomed and homecom-ings to be enjoyed. This is no static eternity, no simultaneity, but a healing of time.

It is a closure with openness at its heart. City and dance, dwelling and movement, are complementary images for the promised end which is nothing less than to move and dwell in God:

No matter what this dance will be here.
Blessed be its weavings and its intricacies.

O fragile city of my trust and desire!
Our glancings. No longer any need to possess.[62]

---

[62] Micheal O'Siadhail, 'Dance' in *A Fragile City* (Newcastle: Bloodaxe Books, 1995), p. 76.

INDEX